T0271290

Institutional Challenges at the Early Stages of Development

Despite strong interest in the role of institutions, methods of operation, underlying political forces and their precise nature are still misunderstood. Partial analysis of specific aspects of public interventions simplified historical examples, or rough cross-country relationships tend to be the main guides to policy recommendations. Along with four in-depth country studies, published in companion volumes, *Institutional Challenges at the Early Stages of Development* gives a thorough review of the experiences of South Korea and Taiwan, offering a new perspective for identifying critical institutional issues. Including those related to state–business relations and the economic structure, and its transformation, analytical tools and concept are provided to help diagnose important hurdles at the early stage of a country's development. This title is also available as Open Access on Cambridge Core.

François Bourguignon is Emeritus Professor of Economics at the Paris School of Economics and School of Advanced Studies in Social Sciences, Paris. He is Former Chief Economist and Senior Vice President of the World Bank and the Co-founder of the European Development Network. His awards include the Dan David Prize and Centre national de la recherche scientifique silver medal.

Jean-Philippe Platteau is Emeritus Professor of Economics, University of Namur, Belgium. At this university, he has been a long-time director of the Centre for Research in the Economics of Development, which he founded. He held two Franqui chairs at the Free University of Brussels and the Katholieke University of Leuven. He is also the Co-founder of the European Development Network.

The Institutional Diagnostic Project

A suite of case-study monographs emerging from a large research program on the role of institutions in the economics, and the political economy of development in low-income countries, supported by a synthesis volume of the original case studies. This program was funded by the United Kingdom's Foreign and Commonwealth Development Office during a period of six years, during which program researchers had regular interactions with its staff, either directly or through Oxford Policy Management (the lead managing organisation).

Books in this collection:

François Bourguignon and Jean-Philippe Platteau *Institutional Challenges at the Early Stages of Development: Lessons from a Multi-Country Study*

Selim Raihan, François Bourguignon and Umar Salam (Eds.) *Is the Bangladesh Paradox Sustainable?*

António S. Cruz, Ines A. Ferreira, Johnny Flentø and Finn Tarp (Eds.) *Mozambique at a Fork in the Road*

François Bourguignon, Romain Houssa, Jean-Philippe Platteau and Paul Reding (Eds.) *State Capture and Rent-Seeking in Benin*

François Bourguignon and Samuel Mwita Wangwe (Eds.) *State and Business in Tanzania's Development*

Institutional Challenges at the Early Stages of Development

Lessons from a Multi-Country Study

FRANÇOIS BOURGUIGNON
Paris School of Economics and EHESS, Paris

JEAN-PHILIPPE PLATTEAU
University of Namur, Belgium

CAMBRIDGE
UNIVERSITY PRESS

CAMBRIDGE
UNIVERSITY PRESS

Shaftesbury Road, Cambridge CB2 8EA, United Kingdom

One Liberty Plaza, 20th Floor, New York, NY 10006, USA

477 Williamstown Road, Port Melbourne, VIC 3207, Australia

314–321, 3rd Floor, Plot 3, Splendor Forum, Jasola District Centre, New Delhi – 110025, India

103 Penang Road, #05–06/07, Visioncrest Commercial, Singapore 238467

Cambridge University Press is part of Cambridge University Press & Assessment, a department of the University of Cambridge.

We share the University's mission to contribute to society through the pursuit of education, learning and research at the highest international levels of excellence.

www.cambridge.org
Information on this title: www.cambridge.org/9781009285704

DOI: 10.1017/9781009285735

First published 2023

A catalogue record for this publication is available from the British Library

Library of Congress Cataloging-in-Publication Data
NAMES: Bourguignon, François, author. | Platteau, Jean-Philippe, 1947– author.
TITLE: Institutional challenges at the early stages of development : lessons from a multi-country study / François Bourguignon, Paris School of Economics and EHESS, Paris, Jean-Philippe Platteau, University of Namur, Belgium.
DESCRIPTION: First edition. | Cambridge, United Kingdom ; New York, NY : Cambridge University Press, [2023] | Includes bibliographical references and index.
IDENTIFIERS: LCCN 2023005681 | ISBN 9781009285704 (hardback)
| ISBN 9781009285711 (paperback) | ISBN 9781009285735 (ebook)
SUBJECTS: LCSH: Developing countries – Economic conditions.
| Economic development – Developing countries.
CLASSIFICATION: LCC HC59.7 .B643 2023 | DDC 338.9009172/4–dc23/eng/20230315
LC record available at https://lccn.loc.gov/2023005681

ISBN 978-1-009-28570-4 Hardback
ISBN 978-1-009-28571-1 Paperback

Contents

Figures

Tables

Abbreviations

AIC	Association Interprofessionnelle du Coton
AL	Awami League
ANDF	Agence Nationale du Domaine et du Foncier
BNP	Bangladesh National Party
CCM	Chama Cha Mapinduzi
CE	School Council
CIS	Country Institutional Surveys
DLHT	District Land and Housing Tribunals
EPB	Economic Planning Board
EWURA	Energy and Water Utilities Regulatory Authority
GDP	Gross Domestic Product
GNI	Gross National Income
GNP	Gross National Product
HCI	Heavy and Chemical Industries
ICA	Industrial Coordination Act
ICBT	Informal Cross-Border Trade
IDP	Institutional Diagnostic Project
IMF	International Monetary Fund
IPD	Institutional Profile Database
ISI	Intelligence Services
JCRR	Joint Commission on Rural Reconstruction
KADU	Kenya African Democratic Union
KCIA	Korean Central Intelligence Agency
KMT	Kuomintang
LAC	Least Advanced Country
LDC	Least Developed Country
MCC	Millennium Challenge Corporation
MFA	Multi-Fibre Arrangement

MITI	Ministry of International Trade and Industry
MLHHSD	Ministry of Land, Housing, and Human Settlement Development
NGO	Non-Governmental Organisation
NPL	Non-Performing Loan
NRC	Natural Resources Commission
OECD	Organisation for Economic Co-operation and Development
POSCO	Pohang Iron and Steel Company
QoG	Quality of Government (database)
RCT	Randomised Control Trial
RMG	Ready-Made Garment
SAP	Structural Adjustment Programme
SEZ	Special Economic Zone
SME	Small and Medium-sized Enterprise
SOE	State-Owned Enterprise
TANESCO	Tanzania Electric Supply Company
TANU	Tanganyika African National Union
TFP	Total Factor Productivity
UMNO	United Malays National Organisation
USAID	United States Agency for International Development
WAEMU	West African Economic and Monetary Union
WGI	Worldwide Governance Indicators

Introduction

Faced with disappointing performance under the 'Washington Consensus', international organisations and bilateral development agencies switched to what was called the 'post-Washington consensus'. This extended set of principles was seen as a way of compensating for the neglect of institutional considerations in the original consensus. Market-oriented reforms thus had to be accompanied by other reforms, including the regulation of various sectors, making governments more efficient, and increasing the capacity of human capital. Most importantly, however, emphasis was also placed on good governance as a necessary adjunct to market-led development, especially in regard to its capacity to protect property rights and guarantee contract enforcement. With time, governance then became a key criterion among donors for allocating aid across low-income countries, and also to monitor its use.

It is fair to say that, practically speaking, governance has been defined and evaluated in a rather ad hoc way, based on expert opinion, firm surveys, and simple economic parameters like the rate of inflation or the size of the budget deficit. The relationship with the nature and quality of institutions is thus very indirect. This still seems to be the case today, even though the recent World Development Report, entitled 'Governance and the Law' (World Bank, 2017), intends to go further by showing how governance, or policymaking in general, including institutional reforms, depends on the functioning of institutions, the role of stakeholders, and their relative political power. Practically speaking, however, there remains something mechanical and schematic in the way institutions are represented in the 2017 report, which is actually more about effective policymaking than about the diagnosis of institutional weaknesses and possible pathways for reform.

If there is absolutely no doubt that institutions matter for development, and for development policies and strategies in the first place, the crucial issue is knowing how they matter. After all, impressive economic development achievements have been observed, despite the presence of clear failures in particular institutional areas. In other words, not all dimensions of governance may be relevant at a given point in time in a given country. Likewise, institutional dimensions that are not included in governance criteria may play a critical role. Despite intensive and increasing efforts over the last few decades, there remains limited knowledge about how institutions affect development, how those institutions are formed, and how they could be reformed in specific contexts.

I SEARCHING FOR EVIDENCE ON THE ROLE OF INSTITUTIONS: THREE APPROACHES

Three approaches have been developed to identify the institutional factors that may hinder or promote development, and to think of ways of remedying or enhancing specific factors. Each of these approaches have their drawbacks.

The first approach consists of historical case studies, understood as in-depth studies of successful and unsuccessful development experiences in history or in the contemporary world. The formation and success of the Maghribi traders' coalition in the eleventh-century Mediterranean basin, the effects of the Glorious Revolution in Britain, the experiences of land redistribution in South Korea and Taiwan after the demise of Japanese colonial rule, the reform programme known as the Rural Household Responsibility system in China, or the violent fight for the appropriation of natural resource rents in several post-independence African states, all epitomise various possibilities of institutional change: while some of them led to vigorous development headed by developmental states of different types, others caused underdevelopment under the aegis of predatory states. Such studies are of the utmost interest because they show, at work, the mechanisms that may govern the transformation of institutions, often under the pressure of external circumstances, and they show the unequal success that can be attributed to institutional change. In *Why Nations Fail*, for instance, Acemoglu and Robinson (2012) masterfully highlight the role of institutions in several historical and contemporaneous cases of development, and in failed development experiences. They place a special emphasis on the key role of inclusive institutions, as compared with predatory ones, and, most importantly, on the role of politics in encouraging or impeding development. The problem, however, is that the lessons from most history-oriented studies are rarely transferable across time or space, and they are not necessarily – or completely – relevant for today's developing countries.

The same conclusion applies to studies emanating from the quickly proliferating strand of economic history research based on natural historical experiments. Variation in some key determinants, whose presence or absence was observed a long time ago, is considered as exogenous, and therefore is used as a valid instrument to explain today's different outcomes. Because many geological and geographic characteristics have the appearance of being deterministic, they are often seen as the deep causes behind the institutional divergence that is responsible for different growth and development trajectories. Two particular difficulties arise here. First, as underlined by Dany Rodrick (2004) and others, it is not because a researcher finds an appropriate econometric instrument that s/he is able to offer an adequate explanation. We tend to agree with Avinash Dixit (2007: 137) that 'the notion that geographic and historical variables are merely instruments for institutional determinants of economic success is supported more by the intuitive appeal of the stories told than by the statistical significance of the tests performed'. Second, results that highlight the role of historical factors, particularly when they are rooted in physical determinants, give no guidance when the problem affects the relevant institutions directly: 'the recommendation to change one's geography or history is useless' (Dixit, 2007: 137).

The second approach to identifying institutional factors that may hinder or promote development involves cross-country studies in the contemporaneous era. It relies on indicators that describe the strength of a particular set of institutions in a country – for example, property rights, legal regimes, the extent of democracy, the strength and nature of controls on the executive, corruption, and so on – with the aim being to identify whether there is a correlation between these indicators and growth or other development outcomes. Institutional and governance indicators are generally based on the opinions of experts, who compare the performance of different countries on which they have specialised knowledge along a number of selected dimensions. As such, they are grounded in largely subjective assessments and lack the precision needed for statistical analysis. This being said, correlations between these indicators and development outcomes are sometimes significant, and they are often intuitive. However, the use that can be made of the results of such cross-country studies is limited since, by construction, they essentially refer to an abstract 'average country'. They may therefore be of little use when it comes to a specific country. Most importantly, they say nothing about causality, and still less about the policy instruments that could improve particular institutions. For example, corruption is generally found to be bad for development. However, we would like to know the direction of causality, and whether this conclusion is true in all countries and in all circumstances. And what should we think about cases where corruption serves to 'grease the wheels' of the bureaucratic system, speeding up procedures in the presence of too stringent administrative constraints? In sum, cross-country analysis is an interesting exploratory approach, yet we need to delve deeper into the issues when focusing on a particular country and trying to conceive of potential institutional reforms.

To understand the third approach to identifying institutional factors that may hinder or promote development it must be borne in mind that in some cases institutional weaknesses or strengths are readily observable, as in the delivery of public services like education or healthcare. For instance, the absenteeism of teachers in public schools reveals a breach of contract between civil servants and their employers, and/or a monitoring failure by supervisors. This state of affairs raises two interesting issues. On the one hand, there are ways of incentivising teachers so that they show up to school. Numerous experiments that have been rigorously evaluated by randomised control trial (RCT) techniques in various community settings have successfully explored such incentive schemes in various countries over the last two decades or so. On the other hand, it is not clear whether there is always the political will, or an adequate coalition of interest groups, to fully correct this institutional failure of civil servants who do not comply with their official duty, and to make successful experimental schemes universally compulsory.

Identification of institutional weaknesses at the microeconomic level, and experimentation to identify ways to correct them, has multiplied over recent years. Yet this line of research generally addresses simple cases that can be suitably designed for experimentation. Identifying institutional failures and devising remedies is much less easy, if not impossible, in more complex situations where a bundle of attributes rather than a single or a few factors seem to play an important role. Moreover, if RCT studies (and this is their strength) are able to establish causality between well-specified institutional interventions and outcomes of concern, they are often less successful when it comes to shedding light on the underlying mechanisms. This limitation makes thinking about the generalisability of their conclusions difficult. This is especially so because the impact that is assessed typically consists of short- or medium-term effects and we therefore need a good theory to persuade us that these effects will endure. Doubts are of course reinforced when comparable studies of the effects of a given intervention in different countries do not converge (see Dal Bo and Finan (2020), for a recent survey of results).

The three empirical approaches to institutions and development summarised above leave a gap between an essentially macro view of the relationship – stylised historical facts or cross-country correlations between GDP growth and governance or institutional indicators – and a micro view that is grounded in, say, the direct observation of the behaviour of absentee civil servants or corrupt tax inspectors. Indeed, it can reasonably be held that economic growth results from the combination of many factors, including structural changes, which depend themselves on the way institutions work. Industrialisation may be made easier because of institutions that are conducive to local entrepreneurial initiative, or more difficult due to institutions that protect importers' rents. Agricultural productivity may grow faster if land rights are well defined and well implemented, yet the need for the state to intervene may be confined to certain situations, which themselves have to be specified. To understand the relationship between institutions and development we must be able to identify how institutions facilitate or hinder the basic changes that govern economic growth.

Moreover, development is not exclusively about economic growth. It is about the structural transformation of the economy and the society. It is about inclusiveness, and therefore the way institutions distribute the products of growth. And it is about sustainability. For another thing, focusing on micro aspects is fine as long as one does not lose sight of the bigger picture. It is almost trivial to say, but it is still worth emphasising, that the fundamental institutional factor(s) behind a specific dysfunction must be uncovered in order to reach a correct diagnosis and to correctly identify the policy implications. There are innumerable instances where, because only proximate causes have been identified, the problem at stake quickly resurfaced after the remedy inferred from an incomplete diagnostic was applied. There are thus many possible causes of corruption among tax collectors, including lack of monitoring, or the propensity of supervisors to take their cut, or of rich taxpayers to bribe the budget minister for looser tax controls. Even if some experimental anti-corruption device is found to work for a given tax and a given group of tax collectors, there is no guarantee that the government will make the decision to implement it on a broad scale and on a permanent basis.

Moving from the rigorous identification of what appears to be an efficiency-improving policy or institutional arrangement to an understanding of the conditions in which it may be effectively put into practice requires that we decipher the surrounding political economy context. In other words, considerations of political feasibility need to be added to considerations of economic efficiency. As we have learned from the political economy approach discussed earlier, politics may act as a constraint, and it is not clear *a priori* how a trade-off between economic efficiency and political objectives should be resolved. Even working in partnership with a government agency and obtaining its agreement on the soundness of a particular treatment that has been revealed in the course of an experiment that was run with its full support does not ensure that this treatment will actually be implemented. Interests or considerations that were abstracted away at the time of the experiment may come into play or may emerge only at the time of implementation.

These limitations of standard analyses of the relationship between institutions and development have motivated the exploratory research undertaken within the Institutional Diagnostic Project (henceforth labelled IDP). Even though we do not claim to be able to close the gap between research on the role of institutions and a diagnostic that will be directly relevant for policymakers, we believe that we can narrow it down somewhat. At least, this is our hope – and that is the purpose of this project. One of the main reasons why we believe that it was worth undertaking is that the above gap is currently quite large – too large, actually. Here, we cannot resist the temptation to cite Avinash Dixit (2007) extensively:

the econometric and theoretical studies are not the best way to generate policy prescriptions. Most cross-country regressions are a far from perfect fit: the myriad explanatory variables that have been tried explain only a fraction of the variance. Theoretical modelling explores the implications of one cause or mechanism in depth, deliberately isolating it from others, whereas policy prescriptions require that one consider all the different causes or mechanisms at work in a country and how they interact. The question policy prescribers must address, is not what creates success on average across countries, but what is going wrong in this country, and how can we put it right. (p. 150)

A similar type of warning has been issued by Jean Drèze (2020) when he stresses that 'policy is not a matter of evidence alone'. Besides evidence, which is about facts, good policy requires understanding, which is often gained through personal experience. Moreover, 'policy-making calls for serious reflection about values and objectives', equivalent to asking for what purpose and for whom findings about 'what works' (as revealed by a RCT, in particular) are to be implemented. Lastly, since policy is a political decision, it requires deliberation. It is when people differ in their understanding and values that deliberation is especially needed and that care should be taken not to de-politicise public policy through exclusive reliance on the advices of experts working behind closed doors.

In short, we readily admit that researchers cannot be good substitutes for policy practitioners and advisors. What we claim, however, is that it is possible to get closer to policy-relevant diagnostics by following an approach that is at the same time more comprehensive and more detailed than conventional approaches. In this new approach, special attention is paid in particular to the roles of context and political economy factors, and to the nature of mechanisms linking critical institutions to relevant outcomes.

II INSTITUTIONAL DIAGNOSTICS AS A NEW APPROACH TO INSTITUTIONS AND DEVELOPMENT

This volume summarises the lessons learned from the IDP, a multi-country IDP project that aimed to design a methodology able to diagnose development-impeding institutional weaknesses, or disruptions, in a country, and to propose lines of reform which take the political context into account. An 'institutional diagnostic' of development must first be seen as an exploration of the way in which various types of institutional features affect the functioning of its economy, its dynamics, and the policymaking process, the ultimate goal being to detect the most serious flaws or ill-boding imperfections in the institutional scaffolding of the country or, by contrast, healthy tendencies which seem to portend continuous progress on the way to development.

But the diagnostic must also come with a reflection on those reforms likely to succeed in removing institutional obstacles and the political economy context in which they would have to be decided and then implemented. It is a new approach to institutions and development in the sense that it departs from the three lines of research mentioned earlier. It is a country-centred approach differing from historical case studies because the focus is not on a particular event, circumstance, or episode but on the overall functioning of a country's economy. It also goes beyond the mere use of governance or institutional indicators, which are deemed much too rough or imprecise when dealing with a real economy, even though they may sometimes be informative. On the contrary, institutional diagnostics are meant to apply to economies taken in all their complexity, including their socio-political dimensions. Of course, they also make use of microeconomic evidence on institutional failures or deficiencies and, where available, of experimental studies conducted in the country concerned.

Within IDP, such an institutional diagnostic was performed on four low-income countries, two of them graduating to lower-middle-income status. This restriction in the choice of case studies was imposed by the funding agency behind this research project, the UK Department for International Development (now the Foreign and Commonwealth Development Office). Accordingly, and within the constraints of the available resources, the following four countries were selected: Bangladesh, Benin, Mozambique, and Tanzania. The rationale for this choice is explained in detail in each individual case study. At this stage, it may simply be noted that, together, they cover a broad range of initial conditions, development trajectories, and achievements. These case studies are published in four companion volumes (Bourguignon and Wangwe, 2023; Bourguinon et al., 2023; Cruz et al., 2023; Raihan, Bourguignon, and Salam, 2023).

The objective of the present volume is twofold. On the one hand, it offers a reflection on the institutional diagnostic methodology in the light of the experience gathered in the case studies. In contrast to the well-known 'growth diagnostic' approach to development developed by Hausmann, Rodrik, and Velasco (2005), there is no simple theoretical framework in the literature that could be used as a logical basis for a comprehensive diagnostic of how institutions may hinder the development of a country. A heuristic approach had to be followed and it should be evaluated. On the other hand, the volume attempts to synthesise the results of the diagnostic established in the four case studies in terms of what they teach about the relationship between institutions and development. In particular, a reflection is undertaken on the comparability of the institutional challenges identified in the various case studies, and some other countries. It leads to a list of 'generic institutional issues', which are of interest per se but also should help in establishing the institutional diagnostic of a particular country.

III STRUCTURE OF THE CASE STUDIES

A brief presentation of the methodology and the content of the case studies may be helpful at this stage to get an idea of the material available for the synthesis undertaken in the present volume.

Each study proceeds in three steps. The first step is rather 'mechanical': it consists of reviewing the economic, social, and political development of the country, surveying the existing literature, examining governance or institutional quality indicators, and soliciting from various types of decision makers, top policymakers, and experts their views on the functioning of the economy and institutions in their country. Based on this material, it will be possible to identify the most obvious 'binding economic constraints' on economic development and the perceived institutional weaknesses by various actors. Regarding economic constraints, hypotheses about whether and how they relate to institutional factors have also to be put forward. This rather straightforward approach to institutions and development in a particular country is also expected to point to several thematic areas of utmost economic importance and where critical institutional factors seem to be at play: commercial agriculture and the legal or informal system of land use transfers, manufacturing development, and the regulation/incentivising of firms, tax collection, delivery of particular public goods, and so on. Yet problem areas are likely to be strongly country dependent.

The second step consists of a thorough analysis of the critical areas revealed by the exploration in the first step. The challenge here is to identify the way in which an economic weakness is the result of institutional dysfunction, and then to unearth the root causes of this particular dysfunction and understand how they could be remedied, while taking account of the stakes involved in the reforms. Using these detailed analyses of key thematic areas as well as the evidence gathered in the first part, the third step of the case studies then consists of synthesising what has been learned into a repertoire of some basic institutional problems that are common to the different problem areas, their negative consequences for development, and, most importantly, their causes, proximate or more distant, as well as the potential for remedies and reforms. This is the essence of the 'diagnostic' that each case study intends to deliver. Practically, all that analysis is summarised in a 'diagnostic table', which thus appears as a short statement of the diagnostic.

What is thus intended is a diagnostic, not a reform agenda. Because there are winners and losers of most reforms, political economy factors, as well as political and economic circumstances, will determine whether they can be undertaken or not. This is thoroughly discussed in the case studies, but it must be clear that no firm conclusion about the political economy feasibility can be reached without a precise evaluation of the distribution of political power in the society – something that goes far beyond the present exercise. From the strict point of view of the diagnosis, however, its most important contribution is to put squarely on the table the nature of the institutional problems, the needed reforms, and the stakes involved. In other words, it is to make sure that all key actors are aware of the most serious implications of the reforms, the ensuing collective gains, and, possibly, the losses for various categories of agents. In theory, and if successful, our approach should clarify among all stakeholders and the public the cost of not undertaking a given institutional reform, the gain of doing so, and who is likely to lose and gain.

In line with what has been said earlier, the ambition of an institutional diagnostic is not to formulate precise policy prescriptions. Moreover, such recommendations would be fraught with uncertainty. The aim is essentially to unveil weak points that have the potential to cause severe problems in the future and the effects of possible remedies. This is with a view to hopefully prompting policymakers to become more aware of them, monitor their evolution, and ponder feasible reforms. For instance, the role of informal rules and institutions, and their interactions with formal institutions, receive great attention throughout the various studies. This is justified, given the important role and the great resilience of traditional local rules and institutions in many developing countries. They permeate the whole social fabric and the question as to how they are antagonised by newly established formal institutions, or complement them, or accommodate them in some way or other, cannot be escaped. This is particularly evident in matters of contract enforcement and land property rights. Reforming by simply changing the law or trying to implement it more strictly, as frequently done by policymakers after long political debates, often proves ineffective.

IV THE ASIAN TIGERS' TAKE-OFF AS A BENCHMARK

Some of the four IDP countries may be considered as development successes according to some criteria, whereas the development performance of others or according to other criteria appears as modest. No country can really be considered as over-performing the others or not subject to substantial uncertainty about its future development. To enrich the comparative perspective of the reflection in this volume, two countries were added to the list of our four in-depth country case studies. These new countries, for which we rely on second-hand literature, are South Korea and Taiwan – at the time they were at a comparable level of income per capita as the IDP countries today, that is, the time of their take-off in the 1960s and early 1970s. The two East Asian tigers are indeed known for their spectacular development records and provide an interesting basis for comparison. However, it bears emphasis that the idea is not to erect these two cases as benchmarks against which institutional imperfections in other, less successful countries must be measured. That one-size-fits-all solutions are inadequate is a principle that should be applied to any attempt to mechanically transplant institutions not only from economically advanced countries of the Western world but also from successful Southeast Asian countries, even at the time of their take-off. The objective is different. It is to use the experiences of South Korea and Taiwan at the beginning of their stellar development to get a better idea of the key issues that a country must tackle in order to develop in a sustainable manner.

To make things more concrete, the point is not to claim that, because these two Asian countries followed such a path, a military-based authoritarian regime is a prerequisite of sustainable development. It is evident that this sort of advice is fraught, if only because it is not known how a benevolent, or at least a development-minded despot can arise in a particular country. In fact, many examples from the contemporaneous world seem to indicate that malevolent military rulers are the rule rather than the exception, as attested by the present-day regimes of countries such as Mali, Myanmar, Pakistan, Thailand, and many others. What is of interest here, and where a lot can be learned from the study of South Korea and Taiwan, is that their military regimes succeeded in preventing business interests from capturing the state and influencing its development policies, as observed under one form or another in the IDP countries. This is an issue which must be addressed and solved in some way or other, and the experiences of these two countries should be considered as sources from which to get inspiration and not as models to copy *in toto*.

V OUTLINE OF THE VOLUME

The outline of the book is as follows. In Chapter 1, we define the concept of institutions and then move forward by discussing interactions between formal and informal institutions and then presenting and illustrating the main existing economic theories of institutional change. In Chapter 2, the methodological approach of the institutional diagnostic is explained and justified. In the four subsequent chapters, the results of the institutional diagnostics based upon the thorough analysis of development in the IDP countries in companion volumes, as well as the salient points of that analysis are summarised: Bangladesh and Tanzania in Chapter 3 and Benin and Mozambique in Chapter 4. We then try to apply a comparable methodology to imagine what would have been the conclusions of an institutional diagnostic drawn at the beginning of the development of the two big achievers: South Korea in Chapter 5 and Taiwan in Chapter 6. Then come the synthesis chapters. First, Chapter 7 summarises on a comparative basis the nature of the obstacles and enablers of structural transformation in the six countries' economies and suggests possible links with institutional factors. Those are taken up more explicitly in the next two chapters, which focus on the set of generic institutional issues found among the case studies and the two Southeast Asian countries. Chapter 8 probes the role of politics and the initial conditions prevailing at the time development efforts were initiated, while Chapter 9 focuses on issues of state capacity and property rights. Finally, Chapter 10 offers a general conclusion, in which basic lessons from the analysis, and the implications for development assistance, are identified.

PART I

APPROACHING INSTITUTIONAL CHANGE: THEORY AND METHODOLOGY

I

Theoretical Underpinnings

The 'institutions matter' slogan appears today as a fundamental truth about development. Widely shared by the development community, including international organisations, it goes with the idea that the benefits of both market operations and state interventions are significantly conditioned by the presence of effective institutions. An abundant literature in economic and political sciences, both theoretical and empirical, has recently suggested that the poor quality of institutions is an important determinant of low development outcomes and the persistence of poverty in the world. In many cases, existing institutions are not well adapted to the challenge of modern economic growth and development. This raises the issue as to how existing institutions can be reformed, which is a particularly hard challenge when they are the embodiment of local cultures and historical legacies. If reform is unrealistic, institutional change will have to wait, and economic progress is then constrained during the time necessary for such change to be induced by a transformation of the environment, whether economic, technological, or demographic. The question is how long the new, better adapted institution will take to emerge. The answer will obviously depend on the type of institutions concerned.

There are two main reasons why, at this early stage, it is appropriate to briefly survey the literature on institutions and institutional change. First, we need to have a basic understanding of what is meant by institutions, so as to avoid using the word as a sort of residual category into which everything that is not production factors and technical progress would fall. The distinction between formal and informal institutions will draw our attention because at the early stages of development informality is an important feature of the society, the economy, and the polity. Second, the survey is intended to supply us with the theoretical underpinnings required to get a good grasp of the generic institutional issues discussed in Chapters 8 and 9. These underpinnings involve both the way in which formal and informal institutions may interact, and the way institutions may change as a result of reforms or other forces, such as the transformation of the environment. In the latter instance, institutional change is clearly induced by material forces, and institutions are endogenous (they result from) to growth rather than the other way around. An important implication is that institutional reforms themselves do not have to be imposed in a direct manner if they can indirectly cause institutions to evolve, perhaps in a gradual manner. This is patently the case when a reform that has the effect of accelerating growth induces changes in social norms, cultural values, and other slow-moving institutions, that is, when an institutional or policy reform in one sector of the society trigger off changes in a different sector.

In line with the above motivations, the present chapter is organised into three main sections. First, we provide a simple definition of institutions and comment upon their main aspects. Second, we highlight various ways in which informal arrangements may interact with formal institutions. In the process we touch on the issue of institutional change, since an important question is how the dynamic of change is affected when formal and informal institutions enter into conflict with each other – say, following the creation of a new formal institution. Third, we address the issue of institutional change by looking at the various theories proposed by economists to explain why institutions may evolve or alternatively persist in spite of a changing environment. Finally, by way of conclusion, we examine various arguments in the debate about radical versus gradual institutional reforms.

I A SIMPLE DEFINITION OF INSTITUTIONS

Many and diverse definitions of institutions have been proposed in books and papers written by economists and other social scientists. Our purpose here is not to offer a review but only to formulate a clear definition to be consistently applied in the following chapters. This definition, which is neither original nor novel, emphasises the most critical features that will come up for discussion in the book, whether explicitly or implicitly. *Institutions are rules, procedures, or organisations, formal or informal, that constrain individual behaviour in such a way that human actions become coordinated. Individual actions are influenced through adhesion or coercion; it is only in the former case that an institution can claim a high degree of acceptance or legitimacy.*

A first implication of this definition is that institutions cover a wide variety of humanly devised coordinating mechanisms, running from state administrations, the judiciary, and the police to religious bodies, tribal chiefdoms, and patronage relationships, passing through social norms, customs, contract arrangements, mutual aid groups, and neighbourhood associations.

A second implication, as underlined in North (1990), is that individual expectations play a pivotal role in the formation and maintenance of institutions. This is true whether the shaping of behaviours takes place through adhesion or coercion. In the case of adhesion, people adhere to an institutional arrangement when they trust it in the sense that they believe that not only themselves, but also other individuals, support it. The arrangement is then considered legitimate by a large number of its users, and this legitimacy means that individuals expect many others to comply with the prescriptions involved. It should be noted that compliance does not necessarily imply that everybody is happy about the institution, or thinks it is the best that can be achieved. What it does imply is that everybody is confident that other people are likely to behave in the way prescribed because this is the normal thing to do or the established manner of behaving in the particular society and context in which they live. Striking illustrations are provided by many social norms and customs, but also by manifestations of voluntary compliance with laws or regulations.

For obvious reasons, adhesion is especially forthcoming when, through some form of collective action, people have themselves decided to set up rules that will constrain them in a way that is ultimately beneficial for all. For example, villagers may realise that when left free to act according to their best private interests, they have a tendency to overexploit a local natural resource (a fishing ground, a pasture, a forest, underground water, etc.). They may then vote to establish regulations that will limit their freedom to exploit this resource – say through the imposition of quotas, harvesting seasons, and rules regarding the characteristics of the produce they are allowed to get hold of (e.g., the size of fish that may be caught or the height of trees that may be felled).

In the case of coercion, expectations formed by individuals also play an important role. Indeed, there can be no coercion without the possible use of sanctions meted out by an authority. And coercion will not be effective if people are not convinced that the rule will be more or less strictly enforced. Just think of tax laws or driving regulations in a democratic country: if citizens do not expect that the rules will be enforced – either because detection of fraud or rule violation is deficient or sanctions are small or easy to circumvent – they will not take them seriously, unless they are imbued with a strong sense of civicness, which is understood as an inclination to follow a law just because it has been enacted by a legitimate authority (the state, in this instance).

A third implication, related to the first one, is that both formal and informal arrangements can be institutions. Institutions are formal when they rest on explicit, written rules that are enforced through official channels. As explained in more detail in Baland et al. (2020), the first requirement (explicitness) means that the rules are stated in a clear and articulate manner so that they are understandable by anyone possessing sufficient knowledge of the language in which they are written, and people are left with little uncertainty about the circumstances to which they apply. By contrast, informal institutions are generally made up of non-written rules or, if they are written, the rules are specific to a particular human community in the sense that their meaning is not easily accessible to outsiders. One important reason for this is that the circumstances and the social groups to which they apply may not be clear for those who are not members of the rule-setting community. They may thus appear to the external observer to be somehow arbitrary. In addition, informal rules or arrangements are often somewhat loose or flexible. This is because they tend to allow for individual circumstances and, relatedly, they involve *ex post* sharing, redistribution, or insurance. In other words, the terms of an informal contract (e.g., the rewards for performing a task) are typically unspecified and frequently contingent on future shocks.[1]

Finally, the rules behind informal arrangements are typically enforced through non-official sanctioning mechanisms. Like official ones, these may consist of punishments meted out by an authority. In this case, the authority is informal, such as a tribal chief, a clan leader, or a landlord-patron. Yet other types of sanctions are also found in the universe of informal institutions.[2] First is the fear of reprisal by a partner or a group that is outraged by the behaviour of a rule-violator, or by an organisation established for that purpose. The latter may be a thuggish or criminal organisation that specialises in the job of intimidating and threatening individuals or families with a view to obtaining redress for a fraudulent or deviant act. Second is the fear of losing a valuable relationship with the cheated or disappointed partner in a so-called relational contracting based on repeated interactions between two agents. The punishment thus involves what Greif (1993) has called a bilateral mechanism of reputation and punishment. Third is the fear of losing reputation inside the whole group, community, sector, or location to which the cheated partner belongs. In this instance, a multilateral mechanism of reputation and punishment is set in motion. It operates in a decentralised manner and in an extreme case can take the form of ostracism. Fourth, sanctions can be internalised through a psychological process, such as social learning and cultural transmission. In the latter case, social norms are instilled in members of, say, a community, a group, a brotherhood, or a sect, with the purpose of driving them to feel guilty whenever they deviate from their prescribed behaviour. Such guilt feelings are often anchored in the idea that deviation amounts to a betrayal of the collective. Internalisation mechanisms of this kind are the functional equivalent of civicness in the sphere of formal institutions. In both cases, individual preferences are shaped through a moral upbringing process that emphasises collective interests at the expense of private interests.

Before turning to an examination of key issues raised by institutions, two remarks should be made. To begin with, there is an interesting parallel between the idea that modernisation is reflected in the growing importance of formal

---

[1] This is especially true in the realm of the family (narrow or extended), where the dominant form of (economic) relationships is gift exchange in which reciprocity is typically delayed and combined with insurance (Fafchamps, 2019).

[2] For more details, see Colson (1947), Sahlins (1965), Hayami and Kikuchi (1982), Greif (1989, 1992, 1993, 1994, 1998, 2002, 2006), Platteau (1991, 1994a, 1994b, 2000, 2006), Fafchamps (1992, 1996, 2020), Aoki (2001), Dixit (2004).

relative to informal institutions, on the one hand, and Greif's idea that development entails a shift from 'collectivist' to 'individualist' societies, on the other hand (Greif, 1989, 1992, 1994). This is because order in collectivist societies is largely based on multilateral reputation and punishment mechanisms, which are essentially informal, while individualist societies cannot function effectively if their bilateral reputation and punishment mechanisms are not backed by formal institutions.[3]

Our second remark is that institutions are not all situated on the same level. There actually exists an institutional hierarchy that is made up of a set of institutions that are vertically entwined with each other. At the top of the ladder are fundamental or constitutional institutions that set the rules around which inferior institutions are grafted. An example of a fundamental institution is a political constitution: it defines a political regime and sets the rules regarding the frequency and mode of elections, the pattern of representation, and the like. It also spells out which liberties and individual rights should be upheld in a country. Within the framework of that constitutive law, other laws and regulations specify how the political system and the fundamental rights of the citizens are to be implemented in more operational terms.

To provide an illustration from the informal domain, let us refer back to the aforementioned example of collective action to ensure the efficient management of local natural resources. In rather egalitarian societies, the principle of equal contributions is considered important, and a convenient way to implement it is by sharing collective duties in a rotary manner among all the (adult) members. When a new initiative is decided, the corresponding rules will typically be inspired by this fundamental rotating principle applied at the highest level of the social and political order. Thus, the burden of monitoring the proper use of a resource – for example, guarding a village forest or fishing ground during periods of prohibited harvest, or ensuring that rights of access to irrigation water are duly respected – will be shared among the resource users according to some form of rotation. In fact, even rights of access to the resource may be organised following the same principle (Ostrom, 1990; Baland and Platteau, 1996).

As the last example indicates, it is impossible to talk about institutions and institutional change in developing countries without paying due attention to informal arrangements, rules, norms, and modes of behaviour, which regulate essential aspects of everyday life. And since we are primarily interested in institutional change (or stagnation), which will be the central focus of our attention in Section III (subsection D), we need to first take stock of the various ways in which informal institutions can interact with formal ones. The

---

[3] In Greif's reading of the history of Western Europe, it was the need to compensate for the lack of multilateral arrangements, itself caused by unstable social networks, that caused the gradual emergence (in cities in northern Italy during the thirteenth century and later) of legal and political enforcement organisations as well as a legal code.

most straightforward case of institutional change arises when a new formal institution is established in a context where informal arrangements exist. The question as to how both will coexist, adapt to each other, or enter into mutual conflict is therefore of great importance – hence our discussion in the next section.

II INTERACTIONS BETWEEN FORMAL AND INFORMAL INSTITUTIONS

A An Illustrated Typology

Any social order is built upon a mix of formal and informal institutions, yet the proportion of either type can vary considerably from country to country for complex reasons that have to do with the political system, administrative traditions (centralised versus decentralised), and cultural influences, in particular. Along the modernisation path of a given country, formal institutions are predicted to grow in importance relative to informal ones. This is not only or necessarily because the former may displace the latter as the result of their being more effective in providing the same service – as witnessed by the replacement of informal insurance or mutual help mechanisms by formal social security systems in advanced Western European countries – but also because they fulfil new functions for which informal arrangements are ill-suited. It is therefore useful to get a better understanding of the way these two types of institutions or rules interact with each other. To help us in this effort, we use a typology proposed by two social scientists, Helme and Levitsky (2004), and we discuss it in a way that extends the presentation made in Baland et al. (2020), a paper to which we directly contributed. Here, we make a special effort to illustrate the different cases highlighted in this typology, which is constructed along two dimensions and provides a static picture (the situation obtained at a given point of time).

The first dimension (represented on the vertical axis of Table 1.1) is the degree to which the outcomes of formal and informal institutions' rules converge or diverge, depending upon whether the latter produce substantively similar or different results from those expected from a strict and exclusive adherence to the former. Divergence points to a substantial discrepancy or contradiction across these outcomes, whereas convergence is obtained when the outcomes are not substantively different. The second dimension (on the horizontal axis) indicates the effectiveness of the formal institutions, understood as the extent to which formal rules and procedures are enforced and complied with in practice. A high level of effectiveness thus means that individuals' choices are actually constrained or enabled, and there is a high probability of official sanctions in the case of a violation of the rules. Conversely, people expect a low probability of enforcement (and hence a low expected cost of violation) when institutional effectiveness is small.

TABLE 1.1 *Typology of interactions between formal and informal institutions according to Helme and Levitsky (2004)*

Institutional outcomes	Formal institutions effective	Formal institutions ineffective
Convergent	Complementarity	Substitution
Divergent	Accommodation	Competition

According to Table 1.1, four different types of institutional interaction patterns can arise: complementarity, accommodation, competition, and substitution. Let us consider them in turn.

B Complementarity

A combination of effective formal rules and convergent outcomes produces complementarity between informal and formal institutions. In such cases, informal institutions may cover contingencies that are not properly allowed for by formal rules, or they may facilitate the pursuit of individual goals within the formal institutional framework, or else they may serve as pillars that support the functioning of formal institutions. In the latter instance, their role is to create or strengthen incentives to comply with formal rules that might otherwise exist merely on paper.

Fafchamps (2020) puts much stress on complementarity when he writes that formal institutions are best regarded as enabling informal ones to perform better. His focus is on the enforcement of market transactions, and his central point is that, since interpersonal relationships are not eliminated by formal institutions (and contracts in particular), the role of good formal institutions is 'to reinforce the forms of social interactions that lead to a more efficient, more inclusive outcome, and to discourage those interactions that reduce efficiency and ostracise certain groups and individuals' (p. 376). Thus, formal institutions promote markets less by enforcing contracts directly than by seeking to reinforce informal contract enforcement mechanisms, especially those based on reputation. More precisely, they contribute to more active and more efficient markets by: (i) providing uniform measurement rules and quality standards; (ii) minimising conflicts stemming from fraudulent information or any form of misrepresentation by one party to a transaction; (iii) regulating fraud, bankruptcy, and the conditions under which a relational contract (e.g., an employment contract, a rental or a land lease contract) may end; (iv) curbing violent forms of informal contract enforcement (the reliance on thugs and criminal organisations, in particular); and (v) offering a strictly organised process for the adjudication of contractual disputes which agents may optionally use (pp. 380–1). This view of mutually supporting formal and informal institutions, long held by social scientists (Polanyi, 1957; Granovetter, 1985;

Ensminger, 1992), is anchored in the idea that economic exchanges take place between individuals who are necessarily embedded within a social context that does not disappear with the introduction of formal institutions.

C Accommodation

When effective formal institutions are combined with divergent outcomes, we have a situation of accommodation between informal and formal institutions. This situation arises because informal institutions create incentives that prompt people to behave in ways that alter the substantive effects of formal rules, yet without directly violating them. In other words, the effect of informal institutions is to contradict the spirit, but not the letter, of the formal rules. Accommodation occurs when a contradiction emerges between outcomes generated by the formal rules and prescriptions emanating from customary or informal rules. What impedes an outright change or open violation of the formal rules is their very effectiveness. Conflicting dimensions are present within the existing formal institutional arrangement, and what accommodation does is to somehow reconcile them through the implementation and interpretation of formal rules by actors that are subject to informal prescriptions.

As an illustration, consider the following example, collected from fieldwork in West Africa by one of the authors. In Mali, judges in the formal court system often deal with inheritance cases involving rural people in ways that rest on a compromise between the formal law and custom. Thus, when one son and one daughter disagree about their entitled share of the wealth of their deceased father, the judge may choose to persuade the defendant (the son who asks for the enforcement of the custom according to which he should inherit the entire wealth of the father) and the claimant (the daughter who asks for the enforcement of the statutory law that has established the principle of gender equality in matters of inheritance) to accept a verdict based on Islamic law (the daughter receives one-half of the brother's share). In this manner, the authority of Islam is invoked (the claimant and the defendant are both Muslims) with a view to avoiding a confrontational approach that is likely to disrupt family relations. This is a typical instance in which an actor, the modern judge, plays upon several legal registers to find a solution that is acceptable to the different parties involved in a case. The formal law is not ignored, since it serves as a reference point with respect to which the compromise with other types of laws is devised. Incidentally, the example shows that the stark opposition often drawn between French colonial countries, which rely on written codes, and British colonial countries, which rely on the common law, may be easily overdone.[4]

---

[4] Accommodation may also be observed in non-market economies, as testified by the critical role of informal exchange arrangements (the 'blat' relationships in the USSR and the 'guanxi' informal exchanges in communist China) in solving problems of shortage caused by central planning

D Competition

The next possibility combines ineffective formal rules and divergent outcomes, giving rise to competition between informal and formal institutions. Here, informal institutions structure incentives in ways that are incompatible with the formal rules: to follow one rule, actors must blatantly violate another. Examples of such situations occur, for instance, when particularistic informal institutions, such as clientelistic relations and clan-based nepotism, arise in various contexts of weak formal political or economic institutions (Hoff and Sen, 2005, 2006; Bardhan and Mookherjee, 2020). Not surprisingly, competing informal institutions are often found in postcolonial contexts in which formal institutions that were imposed on indigenous rules and authority structures dominate, and have been retained by the new independent states. In postcolonial Ghana, for instance, civil servants were officially instructed to follow the rules of the public bureaucracy, but most believed they would incur a significant social cost (such as a loss of standing in the community) if they ignored kinship obligations that made it a duty for them to provide jobs and other favours to their families and villages (Price, 1975). The same attitude of favouritism may be found in non-tribal societies: for example, in India where loyalty is due to the *jati* (subcaste) rather than the kin group (Kakar, 1978).[5] In the worst cases, the main goal of the officials consists of extorting revenue in order to distribute gifts to families and patronage networks. The temptation of such biased behaviour is increased when official posts are on sale, generally within a limited circle of people and groups. The winners are then forced to exact kickbacks to recoup their investment, such as is observed in parts of Pakistan and in Afghanistan (prior to the seizure of power by the Taliban in August 2021).

(Ledeneva, 1998: 182–7, 211). In the case of China, these arrangements struck deep roots in kinship structures inherited from the Confucianist tradition (Greif and Tabellini, 2010, 2017; Fukuyama, 2012: 119–21).

[5] We cannot resist the temptation to quote from the insightful book of Sudhir Kakar (1978), who has emphasised the considerable emotional stress caused by the primacy of relationships, family loyalties, and *jati* connections in Indian society. According to him, the conflict between the rational criteria of specific tasks and institutional goals rooted in Western societal values, and the deeply held belief (however ambivalent) in the importance of honouring family and *jati* bonds is typical among highly educated and prominently employed Indians. As for the vast majority of tradition-minded countrymen:

Dishonesty, nepotism and corruption as they are understood in the West are merely abstract concepts. These negative constructions are irrelevant to Indian psycho-social experience, which, from childhood on, nurtures one standard of responsible adult action, and one only, namely, an individual's lifelong obligation to his kith and kin. Allegiance to impersonal institutions and abstract moral concepts is without precedent in individual developmental experience, an adventitious growth in the Indian inner world. Guilt and its attendant inner anxiety are aroused only when individual actions go against the principle of the primacy of relationships, not when foreign ethical standards of justice and efficiency are breached. (Kakar, 1978, pp. 125–6)

In some countries – African countries in particular – the problem of kin-based favouritism plagues not only the public sector but also, potentially, the private world of business firms (Kennedy, 1988). A series of studies of indigenous and non-indigenous (immigrant) firms located in certain African countries, and based on detailed interviews with a sample of trading and manufacturing firms, reveals interesting evidence (see Fafchamps (2004) for an extended synthesis, and Platteau (2014: 177–9) for a summary). Not only is trade with relatives and friends extremely rare in Africa but, when it happens, it harms firm performance. This suggests that, as much as possible, business-people want to avoid involving their kin networks in their business, for fear of the costs that are likely to follow. Involvement of relatives is 'the surest way to go out of business, while selling on credit to relatives and neighbours amounts to 'signing the death warrant of the firm' (Fafchamps, 2004: 173). Entrepreneurs thus complain that it is difficult to keep business with relatives within the confines of an economic transaction. For example, it is hard to collect payments from relatives, whether in relation to a loan or the delivery of a good. More generally, payment problems are frequent because friendship and family ties get in the way of exerting pressures on clients. In addition, firms buying from family and friends encounter more late delivery problems.

A second relevant finding is the absence of evidence of systematic mechanisms whereby information about trustworthiness of clients is shared among African manufacturing firms, other than direct recommendation by common acquaintances (Fafchamps, 2004: 173, 256–7, 295). Among agricultural traders, too, trust-based relationships constitute the dominant contract enforcement mechanism, implying that trust is established primarily through repeated interactions, with little role for referral by other traders. Information on bad clients does not circulate widely, which severely limits collective punishments for opportunistic breaches of contract (such as non-payment). African-managed firms face more cases of non-payment than other firms, and they also complain more frequently about deficient quality (Fafchamps, 2004: 92, 109, 117, 135). Their transaction costs are consequently higher. By contrast, within stranger communities, information circulates rather freely, and client referral is a common practice. For all these reasons, non-indigenous firms operating in Africa are at an advantage, as illustrated by the fact that in Kenya, for example, it is only within the Indian community that first-time customers are able to obtain trade credit from the date of their first purchase.[6]

Finally, foreign firms hesitate to enter into business relations with indigenous firms, which they generally deem to be unreliable. In particular, they find

---

[6] Moreover, indigenous firms (in Kenya and Zimbabwe) are less likely to socialise with suppliers, and they have more restricted knowledge about them and their supplies, compared to immigrant firms, suggesting that ethnic barriers are more limiting for the former. Since better business contacts allow firms to enforce contracts and economise on screening costs, immigrant firms tend to be more profitable (Fafchamps, 2004: 252–3, 258, 300).

fault with African managers for continuously trying to renegotiate delivery and payment terms *ex post* (Fafchamps, 2004: 110). Clearly, the multilateral reputation mechanism which, according to Avner Greif (1994), characterises so-called collectivist cultures is conspicuously absent in sub-Saharan Africa. What we find, instead, is the bilateral reputation mechanism that is typical of 'individualistic cultures'. This is a rather paradoxical conclusion, yet it is perfectly congruent with the idea that in this region kinship/ethnic ties and their associated obligations are more an impediment to private capital accumulation than a social capital that can reduce transaction costs (Kennedy, 1988). Note that inefficiencies arising from kin-based relations are not only caused by non-contract performance; they are also caused by powerful redistributive pressures exerted on economically successful kin people. In fact, the two problems are often related, since if African businesspeople do not estrange themselves from the realm of the family, they will typically be compelled to sell on credit to their relatives and friends, and the risk will be high that the loans will never be returned. The problem is that borrowers do not feel morally obliged to repay debts incurred from a prosperous relative. Refusing to return a loan is an accepted way to preserve a rough egalitarianism among kin people, or to maintain the prior state of status inequality within the kin group (when a clan leader claims a higher economic position). Insofar as the credit has been granted under this informal pressure, the gift involved results not from a spontaneous but from a forced transaction (Platteau, 2014: 170).

E Substitution

The last type of interaction combines ineffective formal institutions and converging outcomes, and it involves substitution between the two types of institutions. In short, informal institutions achieve what formal institutions were designed, but failed, to achieve. A well-known example is the persistence of traditional and informal forms of intra-community income sharing and mutual help in the face of absent or highly imperfect (formal) insurance markets, due to a lack of verifiability and/or asymmetric information between contracting parties (Scott, 1976; Platteau, 1991, 1997; Dercon, 2005; Udry, 1994). A second illustration concerns the problem of public order and public goods provision. A most glaring reflection of weak state capacity is its failure to provide key public goods, including physical security and protection for its citizens. When this happens, there is a tendency for informal groups, networks, or organisations to fill the gap. There is thus abundant evidence of such groups emerging or extending their role to provide emergency help to people hit by a natural disaster (a flood, a forest fire, an epidemic), to build and maintain rural roads or water control infrastructure, or to supply basic education and health services. When it comes to public order, what springs to mind is the situation of failed states in which, by definition, the state is unable to fulfil its minimal function of guaranteeing law and order to all its people. In such contexts, law and order is generally established on fragmented portions of the national territory, at the level of regions or sub-regions, tribal and ethnic entities, religious communities, and so on. It is implemented by warlords, clan militia, sectarian movements based on religion or a millenarian ideology, or some forms of 'village republic', military groups backed and directed by a foreign government, or criminal organisations.

There is a serious risk that the substitution of informal law and order agencies for state power entail what Chabal and Daloz (1999) have called a 're-traditionalisation of society'. But reality may be more complex and point to various forms of amalgamation of the state system with traditional agencies (Bayart, 1993; Reno, 1995; Jones, 2009). In Liberia, for example, we learn that 'tribalism is not an ancient form of organisation which pre-dates the nation-state, but an essentially modern concept which is inherently connected to that of the nation-state ... It is a political resource which enables individuals and factions to pursue their interests in a national state' (Ellis, 1999: 198). Therefore, 'the apparent uniformity of the formal system of government which has its centre in Monrovia was in reality a patchwork structure in which local communities and their leaders reached a variety of accommodations with the centre, in the process of which old institutions of government, such as chieftaincies and religious sodalities, acquired new characteristics' (p. 207). Interactions between informal and formal institutions may thus evolve dynamically depending on the institutional path followed by society: the two types of institutions influence each other in a dynamic two-way process.

III ECONOMIC THEORIES OF INSTITUTIONAL CHANGE
AND STAGNATION

In the following paragraphs, we address the issue of institutional change by discussing four different strands of economic literature: the induced institutional innovation theory, the evolutionary theory, the theory of external shocks to self-enforcing institutional equilibria, and the political economy approach.

A Smooth Adaptation of Institutions: Price-Induced Institutional Change

One approach to institutional change is to view institutions as more or less smoothly adapting to changing circumstances or a changing environment. This adaptation can be conceptualised either as the outcome of the changing behaviour of rational agents or as an evolutionary process driven by agents with only limited rationality. The former view, which we discuss in the present subsection, is well reflected in the so-called induced institutional innovation theory advanced by Hayami and Ruttan (1985) and Hayami and Kikuchi (1981). The basic idea is that changes in the environment are translated into the price realm, and agents respond to changes in relative prices by modifying not only the technology they use but also the institutions that regulate their lives.[7] The explanation is thus based on an important simplification: institutions are treated analogously to ordinary goods and services, and market forces are conceived as exerting their influence upon them in the same way as they do for goods and production factors. In short, the market is the driver of institutional change.

As Hayami later admitted (1997), this is a quite naïve model, especially because institutional change typically requires collective action, and it is simplistic to assume that it is automatically organised whenever the aggregate social benefit resulting from such a change exceeds the social cost. In his words, 'if such a naïve mechanism of induced institutional innovation always operated, all the economies would have grown smoothly, and no great income gap would ever have emerged between developed and developing economies' (p. 20). Still, the naïve model could well be valid in broad terms of progress in human history, which seems to suggest that, with enough time, people eventually find solutions to overcome the incentive problems that stand in the way of collective action.

It is therefore no coincidence that the work of Boserup (1965, 1981) has been a major source of inspiration for development economists seeking to explain institutional change as a pseudo-market mechanism, that is, as the outcome of changes in relative factor scarcities. In her detailed account of the evolution of agricultural systems and patterns of land use under pre-industrial conditions in both temperate and tropical regions, she persuasively argued that food has been increasingly produced with the help of labour-intensive technologies. The dynamic changes involved – which entailed the reshuffling of land rights, the redefinition of gender roles, and other social and institutional changes – had the effect of increasing land productivity while simultaneously maintaining labour productivity and standards of living in the presence of growing population pressure.

Binswanger and co-authors have followed up on the idea that changes in endowments propelled by population growth are an important source of institutional change. They thus proposed a theory in which agrarian institutions and their evolution are largely explained as a function of population density (Binswanger and Rosenzweig, 1986; Binswanger and McIntire, 1987; Binswanger et al., 1989). More precisely, relative scarcities of key production factors, jointly with material characteristics of agricultural activities and the pervasive information problems associated with them, are seen as playing a major role in explaining changes in contract forms, the intensification of agriculture, and the emergence of small family farms in areas of high population density. The conditions in which plantations exist can also be derived.

---

[7] When applied to technological choices, the theory is known as the induced technological innovation hypothesis, initially propounded by John Hicks (1932). See Hayami (1997: 16–19) for a short presentation.

The idea that under the influence of population growth and market integration informal land tenure rights are gradually transformed into forms closer and closer to freehold rights has been studied in detail by Platteau (2000: Chap. 4, 2004). More recently, Guirkinger and Platteau (2015, 2017, 2020; Guirkinger et al., 2015) have further developed this line of explanation and support it with first-hand empirical evidence about the nuclearisation of farm households in West Africa.

Interestingly, fascinating applications of the approach of induced institutional change have been made to important episodes of historical development in the Western world, Japan, and Russia. Since it is beyond the scope of the present book to review them, we are content with making a passing mention of a few particularly salient studies. To begin with, Smith (1959) has offered us a detailed and original account of the rather gradual transformation of agrarian contracts and the demise of serfdom in Tokugawa Japan. These profound changes are traced back to a major expansion of economic opportunities sparked by the development of rural (silk-producing) industries. This process appears to be in striking contrast to events in Russia, where serfs were emancipated (in 1861) as a result of a top-down, state-directed reform abolishing serfdom. Things may have been more complex, though, since under the initiative of enlightened landlords, gradual reforms were introduced in some estates even before 1861 (Markevich and Zuravskaya, 2018). Another illustration is provided by the work of Voigtländer and Voth (2013), who traced the origin of late marriage in Europe to the Black Plague period. The underlying mechanism lies in a change of the opportunity cost of women's involvement in husbandry production, rather than in grain production, following the abrupt decline of the population caused by this plague. The same line of argument, based on the relative importance of grain and husbandry in the prevailing agricultural system and the specific characteristics of the husbandry technology, has been used by the latter authors to account for the differential evolution of the marriage pattern between northwestern Europe, on the one hand, and Mediterranean and Eastern Europe and even China, on the other hand.

At this final stage of our discussion of the first approach, two remarks are in order. First, in many post-Hayami studies the analytical framework actually departs from the original and crude idea of price-adjusting behaviours by agents endowed with so-called parametric rationality (agents take prices as a given which they cannot influence). The preferred theoretical approach has been the principal–agent model, in which a principal wants a task to be performed by an agent whose actions or characteristics s/he cannot directly observe. Since the agent is then incited to opportunistically exploit the resulting information gap, the principal needs to design a contract or a scheme that will induce the agent to behave in such a way as to satisfy the principal's interests. In this type of model, individuals are assumed to possess strategic rationality, meaning that they are able to anticipate how others will respond to their own decisions. Instead of adjusting to relative prices, they make constrained optimal decisions in which the constraint is often set by relative factor scarcities (in land, labour, or capital) or by the importance of external opportunities (as reflected in the agent's reservation utility).[8]

Second, it is not coincidental that in the above-cited examples, institutional change is largely the outcome of individual decisions taken in a decentralised context. In such instances the induced institutional innovation model does not appear to be too naïve, although it is based on a comparative-static reasoning rather than on a genuinely dynamic argument. When a change occurs in some parameters of the social, technical, and economic environment, the optimal institution, rule, or contract is modified and, being somehow able to recognise this, rational individuals bring about the new arrangement. If that does not happen, the persistence of the inefficient institution is typically attributed to undue meddling of the government or another authority. In contrast to the above approach, the one to which we now turn is truly dynamic in the sense that it depicts the path that leads from one institution to another.

B Smooth (but Slow) Adaptation of Institutions: The Evolutionary View

An alternative view of how institutional change can come about when the environment changes – say because of population growth, the emergence of new economic opportunities, or an external threat or challenge – is anchored in evolutionary theory. According to this view, the emergence, diffusion, and demise of rules or institutions are the outcome of an organic process of Darwinian natural selection, which epitomises the competitive pressures of the market and the invisible hand. Institutions or rules are thus seen as evolving unconsciously and gradually as a result of the pursuit of individual interests as agents repeatedly face the same types of social problems or situations. In the simplest version, inefficient institutions are expected to have a low evolutionary fitness, and therefore they tend to be displaced in the long run by more efficient institutions (see, e.g., Schotter, 1981; Axelrod, 1984; Sugden, 1986, 1989).

Looked at in this way, institutions emerge not as a result of rational, purposeful design by any individual or organisation of individuals, but as the result of spontaneous evolution. This means, for example, that people learn from experience that following a given constraint or custom can actually serve their own individual interests (Aoki, 2001: 40). Possessing a limited (or bounded) rationality, they follow trial-and-error behaviours: what works well for an individual is more likely to be used again, whereas what turns out poorly is more likely to be discarded. They look around them, gather information, and ground their decisions on the basis of fragmentary information. Because they

---

[8] Optima are constrained because in the presence of private information first-best solutions cannot be achieved. What is sought is the best possible contract or scheme from the principal's standpoint.

have only an incomplete idea of the way the world in which they operate works, they do not fully understand the strategic implications of their choices, and may not be especially forward-looking (Young, 1998: 5–6). Thanks to imitation, trials and errors, and takeovers, however, effective strategies are more likely than ineffective ones to be retained (Axelrod, 1997: 47–8).

The key mechanism driving change in the evolutionary setup is the so-called replicator mechanism. Whereas in biology the inheritance of parental genes is the replication mechanism (called natural selection) that ensures the survival of the fittest over successive generations (the more effective individuals are more likely to survive and reproduce), in economics replication is often assumed to be effected through the types of behaviour just discussed: imitation and takeover of unsuccessful agents or firms by successful ones, trial-and-error experimentation, and learning.[9] In such 'reinforcement' mechanisms, it is one's own past payoffs that matter, not those of other agents. The principle is that 'the probability of taking an action in the present increases with the payoff that resulted from taking that action in the past' (Young, 1998: 28). It should be noted that, in line with the assumption of limited rationality, the diffusion of more effective strategies does not require that the agents fully understand the strategic implications of their choices (i.e., they are not assumed to have a perfect ability to reason inductively about a feedback mechanism between their own choices and the choices of the other players). Rather than explaining how they would rationally pick actions in a given situation, evolutionary theorising is concerned with understanding how behaviour evolves or persists over time (Rasmusen, 1989: 121).

Interestingly, many pioneers of the development economics discipline implicitly held a sort of (co-)evolutionary view of institutional and cultural change. Thus, Arthur Lewis (1955) thought that religious beliefs, for example, may evolve and be reinterpreted depending on the economic environment confronting societies. In other words, traditional values and attitudes, whenever they are hostile to economic advancement, will eventually adapt themselves to new economic opportunities (p. 106). And Alfred Hirschman (1958) pointed out that traditional images of change will remain a critical bottleneck for constructive action for economic development until experience modifies them in the appropriate direction (see also Bauer and Yamey, 1957; Meier and Baldwin, 1957; and the discussion in Platteau, 2011).

Unlike what immediate intuition might suggest, and defeating the excessive hopes placed in them by the economists who first used them, evolutionary

---

[9] Since in most standard evolutionary models pairs of players are selected randomly from a 'large' population to play the given game once, and are thereafter returned to the population, imitative and learning behaviour that involves strategy changes during the life of an agent are precluded. Recently, however, economists have paid increasing attention to learning models where the strategy revisions of a given player generate substantial feedback effects by affecting the other players' payoffs, thereby inducing the latter also to revise their strategies subsequently. In all cases, rationality is assumed to be limited.

models do not unambiguously point to efficient adaptation of human institutions: there is absolutely no certainty that optimal rules or institutions will
emerge from evolutionary processes. Contrary to appearances, the evolutionary
theory of institutional change is therefore in clear opposition to the induced
institutional innovation approach, and the former is better able than the latter
to explain diverging institutional trajectories across countries. And since diverging paths are often encountered, the interest of the evolutionary approach ought
not to be underestimated. This is particularly evident in the case of cultural
norms and habits, modes of social interaction, and political regimes.

It would be wrong to think that the competitive selection of group-level
institutions rather than individual strategies might lead to more positive conclusions in the form of more efficient arrangements. In fact, it raises even more
severe problems than those confronting invisible hand arguments applied to
individual traits. Several factors account for this (partial) failure, and they
deserve our attention (see Bowles, 2004: 90–1, Chap. 13).

First, the repertoire of institutions and behaviours among which selection
operates may be highly restricted: being absent from the available repertoire,
many institutions remain unknown or untried.[10] Moreover, 'the creation of
novel institutions is akin to the emergence of new species: it requires the con-
fluence of a large number of improbable variations in the status quo' (Bowles,
2004: 91).[11] Binmore (1992) makes essentially the same point when he stresses
that in many evolutionary models attention has been artificially restricted to a
few strategies, often arbitrarily chosen. No clue is given as to why particular
strategies are there while innumerable other conceivable strategies are ignored
(p. 434). If such an approach allows the evolutionary modeller to derive efficient institutions, it does so without really explaining their emergence, since the
appearance of the beneficial strategies that lead to them is itself unaccounted
for. For example, if followed by everyone, a strategy consisting of respecting a
claim to property made by an individual who first occupied a piece of land can
lead to the establishment of the institution of private property rights. Yet, the
question remains as to how such a strategy did emerge. Also, what happens
when several individuals came to occupy a land at the same time, or believe
and claim that they did, is an unresolved issue.

Second, the existence and efficiency of an institution often depend on the fraction of the population that is governed by it (a characteristic sometimes called

---

[10] In biology, natural selection works on existing genetic material, which need not include the
optimal genetic 'programme', and, if it does not, optimal adaptation is hampered. Moreover,
the fact that gene mutations are blind (their occurrence is assumed to be independent of the
needs of organisms) and can represent only gradual variations of existing genotypes precludes
them from introducing optimal types in the population (Vromen, 1995: 95–6).

[11] An immediate implication of the above point is that it may be impossible to measure inefficiency owing to the lack of a counterfactual. As a matter of fact, it is difficult to compare the
efficiency of a selected institution against another because the latter has not been selected (Platteau, 2008: 460).

strategic complementarity) and on the set of co-existing institutions.[12] Thus, 'some institutions may be complementary, each enhancing the functioning of the other, while some institutions may reduce the effectiveness of other institutions' (Bowles, 2004: 90). As a consequence, there may exist multiple stable configurations of institutions, and some of these configurations may be very inefficient and still persist over long periods of time. Because strategic complementarities or other sources of increasing returns – more particularly, setup or fixed costs that must be incurred to create an institution, or learning effects that raise the effectiveness of an institution that acquires growing influence – may thus give rise to multiple (equilibrium) outcomes, institutions may be path-dependent. When institutional evolution is path-dependent, small initial differences may cause distinct societal histories to emerge. Instead of institutional convergence, what is obtained is then the long-term coexistence of distinct evolutionarily stable institutions (Bowles, 2004: 403–4). The evolutionary process follows paths that have different long-run characteristics depending on where they start and on the order in which agents happen to meet, thus leading to different equilibrium configurations (Young, 1998: 8; see also North, 1990: 92–104).

Third, when the evolutionary framework is enlarged to allow for a coevolution of institutions and preferences (with each exerting an influence on the development of the other), it is quite possible for group-advantageous but individually costly norms and patterns of behaviour to evolve. Thus, between-group competition may have favoured the emergence of groups or nations that have fostered preferences promoting military abilities and war-making capacity rather than individually profitable behaviour. In the process, values centred on glory, honour, valour, and self-sacrifice, as well as the systems promoting them (tribal systems, religions, etc.), take precedence over more selfish individual traits.

Finally, the rates of change induced by selection processes may well be very slow relative to the pace of changes induced by chance events, or exogenous changes in certain key elements in the environment (e.g., knowledge, external influences). If that is the case, and if the outcome of a competitive selection process eventually materialises, it will have become inefficient.

Interestingly, the central message – according to which inefficient (and unequal) institutions can persist over very long periods of time – continues to hold when evolutionary models are made more complex, by bringing multi-level selection into the picture and by introducing players who intentionally pursue conflicting interests through collective action (Bowles, 2004: Chaps. 11–13). We now turn our attention to two remaining approaches which, unlike the above two, are essentially static.

---

[12] Strategic complementarity thus applies to conventions, such as measurement standards or traffic rules: the incentive to adopt these standards or to abide by these rules increases with the number of other people taking the same action. These are typically the sorts of institutions that lend themselves to adaptive expectations 'where increased prevalence enhances beliefs of further prevalence' (North, 1990: 94).

C Institutions as Self-Enforcing Arrangements

This approach, in common with the principal–agent approach, conceives of institutions as self-enforcing (equilibrium) arrangements. However, rather than considering contracts or deals that are entered into in the context of bilateral relationships or multilateral relationships based on pairwise relationships inside a network, it analyses situations in which numerous actors interact simultaneously. Institutions are conceptualised as Nash equilibria because they ensure that beliefs have converged, and actions have been coordinated between individuals. More precisely, all agents choose their own action-choice rules in response to their subjective perceptions (beliefs) of others' action-choice rules, and it is only when these perceptions are confirmed by observation that an institution or rule is well established (Aoki, 2001: 10–11). Institutions are therefore self-enforcing by virtue of the fact that at equilibrium the actors' expectations about each other's behaviour in a particular situation turn out to be consistent with the experience generated by the resulting actions. When this is the case, agents have no incentive to deviate from their own action-choice rule, and institutions represent stable outcomes.

A number of important implications follow from the above characterisation. First, there are multiple possible institutions that can satisfy the requirements of a Nash equilibrium; that is, institutions for which beliefs converge and actions are coordinated. Furthermore, there is absolutely no assurance that they all correspond to socially efficient outcomes. Put in another way, it is only in particular situations, namely in pure coordination problems, that people are indifferent between possible stable solutions: for example, they do not care whether they should stop at the traffic light when the colour is red, green, blue, or orange – the only thing that matters to them is that everybody follows the same rule or convention. Since individual beliefs or expectations play such an important role in many problems of institutional choice, it is highly plausible that people end up coordinating on a rule that is not optimal (in the sense intended by Pareto, that no other rule is available that could improve the situation of one individual without causing a loss of welfare for some other individuals). By definition, if a rule or institution is a Nash equilibrium, people do not deviate from the outcome to which their expectations have led them; cultural inertia appears to be the factor behind this stability (Basu et al., 1987). In the words of Stiglitz (1989), 'individuals know more about the institutions and conventions with which they have lived in the recent past than they know of others by which they might live' (p. 26). Therefore, they tend to prefer the status quo to untried solutions, the effects of which they can only anticipate or speculate on.

Owing to the critical role of beliefs, it is even possible to come across paradoxical situations in which individuals choose to support rules or other institutional arrangements which they do not like, or even find repugnant (such as the caste system in India). As shown by Georges Akerlof (1976) and Timur

Kuran (1995: Chaps. 6–8), it may thus be rational for an individual to comply with unpleasant rules or to obey a totalitarian regime if there exists an effective network of mutually reinforcing social sanctions against disobedience and a system of converging expectations that sustain the existing arrangement. The underlying intuition is that a bad institution or a harmful rule persists due to mutual suspicion between people, and the immediate implication of the existence of a web of self-reinforcing sanctions is that everyone is both a victim and a supporter of a system in which there need not even exist a power-wielding central authority. For these sorts of effective sanctions to prevail, meta-punishment must be applied; that is, an individual is considered disloyal to a regime or a rule if either s/he does not cooperate or s/he maintains relations with someone who is disloyal (Kuran, 1995: 118–36; Basu, 2000: 136–47).

Raising the question of institutional change in this new framework amounts to asking how people can possibly extract themselves from the current arrangement. Logically, they can succeed in this only as a result of exogenous shocks that modify some key parameters of the situation produced by their history and culture. As pointed out by Greif and Laitin (2004: 633): 'A self-enforcing institution is one in which each player's behaviour is a best response. The inescapable conclusion is that a change in self-enforcing institutions must have an exogenous origin'. The shocks can have different sources: they may consist of technological, economic, demographic, environmental, or political changes that end up modifying the payoffs accruing to some or all the agents, of changes that bring new actors onto the scene and/or remove old ones, or of changes that enlarge the repertoire of available actions or alter the expectations of agents regarding others' actions. In such cases, new equilibrium outcomes become possible while old ones may no longer be accessible.

A well-known illustration is based on the distinction between inclusive and extractive political equilibria, as described by Acemoglu and Robinson (2012) and by Sokoloff and Engerman (2000). While the latter are based on highly oppressive economic and political institutions, the former are characterised by participatory politics, checks and balances on politicians, and effective property rights for a broad cross-section of society. Once a country has attained either equilibrium, it gets trapped in it. For precisely this reason, an exogenous shock or a chance event is required to move a country from the vicious (extractive) to the virtuous (inclusive) equilibrium. As in the case of the first approach (induced institutional innovation), though, the theory is essentially static and therefore does not provide clues about the pathway leading from one equilibrium arrangement to the other. Since many agents are now involved, the issue of how they succeed in establishing the best institution following the occurrence of a beneficial shock is even more complicated than in the first approach.

To take another example, consider the aforementioned example of collectivist societies described by Greif: those societies were embedded in an institution that was dominated by the mechanism of multilateral reputations and sanctioning. Grounded in continuous relationships between members of a network, this arrangement enabled merchants to build trust, enforce contracts, and expand their activities in Europe and the Mediterranean during early modern times, and it is not coincidental that similar trade networks, or trading diasporas, have been equally successful in Africa as well (Platteau, 2000: 261–2). As trade opportunities expand, however, the limited size of a network may become a constraint on further capital accumulation and growth. What is needed, then, is a shift of the society from the collectivist institutional setup to a more individualistic setup in which political enforcement organisations operate.

Call 'relation-based governance' the informal mode of contract enforcement documented by Greif (i.e., contracts involving reputational effects arising from repeated transactions), and 'rule-based governance' the system that relies on formal contracts and their enforcement by the courts or the police (Dixit, 2007: 141–2). Li (2003) has aptly clarified the analytical conditions under which each system is preferable to the other, and when the latter should replace the former (see also Dixit, 2004). Relation-based governance has small fixed costs, since it can operate on the basis of existing networks of relatives and friends. But its marginal costs are large, and they increase substantially as the scope of trade expands and requires the enlargement of the merchant network beyond close acquaintances who are generally trustworthy. In contrast, rule-based governance entails high fixed costs in the form of laws, regulations, regulatory agencies, and courts. Yet, once these formal institutions are in place, business deals with strangers can be struck at low marginal cost. The conclusion is rather straightforward: the relation-based system is scale-limited, being better at small scales of transactions but inferior to the rule-based system at large scales. But that leaves entirely open the question as to how, starting from an informal relation-based system, a society succeeds in moving to a formal rule-based system when such a shift becomes necessary.

What bears emphasis is that in most cases countries do not switch entirely to purely formal institutions: a lot of economic activity, even in the most advanced countries, continues to be governed by relational and private ordering 'under the shadow of the law' (Dixit, 2007: 143–4). To the extent that formal and informal rules are complementary, this feature does not create problems but actually helps promote growth in a rather smooth manner (see Section II, subsection B).

A clear advantage of the last two approaches to institutions and institutional change is that they both lead to the conclusion that there is not one but several pathways to modern economic growth and development. The last approach, to which we now turn, comes to the same conclusion.

D The Political Economy Approach: Why Are Institutions and Policies Inefficient?

The discussion of this last approach proceeds in two steps. To begin with, we examine the many obstacles that can block the decentralised mechanisms whereby losers from socially beneficial institutional change are appropriately compensated. The need for an effective state emerges from this failure of a decentralised functioning of the society. Unfortunately, as argued in the second step of our analysis, the state may also fail for reasons that the political economy approach can help us to understand.

1 The Coase Theorem

Consider the frequent situation in which the aggregate benefits of an institutional change exceed the costs, but some individuals or groups are going to lose from the shift to the new institution. The efficiency principle that underpins the well-known Coase theorem indicates that this should not be an obstacle to change: under certain assumptions, through decentralised bargaining and transfer payments, agents should be able to reach an agreement that ensures that the losers are duly compensated by the winners and therefore agree to depart from the status quo. In these conditions, moreover, the choice of the efficient institution, which is supposed to be unique, does not depend on the *a priori* distribution of power between the parties involved. The latter will affect only the distribution of the costs and benefits of the change. In short, the issues of efficiency (selecting the efficient institution) and distribution (how the gains from institutional change are shared among all the participants) are separable (see Milgrom and Roberts (1992: 35–8) for a detailed argument).

The problem is that, whether explicit or implicit, the assumptions required for effective decentralised bargaining and for absent impact of power asymmetries on the efficiency of institutional choices are very restrictive. We review them because their limitations point to important barriers to institutional change. Let us start by stating the efficiency principle: if people are able to bargain together effectively and can effectively implement and enforce any agreements they reach, they should be able to realise all the gains caused by a shift from an inefficient situation to an alternative that everyone would prefer (Milgrom and Roberts, 1992: 24). Two explicit assumptions are: (i) negotiating costs are nil and (ii) no wealth effect is at play. The former assumption is clearly violated when many people are involved, or they have heterogeneous characteristics. It is true that bargaining can be entrusted to group representatives, but then all sorts of collective action problems arise, including the delicate issue of leadership (see Baland and Platteau, 1996: Chaps. 5–7, and 1997, 1998, for an extensive treatment). Moreover, if one party can more easily solve these problems than the other can (think of the old Smithian problem of a well-organised group of colluding producers facing a large group of consumers), the resulting institutional choice will favour the former and not necessarily coincide with the optimal solution. As for the second assumption, it is realistic only when the amounts of the compensatory transfers are small relative to the agents' financial resources; that is, when the stakes of institutional change are not too high. If that is not the case, the very payment transfer process is going to affect the wealth of the negotiating parties, who will then modify their transfer demands (for the losers) or their willingness to satisfy them (for the winners).

But there is another bargaining-related assumption that is often ignored: the reasoning is typically based on a two-agent framework where the outcome of bargaining is rather straightforward. As Shapley and Shubik (1969) have shown, however, when there are more than two agents, a bargaining solution may not exist. More precisely, an efficient solution may exist, yet the parties will not be able to reach it through decentralised bargaining. Moreover, whether a bargaining solution is attainable or not may ultimately depend on the initial assignment of rights to the parties; that is, on the initial distribution of bargaining powers. In this instance, the separability between efficiency and distributive issues is clearly broken (Baland and Platteau, 1996: 51–2).

To these major difficulties a number of other snags must be added. Three of them deserve particular attention (see Platteau, 2008: 447–9). First, people may not behave rationally, implying that they may seem to act against their interests. This is the case not only when they stick to a particular cultural prescription (a social norm may even prohibit compensatory cash transfers, at least when they involve certain categories of people), but also when they are imbued with a strong sense of justice that takes precedence over cold calculus. As an example of the latter possibility, common people may oppose awarding compensation to an erstwhile elite (say, big landowners) who are going to lose from a socially beneficial land reform. Their opposition may be justified by the excessively large benefits that this elite drew from the existing arrangement in the past. Ideology then trumps rational bargaining based on present and future gains.

Second, negotiations are complicated if winners and losers have a different assessment of the costs and benefits of institutional change. Situations that immediately come to mind here are those in which poor people, whose preferences exhibit high discount rates, live in the same institutional setup as richer people, who have more future-oriented time preferences. Asymmetric evaluation of institutional change may also originate in particular worldviews or ideologies rooted in past experiences. An apt illustration is provided by the resistance of domestic producers against an opening of the national economy to external trade on account of an excessively pessimistic evaluation of the costs that such a change would entail for them. Such kind of resistance is expected to be especially strong in countries with a protectionist tradition. Of course, it may just be the case that genuine uncertainty prevails about the benefits and costs of institutional change. It is then highly likely that among the several bodies of knowledge or expertise available, the parties at stake will invoke the one that serves their particular interests best. For example, in fishing conflicts between small-scale fishermen and industrial vessel owners, the former tend to attribute their declining catches to the encroachment of the latter in coastal waters, while the latter tend to blame excessive fishing effort on the part of the former, say as a result of adoption of more effective technologies.

Each party seeks the support of marine biologists who produce evidence in their favour, and while small-scale fishermen demand the enforcement of an exclusive fishing zone for themselves, industrial fishermen and owners strongly resist this demand.[13]

A third source of failure of the Coase theorem is the double commitment problem, which makes the outcome of decentralised bargaining hard to implement and enforce. Potential losers may typically not trust the potential winners' promise to compensate them once the institutional change has occurred. Realising the transfers before the advent of the change is of no help: the inverse problem would then arise, since the potential winners may now fear that the incumbents will opportunistically collect the payment and then oppose the agreed-upon change.

For all of these reasons, efficiency and distributive issues are generally not separable, and institutional choices tend to reflect the distribution of power in society, rather than efficiency considerations. To increase efficiency, the intervention of the state is needed. However, as soon as one drops the naïve assumption of a benevolent state or social planner, that is, the assumption of a central agency that maximises the aggregate welfare of the population, the problem of power resurfaces. Precisely this problem is at the heart of the political economy approach: its main novelty consists of positing the state as a full-fledged actor pursuing its own (selfish) objectives, featuring the relative power weights of the various actors and the negotiating arenas existing in a society (see Acemoglu and Robinson, 2000, 2006a). In the new framework, an efficiency-improving institutional change will not occur if the interests of the state elite are aligned with those of a group of people opposed to that change. This is especially likely if organisations and interest groups that benefit from the current (inefficient) arrangements are able to shape the polity according to their wishes, thus making it still more difficult for change to come in the future. Ideology can also play a role, such as when agents or groups construct rationalisations aimed at vindicating the prevailing rules and structures, thereby accounting for their poor objective performance (North, 1990: 99).

2 The Political Coase Theorem

It is useful to stress the analogy between some of the aforementioned problems undermining the applicability of the Coase theorem in a decentralised context, on the one hand, and the problems that arise when a centralised state exists that fulfils important functions, on the other hand. As argued by Acemoglu (2003), an extension of the reasoning underpinning the Coase theorem to the political sphere would mean that political and economic transactions should push towards efficient policies and institutions (i.e., those that achieve the best

---

[13] This example is based on the experience of one of the authors in the state of Kerala (India) in the 1980s and 1990s.

outcomes for the society), regardless of who, or which social group, holds political power (p. 621).[14] In actual practice, however, politicians and powerful social groups do not typically strike deals with the rest of society for the purpose of adopting policies and establishing institutions that maximise aggregate production or social welfare while ensuring the redistribution of part of the gains to themselves. In short, they do not 'predate efficiently'. At the root of this recurrent state failure or political failure are 'inherent commitment problems associated with political power' (p. 622; see also Besley and Coate, 1998).

More precisely, while the validity of the so-called political Coase theorem rests on the ability of the state to write enforceable contracts, the state, or the social groups controlling it, cannot actually commit to not using their power to renege on their promises, or to not modifying the terms of the contract, if their selfish interests dictate that they should do so. Because contracts written by the state are by definition unenforceable – there is no state above the state – an inherent commitment problem thus arises that prevents efficient outcomes from materialising. On the other hand, if the rulers relinquish their power, the citizens cannot commit to making side payments to them in the future, since they will no longer possess the political power to enforce the agreed-upon promises. This is the political form of the double commitment problem mentioned above. In this view, problems of credible commitment ultimately appear as problems about the future exercise of political power.

Because the relationship between the state and the citizens is repeated, it is possible to conceive some commitment based on reputation and supported by the threat of future punishment (Acemoglu, 2003: 623). This is the function of political constitutions and other institutions (e.g., the delegation of monetary policy to a politically independent central bank) that are intended to provide checks and balances on the power of the rulers. The commitment problem cannot be completely overcome, however, and observation of the reality in many developing countries, in particular, confirms that states often choose inefficient and even disastrous policies and institutions because these choices 'are not made for the benefit of society as a whole, but for the benefit of those who control political power' (p. 648). A powerful ruler can thus flout a constitution that prescribes political mandates of a finite duration or that violates the independence of the central bank.

A general conclusion of the political economy literature addressing the problem of credible commitment is that the degree of inequality in the distribution of the costs of reforms, or of the benefits from the status quo, plays a critical role

---

[14] The distinction between policies and institutions proposed by Acemoglu (2003) is the following: while policies are choices made within a given political and social structure, institutions can be viewed as 'determinants of the political and social structure that are more durable and, as such, constrain future choices and policies' (p. 621, ftn. 2). Although institutions are often predetermined at the time when certain policy choices are made, they are also chosen by the society. Institutions thus correspond to the rules of the game that a society is playing, and these rules have been chosen by its citizens to constrain their future actions.

in determining whether reforms will be feasible or not. More precisely, when the inequality of power, or of the benefits from status quo policies or existing institutions is quite large, elites are prompted to oppose reforms in order to be able to hold on to their power and the associated rents in the future. Because the initial inequality in wealth and power is high, it is then difficult to commit in future to making everyone better off without making the elites worse off (Khemani, 2020: 5). Only through revolution or through a change in the composition of the elites and their preferences can key reforms become possible.[15]

Other reasons than unequal initial endowments can explain political opposition to reforms. These have already been mentioned in our discussion of the failures of the Coase theorem. In particular, uncertainty may exist over the distribution of the costs and benefits from reforms, due to a lack of solid technical evidence, to heterogeneous preferences leading to different evaluations of the pro and contra of a change, or to ideological resistance to available evidence. Regarding the latter source of uncertainty, it is worth noting that propagation of ideological prejudices against a reform may actually be driven by powerful groups whose interests would be harmed by its implementation. In all these cases, commitment problems will necessarily emerge and will block change (Majumdar and Mukand, 2004). Moreover, a bias towards the status quo may be caused by the fact that some of the individual winners and losers from the reform cannot be identified beforehand. For instance, it may be difficult to predict *ex ante* which precise sectors and firms would benefit from trade liberalisation reforms. When individuals ignore how they will fare under a reform, aggregate support for it is likely to be lower than it would have been under complete information. This is true even when individuals are rational, forward-looking, and risk-neutral, and when there is no aggregate uncertainty. Under these conditions it may happen that, once enacted, reforms will receive adequate political support, but they would nevertheless fail to carry the day *ex ante* (Fernandez and Rodrick, 1991).

Clearly, one important objective of the IDP is to reduce uncertainties and information asymmetries so as to ease the reform process by creating conditions conducive to an effective application of the Coase theorem.

3 Norms and Preferences for Public Goods

More recent strands of the political economy literature have turned their attention to problems beyond the credible commitment issue. One of them approaches resistance to reforms through the angle of norms, while the other refers to preference for public goods. The starting point of the norm approach

---

[15] Lizzeri and Persico (2004) have thus argued that the main factor that allowed for deep institutional reforms in the history of nations has typically consisted of significant increases in the elites' demand for public goods. This shift made them ready to give up private rents in exchange for more public goods.

is the idea that if a contract among rival interest groups is not enforceable or justiciable, it has to be self-enforcing. Here lies a prisoner's dilemma, since each group can extract a private gain by reneging. Consider the case where several competing interest groups, acting as multiple principals, attempt to control a government institution or department (the common agency). Each of these groups has an interest in offering the agency a little bit more than what others are offering in order to advance its interest at their expense (Dixit, 1996, 2003). Thus, Dixit (2018) argues that persistent and endemic corruption should be seen as a prisoner's dilemma in which, say, business groups are 'givers' of bribes. Although all of these groups would benefit from reduced bribes when taken as a whole, they stick to their current practice because they believe that this is the best they can do given the behaviour of the others. Absent some coordination mechanism or norm to regulate corruption, the high-level corruption equilibrium will persist.

That such mechanisms or norms are hard to come by is attested to by the general failure of anti-corruption policies, such as those embedded in the creation of the anti-corruption agencies that are so much favoured by the donor community (Olken and Pande, 2012; Khemani, 2020: 7–8). These failures tend to be attributed to the lack of legitimacy of political leaders. A leadership's legitimacy, if one follows Akerlof (2017), is functionally equivalent to agents monitoring each other with a view to ensuring compliance, implying the existence of some norm among peers regarding performing duties that are prescribed by a (legitimate) leader. The problem, however, is that in many instances political leaders are themselves corrupt – they extract rents from public office, indulge in vote buying and the like – or they are perceived as corrupt by the population. Therefore, they are not in a position to implement reforms aimed at combatting not only big cases of embezzlement but also more ordinary forms of petty corruption. Clearly, to break the vicious cycle of corruption, there is a need for exceptional and strong leaders, such as Kemal Atatürk in Turkey or Habib Bourguiba in Tunisia (Platteau, 2022). When available, these leaders can serve as role models capable of starting a virtuous mechanism of 'clean politics'.

When resistance to beneficial reforms is viewed from the standpoint of preference, stress is laid on the fact that citizens may vote in ways that do not properly account for negative consequences. In particular, Stuti Khemani (2020) writes that 'Citizens' preferences for emphasizing private benefits over public goods when evaluating leaders, either delivered by co-ethnic leaders, or through vote buying at the time of elections, appears to be a significant factor explaining the persistence of clientelistic politics in democracies in the poor world and its negative consequences for political incentives to pursue reforms' (p. 11). Citizens actually appear to be cognitively constrained such that they demand policies that confer short-term benefits at the expense of long-term costs (Dal Bo et al., 2017). Clientelistic politics may thus cause public goods or services to be under-provided even when they seem to favour the poor disproportionately, like in the case of primary healthcare and anti-poverty programmes or policies (Khemani, 2015; Anderson et al., 2015; Bardhan and Mookherjee, 2020; Bardhan et al., 2020).

Moreover, because the poor often place a high value upon their ethnic affiliation, leaders and their political parties often find it a more effective strategy to supply targeted private benefits to a special clientele than to supply public goods from which many people will benefit (Banerjee and Pande, 2007). Following this interpretation, political corruption partly stems from the fact that citizens value honesty in their leaders less than they value their ability to supply public resources on the basis of shared ethnic or caste identity. Stark evidence of this possibility has been adduced by Prakash and co-authors (2019): in India people may not hesitate to cast their votes in favour of politicians accused of criminal actions, even though these politicians generate bad economic outcomes (Prakash et al., 2019). In sum, 'vote buying could be a form of political responsiveness to the demands or needs of voters' (Khemani, 2020: 12).

A key problem with the cognitive thesis, however, is that an alternative explanation exists to account for the poor's demand for the wrong kind of goods and services. This explanation also relies on a preference characteristic, namely high time discount rates among the poor. Perhaps the cognitive constraint argument is the most relevant when the poor, as they often do, assign a high value to social events and religious festivals. On these occasions, they tend to spend large amounts of money that could have been used for more welfare-enhancing purposes, even in the short or medium term. But even here, rather than invoking cognitive constraints (or preference patterns that have arisen evolutionarily and have become inefficient), one can conceive of other explanations, such as the importance of social identity in the poor's preference schedule, the need to build up social capital, or the role of the elite in shaping the poor's preference in a way that legitimates their own power and influence.

The problem of reforms is therefore immensely complex, especially when powerful interests derive enormous advantages from the status quo. Lack of information about the value of reforms and heterogeneous evaluation of its benefits and costs among the parties at stake may also constitute a strong impediment. Worse still, even well-informed citizens may oppose a reform if they are reluctant to change their beliefs and preferences even when shown that their beliefs are wrong (Barrera et al., 2020). In the end, the credibility and legitimacy of reformist leaders are a crucial factor for success, but this is not a very reassuring conclusion given that we do not know where credibility and legitimacy come from (Khemani, 2020: 16).

4 The Political Economy Approach: Illustrating State Capture and State Failures

We can now briefly discuss a few interesting applications and illustrations of the argument according to which political elites may drive their societies away from efficient or development-enhancing institutions and policies, as well as of the role of beliefs and preferences. To begin with, we wish to refer to the political theory of economic backwardness, through which Acemoglu and Robinson (2006b) show how and in which conditions state elites may deliberately thwart development. Their basic intuition is that political elites face a trade-off between economic gains and power. All else being equal, they prefer technological progress and prosperity-inducing reforms that might increase their economic rents in the future. Yet all else is not equal because such changes can potentially erode their political advantages relative to other groups. They will thus decide to 'block beneficial economic and institutional change when they are afraid that these changes will destabilise the existing system and make it more likely that they will lose political power and future rents' (pp. 115–16). The theory predicts a non-monotonic impact of political competition on resistance to development: while political elites that are either subject to intense competition or do not face any competition due to their complete domination of the electoral landscape adopt new technologies, elites occupying an intermediate position between these two extremes will adopt the opposite attitude. This is because with intense political competition, elites prefer to innovate lest they should be replaced, whereas strongly entrenched elites do not fear losing political power, so for them there is no trade-off between economic gains and power. By contrast, elites that are 'somewhat entrenched' but are still afraid of being replaced are tempted to block innovation to prevent such replacement from happening (p. 116).

Along the same line, within a framework in which education is both the engine of growth and a determinant of political participation, Bourguignon and Verdier (2000) have looked for the conditions under which an educated oligarchy may have an incentive to subsidise the poor's education and to initiate a democratic transition, thereby promoting the endogenous emergence of a middle class. When these conditions are violated, the oligarchy will undermine universal education. There is evidence that, indeed, the education of ordinary people may be blocked by the elite. For example, in the case of Pakistan, Martin (2016) has observed a tendency among traditional landlords to oppose the (secular) education of their dependents lest they should seek emancipation and develop 'unrealistic expectations, and thereby cause a shortage of cheap agricultural labour (p. 87). Also, assuming a regime of autocracy, Auriol and Platteau (2017a, 2017b) have shown that a ruler may deliberately sacrifice institutional reforms in order to placate the opposition coming from traditional leaders (including religious authorities) who resent that their erstwhile prerogatives will be encroached upon (see also Auriol et al. (2021), where the army is added as a strategic actor). This raises the serious issue of how a modern state can manage the divergent interests of popular masses under the influence of traditional authorities that want to preserve the old order based on the community, on the one hand, and urban elites that have been exposed to Western values centred upon the improvement of the individual, on the other hand.[16]

---

[16] This issue is at the heart of Platteau (2017).

Turning to the role of beliefs and preferences, Chinese history supplies us with an interesting example of the role of ideology. Since the early fifteenth century, Chinese authorities have developed the idea that China does not need to develop its external trade links to become or remain a major economic and political power. Under the influence of the mandarins, who scorned and distrusted commerce, and unlike the eunuchs, who had the opposite interests and beliefs, the new worldview led the Chinese into believing that their country is better off when it relies on its own forces. Carried over well into the nineteenth century, 'this deliberate introversion', a major turning point in Chinese history, proved to be a disaster for the country that was leading the world in many respects several centuries earlier. It could not have come at a worse time, since it disarmed China just as European power was rising (Landes, 1998: 96; see also Jones, 1981: 168–9).

It bears emphasis that in the above discussion the state has been treated as a single homogeneous actor. This is an obvious simplification, not only because it ignores the distinction between the executive, the legislative, and the judiciary, but also because it bypasses possible conflicts existing inside each of these branches. Thus, serious dysfunction of the state apparatus may arise from tensions or contradictions that may come from a variety of different sources: between a government and its administration, between various departments or levels of the bureaucracy, between various political interest groups, or between appointed and elected leaders (say, between district officers and elected councillors). Note that the latter tensions may actually be ignited and nurtured by holders of central power who are eager to 'divide to rule' (for a vivid application of this argument in relation to Pakistan, see Cheema et al., 2005; Malik et al., 2022). Technically, whatever the source of misalignment, the problem can often be framed as one of multiple principals with conflicting interests (Dixit, 1996, 2002; Martimort, 1996; Bolton and Dewatripont, 2005: Chap. 13).[17]

Another important source of efficiency losses lies in the fact that the administration is often undermined by the corrupt behaviour of selfish officers and politicians. Consider the following example of the rise and decline of the effectiveness of land documentation and titling in Kenya (see Onoma, 2010). Although this was embraced by the postcolonial government after independence in 1963 (the system was initiated by the British in the early 1900s), the associated practices were gradually eroded so that by the early 2000s they had fallen into disrepute. Ominous signs of this institutional degradation were visible before, as attested by the cancellation of hundreds of title deeds by Kenya's High Court in May 1991, a dramatic move which led one

---

[17] Among the solutions to this problem that can be derived from this literature are exclusive deals aimed at making a common agent depend on a single principal, a greater role for the autonomy of the agent, a reduced role for top-down hierarchical monitoring, and an increased role for peer-to-peer professional norms (for a few illustrations, see Khemani, 2019: 8–15).

commentator to wonder 'whether the assumption that a title gives one inde-feasible rights to property was still true' (p. 65). Onoma's explanation is that the administration, by exchanging fake land documents for money, largely contributed to the erosion and drift, causing a marked fall in the efficacy of land documentation. At the same time, it appears that civil servants acted under the corrosive influence of well-connected politicians who used land doc-uments to obtain political support. For these politicians, 'issuing and selling land documents became an excellent way of raising cash for electoral cam-paigns, for buying the support of various individuals and groups, and for dissuading would-be opponents' (p. 66).

Onoma sums up his diagnosis by stressing that the problem was not just one of weak state capacity, nor was it that the system of land documenta-tion was not well established in the first place. The problem was rather that state agencies became increasingly less willing to use their powers to stop the fraudulent exploitation of land documentation by people close to the state (p. 66). Herein lies a prisoner's dilemma between the users of the law: an institution serving the common good (an efficient institution) has been created or confirmed, yet key participants find it in their own selfish interests to break the rules and thereby undermine it. At the root of the problem lies a system of political patronage that prompts key political actors to instrumentalise the administration for their own immediate benefit, rather treating it as a vehicle for advancing the national interest.

Other problems have plagued land titling in Kenya, including the usual problem of a lack of proper updating of land records. One of these prob-lems in particular deserves our attention because it vividly illustrates the role of ideology and the political influence of the common farmers rather than the Big Men on whom attention is usually focused. In Kenya, lenders have usually faced great difficulty foreclosing on land mortgages in the face of determined opposition from family and community. The fact of the matter is that 'the presence of many kin around mortgaged land makes it politically unfeasible to auction the holdings of defaulters' (Shipton, 1988: 120; see also Migot-Adholla et al., 1991: 170; Ensminger, 1997; Platteau, 2000: 145–7, 153–6). One important politico-ideological reason behind the government's reluctance to strictly enforce the law after independence was its fear of break-ing the fragile political consensus on which national policies rested. In the words of Bates (1989): 'The cry of land hunger had fed the nationalist rebel-lion that had brought the government to power. To turn people off the lands that they had fought to capture would be to risk the wrath of the true believ-ers in the nationalist revolution' (p. 74). The pressure on the government was all the stronger as the official opposition, represented by a radical party (the Kenya African Democratic Union, KADU) lobbied intensively on the land issue (pp. 67–8).

The stylised approach of the political economy approach has the advan-tage of supplying us with structured treatments of well-defined issues involving politics, as well as useful predictions of the effects of changing components in the environment. However, because the inter-relationships between institutions, politics, and development, and the dynamics of institutional change, are so complex, the approach needs to be complemented by contributions from other disciplines: political science, history, and socio-anthropology in particular. As attested by the above example about Kenya, these contributions are expected to provide a lot of details on the concrete processes of institutional change, as well as the specific problems they raise in particular contexts. The same interdisciplinary perspective and the same concerns with context and institutional details underlie the IDP approach that led to this book.

IV BY WAY OF CONCLUSION: RADICAL VERSUS GRADUAL INSTITUTIONAL REFORMS

The radical approach to institutional reforms views cultures and informal arrangements as powerful and persistent dragging forces that are unsuited to market-oriented growth and social development (Harrison and Huntington, 2000).[18] In this perspective, the discrepancy between people's traditional behaviour, beliefs, social norms, and collective rules and modernity can be overcome only by radically changing cultural traits. This can be done only by imposing new institutions by force, thereby creating an unavoidable tension and conflict between modern elites and traditional power structures.

Under certain circumstances, reformers with enough power and legitimacy may succeed in drastically modifying people's expectations and bringing about radical changes. For instance, Mustapha Kemal Atatürk undertook radical reforms to modernise Turkey, which had the effect of erasing a legacy of dominance by religion and tradition. A comprehensive set of policies was implemented, ranging from compulsory secular education, restrictions on wearing religious symbols in school, and the closure of religious orders, to the extension of women's voting rights, their right to be elected to public office, and separation between governmental and religious affairs in the country. In general, however, state policies directly aimed at top-down institutional change fail to produce effective and long-standing changes to existing traditional institutions. Even the Turkish experience has revealed that bold measures that ignore the deep values and norms of a large number of people have the effect of polarising the society between a modern urban elite residing in big cities and traditional masses inhabiting the countryside and towns. As the rise of an Islamist party testifies, and even though some important achievements were left untouched, some backtracking on previous reforms took place as soon as ordinary people

---

[18] This section is largely inspired by a note written by Jean-Philippe Platteau and Thierry Verdier in 2022: 'Formal and Informal Institutions in Development: Contexts, Resistance, and Leverage', Economic Development and Institutions (EDI) Project, Oxford Policy Management, Oxford.

were given a voice (Platteau, 2022). This is the cultural backlash effect which radical institutional reforms are likely to generate.

One of the factors explaining the strong resilience of traditional structures in the presence of a forced top-down imposition of formal institutions is the internalisation of informal norms and cultural values within individual preferences (Bisin and Verdier 2001, 2011). This internalisation allows for the persistence of traditional values and their transmission to future generations even in the absence of an explicit policy or will to perpetuate them. Another factor relates to the fact that the choice of a non-traditional option may require anticipation of the long-run effects of the policy reform. These effects themselves depend on the way people's expectations converge, and the way their actions, based on these expectations, are coordinated. When a reform implies a departure from traditional ways of doing things, changing behaviour is individually harmful if undertaken alone. Resistance to radical reforms may be all the stronger as these reforms involve egregious changes that destabilise the status quo, and therefore entail uncertain consequences.

Yet not all reforms are aimed at modifying the traditional order of things and at questioning deep-rooted social norms. Trade liberalisation reforms, for example, have no straightforward effect on a country's culture. This is the example chosen by Fernandez and Rodrik (1991) to illustrate their argument in favour of radical reforms. They make the critical but sensible assumption that there is initial uncertainty about the distribution of the costs and benefits of a reform. They show that a radical reform that is initially opposed by important sections of the population may eventually come to receive their support once uncertainty has vanished. Thus, in Taiwan and Turkey, where trade liberalisation was authoritatively imposed by an autocratic ruler against the wishes of the business community, the reform was gradually accepted by important group coalitions once they realised that the net benefits were greater than initially expected.

When cultural rules and social norms are at stake, like in the domains of family law and land tenure rules, however, a stronger case can be made for a more gradualist approach to institutional reforms. A first argument in favour of gradualism is that it avoids the large redistributive effects, both economically and culturally, which are typically produced by radical changes. It may also avoid head-on confrontation with the established power structures. More gradual or stepwise policies, which only marginally affect established interests at a given point in time, may be easier to implement with popular support (Gulesci et al., 2021; see also Aldashev et al., 2012). In their analyses of the policy trade-off between big-bang and gradualist reforms in the transition economies of the 1990s, Dewatripont and Roland (1992a, 1992b, 1995) argue that a gradualist strategy significantly relaxes the political economy constraints of reforms, and may sequentially exploit the fluidity of stepwise reform-supporting coalitions in the process of institutional change. In other words, because they are stretched over a rather long period, gradualist reforms allow political groups, which were not initially in favour of changing the status quo, to gradually emerge and join other groups that were initially supportive.

Relatedly, reforms that have few distributional consequences are arguably easier to carry out, in contrast with those that call into question established hierarchies. Moreover, from a social psychology standpoint, a gradualist approach also keeps socially determined goals and outcomes within the 'window' of the conceivable aspirations of individuals affected by the reform, which helps maintain their motivation and support (see Genicot and Ray, 2020). In this respect, public policies that radically promote Western values may be too distant from local norms, thereby generating frustration, conservatism, or backlash, especially when a large share of the population feels disenfranchised. Interestingly, Islamic fundamentalism was born as a movement of cultural reaction against attempts by colonial powers to annihilate local cultures (Platteau, 2017: Chap. 7).

An institutional gradualist approach has some drawbacks, though. A first issue stems from the existence of complementarities between different institutional dimensions. Introducing some institutional change along one dimension may fail to produce any effective outcome if there is a strong complementarity with another dimension that is not reformed at the same time. A second issue relates to the credibility of gradual reforms: because marginal changes may appear too hesitant and riddled with too many exemptions, the proposed policies do not credibly support a viable alternative. Essentially, the same argument stresses that a reformist government must engage in excessive signalling to distinguish itself from a less purposeful one. In this way, indeed, policy actions will convey useful signals about their intentions to financial markets and investors (Dixit, 2007: 145). More generally, formal institutional reforms that are designed to preserve certain traditional norms and practices may fail to change beliefs about what is the socially appropriate behaviour. Given the resilience of traditional institutions in shaping beliefs and constraining individual behaviour, gregarious practices that are in line with tradition may have a high degree of persistence in the face of moderate institutional reforms. In such cases, a more comprehensive approach may prove more effective.

In the sensitive domains of personal and community life, however, the best way to think of institutional change is in terms of leveraging informal arrangements to the extent that they can effectively promote development, possibly in tandem with formal institutions. Especially useful are informal structures, including support networks relating to reciprocity and mutual help, and traditional common pool management institutions. In addition to being able to fill gaps that are left vacant by market and state failures, these horizontal institutional arrangements based on castes or kinship groups may be better able to adapt to new opportunities and changing conditions. By fulfilling new roles and adapting successfully, they may become stronger and they may persist, even though their original function has vanished. This is the approach actually followed by many non-governmental organisations (NGOs) operating in rural areas of poor countries. Conversely, there is scope to leverage formal institutional structures with a view to indirectly promoting changes in informal arrangements within communities. Thus, within the framework of rural development projects, external supporting agencies often demand that local communities set up organisations that obey certain rules: regarding the creation of a general assembly of members and a management committee, the appointment of a treasurer, the regular convening of the assembly, the laying down of precise accounts about the use of money received, and so on. These rules aim at imparting financial discipline, accountability, delineation of responsibilities, and clear separation between the sphere of interpersonal relations and the sphere of professional activities.

The discrepancy between formal and informal institutions may also be reduced by openly allowing their joint functioning in the same domains. An interesting example is the approach of legal pluralism, where formal law coexists with customary law. Once specific dimensions are fixed by the formal structure, individuals may be left free to choose between various legal systems of arbitration and dispute settlement (formal and informal) in order to resolve their conflicts. This type of mechanism allows for a flexible implementation of the law that is compatible with traditional beliefs and social structures, eventually leading to a convergence of the two systems (Aldashev et al., 2012; Platteau and Wahhaj, 2013). The experiences of legal pluralism in the Ottoman empire, or presently in Indonesia, offer vivid illustrations of the beneficial effects which such an approach may engender (Bowen, 2003; Kuran, 2004a, 2004b).

To sum up, when compared to a gradual approach, a radical institutional approach enjoys the benefits of signalling policy commitment as well as the gains of complementarities across institutional dimensions, which are tackled at the same time. On the other hand, it encounters more stringent political economy constraints, and may induce strong cultural resistance from significant parts of the population, especially in domains where reforms hurt deep-rooted social norms and are easily viewed as an attack on local cultures.

Several implications can be drawn for policymakers and foreign donors. First, when political constraints are particularly strong, a radical approach may not be feasible. In such a case, aid policy should preferably stimulate gradual and marginal changes in endowments and resources so that over time coalitions can be formed along the reform process. Similarly, in domains where cultural resistance is a serious issue, aid policy should favour the implementation of a gradualist approach aimed at supporting mixed institutional reform systems, whereby specific dimensions are fixed by the formal structure while other dimensions are left to the functioning of traditional structures. Finally, individuals may often appear to oppose progressive social changes because they fail to anticipate their consequences and focus therefore on their individual, short-run costs. One way out of this dilemma is to ensure that resources and endowments can be provided to reduce these short-run costs. In these instances, donors can make a useful contribution by stimulating complementary institutional structures that implement transfers of resources through various channels, such as insurance systems, money transfers, information diffusion, and coordination mechanisms.

2

Tools for an Institutional Diagnostic

I INTRODUCTION

The case studies summarised in this volume, and which serve as raw material for our reflection on institutions and development, follow a particular analytical approach. Conceived in the same spirit as the 'growth diagnostic' introduced in the development literature by Hausmann, Rodrik, and Velasco (2005), the institutional diagnostic approach consists of identifying within a particular country at a given point in time which institutional dysfunctions or weaknesses may be responsible for hindering faster, more transformative, more inclusive, or more sustainable development. Based on such diagnostics in several case studies, our final objective will then be to examine whether common weaknesses or 'generic' institutional issues arise, which should help understand better the general relationship between institutions and development and provide a kind of analytical grid to explore development-costly institutional flaws in other countries.

The preceding reference to the growth diagnostic approach to the identification of development constraints must not be taken rigorously. A huge difference between that approach and the institutional diagnostic is that no formal general model linking institutional constraints or deficiencies is available in the latter case. Therefore, neither an *a priori* list of potential institutional constraints on growth and development, nor a specific variable unequivocally signalling the strength of these constraints is available. This is a major difference with the growth diagnostic methodology, which benefits from an *a priori* knowledge of the nature of the economic determinants of growth. Issues involving institutions are more complex. To illustrate, corruption does not necessarily imply slow growth, autocratic leaders are not systematically associated with development failures, and informal institutions may work better than formal institutions in overcoming key economic constraints.

Rather than designing and following a questionable, predetermined analytical path, we adopt for the IDP a methodology that can be characterised as heuristic. For a given country, it consists first of gathering all information available on the quality of institutions and their possible role in constraining development. This includes exploiting the international databases of institutional or governance indicators to see how the country differs from well-chosen comparator countries, and using formal and informal opinion surveys addressed to those local experts and people whose activity is likely to be directly affected by, or who are knowledgeable on the way institutions work. Such a step partakes of a sort of 'mechanical' approach to the identification of institutional weaknesses (mechanical in the sense that ways to process the information are well known). It is succeeded by a more inductive approach. Starting from an in-depth analysis of the historical economic development process of a country, including growth diagnostics when available, the idea is to first identify apparent economic weaknesses – or constraints – and then to ponder over the possible institutional causes behind them. This can be done at the aggregate level or by focusing on restricted thematic areas where the relationship between specific institutions and economic development constraints is likely to be easier to detect.

The final challenge is then to put all the collected pieces of evidence together, and then propose an institutional analysis based on them. This requires that we start by defining what seems to be the most binding institutional weaknesses of a country as well as their economic consequences, and that, thereafter, we diagnose their likely proximate causes and deep determinants. Such an endeavour inevitably leads to the question as to why reforms susceptible of attenuating or removing an institutional weakness were not implemented, which is often tantamount to investigating the political economy aspects of that particular institutional issue.

The above-described steps are presented and discussed in the rest of the chapter, approximately in the preceding order. The first two sections deal with mechanical approaches based on the use of institutional or governance indicators, on the one hand, and on opinion or expert surveys, on the other. The next two sections focus on more inductive approaches to the institution–development relationship in a country. A final section then presents the 'diagnostic table, an instrument that was found particularly helpful to synthetise and summarise what was learned in all the preceding steps. Moreover, it has the advantage of bringing to the limelight the proximate causes and the deep factors at work behind the identified development-constraining institutional weaknesses.

Before getting to the crux of the matter, it is necessary to repeat that the present volume and the IDP case studies it relies upon do explicitly deal with low-income or lower-middle-income countries, that is to say, countries in their early stage of development. Therefore, several arguments developed in the rest of this chapter might not have the same relevance if we were dealing with emerging countries.

II BENCHMARKING A COUNTRY'S INSTITUTIONS USING GLOBAL INSTITUTIONAL/GOVERNANCE INDICATORS

Imagine that a set of indicators is available that describes the quality of countries' institutions in their various dimensions and, as a result of a set of regressions across both countries and time periods, the impact of each indicator on economic growth and several other development outcomes is known. The institutional diagnostic of development in a country would then be greatly facilitated. The set of indicators would provide this right away. The issue would then be to go from the indicators to the institutions whose functioning they describe, and then to investigate how changes can be made to improve their performance.

Unfortunately, things are not that simple. First, the significance of the correlation between the quality of institutions and development outcomes varies according to what development outcome is chosen. Second, when the correlation is significant, the causality behind it is ambiguous: does it run from good institutions to favourable development outcomes or the opposite? Third, it is not clear whether available indicators describe the quality of specific institutions – like the accountability of the executive or the independence of the judiciary – or some joint observable outcome of the functioning of these institutions. Available indicators are often presented as 'governance' indicators, thus describing how the institutional framework of a country makes its governance more, or less, development efficient, rather than describing the quality of a specific institution. Fourth, the precision of indicators is limited so that there would be much fuzziness in using them to benchmark a country relative to others.

This section elaborates on whether the indicators available in various cross-country databases may reveal obstacles to institutional development in a country. Even though such a capacity may be limited, it nevertheless shows how indicators can be used to expose the idiosyncrasy of a country in the space of broad institutional domains, possibly paving the way to a deeper institutional diagnostic. In short, it shows that they can be a useful exploratory tool.

A To What Extent Do Governance Indicators Reveal Institutional Obstacles to Development?

The use of indicators meant to describe the quality of institutions to make a judgement about whether institutions in a country are more or less favourable to economic growth, and more generally to development, is justified by the theoretical arguments surveyed in the preceding chapter and, supposedly, by empirical evidence. The latter is statistically fragile, however, and not without ambiguity. Precautions should thus be taken in using those indicators as a tool to identify institutional strengths and weaknesses. This is even more necessary as the indicators themselves provide descriptions of the quality of institutions that do not exhibit the precision required by a diagnostic.

Empirical evidence points to a strong correlation between institutional indicators and the level of GDP per capita across countries. The problem is that this correlation is consistent with causality going both ways: from better institutions to faster growth and from growth to better institutions. Instrumental variables that are assumed to be correlated with institutional quality but not with the level of development or past growth are used to control for this problem.[1] This procedure tends to confirm that institutions affect economic growth, or the contemporaneous level of income per capita, among developing countries. However, the exogeneity of these instruments with respect to economic development is often debatable. On the other hand, the cross-country relationship between institutional indicators and the average rate of GDP per capita growth over ten- or twenty-year periods of time is weaker. Moreover, when other country characteristics are introduced to control for other exogenous factors that may condition growth it turns out that the effect of institutional indicators and their statistical significance tends to vary with the set of controls being used, which does not suggest a robust relationship.

These issues are thoroughly discussed in a recent survey by Stephen Durlauf (2020) of the imposing cross-country growth and institution literature of the past twenty years.[2] Its main conclusion is that, if there is no doubt about the influence of the quality of institutions in general on economic development, the exact channels for such an influence are essentially ambiguous. As an example, consider the following three well-known studies: Acemoglu et al. (2001) provided evidence on a cross-section of countries that the protection of property rights delivered by a country's institutions matters for development; likewise, Mauro (1995) found with another instrument that corruption significantly and negatively affects growth; whereas Dawson (2003) applied Granger causation[3] methodology on a panel of countries to show that the degree of economic freedom influences economic development. Those three studies show that, indeed, on average across countries, the quality of institutions matters for economic growth, but they do not say much about what institutions matter, and by what mechanisms these relationships are obtained. There are many different types of corruption – high-level politicians or civil servants siphoning away public money, taxpayers bribing tax authority personnel, the petty corruption of police officers – with *a priori* differentiated effects on economic efficiency and growth. A lack of protection of property rights may be due to corruption, to a weak judicial system, or to predatory rulers, while a lack of

---

[1] Thus, the absence of a correlation between the instrumental variable and the development outcome is a sign of causality going from the institutional indicator to development. One famous example of such instrumentation in the development–institution literature is the use of the mortality of fifteenth-century European settlers as an instrument to explain the protection of property rights in today's developing economies. The rationale for the use of that instrument by Acemoglu et al. (2001) is that it determines the quality of institutions set by settlers at that time, which has somehow persisted until now.

[2] An earlier insightful critical survey of that literature can be found in Dixit (2007).

[3] A test of the ability of the past values of a time series to predict future values of another time series.

economic freedom may be due to over-regulation but also to excessive taxation or weak property rights. Surely the fact that significant relationships are found in those three studies, which are very representative of the empirical institution–development literature, means that the quality of 'some' institutions affects growth and development. Yet no one would accept an analyst making a diagnosis about what is wrong or right in a country's institutions concerning economic growth based on those sole relationships.

As can be seen from the previous examples, the difficulty is as much in providing evidence of a causal relationship as in identifying what the institutional indicators used in cross-country analyses of the institution–development relationship stand for. To a large extent, this ambiguity results from the fact that these indicators most often describe the consequences of something being wrong in the way in which institutions function but not what is wrong. In other words, they point to symptoms rather than dysfunctions. Corruption is a case in point. It can always be described as the consequence of a judicial system that is unable to enforce the law – for instance, due to a lack of resources or (honest) personnel – but it may also be the consequence of loopholes in the law or in the regulatory framework that create rent-seeking situations, or of a lack of transparency of operations in the public sector. Yet the information gathered from experts relates to their perceptions of corruption, rather than the relative importance of the institutional causes behind it. In other cases, indicators rely on a set of very precise questions that are then aggregated into a single index. Yet the field covered by these questions is often incomplete. For instance, the 'Rule of Law' indicator in the Global Integrity Index relies exclusively on questions about the independence of the judiciary from political influence and the transparency of judgements, but no information is gathered on the time it takes to clear a case, the degree of corruption of judges and judicial officers, or their level of competence. By contrast, other indicators rely on long lists of questions covering various, often heterogeneous subfields.

Where does all this leave us concerning the institutional diagnostic of a specific country? Mostly to the fact that institutional indicators only provide a measure of the overall quality of institutions and, at best, some more detailed information on the strengths of various types of symptoms that may point to specific institutional flaws. It must be clear, on the other hand, that the measurement precision of these indicators is limited. In the Corruption Perceptions Index published by Transparency International, for instance, accounting for a reasonable degree of measurement error, it is not possible to say whether Kenya, ranked 124, significantly differs from Madagascar, ranked 149, or Egypt, ranked 117. When benchmarking a country relative to others, the lesson is that not too much meaning must be attributed to a country ranking 10 or 15 slots ahead or behind another. Attention should focus on those institutional domains where indicators show substantial differences.

A last remark is of importance when using global rankings of institutional indicators as an input into the institutional diagnostic of a country. It is that the correlation observed across countries between indicators and development outcomes applies to the 'average country', not to all single countries, far from it. In other words, it is not because the Risk of Expropriation of Foreign Investment published by Political Risk Services is shown to affect negatively the level of GDP in a cross-section of countries[4] that a specific country where this risk is perceived to be high will necessarily underperform. There is some strong idiosyncrasy behind statistically significant cross-country relationship, which cannot be ignored when analysing a single country.

B Benchmarking Low-Income and Lower-Middle-Income Countries According to Institutional Indicators

The first question to ask when using institutional indicators to benchmark a country against others is what indicator to use. As mentioned earlier, many indicators are available, and even when they are supposed to cover the same institutional domain it turns out that they may substantially differ in some cases. Aggregating indicators covering close domains is a way of extracting from their diversity more robust differences across countries. This is the approach taken by the authors of the widely used Worldwide Governance Indicators (WGI).[5] An alternative approach, based on the extensive set of institutional and governance indicators stored in the Quality of Government (QoG) database[6] and focused on developing countries only, was also used in the IDP case studies. They are briefly described in turn.

The WGI indicators cover six broad domains: (i) rule of law; (ii) voice and accountability; (iii) control of corruption; (iv) government effectiveness; (v) political stability; and (vi) regulatory quality. Each aggregate indicator results from a statistical procedure that involves extracting from the large number of individual indicators which seem to fit the domain under analysis a 'common factor' in the way these various indicators rank countries. Practically speaking, this is done through looking for a linear combination of individual indicators whose average correlation, so to speak, with each indicator is the closest.[7] This common factor is then taken as the aggregate indicator which best describes the quality of institutions in the domain being considered.

The WGI methodology for defining aggregate indicators regroups individual indicators available in various sources according to the six institutional domains listed above on an *a priori* basis. An alternative approach consists of being agnostic about these domains and regrouping individual indicators

---

[4] This example is taken from Acemoglu and Johnson (2005).

[5] See Kaufmann et al. (2010).

[6] See Teorell et al. (2021) for the current version of the database.

[7] The common factor is the equivalent of the 'first principal component' in a standard principal component analysis of the whole set of individual indicators related to a specific domain and their value in the countries being covered. Some technical complication arises from the fact that the datasets used in this aggregation procedure, or some individual indicators, do not necessarily cover the same set of countries. See Kaufmann et al. (2010) for details.

according to their proximity in the way they rank countries. The number of groupings is decided *a priori*, and a 'cluster analysis' procedure determines which indicators enter each group. In other words, each group comprises a set of indicators that are highly correlated to each other in the way they rank countries, while this common ranking is made to differ as much as possible across groups. Then a common factor is identified in each group that summarises the way indicators in that group ranks countries. As the clustering is the result of a purely statistical procedure operated on the whole set of individual indicators, it is not clear whether they should be conceptually close to each other. Yet it turns out to be the case that they are close, suggesting that available individual indicators from a host of different sources tend to describe the functioning of institutions within a country according to a small number of key dimensions.

In the application of this methodology to some of the IDP case studies, the QoG database was restricted to developing and emerging countries so as to avoid aggregate indicators being mostly based on differences between advanced and less advanced economies, which may be a problem of the WGI indicators. Even though the dataset comprises more than 2,000 indicators, coming from practically all sources of institutional/governance indicators available, only those that were available for all countries in the sample were kept. They numbered 350, which were then clustered in six groups or 'categories'.[8] Upon inspection of the indicators they comprised, the six categories were identified as:

a. democratisation;
b. human rights;
c. administrative capacity;
d. control of corruption and rule of law;
e. conflict and violence; and
f. competitiveness.

It is interesting that some of these categories very much overlap with the WGI domains – that is, 'democratisation' and 'voice and accountability'; 'administrative capacity' and 'government effectiveness'; and 'control of corruption and rule of law', corresponding to the two domains with the same name in WGI. Yet the overlap is far from perfect since the 'human rights' and 'competitiveness' categories have no clear counterparts among the WGI domains, even though the primary sources used to define the latter include datasets oriented towards competitiveness or human rights issues.

With these institutional indicators at hand, a second issue is which comparator countries are to be included in the benchmarking. Clearly, it does not make sense to compare the institutional quality of low- or lower-middle-income countries to countries that are much more advanced in the economic

---

[8] Details of the procedure are given in the IDP Tanzania case study – Chapter 3. The resulting indicators are available on request.

development process, have the resources to maintain better institutions, and whose population demands better-performing institutions. The comparison must allow for income differences, but within a reasonable range of variation.

Two sets of comparator countries were used in the IDP case studies. The first one comprises neighbour countries, with the justification that these may share with the country under analysis a common geo-physical context and, depending on the region, some common cultural or historical references – such as, for instance, the same past coloniser. Lack of significant differences within this set of countries may then reflect the strong influence of this context, as well as some homogeneity in terms of living standards. By contrast, variations across countries could mean either that the geo-physical and cultural context are not major determinants of the institutional features of countries in that region, or that the region is rather heterogeneous with respect to these geographical and historical characteristics. The significance of a country differing from comparators may be stronger in the second case.

The second set of comparator countries consists of countries which were at the same income level as the country under analysis two or three decades ago but that have managed to grow substantially faster since then. The question then is whether some institutional domains were of a better quality in the latter when growth accelerated, compared to the country being studied. The difficulty is that institutional indicators rarely go back as far as two decades or more. The comparison can only be performed on relatively recent years, and, in some cases, there is no possibility of going back in time.[9]

Examples of the kind of benchmarking based on the WGI and QoG-based indicators are given in Figures 2.1 and 2.2 for Tanzania. The radar chart in Figure 2.1 compares that country with its neighbours in 2019. The WGI indicators range from –2.5 (worst institutional quality) to 2.5 (best), and the standard deviation of the six indicators – within the sample of developing and emerging countries – is around 0.5. The radar chart is thus constructed in such a way that the difference in graduations along all axes is precisely around one standard deviation, which allows us to pass a judgement on the significance of differences between countries. On the other hand, country scores tend to concentrate on the negative part of their interval of definition, which means, unsurprisingly, that governance and institutional quality in this set of low- or lower-middle-income countries are below the world median[10].

Looking at the figure from the point of view of Tanzania, the conclusion is undoubtedly that there is no difference when compared to the bulk of its neighbour countries, except Rwanda and Burundi, since differences with other countries never exceed one standard deviation. When restricting the

---

[9] This was the case for the indicators based on the QoG database because of the rapid increase in missing observations of individual indicators when going back in time.

[10] The median is influenced by advanced countries, unlike the aggregate indicators built based on the QoG database and focused on developing countries only.

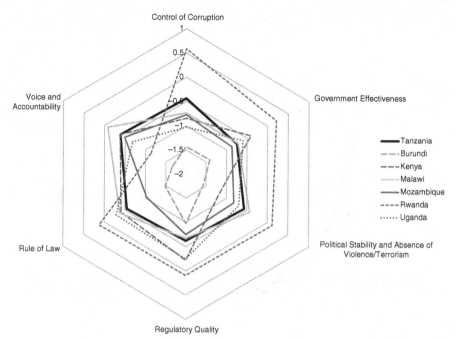

FIGURE 2.1 Comparing Tanzania and neighbour countries according to the WGI indicators, 2018

comparison to these countries, one would tend to conclude, as suggested earlier, that Tanzania shares with them common geographical, demographic, and historical factors that lead to comparable institutional quality features. On the other hand, except for the rule of law in Mozambique, scores tend to be similar across the six institutional domains, so that no particular domain can be singled out for special attention later in the diagnostic exercise.

The chart may also be looked at from the point of view of other countries. If a diagnostic had to be established for Rwanda, for instance, this benchmarking exercise would have led to the conclusion that Rwanda tends to perform better than other countries in the region, except for a very low score in 'voice and accountability': that is, the democratic functioning and transparency of the government's action. This is a valuable clue for an institutional diagnostic. Likewise, Burundi is shown to perform worse than other countries in the region – and as a matter of fact very badly in absolute terms, but a little less badly for 'regulatory quality' – whereas Mozambique would be comparable to other countries if it were not for the 'rule of law' domain.

To evaluate the consistency of using the WGI indicators, Figure 2.2 shows the same benchmarking exercise but now based on the aggregate developing countries' indicators built based on the QoG database using cluster analysis. Roughly speaking, the same proximity among the comparator countries,

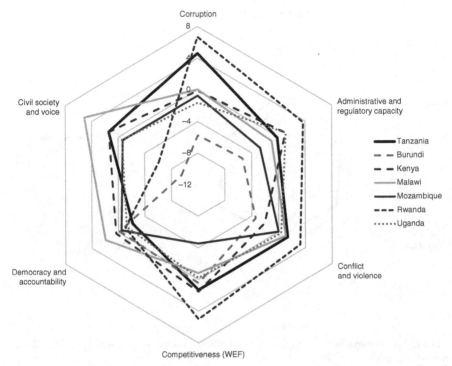

FIGURE 2.2 Comparing Tanzania and neighbour countries according to the QoG-based indicators, 2018[11]

except for Rwanda and Burundi, is observed and most country profiles exhibit the same regularity, with scores comparable across institutional domains, although somewhat less so than with the WGI indicators. The salient features are: (i) the superiority of Rwanda in all domains except 'civil society and voice', and an impressive advantage in 'competitiveness'; and (ii) the inferior performance of Burundi, in all areas but competitiveness and democracy and accountability, where it is similar to all other countries. Mozambique's chart also departs from the mean shape in the 'competitiveness' dimension.

A comparison is now made between Tanzania and countries which, although at a roughly comparable level of GDP per capita in the late 1980s, grew so much faster since then that they have reached an income level double or more that of Tanzania, on average. These are essentially Asian countries: Bangladesh, Cambodia, Lao People's Democratic Republic, and Vietnam. The comparison is made using both 2019 and 2005 WGI indicators, with 2005 being the year when the income gap was roughly half what it is today (see Figure 2.3).

---

[11] For ease of comparison with the preceding figure, QoG-based indicators have been normalised so as to exhibit the same overall mean and standard deviation as in the preceding (WGI) figure.

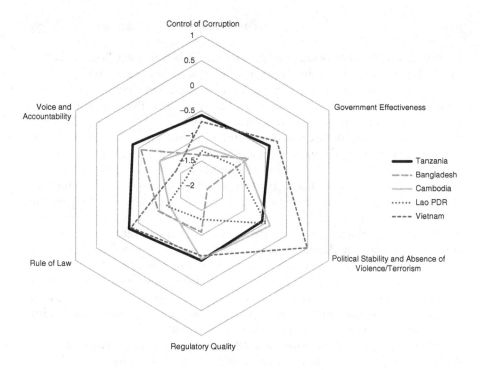

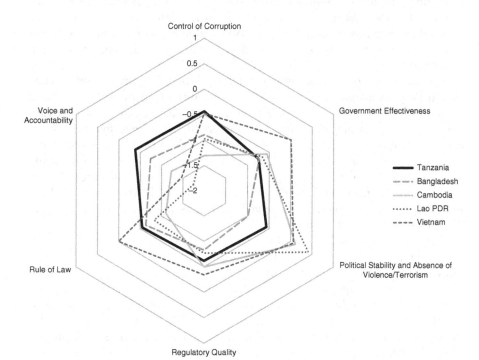

FIGURE 2.3 Benchmarking of Tanzania with respect to fast-growing Asian countries: WGI indicators, 2005 (top figure) and 2018 (bottom figure)

Unfortunately, it is not possible to go back much before 2005 because indicators lack precision, due to the fact that fewer observations are available.

Two lessons may be drawn from this new benchmarking. First, back in 2005, Tanzania's institutions did not seem to be worse than those of Bangladesh, Cambodia, and Lao People's Democratic Republic. On the contrary, Tanzania was surpassing these three countries in almost all institutional domains. It also compared well with Vietnam, except for 'voice and accountability', where Tanzania prevailed, and for 'political stability', where the situation was the opposite. The view that faster-growing developing countries are endowed with institutions of better quality is thus unwarranted when looking at this particular case. The second lesson stems from the rather strong improvement observed in several dimensions among some of Tanzania's outperformers. This is clearly the case of Bangladesh, Cambodia, and Lao People's Democratic Republic, and to a lesser extent Vietnam, but not of Tanzania. It is interesting that Tanzania's development outperformers saw the quality of their institutions improving while growing substantially faster. An obvious hypothesis in the case of Tanzania would thus be that the lack of progress on the institutional front may have delayed progress on economic development.

Other examples taken from the IDP case studies could further illustrate the use that can be made from the comparison of institutional indicators over time and across countries. For instance, a striking example of worsening institutions is Mozambique, whose WGI indicators scored close to the average of the sample countries at a comparable level of income per capita in 2005, and then drastically worsened in practically all domains after 2010 (see Figure 2.4).

This example confirms an important fact to be taken into account when establishing an institutional diagnostic: the quality of institutions, as gauged by institutional indicators like the WGI or the QoG-based indicators, may vary considerably over time, most often following political changes. In other words, it would be wrong to consider that the institutional framework of an economy or, more exactly, the way it is used, has some degree of permanence. Observing an institutional weakness at a point of time may thus result from a real flaw in the institutional framework being temporarily ignored by the power in place. In other words, the law may be flawed, or it may be temporarily disobeyed. The distinction is clearly important.

Overall, aggregate institutional or governance indicators like the WGI indicators, or those indicators obtained by aggregating in a different way those individual, more focused, indicators available in the QoG database, are useful instruments for starting an institutional diagnostic. It is true that the aggregation procedure introduces some imprecision into the description of the quality of institutions, but it is not clear that one would get a better idea of this by considering the numerous and highly diverse individual indicators available, especially because their precision and mutual consistency is often uncertain.

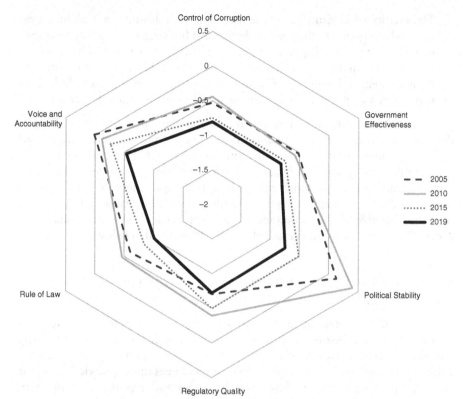

FIGURE 2.4 The worsening of institutions/governance in Mozambique, 2005–2019

The above-noted congruence between the two sets of aggregate indicators is thus reassuring.

Several lessons can be drawn from the few aforementioned examples shown above. They can be summarised in the following way:

a. Not much is to be learned from the absolute level of aggregate institutional indicators when concentrating on low- and lower-middle-income countries. For these countries, scores tend to be low, thus reflecting the causal relationship running from the level of development to the quality of institutions.
b. When considering a single country, the possible asymmetry between scores in various institutional domains is of special interest since it suggests directions for further scrutiny of the functioning of institutions.
c. Benchmarking country A in relation to a group G of other countries requires distinguishing outliers. Comparisons between country A and median countries or against outliers have different meanings.

d. The quality of institutions or the use made of indicators may change over
    time, which points to the need to distinguish between permanent and transi-
    tory elements in the diagnostic to be established. Note that this has implica-
    tions for the analysis of the empirical relationship between institutions and
    development. If the quality of institutions changes over time, it is difficult to
    relate it in a causal way to development indicators over a long period.

This section on indicators has relied on aggregate institutional indicators
defined for a range of general domains and based on specialised individual
indicators – most often based on the opinion of experts. This opinion may differ from the perception that insiders may have of the institutions in their own
country, and most importantly on the practical implications of their possible
dysfunctions. Surveying their views and identifying the weaknesses they point
to is the objective of the second mechanical approach to an institutional diagnostic. The way it was implemented in the IDP is detailed below.

III ASKING PEOPLE: OPINION SURVEYS AND INTERVIEWING
KNOWLEDGEABLE PEOPLE

Citizens of the country under analysis are insiders; they experience the functioning of national institutions on an everyday basis. If they are not necessarily
equipped to compare their country to others, as the experts behind the global
institutional indicators, they may be in some instances more knowledgeable, or
provide a perspective that is closer to reality. A second important tool in establishing an institutional diagnostic consists therefore of simply asking nationals
their opinion on the way institutions work in their country, the most patent
institutional weaknesses, and how they think they could be fixed.

There are various ways of proceeding, depending on whose opinion is
being collected. A representative sample of the population will mostly reveal
how ordinary citizens feel about institutions in their everyday life. Even
though their opinions may reveal differences across various types of institutions being considered, it is unlikely that these appraisals will be enunciated
in terms of the obstacles to, or enablers of, economic development. Only that
part of the population that is used to making decisions that are at the heart
of the economic system, deep observers of the society and the economy, or
people in positions that require an intimate knowledge of how institutions
work, would be able to adopt such a perspective. Especially valuable in this
respect should be the views of those personalities who have, or had, major
responsibilities, such as government members, legislators, top civil servants,
or managers of major firms.

The opinions expressed by these segments of the population must be seen
as complementary, because of their different positions with respect to institutions. Eminent persons have the experience of top decision making: they are

able to provide a rationale for the reforms they think necessary and/or those they try to implement, as well as past successes or failures. Yet they may not appreciate the nature and the strength of the constraints faced by more ordinary decision makers in running small and medium-sized businesses, or civil society organisations. Finally, these views may miss the way the ordinary citizens perceive institutional constraints.

This section elaborates on the experience gained in the IDP case studies in surveying individual opinions about the institutional context of a country at those three preceding levels. It first summarises the results obtained in IDP case studies from a specific survey that was specially designed for this project and intended for small samples of economic and social decision makers. It then offers a few remarks about the experience of the various country teams in interviewing top decision makers and other eminent persons.

A Using Opinion Polls: the case of the Afrobarometer

Opinion polls are conducted more or less regularly in most countries, including low-income countries. Their goal is to get a picture of: (i) individual well-being – income, health, life satisfaction; (ii) opinions on major current policy and political issues; and (iii) the most common appraisal of the functioning of society, including local communities and national institutions. Polls may be conducted for profit, or they may be implemented by non-profit organisations, like the Afrobarometer in Africa. Given the multidimensional scope of these surveys, however, they comprise few questions on institutions or governance per se.

As a way of experimenting with existing opinion surveys, this section makes use of a harmonised opinion poll run at certain time intervals in a rather large set of African countries – the Afrobarometer, nicely subtitled 'A pan-African series of national public attitude surveys on democracy, governance, and society'. It is now in its ninth edition, covering the years 2019–2020, but country surveys have not yet been put together in a single database, as was done in the previous rounds. The rest of this section thus uses Wave 8, taken between 2016 and 2018, depending on the country, and covering some 34 countries in the region.

The questionnaire used in the Afrobarometer is common to all countries. It is rather long, since the codebook comprises some 350 variables, among which 80 questions are about the respondent's evaluation of the country's governance. They include the degree of democratisation, the efficiency of the government in providing services, the areas which the respondents see as the most problematic, their perception of corruption and their trust in the main actors in society (president, government, parliament, military, courts etc.).

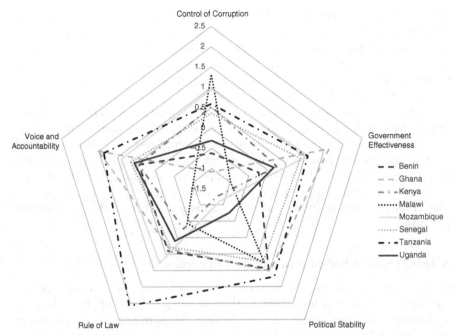

FIGURE 2.5 Comparison of selected African countries, based on aggregated indicators elaborated on the basis of the Afrobarometer: Round 8, 2016–2018

Since it would have been too cumbersome to deal with all of these questions one by one, the same methodology as the one described above to aggregate individual indicators has been followed. Namely, five areas were predefined, closely mimicking the WGI and QoG synthetic indicators in the preceding section. Average question scores for each area were then summarised by their principal component. This yielded an aggregate indicator with a mean of zero and a unit standard deviation across the thirty-four countries present in the eighth wave of the Afrobarometer. Because of non-response in those categories that comprised a relatively small number of original questions, the category meant to represent 'regulatory quality' had to be dropped.

Figure 2.5 shows the results obtained with this procedure for a few countries. As before, attention to each country's institutional profile should focus on two features: (i) the shape of the radar line (i.e., whether it is regular, implying comparable scores on its different branches, or asymmetric); and (ii) how it compares to other countries, keeping in mind that the zero line stands for the mean across all African countries – with no implication whatsoever regarding how African countries perform in comparison to other regions.

Only two countries in the small sample represented in Figure 2.5 exhibit a regular pattern, meaning that there is no specific institutional domain with a noticeable weakness. These two countries are Senegal and Tanzania, although the rule of law indicator is particularly strong in Tanzania relative to other indicators, and relative to all African countries in the sample. All other countries show a bias in at least one or two domains. Thus, it is not surprising to see that 'political stability' and 'absence of conflict and violence' are weak in Kenya (remember the post-election killings in 2017) and Mozambique (on account of the resurgence of the Frelimo–Renamo conflict). This feature may not necessarily be considered as an institutional weakness per se, but it is a strong determinant of the context in which institutions function. More interesting from a diagnostic point of view is Ghana's comparatively weak score on the front of corruption control, which contrasts with quite good scores along all other institutional dimensions. Benin also fares rather badly on the corruption axis, but also on government effectiveness, whereas Uganda fails on corruption and political stability. Finally, Malawi fails in regard to the opinion of the population on both government effectiveness in delivering services and democracy, that is, voice and accountability. If a diagnostic were to be conducted in these last four countries, the Afrobarometer would thus suggest clear directions of investigation.

Despite differences among them, it can be noted that the countries appearing in Figure 2.5 tend to do better than the average African country, since few scores are below zero (which is the mean for the whole sample of countries in every dimension). Equally noticeable is the similarity between the relative scores of countries in Figure 2.5 and comparisons made earlier using the WGI indicators or the indicators constructed from the QoG database. For instance, Tanzania tends to dominate its neighbour countries, as was roughly the case in Figures 2.1 and 2.2, when excluding Rwanda.[12] The similarity is not perfect, however. The 'voice and accountability' score appears to be low in Figure 2.1, based on WGI 2019, whereas it is relatively strong in Figure 2.5, based on the Afrobarometer. Interestingly, this difference likely reflects objective changes that took place between 2017 (the year the Afrobarometer survey was undertaken) and 2019, in regard to the freedom of the press and other media in Tanzania.[13] Overall, it is interesting that a public opinion survey like the Afrobarometer delivers a message about institutional strengths and weaknesses in Africa that is similar to aggregate expert-based indicators.

Even though the discrepancy in the 'voice and accountability' score may have an objective explanation relating to changes in the control of the media by the executive in Tanzania, it raises several issues. First, it is another example of the kind of noticeable change that may take place during a short time span in the evaluation of institutional quality. Second, it may suggest that public opinion is more volatile than that of experts, or that the various factors that

---

[12] Rwanda is absent from the comparison in Figure 2.5 because it is not covered by the Afrobarometer.

[13] See the IDP Tanzania study in Bourguignon and Wangwe (2023: Chap. 1).

should be taken into account in the evaluation of the strength of (democratic) institutions covered under the heading 'voice and accountability' are not given the same weight by citizens and experts. Third, and more fundamentally, the questions asked in opinion surveys like the Afrobarometer bear upon limited aspects of institutions.

Public opinion surveys provide information on individual attitudes and perceptions that seem far away from the institution–development relationship but may nevertheless be of some indirect importance for development. Questions about people's views on basic principles like democracy or justice, about their own moral values, about their degree of trust not only in formal institutions, which are accounted for in the above indicators, but also in relatives and neighbours, surely matter for the way a society – and therefore its economy – functions. Because they were not directly related to the way institutions work, they have not been included in the set of questions used to build the indicators analysed above. Of course, this should not prevent us from considering some of them, especially trust in others, if they appear relevant for a deeper exploration of the way specific sectors of a country's economy work.[14]

B The Country Institutional Surveys (CIS)

Overcoming the limitations of opinion surveys in dealing with such specific issues as the role of national institutions in economic development requires two things: (i) restricting the sample to people with some direct experience in dealing with institutions, or with good knowledge about the way they work; and (ii) orienting the questionnaire towards the institution–development relationship while substantially broadening it to cover the full range of relevant institutional dimensions. The IDP has developed such a surveying tool, whose characteristics are now described, before showing the use that can be made of it.

1 The Structure of the CIS

The CIS implemented in the four IDP case studies is inspired by the Institutional Profile Database (IPD), an expert survey conducted jointly by the economic agencies of the French Embassies, the Centre for Prospective Studies and International Information, and the University of Maastricht (Bertho, 2013). Its questionnaire was taken as a basis for the CIS because of its rather remarkable degree of exhaustiveness. As adapted to the IDP project, the CIS questionnaire

---

[14] The importance of trust among people, relatives, and neighbours in the first place has long been emphasised in the institution–development literature. See for instance Platteau (2000) and (of special relevance in an African context), in regard to the possible link between the slave trade, trust, and development, Nunn (2008). The latter issue is also discussed in the IDP Benin study (Bourguignon et al., 2023).

comprises some 320 questions, covering a broad range of institutional characteristics, structured into nine domains or areas:

1. political institutions;
2. security, law and order, and control of violence;
3. the functioning of public administrations;
4. the free operation of markets (ease of doing business, dealing with land rights);
5. coordination of stakeholders, strategic vision, and innovation;
6. the security of transactions and contracts;
7. market regulation, social dialogue;
8. relations with the rest of the world; and
9. social cohesion, social protection, and solidarity.

Not surprisingly, this list of institutional areas is roughly consistent with the aggregate indicators used in the preceding section to describe the quality of institutions in a country and to make comparisons across countries, though it is slightly more detailed.

A questionnaire with so many questions is clearly impractical if applied to a sample of people who are busy with their own occupations, instead of the experts or observers surveyed in the IPD. Moreover, it is not clear that respondents would have the knowledge that would allow them to cover all the domains set out above. Two solutions were therefore implemented. Both meant a severe reduction in the number of questions – though one more than the other.

The first solution consisted of asking respondents to pinpoint three of the aforementioned areas that they would consider as the most constraining for development, and then to answer the corresponding questions. To make sure all domains were approached, however, respondents were also asked to answer questions in a fourth randomly chosen area. This solution thus yields two sets of information: (i) some ranking of institutional areas depending on the constraints they impose on development; and (ii) in each area, features that were seen as strengths or weaknesses. Overall, the total number of questions turned out to be similar to the original IPD questionnaire, even though many questions were adapted to make them as relevant as possible to the context of the country under analysis, and a few questions were added on country-specific topics. Given the choice of priority areas, the actual number of questions answered by CIS respondents was roughly a third of the total: that is, slightly more than 100 questions. Note that, given the specific structure of the questionnaire, the same question could be relevant under different institutional headings and thus could appear more than once in the full questionnaire. However, as the survey was implemented on tablets, it was possible to code the questionnaire in such a way that a respondent would not have to answer the same question several times.

The second solution was to ask respondents to answer all questions but to simultaneously and drastically reduce the number of questions in the original

IPD questionnaire, while making them more consistent with the economic, social, and institutional reality of the country studied, and while maintaining the exhaustiveness of the areas covered and having respondents answer all questions. This choice did not prevent from proceeding with the initial ranking of institutional areas by perceived severity of the constraints they impose on development. It reduced the detail with which institutional areas were described but added to the representativeness by allowing all respondents to give their opinion on all institutional domains.

The first format of the CIS was implemented in Tanzania, Benin, and Bangladesh, whereas the second one was used in Mozambique. In all cases, variations could be introduced in the list of general institutional areas, depending on the specificity of the country. For instance, decentralisation was considered to be worth singling out in Mozambique, whereas 'political institutions' were split into features referring to the way the executive operates and features describing the functioning of the overall political system in the Bangladesh questionnaire. These variants were generally inspired by the intimate knowledge of the country held by the authors of the diagnostic, or by discussions with key informants within the country, as will be seen below.

In all questionnaires, answers to questions were formatted so that answers could fit a five-point Likert scale ranging from 'not at all' to 'very much', with 'no answer' as an additional option. In aggregating questions together, however, care was taken regarding whether the question being asked was formulated in a positive or a negative way. A high score on the Likert scale would then be taken as favourable in the former case but unfavourable in the latter.

Table A2.1 in the appendix to this chapter, taken from the Bangladesh case study, shows the structure of the questionnaire used in that instance. The complete questionnaires for all case studies are accessible on the Internet.[15]

A last important point to stress about the questionnaires is that answers are necessarily influenced by the current political, social, and economic context. It so happened that the CIS in Bangladesh was conducted at the time of the general elections, so that answers to some questions may have been biased by the arguments exchanged during the electoral campaign. An appropriate discounting of the significance of these answers is thus needed. This being said, most questions in the questionnaire refer to institutional features that are quite persistent. The same situation was found in Tanzania, as the survey was undertaken less than a year after a new president came into power with a rather ambitious anti-corruption programme. Respondents were thus asked to answer the questionnaire in the light of their experience over the last ten years, rather than on the basis of the last few months and the electoral platform of the new president. Still, when they had completed the questionnaire,

---

[15] https://edi.opml.co.uk/wpcms/wp-content/uploads/2020/05/04-Institutional-survey-analysis_
Bangladesh_03062020-edited.pdf, pp. 56–76.

they were then asked how their answers to the questionnaire would possibly be modified if they were to take into consideration the last few months since the presidential inauguration.

As should be clear by now, the CIS is not directed to the whole population but only to those people who are most likely to confront the institutional challenges of a country on a regular basis, either through their occupation or through observation from a particularly informative position. Stratified samples were used, with strata defined by occupation, sector, and high-level positions in several types of organisations. Typically, CIS samples comprised politicians from the ruling party and the opposition, top bureaucrats in ministries and public agencies, business executives in the main sectors of activity, academics, journalists, representatives of civil society, foreign diplomats, and heads of local offices of international organisations. To the extent possible, these strata, of different sizes, were combined with gender and geographic criteria.

The size of the sample differed across surveys. It was slightly more than 100 people in Tanzania and Mozambique, but triple that in Benin and Bangladesh. It is of course always better to deal with a bigger sample. However, because the CIS is meant to reveal the views that decision-making people may have on institutions, rather than to test the significance of such and such an answer to a specific question, sample size should matter mostly in order to make sure that the range of decision-making people who might have different views about institutions is fully covered.

2 Short Overview of Results and Lessons from the CIS in the IDP Case Studies

As the CIS was adapted to the context of the countries in which it was implemented, different definitions of the main institutional areas around which the questionnaire was built were used, while some items were added to or subtracted from the list of the nine areas mentioned above. The customising of the questionnaire also required inserting new questions, deleting others, and framing the remaining questions so that they fit the local context.

Regarding the institutional areas, experience shows, first of all, that for their ranking to deliver information it is important not to have too many or too few of them. In the former case, respondents may find it difficult to differentiate among all the alternatives. In the latter, they will tend to attach the same importance to most of them. The second lesson from experience is that it is important to provide respondents with a general description of the institutional areas they will have to rank, and of the questions they will be asked to answer. However, too general and generic wording may be insufficiently clear. For instance, 'security of transactions and contracts' may not be well understood if it is not specified that it refers to institutions that are supposed to guarantee contract compliance, especially debt contracts, to insolvency laws, to litigation procedures, and to business laws and courts. Likewise, it should be made clear that 'political institutions' without further precision should include not only constitutional matters but also how basic principles are obeyed, political life in general, the control exerted by the executive over political, economic, and civil society actors, electoral procedures, and checks and balances on the government. Incidentally, as this long list attests, this area had to be split into several sub-areas in some surveys.

Then comes the issue of how to articulate the ranking of institutional areas by respondents and their answers to the large number of questions in those areas, and possibly others. These questions are supposed to provide more detail on the reasons why an area is harmful to development. There are two ways of handling them. One way consists of simply ranking them according to the Likert scale and to examine the kind of institutional challenge the most unfavourable answers point towards. The other way consists of dealing with clusters of questions that may be considered as detailed institutional sub-areas – as shown in Table A2.1 – and checking what sub-area exhibits the lowest average Likert scale, bearing in mind the distinction between positive and negative question formulations. The first approach offers the advantage of focusing on extreme weaknesses, whereas the second reveals those sub-areas with a high frequency of mediocre scores.

One way or another, it is interesting that, despite the fact that the respondents to the CIS answered questions in the institutional areas selected by them as the most detrimental to development, the areas revealed by their answers to individual questions do not always fit their initial ranking. This was particularly the case in Bangladesh, where there was very little difference among areas in the initial ranking, whereas answers to questions very clearly singled out as strongly negative 'land rights', 'civil service', and 'political institutions' (in relation to the functioning of the executive). Likewise, in Mozambique, the lack of a 'common vision of the national strategy' and the 'management of public administration' appeared among the most detrimental areas, while answers to single questions suggested that 'legal and constitutional matters' and 'political participation' were the sub-areas where the lowest Likert scores were the most frequently observed. This seems to suggest that general institutional areas may indeed be too general to fully ground a diagnostic exercise because they comprise different dimensions, which may be appraised in different ways by the respondents. In other words, a general institutional area may be seen as mildly constraining for development despite some of its sub-areas being of the lowest quality.

Table 2.1 summarises in a synthetic way the information conveyed by the CIS in the four case studies of the IDP project. As far as the general institutional areas are concerned, whether their ranking was made *a priori* by survey respondents or based on the questions with low scores, it is not surprising to see so much commonality across countries since the options were similar and of a limited number. Yet there are interesting differences. Institutions that affect the business environment are mentioned in Benin and Tanzania, but not

TABLE 2.1 *Synthetic summary of institutional weaknesses and strengths revealed by the CIS in the case studies*

	Bangladesh	Benin	Mozambique[a]	Tanzania
Three worst general institutional areas (*a priori* ranking)	Political institutions: system Justice and regulation Political institutions: executive	Political institutions Public administration Unfriendly business environment	Lack of vision Public administration Management of macro and sectoral policies	Public institutions Public administration Unfriendly business environment
Three worst general institutional areas (based on all questions)[a]	Management of land issues Civil service Political institutions: executive	Public administration Management of land issues Unfriendly business environment	Legal and constitutional matters Limited freedom of information and political participation Constraints imposed by donors	Public administration Management of land issues Unfriendly business environment
Weak institutional sub-areas	Weak checks and balances on executive Excessive centralisation Limited freedom of information Corrupt elections Nepotism Public services Land conflicts	Generalised corruption Opaqueness of executive Imperfect knowledge of the law Mismanagement of SOEs Lack of vision	Corruption Constitutional breaches Elite capture Public goods delivery Land conflicts Aid dependence Separation of powers	Management of land issues Generalised corruption Opaqueness of executive Weak regulation Pressure of lobbies Excessive centralisation
Strong institutional sub-areas	Capacity for informal secure deals with government Role of donors Rigorous macro policies Sense of national identity	Civil liberties State free from traditional norms Role of donors Anti-corruption efforts	Availability of foreign aid Civil liberties State free from traditional norms Sense of national identity	Civil liberties Security Sense of national identity

[a] The question-based ranking of general areas in Mozambique bears upon a slightly different set of areas than the *a priori* ranking.

in Bangladesh and Mozambique. Land issues never appear in the *a priori* rank-ing, but they are present in the question-based rankings in three countries. This divergence may be taken to mean that the handling of land rights is quite bad but that their influence on development is not considered to be of great impor-tance. On the other hand, it is striking, but certainly not unexpected, that the low quality of the public administration, or civil service, appears everywhere as a crucial institutional challenge, the same being true of the way political institutions work. (Remember, however, that this area may in some cases be too broadly defined.)

Comparison with the aggregate governance indicators analysed earlier is not easy because congruence in the definition of institutional areas is limited. Yet it is interesting to note that poor management of the public administration emphasised in the CIS conforms well with the relatively low score of 'govern-ment effectiveness' in Figures 2.1–2.3 for the four case studies.

More detailed information is revealed when scrutinising institutional sub-areas, some of which are reported in Table 2.1 according to their especially low or high Likert score. Many of these institutional weaknesses, or strengths, are analysed in depth in the case studies. Yet even at this aggregate level some interesting features appear. It is indeed at that level of the CIS that corruption is unanimously mentioned, providing another source of consistency between survey results and aggregate institutional indicators. However, the survey gives more detail about where corruption practices are the most salient – that is, at the political level, between business and the executive, and between the pop-ulation and the state bureaucracy. Imperfect knowledge of the law, misman-agement of state-owned enterprises (SOEs), elite capture phenomena and weak regulation of big business, aid dependence, and excessive power centralisation, all uncover precise institutional weaknesses or their consequences, and provide useful directions for further inquiry.

Some of the strengths emerging in Table 2.1 are instructive, too. That the capacity to strike secure informal deals with the executive is found to be a strength in Bangladesh unveils an important characteristic of the institutional framework in that country. That meritocracy – in effect, the recognition of academic credentials in the bureaucracy – is mentioned among the favour-able institutional features in Tanzania is also worth stressing, for this feature coexists with some signs of elite capture and generalised corruption. In both cases, the survey respondents demonstrate a rather flexible conceptualisation of institutions.

The role of donors is stressed at different stages of the survey and arouses ambivalent reactions by the respondents. They generally agree that this is an important aspect of the economic management of their country. In some cases, they emphasise the positive effect of development assistance on national bud-gets, or the usefulness of advice provided by donors. In others, they see aid dependence as severely compromising the long-run development of the coun-try, and donors as constraining policy options too much. This two-sided role has long been underscored in the aid literature, but it is interesting that it is also very present in the minds of decision makers in recipient countries.

Specific questions in the CIS, in contrast to whole areas or sub-areas, may also deliver information that could be relevant in a further stage of the institutional diagnostic procedure. In one country, they may concern public procurement or the reliability of public statistics; in another, they touch upon the presence of discrimination, or the lack thereof; and, in still another, the issue is the unequal geographical coverage of public services.

Another valuable advantage of the CIS is its capacity to differentiate answers by the characteristics of the respondents. Of special interest are differences according to occupation, and especially between business executives and others, in view of the crucial role of the business sector in the development process. In Bangladesh, which is the only case study that systematically exploits that dimension of the survey, it is remarkable that business executives are more severe than politicians, bureaucrats, and academics with respect to the judicial system and the public administration.

To conclude this short synthesis of the CIS expert opinion survey undertaken in the four IDP case studies, it is fair to say that this instrument discriminates better among institutions than the aggregate institutional/governance indicators discussed in the first part of this chapter, and is considerably more instructive than general opinion surveys like the Afrobarometer. This is basically because of its stronger focus on institutions, its more complete inquiry into how well or badly they work, the fact that its set of respondents have some real experience and expertise in local institutions, and the explicit request that they evaluate institutions in regard to how they affect economic development. Despite these advantages, however, the CIS survey must still be seen as a mechanical exploratory tool that suggests areas or sub-areas where institutions do not function well and may be detrimental to development, as well as possibly sub-areas where the opposite may hold. Yet nothing is revealed about what may explain such situations, nor about the channels through which dysfunctional institutions may impinge on, or benefit, development. Executive decisions may be judged 'excessively centralised' or 'opaque', land disputes may be found to be too frequent, or the business elite too powerful, but what are we to infer from these statements that might point to appropriate reforms? It will be the task of the analysts to figure this out at a later stage of the diagnostic.

The format of the CIS evolved over time, from its first edition in Tanzania to the last ones in Bangladesh and Mozambique. In the latter case, the research team opted for a shorter questionnaire common to all respondents and adopted a slightly broader range of institutional areas than in the other countries. Along the initial lines of a longer and, to some extent, customised questionnaire, the Bangladesh survey appears as the most accomplished one, partly because it was able to integrate the experience acquired in the previous editions. The questionnaire was more systematically organised, not only in the main institutional areas but also, within an area, in sub-areas, or 'clusters', and even sub-clusters. This seems to have enhanced the legibility of the questionnaire and eased its statistical treatment. The questionnaire for Bangladesh should therefore be used as a template for a further edition of the survey, if any, unless there are reasons to prefer a shorter common questionnaire.

C Asking Key Informants

The last group of people to be approached for their personal insights into the role of the nature and quality of institutions in their country are those persons who exercise significant responsibilities as politicians in power or in active opposition, top bureaucrats, high-level academics, and personalities of the civil society. Numerous such key informants were interviewed as part of the initial exploratory phase of every IDP case study. In this essentially methodological chapter, the point is to summarise what was learned from them about each country, as this is fully reported and then developed in each case study. The main purpose of this section is to reflect on the way these interviews were conducted and, possibly, on some common features in the opinions expressed by the key informants across countries.

The identity of the key informants varied across case studies, but the choice was made at the outset not to interview high-powered members of the current executive – that is, presidents, vice-presidents, or prime ministers. This choice reflects not so much the difficulty of approaching them, but the concern that their opinion would necessarily be biased, partisan, or too much influenced by current challenges. In this category of informants, interviewees were most often personalities who were in this kind of position in the past and could thus have developed deeper insights into institutional constraints on development-oriented action when they were in charge, as well as today.

Different formats were used to gather the opinions of these particularly knowledgeable persons: seminars, open-ended conversations, or a predetermined set of questions. With retrospect, the latter formula proved the most effective. Yet it requires already having some good intuitions regarding the most relevant issues, so as to avoid losing time on commonalities. From this point of view, the Mozambique experience, with a set of well-chosen questions in each interview, delivered particularly interesting indications.

Several common problems were noticeable among these interviews, which often limited what could be learned from the interlocutors. The first one is that the very concepts of 'institution' and of their role in development were uneasy to convey to the interlocutors. For instance, the view that corruption per se is only the symptom of ill-functioning institutions, the issue being not only the detection and then the punishment of corruption but the circumstances that create the possibility of extracting rents, was not always uniformly shared. Respondents were often satisfied to cite corruption as the main source of problems in the way their country operates and is governed, rather than identifying its deep causes and, possibly, how it could be remedied. A second related common problem was the tendency of key informants to rely on an ideal normative framework without much relevance to the analysis of institutional problems in their country and solutions to them. For instance, the view was often expressed that the reason something does not work well is because it departs from mostly theoretical norms, like a full-fledged democracy with perfect transparency, effective checks and balances on the executive, and complete separation of the executive, the legislative, and the judiciary. Using such a norm as a reference to think about reforms is fine but illusory, since it misses key political economy constraints that precisely explain the persistence of weak institutions and their consequences. The difficulty is that political or political economy issues are still too sensitive for people who have been closely involved in them, whereas opposition members are generally biased, and people who are not directly involved in politics do not always realise the nature of these constraints. A third difficulty experienced during the interviews was the tendency for the conversation to focus exclusively on current public concerns or concerns which left their mark on the minds of interviewees, rather than on what they thought may be key persistent institutional weaknesses in their country.

Another interesting observation that results from these interviews is the similarity across interlocutors and across countries regarding the institutional fields cited as possible sources of hindrance to the process of development. Beyond corruption, practically all informants touched upon the *de facto* functioning of the political system and the judiciary, and the excessive centralisation of power and public decision making. Yet the link was not always drawn with the pace and structure of economic development. Closer to the issue of development, issues like a dysfunctional civil service, limited state capacity, the lack of coordination between public entities, or the management of land issues, were also almost unanimously cited. If the symptoms are clear and were widely shared, however, their causes were rarely discussed and the remedies proposed were not always realistic, often boiling down to wishful thinking: for example, 'eradicate corruption', 'decentralise decisions', and 'have parliament play its role'.

Being what it is, the whole exercise is nevertheless of utmost interest, not only because it allows us to establish a kind of ranking of the most serious symptoms of institutional weaknesses as seen by informed players, and to sometimes have a glimpse into the political-economic factors behind them, but also, and most importantly, because these weaknesses were usually depicted and discussed in a particular sectoral context, be it a specific ministry, local government, the education sector, tax collection, or banking regulation. At a later stage, this observation of institutional dysfunctions within specific economic or social contexts is what may allow for a better understanding of their causes and possible remedies. In that sense, the direct contact with present or past high-level decision makers or observers sheds a different light on institutions than the general description of the quality of institutions and governance that is obtained from the experts consulted in the construction of international indicators, from opinion surveys, and even from the lower-tier decision makers polled in the CIS.

IV RESORTING TO HISTORY AND ECONOMICS

After consulting the opinions of others on their perceptions of the institutional obstacles to, or constraints on, the pace or the sustainability of development, the issue must then be approached from the point of view of economics, and in a more inductive way. The objective of this new stage of the diagnostic methodology is to identify the economic development challenges faced by a country, in order at a later stage to investigate whether and how they may be related to institutional weaknesses. Preparing the ground for this exercise involves more than analysing the current economic situation of a country, as well as its assets and liabilities for future growth. Because development is an evolutionary process, and because present economic challenges most often have some of their roots in the economic, social, and political past of a country, ascertaining their nature and their origin also requires a careful review of the country's political and economic history.

The point is not to propose a methodology for such a review. On the political and social side, we can rely on the existing literature about the country concerned. On the economic side, if available in the recent literature, we may make use of economic diagnostics highlighting the constraints that bear on the acceleration, the sustainability, and the inclusiveness of economic growth. It is not clear, however, that such a diagnostic satisfactorily incorporates all of the roots of these constraints in the past or in recent history. If this is not the case, such a deeper economic diagnostic will have to be established.

Growth diagnostic exercises along the lines of Hausmann, Rodrik, and Velasco (2005) are a useful reference when they are available for the country studied, if they are not outdated. Based on a rather standard model of economic growth, this diagnostic methodology consists of identifying those constraints on economic growth which are likely to be the most binding in the pursuit of faster economic growth.

The idea is simple. Within a standard neo-classical framework, the determinants of growth are the level of investment, the productivity of these investments, and possibly other sources of productivity gains, like a more educated labour force or the adoption of better techniques, or organisation, of production, although the Hausmann, Rodrik, and Velasco approach concentrates on the first two factors. In turn, each of these factors may be hindered by various limitations. Investment may be too low because returns are insufficient or because the cost to finance them is too high. Returns may be low for physical reasons, like the geographical context, lack of human capital, or bad infrastructure, but also due to low appropriability, like excessive taxation, unsecure property rights, macroeconomic volatility, or simply a lack of information on technology or markets. On the other hand, access to finance may be limited because of poor savings, weak financial intermediation, and the unavailability of foreign financing. All of these possibilities form a kind of tree, the top of which is the rate of growth of the economy, with the branches being the immediate determinants of growth, the sub-branches being the channels through which these determinants may fail, and the bottom of the tree being all the potential constraints just listed. The growth diagnostic approach then consists of finding some quantitative measure of the strength of these constraints and looking at those that depart most from some norm. For instance, a higher return to schooling relative to other countries would suggest that human capital is scarce and thus binds economic growth. Likewise, a disproportionately high borrowing rate of interest reveals either insufficient savings or dysfunctional financial intermediation, the same being true of a large gap between the marginal product of capital and borrowing rates. Another example illustrates a deficiency at the level of infrastructure: firms have sometimes to rely on their own generators to palliate frequent electricity outages across the grid, which increases the price they pay for energy. The gap between this price and the posted price of electricity is a measure of how constraining the supply of energy is for firms. Comparing the level of these 'shadow prices' of the various potential constraints on growth with the levels observed in benchmark countries, it is then possible to establish a list of the most binding constraints.

The actual implementation of the growth diagnostic framework goes beyond a few indicators of the type just mentioned. This can be seen, for instance, in the kind of user manual provided by Hausmann et al. (2008) and others. If it is a useful instrument, it has limitations, and practical applications do not always reveal more than what mere intuition would suggest. Among these limitations, one may cite its quasi-exclusive focus on private investment, the inherent difficulty of detecting price or non-price signals, the extreme reliance on inter-country comparisons without clear criteria to select benchmark countries, and the lack of attention to the interaction across constraints and their time dimension (i.e., which one should be handled first).[16]

Another limitation of the standard growth diagnostic approach is its aggregate approach to economic growth and the too-little attention that is given to the structural aspects of development, and especially the structural transformation of the economy that causes and is caused by development, along the lines of the well-known analyses by Kuznets (1955) and Lewis (1954), and the key distinction between formal and informal sectors. This aspect of development is particularly important when dealing with low-income or lower-middle-income countries.

Judging from a few recent applications in the countries covered by the IDP case studies, the conclusions from growth diagnostic exercises are not always very enlightening, even though they are relevant. In the case of Tanzania, for

---

[16] See Felipe and Usui (2008).

instance, such a diagnostic undertaken under the auspices of the United States Agency for International Development (USAID) in 2010[17] pointed to the following major binding gaps: infrastructure, appropriability of returns (due to unsecure land rights for investors), technical skills, and small and medium-sized enterprises' (SMEs') access to finance (including agriculture). A similar study by the Organisation for Economic Co-operation and Development (OECD, 2013) added the weak regulation of business and trade to this list. With a little hindsight, it cannot be said that the lack of infrastructure, of human capital, and of financial resources for small firms were unexpected constraints on growth. In effect, they are common to most low-income or lower-middle-income countries. The issue of land rights may be more specific, and therefore may warrant further investigation. The same would apply to regulation, if the authors had something else in mind than the way the administration deals with the private business sector.

Equally disappointing is the executive summary of an 'Inclusive Growth Diagnostic of Bangladesh – again under the auspices of USAID (Davidson et al., 2014) – which points to electricity and governance as the most binding constraints on faster economic growth at the aggregate level, and, again, to energy and human capital as the most binding constraints on the growth of the garment sector – although education is explicitly mentioned as not binding at the level of the whole economy.

Of course, there is much more than these general conclusions in the two reports just mentioned, especially in the Bangladesh 'inclusive' growth diagnostic, with its focus on specific economic sectors and social issues like women's entrepreneurship. The main point is simply that the approach is too mechanical and too static to take into consideration the past structural evolution of the economy, which may have left heavy sequels in the current working of the economy. Also, it does not anticipate future constraints for which remedies should probably be put in place today. Moreover, it is largely based on information drawn from enterprise surveys, which tend to over-emphasise the practical aspects of business, rather than deeper constraints, and to underplay the macroeconomic aspects of development, despite their utmost importance.

To the extent that growth diagnostics are available, they should be used and updated. If none is available, then a similar approach has to be developed. In both cases, however, it is essential to give more depth to the analysis by incorporating it within a reflection on the long-run evolution of the economy, its potential growth engines, and its current and future likely challenges. Political history and the current state of the political game or the structure of political power are other essential factors that will need to be considered at a later stage of the diagnostic when the causes for the persistence of weak institutional equilibria and the political economy of reforms will be the focus

---

[17] See Partnership for Growth (2011), a document that inspired long-run plans for Tanzanian development – in particular, the 'Vision 2025' plan.

of attention. The overall review of the economy and its political context must rely on the existing literature about the country, but also, where necessary, on original work by the diagnostic team. It is also important that the review covers all aspects of the economy, at macro, meso, and sectoral levels, and that it looks at societal issues too, insofar as institutional weaknesses may be more or less visible, depending on the perspective one adopts with regard to the economy.

The Bangladesh case study provides a good example of the need to go deeper into the analysis of the economy than what a simple-minded growth diagnostic approach does, and to combine it with a review of economic and political history. Bangladesh has grown at a rather rapid rate over the last twenty years or so, very much – but not exclusively – thanks to ready-made garment (RMG) exports. Doubtless, a growth diagnostic exercise would make it possible to identify constraints to be relaxed in order to accelerate growth under this RMG-dominated growth regime. However, an in-depth review of the economic evolution of the country suggested that the long-run sustainability of growth requires a diversification of exports beyond the garment industry. This is unlikely to result from private initiative and would call for an adequate sector-based public policy, such as existed in the past when the textile sector was seen as worth of priority efforts by the government. Lessons can be drawn from this past experience, including not only the policy instruments which were used but also the whole decisions process – by which we mean in particular the relationship between entrepreneurs and the state that allowed for the implementation of the policy drive. The same type of diversification issues arose in the review of the Tanzanian economy.

V PREPARING FOR THEMATIC STUDIES

At this stage of the diagnostic process, it can be considered that most of the more easily accessible materials needed to begin an institutional diagnostic have been gathered. To recap, these are the following:

a. Institution/governance indicators: Which institutional areas appear weaker than the others? How does the country being studied differ from benchmark countries (i.e., neighbour or faster-developing countries)?

b. Which institutions are perceived as weak or most constraining for development by: the whole population, people who are most exposed to the working of institutions, including business managers, politicians, and the civil society, or observers of the way institutions function, and, finally, top decision makers, including past members of the executive, high-level politicians, top bureaucrats, and big business and civil society leaders?

c. A review of the political and economic history of the country, with an emphasis on current and future economic challenges for the acceleration or the sustainability and inclusiveness of growth.

Based on this set of information or evidence, an attempt can be made to bring them together by asking, for instance, whether the identified development challenges relate to specific features revealed by institutional aggregators, or to patterns in the perceptions of people, including experts, about the way institutions hamper faster or more inclusive growth. Digging deeper than simple associations to uncover some logical relationship between these various pieces of evidence might be difficult, however. Some clues will be available in certain cases, particularly when some key informants and analysts concur in the identification of the development challenges confronting their country and provide converging institutional explanations. In most cases, however, further scrutiny will be needed to make the link between development challenges and institutional weaknesses.

The experience accumulated on the occasion of the case studies suggests that this essential step in the diagnostic calls for a more detailed approach than when reviewing general economic development challenges. Some economic challenges will still be too general to be directly related to certain institutional areas, like the rule of law or the quality of regulation in the WGI aggregate indicators, to the problem of corruption in opinion surveys, or to weak state capacity in interviews with key informants. Even in those cases where there apparently is more proximity, such as, for instance, when a dysfunctional public administration is shown to truly exert a major drag on development, a more detailed analysis is needed to determine what makes it dysfunctional. Is it the lack of skill of civil servants, their rent-seeking behaviour, the overlapping of responsibilities, or inefficient management? And then, in every case, what prevents the relevant authority from taking action to remedy those flaws?

Answering these types of questions, as well as addressing the institutional factors behind major economic development challenges, requires getting into more detail about the institutional context in which the economy and the process of economic decision-making works. This cannot be done at the aggregate level – except perhaps when studying possible flaws in macro policymaking – but calls for attention to specific sectors. To take an example, shedding light on the role of institutions behind the absence of firm policies aimed at pushing export diversification in Bangladesh or Tanzania demands a better understanding of the relationship between private business and the state. Likewise, understanding the pervasive infringement of property rights in relation to land, which is found to be a binding constraint in a growth accounting exercise and is stressed by expert opinions, necessitates that we look at the way land allocation issues are resolved through market mechanisms or through the administrative machinery, including the judiciary.

More detailed analysis defines a second step of the institutional diagnostic methodology: *thematic studies* aimed at identifying the role of the institutional context in precise circumstances or sectors, chosen based on the results of the three preceding mechanical steps of the diagnostic (see the two examples just mentioned – export diversification and land rights). This new stage, which is intended to add information for the final phase of the diagnostic, is no longer mechanical. Thematic studies demand research instruments that are adapted to the area being studied and should be left to specialists in that area. These experts will be able to observe, *in situ* so to speak, the role of specific institutional features in producing observed results, including, possibly, the political economy factors that block solutions to the detected problems.

The choice of these thematic studies is best left to the authors of the diagnostic, relying on what has been learned in the mechanical steps: that is, the most salient governance indicators, the institutional features most frequently cited by the people and the experts, or the particular areas highlighted by key informants, and, above all, the main development challenges revealed by the review of economic development and policies. Right away, however, some subjects appear hard to avoid. Think, for instance, of the institutional context of the relationship between the business sector, which is essential for economic development, and the state, the main policy actor. Another key thematic area is the functioning of the public administration, possibly in some specific sector of activity like education, taxation, or land management. Likewise, some space must necessarily be devoted to the strategic sectors of the economy, possibly the export sectors.

VI THE FINAL DIAGNOSTIC AND THE 'DIAGNOSTIC TABLE'

Based both on the general approach to the way institutions may affect development (see the first sections of the present chapter) and on a closer look at how institutions actually affect the functioning of the economy and the political economy of policymaking in certain thematic areas, analysts should then be able to propose a diagnostic of the institutional setup that governs development in the country being studied. Beyond pointing to institutional weaknesses, or possibly strengths, and their implications, they should also be able to speculate on the nature of the reforms to be undertaken and, most importantly, the political economy of these reforms.

More will be said on the methodological framework to be used in this last step of the diagnostic when we summarise the conclusions of the diagnostic performed on the IDP country studies and when we draw broad lessons from the literature dealing with two miracle development experiences of Southeast Asia, South Korea, and Taiwan (see Chapters 3 and 4). Meanwhile, however, it may be useful to indicate the general approach that has been followed in the country case studies, as a way of structuring the elaboration of the final diagnostic.

This approach is summarised in the 'diagnostic table'; an example, drawn from the Benin study, is shown in Table 2.2. This table tries to relate the basic institutional weaknesses identified in the study of a country as practically ubiquitous in all aspects of the functioning of the economy with

TABLE 2.2 *The diagnostic table of the Benin case study*

Deep factors	Proximate causes	Basic institutional weaknesses	Economic consequences

– *Political game* (neo-patrimonialism, with multiple oligarchs)
– *Geography* (small country with a big resource-rich, overly protectionist, neighbour)
– *Multiple ethnic groups and a regional divide*
– *Role of donors*
	– *Policy instability (1)*: frequent law changes
	– *Policy instability (2)*: frequent changes in the organisation of key economic sectors (e.g., cotton sector)
	– Lack of long-term development planning
	– Elite capture of key state functions
	– *Weakness of state,* reflected in its inability to exert control over all its public administration
	– *Existence of rent opportunities* in illegal trade with big neighbour
		– *Widespread corruption* (e.g., in business and politics, lack of independence of tax collectors and magistrates)
		– *Weak enforcement* (and complexity) of laws
		– *Weak regulation* (domination of big business) of key sectors
		– *Lack of state coordination* (e.g., fierce competition between ministries)
		– *Low state capacity* (e.g., under-staffing of key public administrations, low quality of education)
		– Low prioritising of critical public goods (e.g., education or power generation)
		– *Opacity of policymaking and economic management; unaccountability of public agencies in key sectors*
		– *Pervasive informal practices,* magnified by illegal cross-border trade
			– Low quality of education
			– Weak sustainability of the growth pattern:
			  * low productivity growth;
			  * low diversification; and
			  * low level and pace of industrialisation
			– Poor investment climate
			– Lopsided spatial development
			– *Increasing inequality* and slow reduction of poverty
			– Chronic aid dependence
			– *Lack of citizens' trust* in key institutions
			– *Vulnerability* to external shocks

general economic consequences, on the one hand, and proximate causes, on the other. These proximate causes, which are amenable to changes through policies and reforms, must themselves be related to 'deep factors', which may be responsible precisely for whether those policies and reforms can be undertaken or not.

In examining Table 2.2, it is quite important to realise that there is no one-to-one relationship between the elements of the various columns. One institutional weakness does not have a unique general consequence, and has more than one, unique, proximate cause. The relationship between the four columns is essentially multivariate. The important point is essentially the chain of causality. The whole set of institutional weaknesses is the consequence of the whole set of 'proximate causes', which depend themselves on the whole set of 'deep factors'. At the other end of the chain, the set of institutional weaknesses affects how the economy works. Of course, looking at the whole chain, it can be said that the 'deep factors' are the ultimate determinants of economic performance. This would be correct, but not necessarily interesting from a diagnostic point of view. The important element in the whole chain is the proximate causes because they are amenable to changes through policies. This is much less the case for deep factors. Yet they are essential in order to understand why policy reforms are not taking place or why certain policy choices are made and, as such, they are an intimate part of the diagnostic. For instance, if the structure of political power prevents a reform that will help resolve some institutional weakness being undertaken, the only thing the analyst can do is, on the one hand, to identify the winners and losers of the reform and understand the nature of the blockage, and, on the other hand, to take firm notice of it in the diagnostic.

VII CONCLUSION

In concluding this chapter, it is important to stress the radical difference between our all-encompassing approach and the purely mechanical approach based solely on more or less disaggregated governance indicators or specialised surveys. The shortcoming of the latter comes from the fact that it is implicitly based on relatively loose relationships between institutions and development, as can be derived from the empirical cross-section growth literature. Equally striking is the difference between our approach and theoretical approaches to the role of institutions in development, which are necessarily simplified and rely on rough stylised empirical facts for confirmation. By deliberately probing the details of how the institutional context of a country affects the functioning of its economy, or at least some key aspects of it, including economic decision making at all levels, and how it interacts with political economy factors, we hope that a finer diagnostic can be achieved that improves our understanding of the institution–development relationship in the case of specific countries.

A last remark is in order. Its purpose is to dispel the idea that the institutional diagnostic approach described in the preceding pages is holistic. The approach starts with a long exploratory phase aimed at: (i) getting a rather comprehensive view of a country's economic achievements and failings; and (ii) uncovering some salient aspects in which it differs from *a priori* good comparator countries, possibly emphasised by knowledgeable citizens. To help articulate the various ingredients of this exploratory phase, a structural standpoint is adopted, which looks at how resources are moved from one sector to another, privileging the Kuznetsian and Lewisian distinction between low-productivity (generally informal) and high-productivity (typically formal) sectors. It also looks at the intra-sector dynamics and the way both inter-sectoral transfers and intra-sectoral changes affect and are affected by macro-level economic policies and constraints.

From there, the analysis proceeds by delving into the key issues identified so far, whether they pertain to specific sectors or to the more general functioning of the economy. It is at this stage that attention is deliberately focused on the institutional underpinnings of these issues. In dealing with them, all kinds of possible intervening factors are subjected to scrutiny: economic, demographic, social, historical, and political. In other words, the eyes are kept wide open, and all disciplinary boundaries can be traversed in order to get a deep and complete grasp of the roots and the proximate causes of institutional failures or dysfunction. In searching for the ultimate or near-ultimate causal factors, the possible role of politics is not eschewed, as is typically the case in conventional country diagnostic studies (see, for instance, the World Bank report, 'The East Asian Miracle', where little is said about the political context of the 'miracle', despite its obvious relevance). Furthermore, in addressing politics care must be taken to go beyond cursory or perfunctory mentioning of the broad issues at play. This means that effort is undertaken with a view to elucidating the precise ways in which a political system functions and interacts with economic and social agents or groups.

As should be evident from the above summary, our approach is structured, and its encompassing and transdisciplinary character manifests around privileged axes of analysis that are not predetermined but that emerge from a methodologically constructed exploratory phase.

TABLE A2.1 *A Structure of the Bangladesh CIS questionnaire*

Institutional area	Cluster	Questions
Political institutions: Executive	Quality of governance	How strictly would you say representative political institutions (parliament, executive) operate in accordance with the formal rules in the Constitution?
		How free would you say the press, and the media at large, are from political influence ?
		...
	Reporting and planning	What is your take on the accuracy of national accounts, price indices, and financial statistics?
		To what extent do major policy decisions and reforms rely on rigorous analysis of their economic and social impact?
		...
Political institutions: system	Politics in system	Alongside the legal institutions, how influential are certain non-political organisations (e.g., religious, ethnic, trade unions, lobby groups) on government decisions?
		In your opinion, how important are networks (e.g., family, clan, social group) in determining the selection of senior government officials?
		...
	Evaluation of the system	To what extent are statistics on poverty and inequality regularly debated in parliament?
		...
	Influence of civil society	How free do you feel people actually are to get together to debate, demonstrate, or protest?
		...
Justice and regulation	Judiciary in business	In your view, how impartial are judicial decisions in commercial matters involving the state and private stakeholders?
		...
	State and judiciary	How independent is the judiciary vis-à-vis the state?
		...
	Judiciary in labour market	How frequently do labour inspection services raise a case against employers who are at fault?
		...

PART II

LESSONS FROM COUNTRY CASE STUDIES

INTRODUCTION TO PART II

At the core of the IDP is the idea that we can gain more knowledge about the role of institutions by undertaking in-depth country case studies than by carrying out broad quantitative exercises based on a large sample of countries. The reasons behind this research strategy have been explained in detail in Chapter 2. We believe that any institutional analysis that ignores the precise context in which institutions operate is destined to generate only limited insights. The value of large data-based cross-country exercises is essentially exploratory, while the relevance of more sophisticated exercises that overcome the problem of causality – micro-historical studies using regression discontinuity and similar methods in particular – is all the greater as they are seen as complementary efforts to the sort of investigation conducted in this book.

In-depth country case studies not only have the advantage of throwing light on the conditions and circumstances that form the context in which development policies must be understood, but they also enable us to get a grasp of the dynamic processes under way. Policy decisions and institutional choices can thus be analysed in their context and in the light of their succession over time, in the form of a series of steps that could help consolidate a rather well-defined development trajectory or correspond more to strides ahead followed by backward moves, or to temporally inconsistent paths. Clearly, this sort of dynamic analysis necessitates a political economy approach in the sense that institutional choices are not seen as the simple outcomes of decentralised decisions by a multiplicity of private actors, but rather as outcomes decisively influenced by political actors or state agents who have their own preferences and interests (see Chapter 1).

To the six country case studies presented below, we apply the institutional diagnostic approach outlined in Part I. They therefore provide us with many opportunities to test its pertinence. As explained earlier, four country case studies are original: they rely on our own in-the-field investigations of many aspects of their institutional setup and their contexts, both static and dynamic. The countries selected for this purpose – Tanzania, Benin, Bangladesh, and Mozambique – are not trapped in the rather extreme situations of the so-called fragile countries. They offer hope and potential for development, and their study is therefore capable of highlighting the extent to which, and the ways in which, critical institutions may propel or constrain development. The other two countries that will receive our attention, South Korea and Taiwan, are different since they have already completed their take-off into sustainable development and have done so in a remarkably short period of time. Because of this performance and the important contributory role of successful institutions, we wanted to revisit their experiences in the light of our institutional diagnostic approach. Here, instead of in-the-field investigations, we rely on the available literature.

The above case studies are presented in the following order: Bangladesh and Tanzania (Chapter 3), Benin and Mozambique (Chapter 4), South Korea (Chapter 5) and Taiwan (Chapter 6). The reason why we devote less space to the former four countries is that, as has been pointed out earlier, each of them is the object of a separate book and the final chapters of these books offer synthetic analyses on which the present accounts could be anchored.

3

Uncertain Development Trajectories
in Bangladesh and Tanzania

I BANGLADESH

A Is the 'Bangladesh Paradox' Sustainable?

The Bangladesh paradox consists of the apparent contradiction between the superior growth performance of the country over the last two or three decades and the dismal state of its institutions, at least as gauged by most international governance indicators. The IDP case study on Bangladesh attempts to explain this paradox and address the issue of its sustainability.

What follows is a short summary of this case study conducted according to the methodology described in Chapter 2. It starts with a brief presentation of the geographical, demographic, and historical context of development in Bangladesh, before focusing on its economic achievements but also on its challenges going forward. Institutional issues are then taken up, before presenting a full institutional diagnostic of Bangladesh's development perspectives and then concluding.

B The Geophysical and Population Context

Occupying the delta plains of major South Asian rivers – the Ganges, the Brahmaputra, and the Meghna – Bangladesh covers a 150,000-square-kilometre tract of land surrounded by India, except for a short border with Myanmar in its southeast. With 165 million inhabitants, it is the most densely populated country in the word (excluding city-states like Hong Kong and Monaco). It has a tropical monsoon climate with heavy seasonal rainfall, hot temperatures, and high humidity. The combination of its climate, its dense river network, the low elevation of most of its land above sea level, and its geographical position at the very back of the Bay of Bengal make it prone to frequent natural disasters, including floods, cyclones, and tidal surges. For the same reason, it is one of the countries that is most threatened by climate change.

These natural conditions affect the country's development potential and some of its development features. The scarcity of land is especially important since it affects agricultural production and constrains the extension of cities and non-agricultural activity. Over time, arable land as a proportion of total land has shrunk, the average farm size has fallen – it is today around 0.6 hectares – and landlessness has increased in rural areas. Meanwhile, urbanisation has progressed rapidly – at an annual rate of almost 1 per cent of the population – so that the competition between agriculture and other activities for land is fierce.

Land scarcity would be even more worrisome if the rate of population growth had not fallen in a rather spectacular way over time. The fertility rate was above six children per woman at the time of independence in 1971. It is now close to two. Consequently, the annual population growth rate has declined from 3 per cent to less than 1 per cent. Ethnically, the population is extremely homogeneous: 98 per cent of the population belong to the Bengali ethnic-linguistic group, while the remainder comprise several tribal groups in the hilly parts of the country. The same homogeneity is observed with regard to religion, with more than 90 per cent Muslims and 8 per cent Hindus.

This religious homogeneity, as compared to Bangladesh's neighbour India, is mostly due to the historical origins of the country as the isolated eastern part of Pakistan, itself the result of the partition of the Indian provinces of Punjab and Bengal along religious lines at the time of India's and Pakistan's independence in 1947. Today's Popular Republic of Bangladesh thus results from a sequential process of independence: from India or the United Kingdom at the time of the partition, and from West Pakistan twenty-four years later, after a short but deadly war in which dissident Bengali forces defeated local West Pakistani forces thanks to the support and very effective involvement of the Indian army.

C A Short Political History of Bangladesh

Independence was proclaimed on 16 December 1971. Since then, however, the political history of Bangladesh has been rather turbulent, at least until a little more than ten years ago. As it had a clear impact on development, and on the evolution of institutions in Bangladesh, it is worth briefly listing the main episodes in that history, and the enduring struggle between the two main political parties, the Awami League (AL) and the Bangladesh National Party (BNP).[1]

---

[1] This section borrows from Raihan and Bourguignon (2023), as well as from Lewis (2011).

1 *The Difficult Advent of Democracy (1971–1990)*

The AL had been in existence practically since the creation of Pakistan, at the time of partition. Of a clear socialist bent, the party relentlessly pursued autonomous status for the eastern part of the country, starting with the right to use the Bengali language rather than the Urdu spoken in the western part. Mujibur Rahman joined the League shortly after its creation and soon became its main leader, attracting as much popular support for himself personally as for the League itself. This backing was so strong that the AL won the 1970 national election against the main western party. Violent repression by the defeated government followed, which triggered the independence war, which was deadly but short. The East defeated the West with Indian support. In 1971, Mujibur Rahman became the president of the now independent East Pakistan, which was renamed Bangladesh – 'Bengali land'. At the same time he won the title of 'father of the nation'.

After a violent war, which had followed a devastating cyclone, Bangladesh was in a dire state. Mujibur Rahman almost had to reconstruct the country. His period of leadership was short but intense. Guided by four fundamental principles – 'nationalism, secularism, democracy, socialism' – he laid the foundations of a new state along socialist lines, including the nationalisation of many industries and businesses abandoned by the West Pakistanis after the war, land reform and the introduction of agricultural cooperatives, and the expansion of primary education and other public services. Time was too short for Rahman to see the result of these initiatives. Showing a personal inclination towards religious movements, Rahman's rule was soon violently opposed by Communists, while, paradoxically, Muslim extremists reproached him for the secularist principle he had enshrined in Bangladesh's constitution. Sheikh Mujib, as Rahman was known, ruthlessly repressed these movements, jailing and often eliminating opponents to his rule, progressively transforming a liberal parliamentary political system into a single party (AL) authoritarian regime.

Rahman was assassinated in a coup managed by young army officers in November 1975. A period of disorder comprising various coups, counter-coups, and assassinations followed, until army chief Ziaur Rahman ('General Zia') took power in 1976. After running the country as 'chief martial law administrator' for some time, amidst continuing disorder and coup attempts, Zia overwhelmingly won the presidential election that was called in 1978. Soon after, he founded the BNP with a view to uniting people behind principles different from those promoted by the AL, particularly secularism and socialism. He also reinstalled the religious Jamaat-e-Islami party, which had been banned after independence on charges of complicity with West Pakistan.

Zia's rule was short too, though less disorderly than Sheikh Mujib's. In effect, he put the Bangladeshi economy back on track. On the economic front, he focused on boosting agricultural and industrial production by promoting private sector development, export growth, and the reversing of farm collectivisation. Production quotas and other restrictions on economic activities were lifted. A rural development programme was implemented, which comprised innovative social aspects as well as measures to control population growth. Major infrastructure projects were launched, including irrigation canals, power stations, and roads. On the political front, Zia reversed the strong secularist principles imposed by Sheikh Mujib, giving more public space to religion and a greater voice to Islamic movements in a restored multi-party system. Once elected as president, he normalised political life, re-established public order, and tried to rein in the military.

Zia, too, was assassinated in 1981 by a previously high-ranking officer who had been demoted. The rebellion was quickly put down and a civil caretaker government was put in place. Yet the army was not willing to step aside. Another coup soon unfolded, and power fell into the hands of General Ershad, the very officer who had subdued the uprising that followed Zia's assassination.

When he declared himself president in 1983, Ershad immediately faced violent protests from most political parties, as well as from university students and the civil society in general. Thanks to the army's support, he managed to stay in power; he created his own political party, the Jatiya Party, and called a parliamentary election in 1986. The AL, small left-leaning parties, and Islamic parties participated in the election, but the BNP boycotted it. The election was won by the Jatiya Party, amidst allegations of election-rigging and manipulation.

In 1989, General Ershad passed through parliament an amendment to the constitution that made Islam the 'state religion'. Protests amplified, huge marches took place in the later months of 1990, and eventually the military also withdrew their support for the general. Ershad resigned and handed over power to a neutral interim caretaker government, which was mandated to hold free and fair national parliamentary elections within the following 3 months. This was the end of the military rule in Bangladesh and the beginning of democracy. But politics did not become more peaceful.

2 The Competitive Democratic Era (1990–2011)

Two strong personalities have marked Bangladeshi political history since the return to democracy and the 1991 election, who perpetuate the dichotomy that appeared soon after independence between the two differing approaches of Sheikh Mujib and General Zia to the economy and the society. In the post-1990 period, the daughter of the former, Sheik Hasina, headed the AL, whereas the widow of the latter, Khaleda Zia, led the BNP. The political history of Bangladesh in the 1990s may be summarised as a continuous struggle between these two personalities who democratically succeeded each other at the helm of the country but, at the same time, did all they could, often undemocratically, to eliminate their competitor from the political map. One of them eventually won.

It cannot be said that the struggle between the two parties had greatly to do with different views of, or strategies for, Bangladesh's development; rather it had to do with personal animosity between the party leaders and, more decisively, the control of the society and sources of rent within it. All means to win the fight were used, from organising violent protests, to election-rigging, to jailing opponents, to boycotting elections with the hope of nullifying them, to buying support. If the regime was officially democratic, political practices were not.

The BNP won the 1991 election and Khaleda Zia became prime minister after a vote on the constitution transformed the presidential system set up by General Zia into a parliamentary regime. Accusations of election-rigging in the replacement of one particular MP triggered a protest and a general boycott of parliament by the opposition, led by the AL. Likewise, the 1996 election, initially won by the BNP due to the opposition boycott, raised so much protest that the government had to accept new elections under the aegis of a caretaker government. The AL won, and Sheikh Hasina became prime minister. The economy of Bangladesh grew steadily during Sheikh Hasina's tenure as prime minister, yet politics remained very tense, with several protests and strikes led by the BNP, political violence in the streets, and boycotts of parliamentary proceedings.

The rotation in regard to which party held power continued. The BNP prevailed in the 2001 election, organised again by a caretaker government. Khaleda Zia returned to power with a strong anti-corruption programme, which led to her government jailing Sheikh Hasina for a while on corruption charges. Towards the end of 2006, as new elections approached, the country again witnessed serious political unrest, with a demand for a 'free and neutral' general election under a neutral caretaker government. This led to the formation of a 'civil' caretaker government backed by the military in January 2007, which ruled for the next two years while trying to 'normalise' the political game, including through a failed attempt to exile the two 'begum'[2] contenders.

In the December 2008 national election, the AL returned to power, with 230 out of 300 parliamentary seats, and Sheikh Hasina returned as prime minister. In May 2011, the Supreme Court ruled that the system of the interim caretaker government was unconstitutional – a decision that was motivated by the experience of a two-year period during which the caretaker government practically abolished political parties and launched policy reforms, which was not within its formal mandate. This ruling *de facto* reinforced the party in power. The BNP boycotted the 2014 election, fearing it would be fixed and amidst severe repression by the AL government. It failed in imposing

---

[2] This was the popular title given to the two ladies at the head of the two main political parties. Begum, originally an Indian name for princesses or kings' spouses, is a Muslim honorific title for a respectable lady.

a caretaker government arrangement for that election. Consequently, the AL found itself with an overwhelming majority of seats in parliament. It has remained in power until now.

3 The Era of the Dominant Party

After again winning the election in 2020, Sheikh Hasina has now run the Bangladeshi government for fourteen years. The question then arises of whether this longevity is the result of an effective steering of the economy and the society, or of specific policies implemented by the AL, or the vanishing of the main opposition party.

Most Bangladeshi political commentators seem to agree on the fact that ideological differences between the two parties are small. The AL is considered to be positioned on the centre-left, with possibly more liberal views than the BNP, which is more centre-right and conservative, in part because it is closer to Islamic values. However, this can hardly be taken as the reason why the latter has lost traction with the public. Doubtlessly, being in power helped the AL weaken the BNP – for instance, by jailing Khaleda Zia, whose son seems not to have been an effective substitute for his mother. But it is equally certain that the BNP has made political mistakes that have progressively driven it away from its electoral base. In fact, many people feel that the two parties are equally corrupt, undemocratic, and ideologically neutral, but also that Sheikh Hasina has been smarter and shrewder than her opponent.

In any case, since 2008, Bangladesh has clearly entered into an era of a dominant party whereby the AL not only steers the country but also exerts tight control over the whole society, thanks in particular to a ubiquitous presence in rural areas and effective networking in urban areas. With Khaleda Zia jailed on corruption charges for several years since 2018 and her son Tareqe in exile, and also sentenced to multiple years in prison in Bangladesh, the BNP has been decapitated. In the absence of effective and dynamic substitutes for the historical leaders of the main opposition party, the AL seems to have few obstacles to a long tenure in power.

Compared to the tumultuous past, this dominant party regime provides a degree of stability in the political system never seen since independence. This has undoubtedly had a favourable impact on economic development, even though, interestingly, growth was apparently little affected by the political turbulence of the competitive democracy era. However, this political stability should not be confused with progress towards democracy. Recent national elections, and many local-level elections, aroused allegations of irregularities. A decline in participation in elections is observed. There are concerns that the national parliament is dysfunctional when it comes to having meaningful debates on development issues, democratic rights, and freedom of expression. There are also concerns among civil society about the squeezing of the democratic space. It remains an open question the extent to which this state of affairs threatens political stability and the AL's dominance in the future.

D Sources of, and Challenges to, Economic Growth

Bangladesh's experience in regard to economic growth and development over the five decades since independence has generated much interest among academics and development practitioners, both at home and abroad. From its war-torn economy of 1972 until now, Bangladesh has been able to increase its per capita GDP in real terms 3.7 times (from US$460 in 1972 to US$1,700 in 2018),[3] cut the poverty rate from as much as 71 per cent to 20.5 per cent over the same period, become the second largest exporter of RMG in the world, and registered some notable progress in social sectors. In 2015, it graduated from the World Bank's low-income category to lower-middle-income country category. Also, Bangladesh is now on track to meet the criteria for graduating from least developed country (LDC) status by 2024. At the same time, however, Bangladesh's development has happened in a widely recognised context of weak institutions. It has always been ranked in the very bottom of most international rankings of governance indicators. As was just seen, up to the late 2000s, its political climate was extremely tense, unstable, and often violent. All of these factors have prompted some analysts to term Bangladesh's economic development success as the 'Bangladesh paradox' or the 'Bangladesh surprise'.[4] The rest of this short summary of the IDP Bangladesh case study is devoted to explaining this paradox and, most importantly, to assessing whether it can be sustained: namely, whether growth can continue at the same speed without a major change in the institutional setting.

1 Growth Performance

GDP growth in Bangladesh has accelerated continuously since the days of independence. From an annual rate of around 3.7 per cent in the 1970s, it reached 4.7 per cent in the 1990s, and has gained 1 per cent every decade since then. It was close to 7 per cent just before the break caused by the COVID-19 pandemic in 2020. With an annual population growth rate now of around 1 per cent, GDP per capita has followed a growth trend of 6 per cent over the last ten years or so. Few countries can boast such performance.

From an accounting point of view, roughly two-thirds of the increase in GDP per worker results from capital accumulation and one-third from total factor productivity (TFP). Within a causal perspective, however, three main factors are behind Bangladesh's growth performance: (a) RMG exports; (b) hard currency remittances from the huge and growing population of Bangladeshi workers abroad, predominantly in the Gulf countries; and (c) a reasonable macroeconomic management.

2 The Key Role and Challenges of the RMG Sector

The growth of Bangladesh's RMG exports has its origins in the international trade regime in textiles and clothing, which, until 2004, was governed by

---

[3] At constant domestic prices in 2018 US$.
[4] See World Bank (2007) and Mahmud et al. (2010).

Multi-Fibre Arrangement (MFA) quotas. This quota system restricted competition in the global market by providing reserved markets for numerous developing countries, including Bangladesh, where textiles and clothing items were not traditional exports. Bangladeshi entrepreneurs were smart enough to seek help from South Korean companies in setting up their operations and making sure they would reach their quota. They were also able to make deals with the government to obtain exceptional facilities. Yet the real surge in RMG exports took place after the MFA regime ended, when the international market was liberalised and the RMG Bangladeshi sector appeared as particularly competitive, partly because of its previous experience within the quota system and partly because of its very low labour cost, relative to other producers in developing countries (outside China). RMG exports thus increased from US$5 billion in 2003 to US$40 billion in 2019 (at 2015 prices), an annual growth rate of 13 per cent.

The growth of RMG exports has been one of the main growth drivers of Bangladesh's economy over the past three decades. By its forward and backward linkages, and by the hard currency it provides to the whole economy, its contribution is much larger than a simple calculation based on its GDP share would suggest. An econometric exercise has suggested that the elasticity of GDP to the volume of exports is around 22 per cent. Since 2004, it would thus have contributed almost 3 percentage points to overall GDP growth – about half of it.[5]

Despite this impressive growth record, it bears emphasis that the export base and export markets have remained rather narrow, which is a matter of great concern. Undiversified exports, both in terms of market and product range, are likely to be much more vulnerable to external and internal shocks than well-diversified exports. Despite repeated government statements, and even commitments, Bangladesh's diversification of manufacturing exports seems to have failed. UNCTAD's[6] export concentration index even suggests that, instead, export concentration has increased over the last two decades. It is higher today than in the average low- or lower-middle-income country. The performance is equally dismal with respect to the Economic Complexity Index, thought to be related to the process of economic growth.[7]

This situation is still more worrying today as graduation from LDC status will terminate the trade preferences Bangladesh enjoys in advanced economies' markets, as pressure increases internally to improve the conditions of RMG workers, and as technological progress drastically modifies production conditions in the RMG sector.

3 The Role of Migration

It is estimated that 10 million Bangladeshis are working abroad today, three-quarters of them in the Gulf countries. They send home some US$22

---

[5] See Raihan et al. (2020: Chap. 2).
[6] United Nations Conference on Trade and Development.
[7] See Hidalgo and Hausmann (2009).

billion in remittances. This is approximately half the export revenue of the RMG sector. Unsurprisingly, the amount remitted – and, presumably, the number of migrants – closely follows the level of economic activity in oil-exporting countries. Remittances rose from US$2 billion in the early 2000s to US$16 billion in 2014, as the price of oil roughly doubled during that period. They then stagnated, before recently rising again.[8]

In the econometric exercise referred to earlier, which estimates the sources of growth in Bangladesh, the elasticity of GDP growth to remittances, after deflating them by the appropriate price index, turned out to be 0.14. Given an average growth rate around 11 per cent, real migrant remittances explain approximately 1.5 percentage points of the annual growth rate of GDP over the last two decades or so. Together with RMG exports, they thus represent practically two-thirds of overall GDP growth performance.

There are no precise data on the gross or net annual flows of migrants from Bangladesh and back. From the national economy perspective, it is the net flow that matters.[9] Based on rough estimates of the number of Bangladeshi workers abroad, the average net outflow might have been as high as 400,000 workers a year over the last two decades.[10] Such a figure suggests that roughly 30 per cent of the net annual increase in Bangladesh's labour force is employed abroad. In other words, the increase in the local labour force would have been 40 per cent higher without the migration outlet. The stock figure is a little less alarming: if all Bangladeshis working abroad were to return, the labour force would grow by 15 per cent.

Based on these estimates, not only did migration contribute to growth through remittances it also considerably eased the pressure on the supply side of the labour market, especially for low-skilled work.

4 Structural Economic Transformation in Bangladesh

Bangladesh may be considered the typical country as regards the Kuznets/Lewis theory of dual development (Kuznets, 1955; Lewis, 1954). Overpopulated, with huge pressure on land, without natural resource rent, the economy is divided into two sectors: a traditional, mostly agricultural, sector that is home to a majority of the population, but with surplus labour, low marginal productivity, and low average income; and a modern or formal sector employing people at a higher level of productivity and with higher wages but where employment is limited by available equipment. Capital accumulation in that sector, most often assimilated to manufacturing and associated upstream and

---

[8] See Raihan et al. (2020: Chap. 2, p. 13). On the correlation between migration and oil prices see Bossavie et al. (2021).

[9] A recent official statement refers to a plan to 'export 1 million migrant workers to different countries around the world' in 2022, and boasts a successful COVID vaccination programme that can help reach that goal. 'Bangladesh sets target to send 1 million workers abroad in 2022' (Arab News, 2022).

[10] This is based on the stock of workers abroad having increased from 2 to 10 million between 2000 and 2014 – see Raihan et al. (2020: Chap. 2, p. 12).

downstream sectors, is the engine of growth of the economy. It generates both aggregate growth and structural transformation by employing a rising share of the labour force, thus reducing the employment share of the agricultural sector, lowering the extent of surplus labour, and increasing average income. If accumulation takes place at a rate that is fast enough, a time comes when surplus labour has been eliminated from the traditional sector, the marginal labour productivity gap with the modern sector starts to shrink, and the traditional sector modernises. At the same time, clear improvements take place in terms of poverty and income distribution.

Such a view of development is extremely schematic. Actual development processes are much more complex than this simple accumulation and sectoral transformation mechanism. Moreover, there are many factors that may derail this mechanism, starting of course with a low accumulation process in the modern part of the economy. Yet this model provides a simple benchmark by which to evaluate development progress: in particular, the capacity of the economy to absorb the huge pocket of poverty in the traditional sector.

Where does the economy of Bangladesh stand on this dualistic path? Without any doubt the structure of the economy has drastically changed over the last two or three decades. The GDP share of the agricultural sector fell from 32 per cent in 1991 to 13 per cent in 2018, whereas its employment share plummeted from almost 70 per cent to 40 per cent. Overall labour productivity thus increased thanks to this major structural shift. An interesting feature of that process, however, is that within-sector productivity also increased at a fast speed. This is true of the manufacturing sector, where it was multiplied by almost eight, in part thanks to the increasing specialisation in RMG, but also in agriculture, where average labour productivity was multiplied by four.

The possibility that the average labour productivity gains in agriculture might be essentially the reflection of less underemployment in farming has to be examined. In fact, something of this type may have occurred in the early 2000s, when the absolute number of people employed in the agricultural sector declined rather sharply, at the same time as average productivity was increasing. From the mid-2000s on, however, the number of workers has remained approximately constant, while productivity continued to increase at a fast speed. This logically leads us to conclude that surplus labour was eliminated around that time in Bangladesh. Even though the productivity gap between agriculture and manufacturing keeps widening, this is not the case when the comparison is made between agriculture and the rest of the economy: here, the gap is closing.

This apparent success of the Bangladeshi economy in completing the first step of the structural transformation while recording substantial progress in productivity across sectors must nevertheless be mitigated by the key role played by migration. Per se, it is unlikely that the dynamism of the manufacturing RMG sector and its backward and forward linkages would have been strong enough to achieve the structural transformation just described. In the absence of migration, and over two decades, the non-agricultural sector should have absorbed 8 million more workers – roughly a third of the jobs that were actually created.

As for overall growth, Bangladesh's success in triggering this structural transformation of its economy, and the subsequent drop in poverty, is, in major part, the result of RMG exports and migration. Yet the fragility of this twofold engine of growth and structural transformation cannot be underestimated. On the one hand, remittances depend on oil and gas price cycles in Gulf countries at a time when efforts will be made in the world to reduce fossil fuel dependency. On the other hand, RMG exports may be affected by the loss of LDC status in a few years, by harsh competition in the world, and by the need to lift the pressure on labour cost that has led to an almost continuous increase in income inequality over the last three decades.[11]

E Social and Institutional Challenges of Bangladesh's Development

Bangladesh's undeniable success in terms of economic growth and structural transformation, particularly over the last two decades, hides not only some fragility but also deep weaknesses, which may develop into a true handicap in the future. As is well-known, Bangladesh ranks near the bottom of most international governance scales, be it in terms of the control of corruption, state capacity, or the rule of the law. In-depth analysis of several sectors, as conducted in the IDP case study of Bangladesh, makes it possible to document more precisely the flaws in the management of the economy that lie behind this dismal ranking. Such flaws can be observed in most sectors, from infrastructure, to tax collection, to the disastrous regulation of the banking sector, to the judiciary, and to the state bureaucracy, as exemplified in the educational sector. It is fair to say that some progress is being made in some domains, in particular in the provision of energy and the electrification of rural areas, and in school enrolment. It is also the case that, in social matters, an extremely dynamic NGO sector, some parts of which have a worldwide reputation, like Grameen Bank and BRAC, is partly remedying the weaknesses of the government's management, especially in the fields of health, education, and the fight against poverty in general. Yet huge progress is still to be accomplished, as can be seen from the few examples briefly summarised below.

Little will be possible, in fact, if public resources remain as limited as they are today. With total *tax receipts* below 9 per cent of GDP (among the lowest in the world) and limited non-tax public revenues, Bangladesh's public sector suffers from severe atrophy and has a restricted capacity to provide the public goods and services that are needed to extend the industrialisation process beyond RMG exports and to cover basic social needs in the areas of education and healthcare.

---

[11] See Raihan et al. (2020: Chap. 2, p. 27).

On several occasions, the present government has explicitly mentioned the need to raise taxation. Analysis shows that a large part of the problem comes more from tax collection than from too low tax rates or too narrow a definition of taxable assets. No reform has been implemented so far. An ambitious reform of VAT collection was proposed a few years ago but was cancelled at the last moment. The blockage seems to come from an implicit coalition between tax personnel and politically powerful taxpayers, which successfully prevents the introduction of automated procedures that would improve asset transparency, both for direct and indirect tax, and therefore tax collection. The consequence of this situation is not only a dearth of public services, but the informalisation of the economy, since a majority of small and medium firms are able to evade taxation.

The *banking sector* is another area where corruption is a source of inefficiency. Bangladesh is at a stage where this sector, which was initially completely state-owned, has been substantially privatised, with several new banks recently licensed. Yet some important banks and financial institutions remain in the hands of the state, leading to a dual structure of the whole sector. If, overall, the sector has been, and still is, effective in supporting the development of the RMG and other sectors, most often through exclusive deals made between powerful entrepreneurs and private banks, it also shows major weaknesses and exhibits serious failures of regulation, most notably apparent in recurrent excessive non-perfoming loans (NPL). Often caused by fraudulent behaviour rather than problems of profitability, NPLs exert adverse effects on the efficiency of the economy, reinforce the culture of corruption in the country, and contribute to rising inequality. Several major scandals have occurred, showing how deep corruption may be entrenched in this sector, despite, paradoxically, its capacity to finance the dynamic part of the economy.

A major institutional weakness of the banking sector is the lack of autonomy of the central bank in regard to regulating the sector, because of the clear subordinate position of the governor with respect to the government, and, through political links, private bankers. In this respect, the Bangladesh Association of (private sector) Banks, and the increasing political support it can command, represents a major obstacle to effective regulation.

Primary schooling may serve as a good illustration of the issues that are typical of the delivery of public services in Bangladesh: positive efforts are made but their results fall short of what is expected. In primary education, the government boasts an impressive record in regard to increasing enrolment and achieving gender parity. But this is tempered by the growing body of evidence showing that learning outcomes for many children are extremely poor. The main systemic challenges in this sector can be categorised as follows: (i) a complex coexistence of various actors faced with confusing and sometimes conflicting divisions of responsibility; (ii) a lack of resources – Bangladesh devotes only 0.8 per cent of its GDP to primary education, infrastructure is poor, and teachers' salaries are abnormally low, being slightly under per capita GDP; and

(iii) in regard to teacher recruitment and management, recruitment is flawed, with corruption problems including political influence and bribing, while the monitoring of teachers (absenteeism or performance) is weak.

Although the problems in Bangladesh's education system, and indeed in its public services more generally, are both severe and deep-rooted, there are various reforms which could and should be undertaken but which have been set aside. The historically low budgetary allocation towards primary education suggests that an increase in resources to the sector ought to be a major political priority, even though it will not solve all the problems.

Land markets raise important institutional issues in many developing countries but especially so in Bangladesh, as land is so scarce, and the population is so large. The way they function in Bangladesh leads to two major difficulties: an inequitable and not necessarily more effective distribution of land, and constrained industrial development. The growing inequality in the distribution of land results from arrangements that involve corruption, nepotism, and the interference of business elites acting through political parties, rather than neutral market operations. Consequently, the land administration has not only been captured by elites but has also become resistant to reform or effective regulation, and the more the system works in their favour the greater their resistance to reform. The same analysis applies to Bangladesh's attempt to use Special Economic Zones (SEZs) to attract industrial investors despite the scarcity of land. The institutional mechanisms for acquisition and compensation are subject to a range of corrupt practices, which in turn create vested interests that resist change and a bias towards politically connected purchasers, or towards those who are willing and able to pay bribes. Such an environment is inimical to a good business climate and undermines the potential industrial incentives provided by the SEZs.

Another consequence of the way land reallocation operates is the dispossession of some landowners, who then become pure land tenants. Landlessness has greatly increased in rural areas, with the proportion of pure tenants surging from 45 per cent to 65 per cent since 2000 (Sen, 2018). Moreover, a survey conducted by the Manusher Jonno Foundation in 2015 found that around 70 per cent of households reported losses of land in the previous ten years, with 17 per cent reportedly the victims of land grabbing (MJF, 2015). Such a situation reveals not only illegal land acquisitions but also the incapacity of the judiciary to handle such abnormal behaviour. *Weak judiciary systems* are a feature of most developing countries, if only due to a lack of resources and a lack of human capital. In the case of Bangladesh, however, the situation is worse because of an implicit coalition of most actors within the judiciary, from clerks to lawyers to judges, in delaying the conclusion of cases, and repeatedly bribing plaintiffs to supposedly accelerate procedures. Meanwhile, land grabbers exploit the lands they have seized.

One could multiply the examples of ill-functioning public entities. What is surprising is that these are often well documented in the media and yet do not arouse any real corrective reaction by those government agencies that are supposed to control, in an independent way, behaviour that deviates from legal norms. The reason is that those agencies are, in effect, tightly controlled by the government. As an example, the head of the Anti-Corruption Commission is appointed, and may be dismissed discretionarily, by the government. In addition, the Commission must obtain the government's permission to investigate or file any charges against bureaucrats or politicians. Even when granted such permission, the Commission may end up declaring suspected government members innocent, against existing evidence. This has recently occurred in the case of a widely publicised scam.[12]

An interesting question in view of this situation is why such scandals do not help the opposition parties gain more support. One reason is their present weakness. Another is the conviction among the public that they were equally corrupt when in power, and would still be if they were to come back. This kind of affair is therefore considered something almost 'ordinary'.

One could also consider that the abnormally low level of governance quality in Bangladesh is of lesser importance in the public opinion than the good performance of the economy. After all, incomes are growing and poverty falling, and even though inequality is increasing, most people have seen their standard of living improve. Thus, why should they care about poor governance?

Of course, this is fine as long as growth continues to be strong, with more RMG exports and more people going to work abroad. The challenge is that this may not last if no action is taken to diversify the economy and to prevent the growth engine slowing down in the coming years. Ill-functioning institutions may hinder a positive turnaround. This is one of the key elements of the institutional diagnostic that was established for Bangladesh.

F The Bangladesh Institutional Diagnostic

Medical diagnostics start with listing symptoms, before elaborating on the proximate causes of those symptoms and then identifying the deep factors that may permit or prevent correction of them. Our institutional diagnostic follows the same logic.

1 Institutional Weaknesses and their Economic Consequences

In establishing an institutional diagnostic of economic development in Bangladesh it is first necessary to identify the obstacle that prevents the implementation of a strategy of diversifying manufacturing exports, which will avoid a future slowdown of the pace of growth and structural transformation.

---

[12] In 2016, the World Bank cancelled a US$1.2 billion loan for the construction of a bridge because of some evidence that the Canadian company that had won the bid had bribed Bangladeshi officials. The case was investigated by the Anti-Corruption Commission, which finally declared the suspected government members innocent despite the evidence against them.

It should be noted, moreover, that this diversification should take place as much within the RMG sector, the production of which remains extremely concentrated around a few limited ranges of products, as in other labour-intensive sectors like footwear or leather products. The in-depth analysis in the IDP case study of Bangladesh suggests that, following Hassan and Raihan (2017), this obstacle is to be found in the culture of 'deals' that characterises policymaking in Bangladesh. To be sure, planning exercises are undertaken at five-year intervals, and these prioritise manufacturing export diversification through a list of sectors supposed to benefit from the same advantages as the RMG sector. There were some fifteen such sectors in the last five-year plan. Practically speaking, however, decisions about implementation are taken based on arrangements between the political elite in power and dominant entrepreneurs, or sectoral representatives in the case of the RMG sector, without real consideration in regard to the priority list. As a result, most support to exporting activity and infrastructure investment is concentrated in the latter.

Although this *supremacy of deals over formal industrial policymaking* has worked in the past, as exemplified by the phenomenal development of the RMG sector, it has now become an institutional obstacle to the diversification of the economy. This is due to a kind of capture of the government by part of the business elite, and the short-sightedness of both sets of actors.

A second generic institutional weakness that comes out of the analysis in the previous section is the *ineffectiveness of the regulation* that the state is supposed to exert over economic activity to prevent inefficient and inequitable outcomes. This is evident in the dysfunction of the banking sector, the failure to regulate labour conditions in a key sector like RMG (as evidenced by the Rana Plaza accident[13] and the downward pressure on wages), the dismal performance in regard to taxation, and the poor performance in many other areas, including transport, drug administration, and, of course, the Anti-Corruption Commission.

The third major institutional weakness is *state capacity*. This major governance failure in Bangladesh takes different forms. Some are readily apparent, such as the lack of public resources and therefore the limited provision and low quality of public goods, the lack of skills in public service, and an inefficient administrative organisation. These are common across low- and lower-middle-income countries. Other forms of governance failure are more obscure, though equally devastating. This is the case of the high level of corruption found in most administrative clusters, which tends to make the delivery of public services both inefficient and inequitable, reduces revenues, and often discourages economic initiatives.

These generic institutional weaknesses of the Bangladeshi economy are not independent. Moreover, they must be considered more as the symptoms

---

[13] In April 2013, a Dhaka garment factory collapsed causing the death of more than 1,000 workers.

TABLE 3.1 *Institutional diagnostic table for Bangladesh*

Deep factors	Proximate causes	Institutional weaknesses	Economic and social consequences
Political settlement (political and industrial elites against labour) Winner-takes- all electoral democracy Vertical structure of political parties Vibrant civil society Population pressure on land (migration) Role of donors	Elite capture of government (e.g., RMG entrepreneurial class) Weakness of labour organisations Lack of resources and skills in the public sector Corruption equilibrium: – anti-reform coalitions – clientelism Inadequate laws and administrative organisation Opacity and unaccountability	Supremacy of 'deals' over formal industrial (and development) policymaking Ineffective regulation – banking system – tax system – labour conditions Weak state capacity: – weak delivery of public goods and services – ineffective and corrupt judiciary – corruption – ineffective and corrupt judiciary	Past successful development based on RMG exports but threats to future growth Excessive export concentration Suppressed labour regime Gender discrimination NPL leakage of resources Misallocation of investments Unattractive investment climate Abnormally low tax revenues Limited quantity and quality of public goods (education, infrastructure) Rising inequality and slowing down of poverty reduction Compensation for limited public goods by, and poverty reduction role of, NGOs

than the causes of ill-functioning institutions. A more complete picture of the institutional diagnostic appears in Table 3.1, which tries to put the preceding weaknesses in a double perspective: it shows, on the one hand, the social and economic consequences of the preceding weaknesses, and, on the other hand, the proximate causes and deep factors behind them. In reading this table, though, it is important to keep in mind that there is no one-to-one relationship between items at the same level in various columns. Causality must be understood as proceeding from column to column rather than from item to item.

2 Proximate Causes

Six items appear in the 'proximate causes' column. Some of them are rather obvious. *The lack of resources and skills* or the *culture of corruption*, where every actor expects others to behave in a corrupt way, are directly responsible for the weak state capacity and the ineffective regulation of the economy by the state. It bears emphasis in the case of Bangladesh that the lack of resources is partly self-inflicted since it is largely due to the abnormally low level of taxation. There is thus a circular relationship between the proximate causes and the symptoms of institutional flaws. It is also clear that the *elite capture* of the government by the entrepreneurial class, particularly from the RMG sector, explains the supremacy of deals over formal industrial policy. As the sector gained in importance, both through its size in the domestic economy and its dominant role in exports and general economic growth, it quickly acquired considerable leverage over the government, whichever party was in power at the time. Equally clear is the role that the *weakness of labour organisations* and their acceptance of low wages play in helping the RMG sector maintain its global competitiveness, and therefore its dominant position in the home economy. Here, too, the relationship is circular.

Several *laws and administrative organisations* are obsolete or inadequate, and weaken the institutional framework. This includes some land laws inherited from the colonial or the pre-independence period, and overlapping administrative responsibilities in land matters, primary education, and the regulation of banking. The independence of regulatory agencies from central power is another area that needs reform. As they presently stand, these agencies favour the *opacity and unaccountability* of the public sector and severely limit its exposure to the public opinion, despite a vibrant private mediatic context.

3 Deep Factors

Deep factors are those factors that constrain reforms that would remedy the proximate causes of basic institutional weaknesses. It bears emphasis that the term here refers to institutional factors that may hinder development, and not to development itself. For instance, the geopolitical location of Bangladesh is a deep factor that influences its development, but it is not clear that it plays a direct role in explaining the basic institutional weaknesses or the proximate causes set out in the diagnostic table above. Unsurprisingly, many of these deep factors are thus of a political economy nature.

The *political settlement* between the industrial elite and the political elite, whatever the government in place, is a case in point. This factor echoes the elite capture proximate cause discussed above but is more fundamental. The political settlement factor refers to converging interests between whoever is in government and the industrial elite, especially the RMG business leaders. The implicit agreement provides that the government will provide strong support to the rapid development of RMG exports, at the cost of repressing labour, a condition that may be necessary to maintain the global competitiveness of the sector. Overall economic growth is the government's reward, the growth of their profits is the industrial elite's reward. As long as growth prospects remain favourable, and in the absence of major political change, this settlement may persist.

A second deep political economy factor refers to the *winner-takes-all* type of political confrontation between the two main parties in Bangladesh during the so-called competitive democracy regime described earlier. It may explain the absence of long-run structural reform during that period, as parties in government were too busy reinforcing their political base to win the next election. It is now the third time in a row that the AL has won elections, so that one may reasonably question whether a profound change has taken place in Bangladeshi politics. It must be recognised, however, that the democratic debate about long-run development objectives has always played a limited role in Bangladesh. This is even more true today, when the party in power has been able to successfully weaken and repress the opposition. Nor is a democratic debate taking place within parties. The two leaders have managed their respective parties with the same iron fist for the last thirty years, with little space left for dissenting minorities. The dynastic nature of power within the two parties does not suggest that this state of affairs is about to change.

The existence of a *vibrant civil society*, most notably NGOs, is another factor that has sometimes been proposed to explain the relative inertia of successive governments on the social front. Yet the substitutability between the government and NGOs is necessarily limited. The size of needs in areas like education and healthcare is such that NGOs can only play a marginal role, even though that role is crucial for the poorest segment of the population.

The inclusion *of population pressure* among the deep factors is meant to stress the high specificity of Bangladesh in this respect, and, implicitly, the major role of migration in reducing that pressure from an economic, social, and political point of view. Likewise, the mention of *donors* is made to recall the role they played in the past in financing the development of the economy and, in several instances, guiding its macroeconomic policy. Bangladesh's aid dependence has been limited over the last decade – that is, 1 per cent of GDP on average.

In the field of medicine, a diagnostic normally ends with a prescription. In the present case, the prescription would consist of those reforms meant to correct for the causes of institutional weaknesses, as identified by the diagnostic. The nature of reforms that would improve state capacity and the delivery of public services, modify inadequate laws, fight rent-seeking and corruption, and efficiently regulate the banking sector are rather evident. They are listed and discussed in the IDP case study of Bangladesh. More important is the political feasibility of these reforms, which depends on the deep factors that have just been listed but which may take on a different aspect in the particular context that characterises Bangladesh today.

G Conclusion

The preceding diagnostic may seem unduly negative. This is essentially because it is in the nature of a diagnostic to identify existing flaws and potential obstacles to progress, rather than positive factors. Despite an institutional framework that is extremely weak by international standards, the Bangladeshi economy has been able to grow at a fast pace, to reduce poverty, and even to undertake important reforms in the past decades. Even within a turbulent political context, Bangladesh's governments have shown a strong political will for reform on multiple occasions in the past, such as when they supported the RMG sector at an early stage, when they opted for rigorous macroeconomic policies, when they invested massively in power generation or liberalised imports, and when they opened up the economy. Political power, political determination, and policy wisdom were present in many uneasy but key decisions, as, for instance, when food rations were abolished on the grounds that they were a costly way of supporting the urban middle class, rather than the poor, or in the case of the pioneering introduction of food and, later, conditional cash transfers to accelerate universal primary school enrolment. In one way or another, the main question that arises from the preceding diagnostic is thus whether reforms aimed at eliminating notorious rent-seeking opportunities are much more difficult to achieve. Is the present Government of Bangladesh in a situation to undertake them, and is it willing to carry them out?

That the government is in the hands of a strongly dominant party ensures that political leverage for reforms does in principle exist. But at the same time the weakness of the opposition is a disadvantage because the threat it can issue against a wavering government is weak. Up to now, moreover, the economy has done well, with solid growth benefiting most of the population – though more so those at the top of the income scale – and without preventing part of the population having to go abroad to support their family. On grounds of pure political strategy, the incentives for reform may thus seem relatively weak. However, the present diagnostic has exhibited the serious risks to the future rate of growth in Bangladesh. At the top of the list, the COVID-19 pandemic has already slowed down growth, and potential geopolitical tensions in the post-COVID world add to the uncertainty arising from too specialised a development strategy. Taking advantage of the present political situation to launch reforms and to show results regarding both economic diversification and governance would do much to reinforce the party in power. If a power rotation takes place, on the other hand, these reforms would constrain the new government to follow the same principles of good governance and a sound rule of law, thus weakening its control over the opposition. For the party presently in power, and for the whole society, this is clearly a win-win strategy.

As mentioned at the beginning of this summary, the dichotomy observed in Bangladesh between weak institutions and robust growth was termed the 'Bangladesh paradox' or 'Bangladesh surprise'. At the end of this diagnostic one may ask whether such a paradox or such a surprise will persist. The answer is most probably not. Either growth will slow down without institutional improvement, or growth, and the transformations that come with it, will continue at the same pace but institutions will have been reformed. It behoves the present government to decide which direction to choose, considering that the political opportunity for ambitious institutional reforms may not last.

II TANZANIA

The following pages summarise an in-depth study of the relationship between institutions and development in Tanzania conducted following the methodology set out in Chapter 2. Only the essence of the original study is reproduced in this summary, but it is hoped that its main lessons for the understanding of the economic challenges faced by Tanzania, and the way they depend on institutional weaknesses, are truthfully presented here.

The summary is organised in the same way as the original study except for the thematic studies, which provided detailed examples of the way the nature and functioning of institutions affect Tanzanian development. Instead of summarising these, the summary focuses on what was learned from these studies about possible institutional obstacles to an acceleration of development.

A Geographical and Demographic Context

Today's United Republic of Tanzania results from the union of Tanganyika – a large area a few degrees below the equator on the shores of the Indian Ocean – and the Zanzibar archipelago off its coast. Tanzania is the biggest of the eastern and southern African countries, excluding South Africa. Except for the coastal area and Zanzibar, it consists of extensive rolling plains, interrupted by the Great Rift Valley, which cuts across the east of the African continent from north to south. The Rift crosses Tanzania in its western part, where it is interspersed by Africa's three great lakes – Victoria, Tanganyika, and Malawi (or Nyasa) – the shores of which are shared with neighbouring countries. Four major ecological regions are usually distinguished because of their highly differentiated climates: the mountain lands in the north (home to Kilimanjaro) and in the southwest receive generous amounts of rain; rainfall is also satisfactory in the lakeshore regions, especially lake Victoria's; however, the high plateaus that fill the centre of the country are semi-arid, whereas the coastal area is both hot and humid.

Overall, the country enjoys a high agricultural potential, which is presently far from being fully exploited. Only 30 per cent of the land suitable for cultivation is being farmed, often under harsh conditions, despite numerous rivers and lakes, which offer a huge potential for irrigated agriculture. Other natural resources include minerals like gold, some other metals, and gemstones, and fuels (essentially coal and gas), of which abundant reserves have recently been discovered offshore. Another natural resource is the beauty of the country's mountainous, sea, and savannah landscapes, as well as its world-famous reserves of wild animals, which altogether attract a considerable flow of tourists.

Tanzania is home to some 60 million people. Given its size, it is sparsely populated. However, as in most African countries, its population is growing very quickly and will reach 100 million before 2040. Because of the pace of demographic growth, the fast increase in the degree of urbanisation has not prevented the population density doubling in rural areas over the last thirty years, making land progressively less abundant.

The ethnic composition of the population is somewhat remarkable for its diversity, which is thought to have had a favourable influence on the early development of this part of Africa. About 120 different ethnic groups, most with their own language, cohabited for two centuries before colonisation, without any of them trying to dominate the others or to control the whole area. Still today, the largest group represents only 13 per cent of the population and the second largest only 4 per cent. Such an ethnic diversity is without any doubt due to the size of the area, the variety of its habitats, and the relative impracticability of travelling long distances. There is no doubt either that this demographic feature of Tanzania partly explains the political stability of the country once those heterogeneous groups were integrated into a single nation with a common language – the Swahili – and political institutions after independence. It also explains why Tanzania differs from its neighbouring countries and most sub-Saharan countries, where ethnic rivalry is frequent and has caused friction and conflicts that have proved harmful to development.

The presence of non-African racial minorities is another element in the heterogeneity of the population, with rather different implications. Arabs and Indians had always been present in the coastal area, the former being especially powerful when Zanzibar was the home of the Sultanate of Oman and controlled the whole East African shore from the late seventeenth to the late nineteenth century. More Indians arrived during the period when both Zanzibar and the mainland were under a British Protectorate. Like Arabs, Indians were especially active in trading, and more recently in light manufacturing. Both groups remain small minorities today, but their early business specialisation gave them economic power that is out of proportion to their demographic weight. The social distance between these groups and Tanzanian Africans is still detectable nowadays.

The European presence goes back to colonial times in the late nineteenth century, when Germany colonised the interior part of what is today mainland Tanzania, under the name of Tanganyika.

B A Short Account of Tanzania's History Up to Independence

German rule did not last long since the Germans were forced to leave after being defeated in World War I. Yet, despite fierce hostility from the indigenous population, the German colonisers were able to develop major export crops (sisal, coffee, cotton), to start the construction of a railroad network, and to lay the foundations of an administrative structure, as well as an educational system.

After the German defeat in 1918, Great Britain was entrusted with the Protectorate of today's mainland Tanzania. The country was then in a state of extreme underdevelopment, which had even worsened as a consequence of the fierce battles fought in that part of Africa between German, British, and Belgian colonisers, during the war. Yet two major factors prevented an economic development comparable to what could be observed in neighbouring British colonies. One was the relative lack of fertility of a large area in the interior of the country, which was invaded by the tsetse fly as a consequence of the war. The other was the limited attractiveness for European settlers of a territory whose political status was uncertain – being neither a colony nor an independent state. These may also be the reasons why the British administration was initially rather unambitious in its management of the country, mostly perpetuating the German colonial policies.

Things started to change after World War II as the newly created United Nations strengthened its control over territories with Protectorate status and pushed for more participation by the indigenous population. British 'indirect rule' was replaced by formal local governments with a multi-tier structure and increasing African involvement, while the Legislative Council of the Protectorate was progressively opened up to elected African members.

Independence was obtained peacefully. Under the leadership of Julius Nyerere, the Tanganyika African National Union (TANU) won practically all the seats on the Legislative Council open to election in 1958, and again in 1960. The British colonial secretary then acceded to TANU's demand for a 'responsible government' by Africans. One year later, independence was declared, with TANU as the party of government and Nyerere as prime minister. Three years later, the new Republic united with Zanzibar, where a violent revolution against the Arab minority, which ruled the islands, had just brought to power an African-dominated party. Together, they formed the United Republic of Tanzania, with Nyerere as president.

C A Synthetic View of Tanzania's History since Independence

1 *The Socialist Era*

Very much marked by neo-colonialism, development during the first years after independence was disappointing; an alternative strategy was called for. The president spelled out such a strategy in his famous 'Arusha Declaration' in 1967. It was a socialist-oriented development programme adapted to the African context under the label 'Ujamaa' ('familyhood' in Swahili). It comprised three dominant approaches: (i) an emphasis on the agricultural sector and the urgent need to improve its productivity, most importantly through regrouping dispersed subsistence farms into Ujamaa villages, which involved displacing part of the population; (ii) state control of the means of production and exchange, and thus nationalisation of a major part of the non-agricultural sector; and (iii) addressing the social demand for education, health, equality, and participation in public decision making.

Ten years later, the results of this strategy were far from spectacular. Nationalisation did not deliver on its promises because of mismanagement by bureaucrats, interference between managers and politicians, and mounting corruption at the head of nationalised companies. The results were especially bad in the agricultural sector. Although some productivity gains were achieved in the extensive cultivation of some export crops, the collective farms proved disappointing and villagisation essentially disrupted production processes. In a few years, Tanzania passed from being a net exporter to being a net importer of food crops. GDP growth slowed down, and income per capita started to fall after 1976, while severe balance of payment problems developed due to the poor outcomes of the Ujamaa strategy, a costly war with Uganda after the latter invaded the north-western part of the country, and strongly adverse changes in the terms of trade.

A National Economic Survival Programme was launched in the early 1980s, but it came too late and the international development community was called in to rescue the country. Nyerere resisted the pressure of donors and the IMF, which made their aid conditional on his amending his socialist strategy and implementing a return to market mechanisms. As the economic situation of the country continued to deteriorate, however, he was finally forced to accept a stand-by agreement with the IMF in 1985, after having broken off relations with that organisation a few years earlier. This agreement prefigured the Structural Adjustment Programme (SAP) signed later with the World Bank, whose aim was to see Tanzania transition back to a market-led economy and, as a matter of fact, to undo much of Nyerere's efforts to build a socialist economy. Nyerere then decided not to run for a new presidential mandate and left to his successor the task of managing the transition.

If the economic achievements of the Nyerere era were disappointing, the same cannot be said in the non-economic sphere. The nation-building project, which Nyerere embarked on notably by disbanding the multiple chiefdoms existing in the country and promoting Swahili as the lingua franca, brought about national unity and deep cohesion. This successful national integration drive was complemented by major social investments in literacy, education, and health programmes. In comparison with many other African countries, Tanzania is exceptional in the political stability it has experienced since independence, under the influence of Nyerere's probity and respect for constitutional rules. It is thus not surprising that, despite a failing development strategy, Nyerere is considered by a large majority of the population as the father of the nation.

2 The Return to a Market Economy

At the time of Nyerere's retirement in 1985, Tanzania was among the poorest economies in the world and faced a double challenge: to reduce poverty and to transition to a market economy regime.

If the disorder caused by the transition was particularly noticeable during the first five years after the Nyerere era, it took substantially longer for this

process to be completed and fully consolidated. Judging from the rate of inflation it was only slightly before the turn of the new millennium – that is, roughly
fifteen years later – that the economy seems to have stabilised. The adjustment
to a new regime indeed required major changes, from reactivating the price
system and the agricultural distribution network to privatising the multitude
of state-owned enterprises (SOEs), including in the banking sector, to disman-
tling privatised monopolies, and to downsizing and reforming the civil service.
Overall, this heavy agenda was successfully and rather peacefully managed by
the administrations that succeeded Nyerere.

Advances were also made on the front of political institutions, with two
major constitutional changes taking place. The first change limited to two the
number of five-year terms that a president can serve consecutively. The second
change, common to many African countries, abolished single party rule. While
the dominant single party, which had morphed from TANU to Chama Cha
Mapinduzi (CCM) after the union with Zanzibar, remained foremost, opposition parties started to play a significant role in the political debate.

Quite remarkably, all of these changes in both economic and political institutions took place peacefully. The three presidents in command since the launch
of the SAP in 1985 each ruled for two consecutive terms before leaving the
political scene and letting new general elections – usually considered to be fair
by outside observers – to take place in a rather quiet atmosphere (the elections
to the autonomous government of Zanzibar being an exception). It is only in
the last two presidential elections that serious accusations of vote-rigging have
been put forward, at the same time as open political tricks appeared. In 2015,
CCM nominated John Magufuli as its candidate, instead of former prime minister Edward Lowassa, who was the frontrunner but who had been involved
in a big corruption scandal. The latter then defected from CCM and ran for
president as the candidate of the main opposition party, which suggests that
little ideological differentiation exists across the political scene. Lowassa was
defeated and unsuccessfully charged the government with rigging the election.
The situation was considerably worse in the 2020 election when Magufuli
was re-elected with a suspicious lead over the other candidates, commonly
attributed to harsh repression, manipulation, and widespread fraud. Magufuli
died – probably from COVID, after having denied the reality of the pandemic –
shortly after his apparently fraudulent re-election and was replaced at the helm
of the country by his vice-president. At the time of writing, it is too early to
know whether his move towards authoritarianism and away from the democratic practice which had prevailed since independence will persist.

Corruption has always been behind most Tanzanian politics and may be
considered an inherent weakness of the country. Yet over time scandals have
tended to become more frequent and to involve larger amounts. This has sometimes reached such an extent that donors, who are particularly important in
the funding and designing of Tanzania's development strategy, have in various instances suspended their assistance. Magufuli was chosen as the CCM

candidate in 2015 mostly because the party had been badly discredited due to a series of high-profile corruption affairs, and he was elected thanks to his anti-corruption image, acquired while he was Minister of Public Works in the previous government. Some considered his authoritarianism necessary to fight corruption and there are indeed some signs that corruption has receded. It remains to be seen whether this will be confirmed in the coming years.

D Economic Development Challenges

It would be tempting to say that the development of Tanzania since the mid-1990s – that is, after the transition to a market economy was fully achieved – has been a success story. On average, GDP grew at the rate of 6.2 per cent a year but, because of fast population growth, the growth rate of GDP per capita was only 3.4 per cent. Income per capita almost doubled over the last two decades, and Tanzania recently graduated from low-income to lower-middle-income status in the World Bank's country classification. However, a careful review of the Tanzanian economy suggests that maintaining past rates of growth may raise serious challenges.

The first cause for concern is the uncertainty about what could be Tanzania's long-run engine of growth. To a large extent, growth during the last two decades was pushed by the demand side of the economy, itself fed by increasing export revenues arising from improving terms of trade, and foreign financing. A sign of that bias is given by the exceptional dynamism of the construction sector, which grew twice as fast as the whole economy over the whole period. On the supply side, manufacturing has done slightly better than the rest of the economy, especially on export markets, but it is presently too small – less than 10 per cent of GDP – to significantly pull the economy forward. Agricultural exports have not over-performed either. Overall, it turns out that a good part of overall productivity gains over the last twenty years was due to a net reallocation of labour away from low-productivity agriculture to the rest of the economy. However, instead of being in favour of the high-productivity sectors, as in the celebrated Lewis model, the reallocation has concentrated on low-productivity sectors like retail trade or social and personal services. That such productivity gains are not sustainable in the long run is exemplified by the fact that productivity in these sectors has fallen, precisely because of the net influx of workers from agriculture. As high-productivity sectors absorbed only a tiny share of the net migration of workers, there is a risk that, without a powerful engine of growth in high-productivity sectors, labour will remain highly concentrated in the low-productivity part of the economy, thus contributing to slow overall economic growth, a slow reduction of poverty, and increasing inequality.

A second related challenge is precisely to selectively improve within-sector productivity, not to save on labour – the absorption of which is per se a major challenge – but, quite the contrary, to increase competitiveness in tradeable and reasonably labour-intensive sectors where autonomous development looks possible. Maintaining the investment rate at the 35 per cent of GDP level observed today should significantly contribute to this goal by drastically improving the infrastructure needed to achieve this objective. But such a high investment rate is itself a challenge. Exploiting untapped sources of efficiency gains is also needed. For instance, the difficulty of establishing firm land rights is often mentioned as a disincentive for innovation and investment in modern agriculture and agroindustry. The same is true of the lack of some skills in manufacturing, or rent seeking by bureaucrats.

The third challenge lies in freeing the economy from its strong dependency upon foreign financing. Even though it has declined over the recent years, foreign financing has always been sizeable. Official development assistance still represents 5 per cent of GDP – that is, a bit more than a quarter of the government budget and 14 per cent of gross investment. On various occasions, donors have mentioned their wish to reduce their support, arguing that this would be an incentive for the economy to become more autonomous. The Tanzanian government has explicitly concurred with this view. Yet it is unlikely that the current growth trend would be maintained if this flow was to dry up. Private foreign funds are not negligible either. Since the mid-2000s, foreign direct investment amounted to a little more than 3 per cent of GDP.

An important unknown for the future development of Tanzania is the fate of its huge offshore natural gas reserves, which were discovered in 2017. These could provide Tanzania with substantial additional revenues for twenty to thirty years after a five-year investment period. Their extraction cost is apparently high, so profitability requires an export price higher than has been observed throughout the 2010s. Negotiation with foreign companies for extraction, liquefaction, and export of gas broke down a few years ago, but they have just been reactivated. There is still much uncertainty about the extra income flow Tanzania could get in the long run from its gas reserves, even though earlier estimates suggested it could be modest if prices stay on their long-run trend.

A final cause for concern relates to the social side. Inequality has been increasing and poverty has receded at an unexpectedly slow pace. That growth has not trickled down more vigorously to all segments of the population is a challenge for the future. Increasing inequality may have adverse effects on future development through the demand side of the economy, by reducing the aggregate propensity to consume, and more fundamentally by undermining the social and political climate. The same remark applies to the stagnation of school enrolment, which is somewhat below universal primary schooling, and the low quality of the educational system in general, which may put future growth, poverty reduction, and the social equilibrium at risk.

More direct diagnostics of development challenges and firm manager surveys in Tanzania point to the lack of infrastructure, notably in electricity, the limited supply of skilled labour, and the low quality of the civil service and public service delivery as obstacles to accelerating, or even maintaining, the pace of economic growth. These obstacles are common to most low-income or lower-middle-income countries, however, so the real issue is whether Tanzania is successful in progressively overcoming them.

E The Perceived Quality of Institutions

The capacity of the country to address the development challenges summarised above depends on the quality of its institutions, which themselves will determine the effectiveness and inclusiveness of the policies that must be put in place. This is the goal of the in-depth study of Tanzania that is being summarised here. Before synthesising its conclusions, however, it is worth recalling the results of the thorough review of institutional indicators, and of opinion surveys undertaken in Tanzania, with the objective of getting a first idea of possible obstacles to future development.

According to several international databases on governance indicators, the most fragile institutional areas in Tanzania are the control of corruption, on the one hand, and government effectiveness, or administrative capacity, on the other. What is remarkable, however, is that in these two dimensions, as well as others, the quality of Tanzanian institutions turns out to be fully comparable to, and sometimes better than, its neighbours' – except Rwanda for the business environment – and even institutions among low-income countries, which have done significantly better over the last three decades. Opinion surveys among the Tanzanian population and among various types of decision makers also point to corruption as a severe institutional weakness, and further stress several institutional factors that may hinder future development. These include land rights issues, ineffective checks and balances on the executive, weak regulation of big business and utilities, a poor investment climate, and an inefficient civil service.

Of course, the institutional indicators and the preceding list of shortcomings are mixed bags. Yet the general picture they draw of economically relevant institutional challenges in Tanzania is consistent with a cursory review of Tanzania's political and economic history over the last three decades or so. It should also be noted that, when gathering personal opinions on the matter, we often heard that the control of corruption or state capacity are not worse in Tanzania than in comparator countries, and therefore cannot be considered as specific problems hindering Tanzanian development. This is not a convincing argument, though. Of course, these institutional weaknesses may have a negative impact in the other countries too. That they are present elsewhere does not mean that making progress at home on those institutional dimensions would not yield substantial benefits.

F Identifying Major Institutional Weaknesses

Having reviewed the main challenges of economic development, as well as the current political context of Tanzania, it is now time to focus more closely on institutional issues. Following the methodology set out in a previous chapter, the next step is to consider several thematic areas where development challenges are most apparent and are likely to provide evidence or hints on the way institutions help or hinder those changes that make development. Five such studies were conducted in the case of Tanzania. They focused on the following topics: (i) business and politics; (ii) state coordination and decentralisation; (iii) the civil service; (iv) land management; and (v) the regulation of the power sector. The main institutional weaknesses revealed by these studies are succinctly analysed in what follows.

The relationship between big business and politics has shaped Tanzanian development ever since independence. It is thus crucial to understand the nature of the forces that shape it, and their outcome.

A word about the players first. On the business side, most European capitalists left at the beginning of the socialist era and business was then essentially in the hands of Tanzanian Indians and, later, Arabs, a natural extension of the control they had very early on in trade activities. As a matter of fact, indigenous entrepreneurs at the head of medium and large firms or groups have always been a minority in Tanzania, to such an extent that there is only one African Tanzanian name in the list of the twelve richest businessmen in the country. On the political side, the government should be the main actor. However, the dominant party (CCM) has also played an important role because of the fragmentation of political power within the party – that is, the presence of several groups with major influence and with possibly diverging views on the 'right' policy. Nyerere was able for some time to control them, so that political power was reasonably centralised in the hands of the president, yet his grip had started to loosen by the end of his last term, possibly because of the disorder created by the nationalisation process and the multiplication of sources of rents linked to the expansion of parastatals and resulting from increasing disorganisation. Things became worse during the transition back to a market economy. On top of the opportunities arising from the privatisation drive, politically powerful individuals within CCM were able to make deals with businesses for their own interest, and then to impose them on the party and on the executive, using the prospect of party dismantlement as a threat. Deals could be of varying kinds. They could involve conceding competitive advantages to a business group against campaign financing, other indirect electoral benefits, or personal enrichment, or syphoning public resources through schemes involving private business. Major corruption scandals arose in those days, to such a point that donors suspended their aid on various occasions. A climax seems to have been reached at the end of the second term of Kikwete, Magufuli's predecessor. The dominant party's popularity was thereby severely damaged, and the party had to opt for an openly anti-corruption candidate to have a chance of winning the election. Over the last few years, the new president tried to turn the tide by attempting to regain the full control of the party, partly through internal politics, and partly by working to dry up those sources of rents originating in deals with the private sector, a strategy that led him to be particularly tough with both domestic and foreign big business.

Whether this strategy was successful, and whether it will be maintained, is still to be seen. Yet several interesting lessons can be drawn from this sketchy history of business and politics in Tanzania.

A first lesson is the utmost importance of the structure of political power. In Tanzania, the business–politics issue is not a 'government versus private sector' story only: it also comprises the control of the president over the dominant party. It is because the unity of the party is decisive at election times that it is difficult for the president to openly sack powerful party members who use their influence to sell competitive advantages to big business. This is a game with a bad equilibrium, where no player has an interest in making clean moves, with some entering into illegal deals and others not sanctioning departures from good conduct. At the end of the day, the personality, legitimacy, and authority of the leader is determinant.

A second lesson concerns the ineffectiveness of industrial policies, or even their fuzziness in a country where firms can buy direct competitive advantage through political friends. In Tanzania it has long been the case that 'traders' have an advantage over 'industrialists' because they are able to generate more resources and so to convince policymakers to maintain low tariffs on some strategic goods, the imports of which they control. Sugar and rice are typically goods which need some initial protection to generate the economies of scale that would make their cultivation and industrial transformation competitive. Absent this protection, they would be outcompeted by the imports favoured by the traders.

A third consequence of the varying relationship between business and politics since independence, and possibly of the dominance, until now, of big business by Tanzanian Asians and Arabs, is some heterogeneity or hesitation among policymakers about the latitude to be left to the market with respect to state authority. This situation creates some uncertainty, which is necessarily harmful to the economy.

Having established such a diagnostic, two questions should be asked. First, if vertical industrial policies fostering specific activities that are against the interests of dominant business groups are politically difficult to implement, why not promote horizontal policies that simply consist of improving the investment climate for all businesses by getting rid of numerous administrative frictions and burdens, whose main function is often to provide rent opportunities to certain bureaucrats? The point here is that corruption is contagious: it cannot be stopped in the middle range of the bureaucracy when illegal deals continue at the top. Also, it is not clear that dominant business interests could get a better investment climate than the one they enjoy through their partial control of politicians.

Second, can it be argued that the Tanzanian economy is doing relatively well, so that the business–politics collusion issue may not really be a big problem after all? Maybe, but the key question is whether it is possible to accelerate the present trend and, most importantly, to make it more sustainable and less uncertain in the future, when the external context may change and become less favourable? The relative weakness of tradeable sectors like agroindustry and manufacturing was underscored above, and it may be the case that the nature of the business and politics relationship bears some responsibility here. Yet progress has been made and it is unlikely that big business would not seize opportunities if they existed in these areas. On the other hand, choices may have been made that have curtailed these opportunities: think of the case mentioned earlier of the capture of some import markets that may have outcompeted domestic production.

This issue of central control, which is so clearly illustrated by the inherent difficulty faced by the executive in regulating big business groups, despite their crucial role in the dynamics of the economy, is present in other aspects of public management. Paradoxically, successive administrations have apparently been strongly determined to centralise decisions and control, even though such a move was not justified in some cases, while a deficit of coordination exists between the executive and various decentralised administrative units and public agencies. That lack of control gives some leeway to civil servants operating in those entities – and therefore provides rent-seeking opportunities, which they are happy to exploit.

There are various reasons for such a situation. First, it is objectively the case that some sectoral administrations are simply ill-structured, which sometimes results in overlapping responsibilities, inefficient management, and possibly rent seeking. Examples include the following: land management, with a National Land Use Planning Commission that is redundant due to the presence of the Direction of Urban and Rural Affairs in the Ministry of Agriculture; the lack of coordination between the Tanzanian Revenue Authority, responsible for tax collection, and the Minister of Finance, which decides about tax schedules; confusion of mandates between local government executives and central government-appointed officers; or the intricate set of relationships between local government authorities, the Prime Minister's Office, the Minister of Finance, and various other ministries. Likewise, firm managers insist they must obtain the agreement of an abnormally high number of government agencies before they can market a new product or service, when only a couple of them could do the same job.

A second reason for coordination failures may be found in the complexity of various laws. The laws that govern the acquisition of land rights are especially intricate and require a heavy administrative apparatus, from central government to local village level. It is tempting for those in charge, and who are supposed to know the law, to take bribes from those who do not, or who are confused about certain aspects of the law. This is true at all levels: from an investor wishing to develop a large plantation to villagers concerned with the implications of leasing some of their land. The sensitivity of land rights in a country where a sizeable proportion of the land is cultivated by small farmers and is exchanged or transferred according to local customary laws is high. Hence the need for safeguards designed to avoid awkward situations in which villagers come to lease part of their land to a big company without knowing all the implications of such a transaction. The complexity of the existing law has been abundantly stressed and commented upon. Several reports have been commissioned which make suggestions for improving it, and successive governments have declared they would follow suit. Yet nothing has been done for the moment. The same complexity and procrastination is observed in the relationship between the central and local governments: a reform was voted on in the late 1990s and was supposed to be implemented by 2008, yet it is still pending more than ten year later.

Both the intricacy of the structure of public management and the complexity of the law may be related to another specificity of the Tanzanian economic culture: a selective distrust of market mechanisms. Such an attitude may be inherited from the socialist era, although the generation that had some responsibility during that time is now retiring. It is more likely due to the multiple cases of corruption that took place during the period of the return to a market economic regime – a period that was nicknamed *Mzee Riukhsa* ('everything goes') by Tanzanians. Likewise, in the 2010s, the leaders of CCM were afraid they would lose the coming election because of their tarnished image due to multimillion-dollar scandals. It is striking, too, to see how, in some respects, land laws appear to be reminiscent of the planning era and its deep suspicion of market mechanisms, and this despite the fact that the law was voted well after the end of the socialist regime. There may be good reasons for this, but too rigid a process of land allocation entails various types of costs and leads to missed economic opportunities that would benefit the whole country. Moreover, since market mechanisms will become more pervasive in the not-so-distant future, it may be good policy to quickly engineer a smooth transition to a more market-friendly environment.

The will to maintain electricity production and distribution as much as possible as a vertical public monopoly also betrays this bias against market mechanisms. It may be a holdover from the socialist era and the view that such critical goods as power should be publicly managed. However, it is more likely a reaction to earlier corruption scandals linked with the subcontracting of power generation to private firms. Despite such scandals, a public monopoly continues to be seen by the public, and by many policymakers, as a guarantee against private providers charging exorbitant prices. But it also provides influential politicians with rent-seeking opportunities, particularly in procurement operations, including with private power providers.

Institutional weaknesses in Tanzania's public sector are also observed at a more basic level. Comparative institutional indicators, opinion surveys among ordinary people and various types of decision makers, and most policymakers converge in considering the under-performance of the civil service as a serious development impediment. The lack of resources, due to both the low level of income per capita and the limited share of recurrent public expenditures devoted to this service, certainly bears some responsibility for such a situation. But the overall setup of the delivery of public services plays a role too. The misalignment of civil servants' incentives, the lack of effective monitoring and evaluation capacity, the high degree of corruption, as well as under-skilled staff and weak management of administrative units and government agencies, have also been regularly denounced. Two Public Service Reform Programmes have been carried out, which were supposed to make recruitment more rigorous and to introduce a dose of performance-based staff management. Improvements were noted, but serious challenges remain, and several observers felt – a few years ago – that some progress had even been reversed (see Mukandala, 2023). The culture of promotion based on seniority or partisan links, rather than merit, of recruitment based on other grounds than capacity, of shirking, of diverting resources, and of taking bribes is said to be still very present today.

All of these failings are difficult to quantify. Measurement of their economic consequences is still more of a challenge, except maybe in a few sectors. Because of the service it delivers and the size of the staff it employs, the education sector has been subject to more quantitative evaluation exercises than any other. There, the picture is far from favourable. On the supply side, teachers have long been castigated for their absenteeism – found to be as high as 31 per cent in a survey conducted in 2014. They are also frequently under-qualified, with a minority of them achieving the required standard in maths or English tests. The result is that even though school enrolment has progressed – though it is not yet fully universal – learning outcomes are poor. Half of Grade 4 children were not able to carry out two-digit subtraction in 2016. Although progress has apparently been made over recent years, a report by the World Bank concluded in 2018 that a 'learning crisis remains in Tanzania'. Even though this kind of quantitative evaluation can hardly be performed in other areas of public sector activity, there is no reason to believe that their outcomes do not suffer from the same deficit of quality.

Results of surveys about the relationship between firms and the public administration, and anecdotal evidence, confirm the foregoing statement. They also suggest that corruption, in the form of giving and accepting bribes, is widespread. It has already been mentioned that Tanzanian political life has been interspersed with increasingly frequent and large corruption scandals, which are probably just the tip of the iceberg. The concern here is about ordinary corruption that is taking place between middle-tier civil servants with some rent-seeking power and firms or citizens. The root cause lies in weak or ill-defined institutional rules. Here, too, the perception is that progress has been made recently thanks to the energetic anti-corruption policy launched by President Magufuli. Judging from the absence of big scandals in recent years, this is probably accurate. At the ordinary level, however, data are not available to know whether Tanzanian society is in the process of moving away from this equilibrium whereby corruption has become a kind of social norm.

Infrastructure development, electricity in particular, is another area where the score of public management is pretty low by all standards, despite its crucial importance for economic development. As mentioned earlier, the production and distribution of electricity are managed by a public monopoly, TANESCO (Tanzania Electric Supply Company). This national company produces around half of the electricity it distributes, the other half being provided by private producers – after, occasionally, resounding corruption scandals relating to the way they were selected. Electricity has long been priced at a rather low level, which has prevented the public company expanding production and meeting demand, a situation that has resulted in economic growth not being as fast as it could have been with a proper power supply. The sector is regulated in parallel by the Ministry of Mining and a regulation agency, EWURA (Energy and Water Utilities Regulatory Authority), in another case of overlapping responsibility. A few years ago, EWURA endorsed an increase in the electricity prices charged by TANESCO, which was long overdue in view of inflation. Recently, the late President Magufuli opposed that increase. Despite the measure being fully justified and EWURA being internationally praised for its impeccable professionalism, its director was sacked. This was possible because in Tanzania the president has the power to singlehandedly appoint and fire the managers of public agencies, including EWURA, but also the Fair Competition Commission, the Central Bank, and the Commissioner Auditor General. The reason invoked for the sacking was that the price increase would hurt poor people and the ensuing social cost would allegedly be worse than stagnating production capacity in the future. This may well have been the opinion of the leadership, whereas the regulators thought differently. The institutional failure here may originate in either of the two following sources: the social criteria applied by the leadership were inadequately specified in its mission order, or the late president took the liberty of ignoring, and even criticising, legal expert opinion.

There thus seems to be a paradox in regard to the type of leadership exerted in Tanzania. Centralisation appears extreme, and probably excessive, in some areas, whereas in areas where it would be most needed it meets obstacles arising from the fragmentation of political power.

G The Institutional Diagnostic

We could continue to review evidence of institutional weaknesses in Tanzania, but the main conclusions to be derived from the thematic studies undertaken as part of our in-depth diagnostic methodology should be clear by now. Summarising as much as possible the points made in the preceding pages, the institutional challenges in Tanzania come under the few general headings shown in the right-hand-side column of the diagnostic table shown in Figure 3.1. In

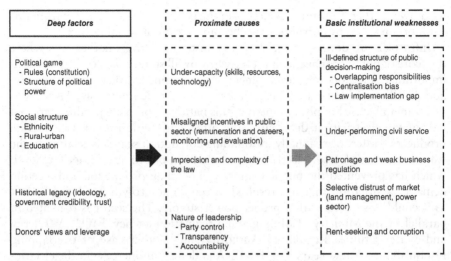

FIGURE 3.1 Institutional diagnostic for Tanzania

reading the table it must be borne in mind that its entries are not independent. For instance, rent seeking and corruption, which are seen to be ubiquitous in Tanzania, are partly caused by the inadequate structure of decision making and the weak regulation of business, as much as they are partly responsible for the under-performance of the civil service, including business regulation. Also, the order of appearance of the various headings is not necessarily related to the severity of the corresponding institutional challenges. As a matter of fact, their mutual dependency prevents us from establishing such a ranking.

Taken together or separately, these institutional weaknesses explain the economic challenges confronting Tanzanian development. For instance, it is easily understood that the difficulty of diversifying exports through appropriate industrial policies is related as much to the uneasy regulation of business, given its relationship with politics, the lack of coordination across administrations, and the poor investment climate created by the under-performance of the civil service. The same factors – and others – may explain the slow productivity gains in agriculture, or the lagging development of infrastructure – at least until the Magufuli administration. This relationship between institutional weaknesses and economic challenges is analysed in more detail in the original Tanzania case study.

Identifying and recording institutional challenges is one thing. However, a diagnostic would not be complete without an analysis of the factors that are responsible for them. The identified weaknesses are the symptoms, while the underlying problem may lie elsewhere. Most causal factors have been alluded to in the preceding pages and are listed in a summary way in the middle column of Figure 3.1. In reading it in connection with the column to its right, it is important to note that items at the same level in the two columns are not necessarily to be associated one to one. The misalignment of incentives in the public sector directly weakens the performance of the civil service, either directly through absenteeism or loose monitoring and evaluation, or indirectly through rent-seeking. At the same time, the poor delivery of public services may result in large part from the lack of skills or resources. Likewise, the nature of the leadership and, most importantly, its control over powerful factions within the party in power is essential to understand the structure of decision making, the extent of rent-seeking and corruption, and the difficulty of regulating business.

This control of the party is partly influenced by voters' support, since political allies will defect if they expect a defeat in the next election. In turn, voters' support depends on the trust inspired by the leadership through the transparency and accountability of its actions. The ability of a leader to oversee the public administration and the whole public decision-making process thus strongly depends on his/her personal capacity to control the political scene and to inspire trust in the population. Needless to say, the nature of the leadership item among the proximate causes of institutional weaknesses also includes the very motivation of the leader. In most preceding points it is implicitly assumed that the leader pursues the common good more than his/her personal interest or that of his/her clique, which indeed seems to have been the case in Tanzania since independence.

Finally, the issue arises of what could be done to combat those proximate causes of the identified institutional weaknesses. Getting more resources to improve the quality of public services, realigning incentives in the public sector, simplifying laws that are felt to be unnecessarily complex, and promoting transparency and accountability through more systematic monitoring and evaluation of the public administration and agencies are obvious measures that would improve the institutional framework of development. They are discussed in some detail in the Tanzania volume. They may raise trade-offs with economic efficiency, however, particularly when they require the collection of additional public resources. Most importantly, they generally generate both winners and losers, at least in the short and medium run, so that their implementation heavily depends on political economy factors. Beyond the proximate causes of the institutional weaknesses, there are deep factors which make the effects of these causes more or less easy to reduce. They appear in the left-hand column of Figure 3.1.

The nature of the political game that is played out in society is the first of these deep factors. On the one hand, the constitution sets the rules, assuming of course it is strictly applied and cannot be easily modified. For instance, it may be the case that it gives too much power to the executive in some areas – for instance, in appointing and suspending people in key positions. On the other hand, in any period there is a structure of political power which evolves only slowly over time – possibly as a function of the pace and structure of economic development – and which makes some reforms possible or impossible. After

Nyerere in Tanzania, the fragmentation of the dominant party (CCM) into several factions made it difficult for the executive not to satisfy the demands of powerful factions since the risk would be the dismantlement of the party and the loss of power. As factions were often associated with business interests that provided them with political, if not monetary, benefits, the state was partly captured by business interests and, in some areas, unable to implement policies that would be detrimental to some of them although beneficial to the country. Modifying this equilibrium involves pure political confrontation between the main actors rather than policy reforms. Magufuli wanted to achieve such a change in the deep factors. It is not clear that he succeeded.

The ethnic structure of the population, including the concentration of big business in non-indigenous hands, or the presence of ethnic cultures and customary laws that sometimes conflict with the statutory law, and the historical legacy in terms of culture, ideology, religion, or trust among citizens, call for the same type of observation. These are deep factors which may affect the proximate causes of institutional weaknesses and may be subject to changes, most notably as a result of development itself, progress in education, or contacts with the rest of the world, but only over a long period.

Among the deep factors, the reference to the role of donors deserves some remarks. In the past, donors have clearly played a huge role in triggering major institutional changes in the way the Tanzanian economy works. This was obviously the case with the SAP, which caused the return to a market economy in the second half of the 1980s, but it has also been the case on several other occasions since then. The weight of donors in pushing reforms derives from the sizeable contribution of aid to the public budget and the domestic economy in general. For instance, the World Bank, which has always pushed for an ambitious decentralisation programme, suspended part of its funding in an effort to impose the decentralisation of the collection of the property tax in 2014 – which was nevertheless re-centralised a few years later. Likewise, donors have cancelled payments several times to protest against big corruption scandals involving government officials, and successfully requested that the latter resign from their positions. Outside these extreme cases, project and programme financing by the World Bank and other donors gives them the opportunity to express their views about the direction in which some institutions like the judiciary or tax collection authorities should be reformed. Even though it is up to the government to decide whether to accept such programmes or not, the funding provided by donors is not a feeble argument.

H Conclusion

The preceding remarks about the deep factors behind the proximate causes of the identified institutional weaknesses may be deemed overly pessimistic. They seem to imply that, at the end of the day, reforming institutions to make them more development-friendly is essentially a matter of politics, or possibly the endogenous consequence of development itself, or the long-run effect of educational progress. This pessimism must be somewhat tempered, though.

First, if big reforms are politically hard to impose, smaller reforms address-ing some of the weaknesses detected at a minor level of political sensitivity might be consensual. It is probably in everybody's interest that the educational system is run more effectively, bureaucratic services are competently and hon-estly delivered, and land management is more efficient. A lot of experimental work has been done in these areas in the economic development literature, which might be a source of inspiration for the design of these reforms. It is not the purpose of the present diagnostic to delve deeper into that kind of detail and it is sufficient to recognise that institutional improvement is now possible in specific sectoral areas.

Second, the Tanzanian economy has done rather well over the last two decades despite the institutional weaknesses uncovered in this in-depth institu-tional diagnostic exercise. We have stressed the fact that the weaknesses that were identified concerned the acceleration of the present pace of growth and its sustainability in the case of substantial changes in the international context. It cannot be excluded that the deep factors that are found to be obstacles to substantive institutional reforms may be progressively altered with the con-tinuation of present development trends in the coming one or two decades. If this happens, some of the reforms suggested by the diagnostic might become more feasible, especially so if the political elite undertakes its own institutional diagnostic along the lines of the present exercise.

Instead of pessimism, lucidity is the right attitude to adopt in the face of the complex relationship between political economy institutions and development uncovered by the present diagnostic.

4

Distorted Development in Benin and Mozambique

I BENIN

A Defining the Question behind the Institutional Diagnostic

The Republic of Benin (formerly known as Dahomey) is a country in West Africa that is bordered by Togo to the west, Nigeria to the east, Burkina Faso to the northwest, and Niger to the northeast. It is a rather small country, with a population of approximately 11.49 million people (2018 estimate) and it is about the same size as three of its neighbours yet is considerably smaller than one of them, Nigeria, which has a population close to 200 million.

There are several reasons why Benin is an interesting country to study, and some of them have no doubt contributed to making it an aid darling for many donors. First, although it is made up of an extraordinarily varied mosaic of peoples and ethnic groups, this does not seem to have created serious problems as in certain other parts of sub-Saharan Africa. Second, it is a place with a long legacy of all sorts of political entities, running from old kingdoms or empires to principalities and microstates (possibly born of the breaking up of kingdoms or empires), which have also coexisted with stateless areas dominated by non-hierarchised families and clans. Because over the last ten centuries the country has been the locus of numerous waves of migration from neighbouring countries, it is a multinational state with strong links to its neighbours, and has porous and flexible borders considered from the standpoint of human settlement. Relatedly, with its direct access to the sea in its southern part, Benin has long been a nexus of trade networks and routes actively engaged in regional and even external commerce. These seem to be ideal conditions for long-term development based on an open (small) market economy. Third, although it was subject to a long-enduring Marxist-Leninist military regime under Lieutenant-Colonel Mathieu Kérékou (1972–90), Benin has proven able to transition to democracy peacefully and then to enjoy political stability through a long period of regular democratic elections. Fourth, being deprived of mineral and non-mineral resources, the country is apparently in a position to eschew the resource curse that has impaired growth and development in many African countries endowed with abundant such resources.

The picture appears less rosy, however, when completed by a number of hard facts. Ranked among the world's poorest countries at the time of independence (1960), Benin has barely succeeded in improving its position since then: although quite volatile, the annual growth of its GDP per capita hardly reached 1 per cent, a disappointing performance partly explained by a very high population growth rate of close to 3 per cent. In addition, improvements in the standard of living have been not only slow but also unequally distributed. The coastal cities of Porto Novo and Cotonou, together with their hinterland, constitute the growth pole of Benin's economy. It is in their tiny departments that poverty is kept under control, unlike in many other parts of the country, where it remains intolerably high. The northern and rather remote part of the country, in particular, suffers from neglect, in the form of a lack of critical public investments, and this is despite the fact that its political representatives have not been consistently deprived of access to the highest levels of state power. Not surprisingly, achievements on the poverty front are also dismal since there does not appear to have been a noticeable reduction in the incidence of poverty during the last decades. Moreover, there is evidence that the severity of poverty has increased significantly, as reflected in the decline of the real expenditures per capita of the bottom 40 per cent of the population. Since the same holds true for income inequality, it can be confidently said that growth in Benin has not been inclusive, to put things mildly: the gains from growth have disproportionately accrued to the top of the living standard distribution.

As could be expected on the basis of the low per capita income growth performance, the economy of Benin is afflicted by low rates of labour productivity growth throughout most sectors. It is striking that capital per capita has contracted over the whole period since 1970. It thus contributed weakly to growth of per capita income, which largely resulted from TFP growth. In addition, the observed change in TFP largely reflects major changes in the sectoral structure of the economy, away from agriculture and towards manufacturing and, above all, services. Here, too, the situation is rather worrying: while most of the limited overall productivity gains can be attributed to labour movements from lower to higher productivity activities, they have come at the cost of decreasing productivity in many of the latter activities. In other words, no sector emerges as a genuine growth engine. A possible exception is perhaps the financial sector, but this has practically no impact on employment. From an examination of the evolution of the structure of output, employment, and productivity, it therefore appears that most TFP growth is due to net labour migration out of agriculture, with no autonomous productivity gains in the destination sectors.

The question that then arises is how Benin came to waste its development potential. Any institutional diagnostic of the country must attempt to provide an answer to that question. This is the task to which we now turn.

B Two Pseudo-Engines of Growth

A valid starting point is the observation that Benin's economy has rested on two pseudo-engines of growth: the cotton sector and the illegal cross-border trade with Nigeria. Cotton is the backbone of the formal Beninese economy, representing a large share of its export revenues, tax proceeds, manufacturing output, and (formal) employment. As for its contribution to GDP, it is of the order of 10 per cent or more. It is well known that the price of raw cotton is subject to wild world price fluctuations, hence the need to smooth their impact on producers and to diversify the sector by encouraging the production of cotton-based textile products. If the former requirement has been satisfactorily met, the same cannot be said of the latter, which raises the whole issue, to which we shall return, of the reasons underlying the weak performance of the manufacturing sector. Moreover, it appears that over long periods of time Benin's cotton sector has performed much more poorly than its two main rivals in West Africa, Burkina Faso and Mali. Thus, after substantial growth from 1980 to the mid-1990s, production did not grow for the next twenty years, and it even fell dramatically in the mid-2000s. It is only recently that production has been able to overtake its 1996 record level.

Because Benin did badly compared to its regional competitors during a prolonged period, we cannot account for the erratic performance of its cotton sector by simply referring to depressions in world prices or adverse weather conditions in the country. More structural factors specific to Benin must therefore have been at play. The first thing to note here is that the general organisation of the cotton sector does not essentially differ between the three main West African producer countries, and producer prices are also comparable. Activities ranging from the provision of inputs and credit to producers to the collection of cotton seeds and the purchase and ginning of their harvests are integrated under a monopolistic structure. Whereas in Mali a national company is in command of the whole sector (except production), in Burkina Faso and Benin an *Association Interprofessionnelle du Coton* (AIC) is in charge, which comprises several private or semi-private companies. In the case of Benin, however, the organisation of the cotton sector has been deeply unstable until recently. After the demise of Kérékou's Marxist regime, it was subject to periodic stints of privatisation, re-nationalisation, and re-privatisation. Behind all of these destabilising moves there has been cutthroat competition between powerful men eager to control the sector and its juicy rents. And if some stability has eventually returned to the sector, allowing for its recent improved performance, it is only because it has now fallen under the indisputable control of a unique businessman who also happens to be the President of the Republic, Patrice Talon. Talon has been nicknamed the 'king of cotton' by the people.

By 2019, when Nigeria decided to close its land borders to goods movements, informal cross-border trade (ICBT) had developed into an important segment of Benin's economy. First, Benin had huge unofficial re-exports to Nigeria, and second, it fraudulently imported a sizeable share of key imports from its big oil-producing neighbour. The illegal nature of this cross-border trade, favoured by the porosity of the borders and the heavily protectionist policy of the Nigerian government, needs to be stressed: goods re-exported to Nigeria, which were legally imported into Benin, faced stiff tariffs or were banned from import into Nigeria. At the port of entry in Benin (Cotonou), the destination of these goods declared at the customs was either a landlocked neighbouring country, for which import taxes and customs duties are low, or the domestic market. Once customs had been cleared, the goods were diverted to Nigeria via a network of informal intermediaries who organised their transportation and smuggled them over the border. Similarly, the large flow of goods imported by Benin from Nigeria, consisting mainly of products that are heavily subsidised in the latter country (oil, in particular), and of other consumer, intermediate, or capital goods, were smuggled into the former country. They thus escaped tariff duties and were sold on the domestic market through informal channels similar to those operating in the re-export sector. Quite evidently, the illegal character of this trade induced its informal organisation.

Dating back to the first oil shock in the 1970s, it is Nigeria's oil rent which fed ICBT: Benin's re-exports were driven by Nigerian demand, itself heavily dependent on oil revenues. On the other hand, Benin's cross-border imports were partly driven by the share of the oil rent that the Nigerian government decided to allocate to the subsidisation of its domestic oil prices, thus creating a positive income effect for a large mass of the population. In this way, Benin shared the oil rent with Nigeria, including through low prices for fuel, and its institutions and policies were shaped by a sort of 'entrepôt state' strategy aimed at transforming the country into a regional trading hub centred on the port of Cotonou. Because there was full knowledge that goods imported into Benin in a fully official and legal way were to be *de facto* diverted to Nigeria in fraudulent ways (that is, by circumventing Nigeria's import tariffs), we can safely say that Benin's strategy was not only to tolerate but also to encourage the informal, fraudulent re-export trade.

That ICBT has been a major sector of activity in Benin can be judged from the following figures: at peak times of the trade, Benin's estimated gross value of imports of products typically destined to be re-exported to Nigeria represented more than 25 times the gross value of Benin's official exports to Nigeria (Golub and Mbaye, 2023). Still more strikingly, the contribution of ICBT to Benin's GDP is estimated to have been in the range of 10–12 per cent, including customs and other tax revenues (6 per cent of

GDP). It has also been a major provider of informal jobs, a direct upshot of the labour-intensive character of many activities involved. Seen in this light, ICBT seems to have played an important role in the economic development of Benin. But there are several flip sides of all these achievements, which we mention now.

The first shortcoming of the situation is the presence of effects akin to those of a Dutch disease. Strictly speaking, Dutch disease occurs when a boom in an export sector (for example, natural resources) causes a decline in other sectors (like agriculture or the manufacturing sector) as a result of an appreciation of the country's currency. The consequence is that the country's other exports become more expensive while its imports become cheaper. The latter effect causes the domestic production of importables to be less competitive. While Dutch disease is most often sparked by the discovery of new natural resources, it can also be caused by any development that results in large inflows of foreign currency, including a sharp surge in natural resource prices, in foreign assistance, and in foreign direct investment.

In the case of Benin, such Dutch disease-type effects can also be observed but, as seen above, the causes are rather different, consisting of a combination of policies based on trade quotas and tariffs, as well as high oil prices in Nigeria, coupled with the use of the resulting rents to illegally import re-exported goods from Benin. The latter thus benefits from effectively higher export prices in the sector of goods illegally re-exported to Nigeria, and from a stronger Nigerian demand for these goods than would be the case under a free international trade regime. It also enjoys lower prices for the goods which it itself illegally imports from Nigeria and which are subsidised by the Nigerian government (oil products, in particular). Such price and quantity effects discourage domestic production, as epitomised by the fate of formal activities of gas distribution, cement factories, and breweries, which have been partly driven out of business.

A second shortcoming arises from the tax losses caused by the informal nature of trade transactions based on imports from Nigeria, and the taxes foregone as a consequence of the displacement of formal domestic activities sparked by these imports. As a third shortcoming, there is the fact that, because the illegal trade is carried out on a large scale, bribery and corruption are pervasive at each stage of the process. A critical level at which malpractices occur is the customs office at Cotonou port facilities: given that it can provide regular and considerable rents, powerful people strive to capture this key office and, given the high stakes involved, the struggle has been unsurprisingly fierce. It is actually revealing that the same man who succeeded in gaining control of the entire cotton sector also ended up owning the customs office. Here is another facet of the resource curse problem that typically harms countries enjoying abundant and valuable natural resources. In this specific case, the valuable resource consists of imports that can be re-sold at much higher prices to a vast neighbouring country.

Finally, grounding growth in ICBT is highly risky as it requires two parties to play the game of undertaking illegal activities. The risk is especially high when the two parties are of significantly different sizes, so that the distribution of bargaining power between them is very unequal. Thus, when in 2019 the Nigerian government abruptly and unilaterally decided to close its land border with Benin, the Beninese government was taken off guard, and a critical source of the country's economic prosperity was disrupted overnight. To the extent that ICBT activities are nevertheless pursued, they now involve much higher risk premia, resulting in lower profits, lower employment, and business failures.

There are two immediate lessons to be learned from the above account: (i) Beninese growth has been anchored in two fragile sectors of activity, thereby calling into question the sustainability of the underlying development strategy; and (ii) the concentration of economic power in the hands of a small clique, and even a single businessman, augurs badly for the possibility of a competitive environment. The first problem means that Benin is, and will remain, highly dependent on external financing, and on foreign aid in particular since its attractiveness for foreign direct investors is low. An ominous sign of its excessive external dependence is the rapid growth of its external debt as a percentage of GDP after the major debt write-off that took place in the early 2000s. As for the second problem, it is the more serious because of the close connection between business and politics, which is our next point.

C Political Instability and the Confusion between Business and Politics

Politics in Benin has always been characterised by a deep intrusion of business interests. This was even true under the Marxist-Leninist regime of Kérékou, which was marred by numerous scandals resulting from the lust for private wealth accumulation among Kérékou's ruling inner circle. After the demise of this pseudo-socialist regime, came the *Renouveau Démocratique* (Democratic Renewal), with its promise of a more transparent and competitive political game that would put an end to kleptocratic practices and blatant favouritism. Unfortunately, these hopes were soon shattered as the old game continued to be played by new actors. In essence, the political system remained patrimonial, in the sense that wealth and power are narrowly intertwined.

At the root of the problem lies the critical role of private financing of electoral campaigns. As has been substantiated in the companion book on Benin, empirical evidence shows that firm owners tend to provide financial support to local politicians in exchange for policy concessions. The most important of these concessions are public procurement arrangements, policy commitments aligned with the firm's interests, and direct appointment to the bureaucracy of relatives and other acquaintances of the firm's owner. Interestingly, it appears that their order of importance varies depending on the degree of political uncertainty: when election results are more uncertain as a result of a higher number of candidates, business firms tend to lay more stress on the second and third types of demands. Moreover, their requests for influence and control over the recruitment of officers in all sections of the public sector increase. Finally, in the absence of what they consider to be a 'good candidate', the option of themselves running for elections, which amounts to direct state capture, becomes more attractive.

In such a context of pervasive attempts at direct and indirect state capture, it is not surprising that the number of political parties soared to reach the astronomical figure of 250 by the late 2010s. This number considerably exceeds the number of ethnic groups in the country, although the latter is quite large, testifying that many of these parties represented narrower factions inside ethnic groups or regroupings stretching across clans and based, for example, on local and regional identities. Far from being strong organisations articulated around programmatic and ideological platforms, political parties are patronage machines led by powerful and wealthy men. Because of the large rewards of political power (remember the juicy rents created by the ICBT and the cotton sector, in particular), these oligarchs or faction leaders (often called 'Big Men') are involved in nasty fights that cause a lot of political instability in the country. Especially destabilising is the opposition between the three main factions composing the dominant ethnic group (the Adja-Fon). Perhaps paradoxically, the other three main groups, namely the Yoruba, the Bariba, and the Atacora, have continuously played a mediating role which has sought to reduce the resulting tensions, whether in an authoritarian (the Kérékou regime) or a democratic setting. Behind this political instability are the constant manoeuvres and shifting alliances and loyalties (including party switching) in which Big Men indulge, depending on their interests as they perceive them at particular moments.

In addition to encouraging political instability, the Big Men system has had a demoralising effect on the population. People witness a succession of obscure political moves and subsequent institutional changes (think of the back-and-forth movements between the public and private status of the companies or agencies in charge of the cotton sector since 2000), as well as scandals whose most common manifestations are sheer favouritism, abuse of public positions, tax evasion, and the embezzlement of public resources. Accusations of embezzlement and rent capture concern not only prestigious construction projects but also programmes that are critical for the well-being of the population and the long-term development of the country (such as water, electricity, and other vital infrastructure projects). Given that most of the misdeeds and cases of extortion go unpunished or uncorrected, it is understandable that the population nurtures a deep mistrust of public institutions. This is especially true of the tax authorities and the judicial system, for which Benin exhibits worse trust indicators than many other African countries.

It is too early to tell how much the rise of Patrice Talon to the presidency is a game-changer. One thing is certain, however: his chaotic ascent to supreme power, itself a reflection of astute tactical moves based on coalitions and counter-coalitions, has been aimed at suppressing instability and establishing law and order in the country, at the price of sacrificing democratic principles. The difference with the experience of Rwanda, which Talon holds in high esteem, is that while Rwanda's leader is himself the richest businessman in his country he also has a reputation of being incorruptible. The story of Talon's rise to the presidency is so revealing of the way politics works in Benin that we cannot resist the temptation of telling it to the reader. In order not to break the continuity of our general argument, however, we have deferred the story to an appendix. Here, we want to stress that, in acceding to the presidency after having gained control of the most important sectors of the Beninese economy, Talon put an end to an era in which political leaders were frontmen acting at the behest of powerful businessmen, rather than these businessmen themselves. In this sense, the democratic façade behind which the latter could previously hide themselves has collapsed to reveal the true nature of Benin's political system.

D Neglect of Critical Public Goods

We have emphasised above some adverse effects of a political system that is penetrated by business interests: namely, political instability and the diffusion of a culture of corruption and cronyism. We now want to add a number of other, equally important, effects. To begin with, the patronage logic governing politics implies that priority is given to pork-barrel projects: transfers that do not typically benefit the poorest sections of the population, and the delivery of local public goods targeted at specific groups. General public goods, such as health, education, nationwide communication, and power infrastructure, tend to be neglected. It is true that efforts have recently been made to fill some of these gaps, yet they still do not reflect sufficient awareness of the critical role these factors play in sustained growth and development. Thus, while the construction of main roads is essentially financed by external aid (think of the two parallel highways linking the southern and northern parts of the country), the building of rural, farm-to-market roads in remote areas, which should be the responsibility of the national government, has not received the attention it deserves. Also, the costs of electricity and telecommunications services are generally higher in Benin than in other African countries, and their quality is often mediocre. Revealingly, access to electricity is the constraint most often cited by economic operators.

The education picture is dismal, as attested to by the catastrophic record for literacy achievements: on this front, Benin ranks among the worst performers in the world. Increasing enrolment at both primary and secondary levels has been actively pursued during the last decades, yet at the price of stagnation – and perhaps even deterioration – of schooling quality (as measured by learning outcomes). These disappointing results are less of a mystery when we learn that the activities of the teacher training schools in Benin were discontinued during the 1990s, which immediately caused a severe shortage of teachers in many parts of the country, particularly in the north. There, out-sized classes (with classes reaching up to 120 pupils in Natitingou), teacher absenteeism, and substitution of poorly trained teachers for the missing qualified staff attained unprecedented levels, thereby increasing the inequality between the north and the south in terms of the quality of basic education. Drastic cuts in the budget of the Education Ministry actually followed a policy of fiscal restraint imposed by the IMF and the World Bank within the framework of three successive Structural Adjustment Programmes (SAP 1989–99). More efficiency in the use of the diminished public resources available was expected by the World Bank, particularly in the form of training and upgrading of government staff, yet this did not come about. However blame is apportioned for the situation, the resulting discontinuation of teacher training schools has been disastrous and in blatant contradiction of the World Bank's sectoral strategy.[1]

Being deprived of mineral and non-mineral resources, Benin needs to base its long-term growth strategy on the emergence and rapid development of sectors that create substantial added value, whether in the processing of agricultural goods, the production of simple manufactured goods, or the delivery of services. In the absence of serious investment in human capital formation and improvement of physical infrastructure, foreign investors will not be attracted to Benin and the country will remain heavily dependent on foreign aid.

E Low State Capacity and Weak Public Management

A political system captured by private interests can negatively affect state capacity in several ways. It can lead to the understaffing of administrative departments that are not considered a priority by these interests, and may even be seen as antagonistic. This seems to be the case for the tax collection department, whose size is clearly below that required to function effectively. Departments can also be captured through the appointment of 'yes people' or the exertion of strong pressure on the decision-making process. In Benin, this applies to the judiciary, whose officers comply with instructions coming from high-level politicians or officers belonging to the executive. It is therefore no wonder that people in Benin have a particularly deep mistrust of the representatives of these two institutions: tax collection officers and judges.

---

[1] The World Bank actually developed a new sectoral strategy for education (and health) aimed at raising literacy and enrolment rates, restructuring the Ministry of Education, improving educational performance through the distribution of textbooks to pupils and students, encouraging parent–teacher associations, the recruitment of contract teachers (with a view to reducing drop-out and failure rates), and better spatial distribution of teachers, between urban and rural areas in particular.

Moreover, under the influence of various lobbies, different parts of the administration and the government may make uncoordinated, divergent decisions that contribute to creating a chaotic and confused legal environment. Land laws and their implementation are an example that comes to mind here. In this matter, indeed, the reform process has been immensely complex, volatile, and non-monotonous. Many changes thus succeeded each other, involving backtracking, not only with respect to the provisions of the successive laws but also with respect to the institutions in charge of their implementation. Regarding the first source of instability, as a result of regular shifts in the relative bargaining power of various interest groups, the law has remained largely unpredictable. Uncertainty exists about (i) whether and to what extent the current law is going to be implemented, and (ii) about whether the current law will be replaced by a different law in the (near) future. Some provisions, such as the authorisations required to buy rural lands, the obligation to officially record rural land transactions, or the possibility of forcing the owner of uncultivated rural land to rent it out, are clearly unenforceable and people do not seem to care about them. Others, however, create a genuine uncertainty that can discourage investment, particularly in urban and peri-urban areas or in areas where migrants coexist with autochthonous populations. To some extent, the issue here is one of misalignment of the law with respect to state capacity: a complex law is enacted for which the state does not have the administrative resources required for effective implementation. Of course, if the provisions of the law are misguided or superfluous, it may turn out that this misalignment is of no direct consequence.[2]

Regarding the second source of instability, the fact is that many institutional choices appear to be the outcome of fierce struggles among rival administrative entities. This is particularly evident at the highest level of the state, where there has been constant wavering about whether to assign the responsibility for land regulation to the Ministry of Agriculture, the Ministry of Town Planning, or the Ministry of Finance. Another example is the strong resistance of rural municipalities to attempts to reduce their prerogatives in land matters. Their resistance paid off, since the right to deliver attestations of customary ownership, which belonged to the *Agence Nationale du Domaine et du Foncier* (best translated as National Agency for Land Administration) under the 2013 law, was shifted to municipalities under the 2017 law. Rural municipalities also successfully opposed the complete suppression of sale conventions, through the requirement that land transactions must be instantaneously registered by

---

[2] For example, we ourselves could verify that informal land rights do not seem to have hindered the expansion of pineapple production in the southern part of the country. Active land sale and, above all, land rental markets have rapidly developed in response to the new export opportunity. The lack of more or less formal land certificates has not been a noticeable problem, and strictly informal land deals appear to satisfy the transactors in the area. The only serious reported constraint is that, when it is possible, women prefer to let their husband act in their name when seeking to access additional land (Broka et al., 2021).

notaries. Finally, the professional bodies that earn incomes from land regulation – notaries, barristers, architects, and land surveyors in particular – played a decisive role in killing the provision of the 2013 law regarding the five-year confirmation period during which property rights must be verified.

F Institutional Diagnostic of Benin: A Compact View

Having expounded the critical elements of the diagnostic, we can now take a comprehensive view in which the institutional weaknesses of Benin are traced back to their deep and proximate causes, and their economic consequences are brought into relief (see Table 4.1).

In short, five deep factors ultimately help to account for the key institutional weaknesses detected in Benin: (i) a political system that is characterised by a neo-patrimonial logic and where there are multiple contenders; (ii) a social landscape in which multiple ethnic groups have coexisted for a long time; (iii) a geographical/neighbourhood landscape in which small Benin has a long border with a big neighbour (Nigeria); (iv) a legacy of centralised management of key economic sectors (the cotton export sector, in particular) dating back to the colonial period; and (v) the heavy presence of aid agencies, which tend to shut their eyes to the dysfunctional aspects of the political system.

Political instability and the lack of long-term economic planning are the result of unruly competition and factional bickering between Big Men who are uncertain about their political future. This competition is especially fierce, and uncertainty especially great, because of the division of the Beninese society into multiple ethno-regional groupings. Key state functions are captured by the dominating faction(s), resulting in a weak state that is unable to exert control over all its administrations, a difficulty that is compounded by a lack of administrative resources (skills, staff, and equipment). This situation of low effectiveness in the management of the public sector and unfair distribution of the country's rents is not adequately mitigated by the pressures emanating from external donor agencies or international (African) institutions. It is not mitigated either by pressures to open up key economic sectors (the cotton sector, in particular) to competition, owing to a long tradition of public monopoly that is easily transformed into private monopoly. As for geography, the presence of Nigeria at the border of Benin gives rise to considerable opportunities for rent that can be earned through illegal trade.

The main economic consequences are as follows: a spatially lopsided development pattern that is, moreover, precarious (subject to external shocks) and unsustainable; chronic dependence on foreign resources resulting from slow productivity growth and pervasive inefficiencies in the running of the state; and a bad investment climate caused by poor governance, widespread corruption, and confusing and loosely enforced laws and regulations. Since foreign direct investment is therefore deterred, foreign aid is the buoy that keeps the country's finance afloat.

TABLE 4.1 *A synthetic ordering of the institutional factors impeding Benin's long-term development*

Deep factors	Proximate causes	Basic institutional weaknesses	Economic consequences
Politics dominated by big business Multiple ethnic groups and a regional divide Geography: a small country with a big and resource-rich neighbour Colonial legacy of top-down management of key economic sectors (cotton, in particular) Accommodating donors	Policy instability (1): frequent changes in law Policy instability (2): frequent changes in the organisation of key economic sectors (e.g., cotton sector) Lack of long-term development planning Elite capture of key state functions Weak state, unable to control administrations, and with insufficient resources for an efficient management of the public sector Existence of rent opportunities in illegal trade with big neighbour Lack of genuine competition in the cotton sector	Widespread corruption and cronyism Weak law enforcement and legal instability Weak regulation of key sectors dominated by big business Low state capacity: understaffing or capture of key administrations; poor inter-department coordination Neglect of critical public goods (e.g., education or power generation) Opacity of policy decisions and economic management; lack of accountability of key public agencies Outsized informal sector driven by ICBT	Low quality of education Low sustainability of the growth pattern: weak productivity growth; low diversification; low level and pace of industrialisation Poor investment climate High, rising inequality between people and regions; slow progress on the poverty front Chronic aid dependence Lack of citizens' trust in key institutions (the judiciary and tax collection) Vulnerability to external shocks

G Policy Implications and Recommendations

Priority attention in any reform process ought to be given to ways of breaking the link between politics and business, which is at the root of many institutional failures and economic problems. Since the financing of electoral campaigns provides oligarchs with a privileged channel for influencing politics, it should be regulated by law. Here we can think of capping the amount of financial contributions to politicians and imposing rules requiring transparency regarding the amount and the source of donations. The problem with such rules is that in weakly governed countries they tend to be ignored whenever they are enacted. This is illustrated by Benin, where they indeed exist but are not strictly enforced. The same restriction probably applies to all rules prescribing rigorous impact evaluations of public sector actions so as to achieve greater accountability of major actors at the state level. And it also applies to many laws, decrees, and regulations that ban day-to-day malpractices, such as the taking of bribes, petty corruption, and money extortion by local officials. Thus, although signboards warning against practices of bribery are displayed in local police offices, nobody really cares.

Clearly, attacking the key issue of the intrusion of business into politics upfront is unlikely to bear much fruit. This is especially true today since the richest businessman in the country holds supreme political authority. More feasible reforms should aim at radically transforming the Beninese economy so as to increase the average income per head of the population and to anchor growth in more sustainable sectors than cotton and the ICBT with Nigeria. Since Nigeria's borders have now been abruptly closed to flows of goods, the latter sector has ceased to be a reliable source of incomes and employment for Benin. The path forward must therefore be based on a sectoral transformation of the economy and strong measures to improve labour productivity in key sectors.

Regarding the first dimension, a realistic strategy consists of promoting agro-processing industries outside the cotton sector. This involves: (1) the identification of agricultural products for which the country's natural conditions are appropriate and which can generate enough added value; and (2) the integration of their producers and intermediaries into a value chain that includes input and credit supply; collection of the produce; and its transportation, storage, processing, packaging, and marketing up to the point of the final consumers in rich countries, if needed. In a country like Benin, where there are many experienced traders and middlemen (including those of Indian or Pakistani origin who criss-cross the country) this is best done through a great deal of market activation or facilitation. On the part of the state, the main tasks required are the construction and maintenance of rural feeder roads, which can be branched off into the main grid, and the effective suppression of all of the money-extorting posts on the routes used by producers and traders.

Valuable efforts in this direction have actually started to be made. Thus, for example, schemes for the production and export of pineapples and pineapple products (like juice or jam) have recently been launched under the impulse of the present government and with the financial and logistical support of several aid agencies and development cooperation programmes (French, Belgian, Canadian, etc.). The organisation of the value chain up to a European food distributing company (the Carrefour chain of supermarkets in France), the high quality of the product, and the quick supply response from the farmers in the Allada region are important advantages for the success of this initiative. To the extent that fertiliser use is almost non-existent in the cultivation of pineapples in Benin, and provided that some logistical and other difficulties are overcome, a promising niche is the market for organically produced, fresh pineapples.[3] When pineapples are processed into juice or jam, expansion is mostly constrained by foreign competition, especially in the European markets, where Chinese and Thai exporters presently enjoy a price advantage. Beninese firms must therefore look for closer foreign markets, such as Burkina Faso and Nigeria, until they improve their competitiveness (through the development of by-products, for example).

Clearly, in the context of a competitive world market dominated by big value chains, the government has a key role to play in the detection of profitable opportunities, the organisation of effective linkages with distant markets, research and development destined to improve the quality of the product and uncover promising by-products, and the like. These are complex tasks requiring appropriate skills, learning by doing, exposure of management staff to foreign experiences, and well-functioning infrastructure (adequate harbour facilities, non-corrupt customs, good roads, reliable internet and mobile phone services, and a regular supply of electricity).

Increasing labour productivity in industrial ventures is another pressing challenge for Benin. This requires not only that more efficient production techniques and capital equipment are used but also that better management systems are put in place. The most effective way to attain this objective is to mobilise foreign direct investment, but that requires, in turn, that governance conditions are improved in the country, so as to reassure potential investors.

Finally, one of the most pressing challenges confronting Benin is education. If significant efforts have been made to increase enrolment, much remains to be done to improve educational quality to reach decent standards, starting with the primary school level. Furthermore, technical and professional schools must be created to help fill the prevailing skills gaps in the labour market. In the absence of significant improvements in educational quality, it is difficult to see how labour productivity can be raised, technical and organisational innovations adopted, and foreign direct investment attracted so as to gradually move Benin to the status of an economy with an intensive degree of skilled labour, as befits a country that is deprived in terms of mineral and non-mineral resources.

Benin is endowed with entrepreneurial people and well-experienced traders and merchants, as well as a good climate and fertile agricultural lands in certain parts of its territory. It has a comparative advantage not only in traditional products such as cotton but also in new agricultural products that can be processed and sold at remunerative prices in the international, regional, and domestic markets. In sum, Benin has a strong potential for development that

---

[3] In particular, pineapples grown in Benin have a shape and a colour to which European consumers are not accustomed and they are more difficult to transport and conserve than pineapples from competing countries (Costa Rica, for example).

can be unleashed if only the right institutional and policy environment can be established. Whether this can be done while the link between business and politics remains unbroken is a pivotal question. What needs to be stressed is that Talon's accession to the presidency has perhaps changed the rules of the game by ending the noxious competition for political leverage between a few oligarchs. It will therefore be especially interesting to see how far his regime will go towards transforming the economy, controlling corruption, and improving the country's human capital and infrastructure.

It cannot be denied that the main planks of Talon's reform programme closely match our own recommendations. Think of his reforms of the education system (with an emphasis on the creation of technical schools and training institutions), his plans for infrastructure expansion (including the improvement of the generation and distribution of electricity, considered as a critical constraint on industrialisation), and his measures intended to diversify the economy in the sense of adding value to agricultural and raw material (e.g., cotton) products. However, given the concentration of economic and political powers in his hands, it is legitimate to ask how he will be motivated to bring more competition to key sectors of the economy and fight 'grand' corruption, rather than only petty corruption and small-scale bribery. In addition, in a country where freedom of expression is highly valued and where free elections and changes of incumbents became a regular feature of the political scene during the last decades, the question arises as to how sustainable his undemocratic regime will prove to be.

II MOZAMBIQUE

A Defining the Question behind the Institutional Diagnostic

Mozambique is a large, sparsely populated country with twenty-five main rivers that empty into the Indian Ocean and that physically divide the country. The main river is the Zambezi, which is navigable for 460 km out of a total of 820 km and flows eastwards across the territory. Located on the east coast of southern Africa, Mozambique, whose population is around 30 million, borders six other countries: Tanzania in the north, Malawi, Zimbabwe, Zambia, and Swaziland to the west, and South Africa to the south.

There are several reasons why Mozambique is worth studying, and some of these reasons have no doubt contributed to making it an aid darling, like Benin, for many donors. First, the country attained its independence late in the process of decolonisation, in which respect it is similar to other Portuguese colonies in Africa (Angola, Cape Verde, and Guinea Bissau). Moreover, it started from a very low base in terms of infrastructural development, education, and levels of living of the autochthonous population. Outright chaos broke out at the time of independence (in 1975), following the massive outflow of Portuguese settlers, who had occupied central positions in every layer of the economy. The country was then the poorest in the world and was in blatant need of external assistance. Second, like Angola, Botswana, Namibia, and Zimbabwe, Mozambique has been governed by the same party that took over after white rule ended (Frelimo). This party historically enjoyed huge prestige and legitimacy, and therefore embarked on a nation-building process under auspicious circumstances. At the same time, however, it quickly declared itself a Marxist-Leninist vanguard party, dedicated to central planning and opposed to private sector development. Third, because it has a long coastline and has enjoyed the presence and influence of Arab traders for a long time, Mozambique has potential in terms of developing trade links, while the proximity of South Africa, and its sizeable and more sophisticated economy, offers many attractive opportunities.

To date, however, the hopes placed in Mozambique's development have largely been disappointed: economic growth has been below potential, social progress has been slow, structural transformation of the economy has barely begun, growth has been unequally distributed across the national territory, and dependence on external financing (development aid in particular) has not abated. Regarding the first point, it is noticeable that until the early 2000s, the donor community generally considered Mozambique a development success story: after the end of the internal war (between the ruling Frelimo and the opposition party, known as Renamo) in 1992, real GDP growth (per capita) was vigorous, easily outstripping the global average and surpassing many other countries in the region. This performance reflected the combination of a return of displaced people to their homes, the rebuilding of private and public infrastructure, supported by foreign aid, and private investment (domestic and foreign).

The trend was not sustained, however: the pace of real aggregate growth peaked at the turn of the new millennium and then slowed moderately during the 2000s (when the rate of real per capita growth was equal to 3.4 per cent per year). As a result, Mozambique is no longer a star growth performer and lags behind its peers in the region (Ethiopia, Ghana, and Tanzania). Similarly, if particularly strong gains were obtained on the poverty front in the immediate post-conflict period, less impressive gains have been recorded since then. Mozambique thus remains a very poor country by any measure. In 2017, it ranked 180 of 186 countries in terms of real GDP per capita, and 180 out of 189 on the United Nations' Human Development Index.

During the decade starting in the late 1990s and ending in the late 2000s, Mozambique showed a promising trend, characterised by vigorous growth in the manufacturing sector, dominated by large-scale capital-intensive investments (particularly in the Mozal aluminium smelter), and by robust service sector growth. Then a turning point was reached, which was triggered by important foreign direct investments in the natural resources sector, mainly coal extraction and natural gas development, following the discovery of abundant reserves in Cabo Delgado. The same period also witnessed a rapid growth in private services, financial services included, but a declining trend in the contribution of agriculture to growth.

Much of Mozambique's growth has been fuelled by significant inflows of foreign exchange, both public and private. These inflows have generated spillovers, either directly into consumption – total consumption has consistently equalled about 90 per cent of GDP– or indirectly into income through investment. Moreover, their pattern has shifted increasingly towards capital-intensive natural resource investments, and it seems highly likely that this trend will persist in the foreseeable future. What is worrying is that the economy seems to have become less diversified over time, as revealed by the shifts in the composition of its exports. Thus, manufacturing exports (aluminium) plateaued by the later 2000s, while, starting roughly in 2010, natural resources exports (mainly coal) have quintupled in value and now account for around 50 per cent of all exports. Correspondingly, there is a relative shift towards lower value-added exports.

Finally, the authorities, in spite of the consistent political domination of the Frelimo party, have signally failed to reduce regional disparities and to therefore tame the resentment of people who do not live in the country's prosperous south. This failure is tragically attested to by the insurgency that broke out in Cabo Delgado in 2018.

B Difficult Initial Conditions

Modern Mozambique was born in especially difficult circumstances, not only because of the sudden departure of 80 per cent of the Portuguese settler population but also due to its geopolitical position in the context of the Cold War. The situation was complicated by the fact that Frelimo, which led the liberation war against the colonial power, came to exert a decisive political influence when the new People's Republic of Mozambique was founded and proclaimed as a one-party socialist state. This posed immediate threats to Rhodesia and South Africa, which feared a Communist presence on their borders. Furthermore, the decision of the Mozambican government to enforce UN sanctions against Rhodesia in 1976 increased regional tensions, so much so that Rhodesia and South Africa moved to support and finance Renamo, the movement opposed to Frelimo's socialist orientation and whose leadership came from the centre of the country. After Zimbabwe (formerly Rhodesia) attained independence in 1980, the apartheid regime of South Africa continued to stir ethno-regional differences and grievances in Mozambique, and it turned Renamo into a significant military force capable of disrupting and sabotaging facilities in large parts of the country. The war rapidly escalated and Renamo's ruthless warfare contributed to undermining Frelimo's nation-building efforts and to destroying valuable infrastructure.

It was only in 1992, following the demise of apartheid in South Africa, that a peace treaty was eventually signed between the two contending parties, thereby opening the way to less chaotic progress and a more stable security situation. Two years later (1994), the first multi-party elections were organised, which, like all the subsequent ones, confirmed the domination of Mozambican politics by Frelimo. Simultaneously, as an aftermath of the collapse of the Soviet empire, the international environment was dramatically modified, and Frelimo was forced to change course. Suddenly deprived of its main external financial support, the government had no other choice than to turn to Western donors (beyond the Nordic countries of Europe, which had been present much earlier) and to accept the free-market policies which they imposed. This implied the forsaking of the central planning strategy centred on import substitution and the forced mechanisation of agriculture, which Frelimo actively pursued after its transformation into a Marxist-Leninist party in 1977. Aid then flowed to the country which was now widely perceived as a donor darling.

Why is it that the strong growth that ensued, largely as a result of the return of a large number of refugees, did not lead to a significant structural transformation of the economy and to sustainable growth at the same level? And why is it that it did not lead to noticeable social achievements, greater national integration, and deep institutional change? This is the question that we now want to address. In order to answer it, we need to lend special attention to geographical and political factors, which appear to have had a determining impact on policies and institutions.

C Geographical Constraints

A basic fact about Mozambique is its low population density: equal to 40 people per square kilometre of land area, which is perceptibly lower than the average for sub-Saharan Africa (48 people per square kilometre), itself much below that observed for East Asia and South Asia (excluding high-income countries) – respectively, 131 and 389 people per square kilometre (United Nations Food and Agriculture Organisation and World Bank data). An immediate consequence of a low population density is the high per unit cost of providing and maintaining infrastructure (transport, telecommunications, electricity, etc.), and of delivering public services. It is therefore no wonder that sub-Saharan Africa generally has a low density of paved roads, particularly rural roads, and a low density of railways links. Nor is it surprising that in remote areas the communication links that exist are often badly maintained, and, as a result, the operating costs of the vehicles tend to be abnormally high, with adverse effects on the efficiency of transport services (see Platteau, 2000: Chap. 2). Equally serious are the effects of low population density not only on the amount and quality of health and education services but also on the amount and quality of other state-provided services, such as agricultural extension, training, irrigation, and various support services to farmers and small-scale entrepreneurs.

Quality is affected insofar as it is difficult to attract skilled labour to isolated places that lack many of the amenities that can be found in areas of higher population concentration.

All of these forces arising from the same fundamental cause, low population density, help explain why distant areas in which the population is highly scattered are backwards and remain so. High transaction costs – transportation and communication costs, in particular – are responsible for low human capital development and slow economic growth, which themselves tend to determine such high costs. Behind the nasty feedback effect that causes low-level trap equilibria in remote areas, two mechanisms (at least) are at work. On the one hand, out-migration resulting from a lack of economic opportunities raises the per unit costs of public goods and services even further and, on the other hand, slow growth implies that business activities are not brisk enough to create a strong demand for transportation and communication, as well as for training, irrigation, and extension services. In rich countries, the vicious circle just described may be broken because income redistribution between different regions is both more affordable and better organised, and public service delivery to isolated areas is often subsidised by taxpayers living in thriving urban environments.

The tendency of poor countries to neglect maintenance of infrastructure, which was pointedly stressed by Alfred Hirschman (1958) a long time ago, is certainly verified in the case of Mozambique. Routine maintenance is generally delayed and migrated from the recurrent to the investment budget, where donors are more likely to help finance major rehabilitations once the infrastructure has degraded substantially. This sort of last-minute rehabilitation is a much more costly solution than regular maintenance, both in terms of the civil engineering work itself and in terms of vehicle operation costs (since the infrastructure remains degraded for a longer time). In addition, major rehabilitation work is not easily contractible to small local firms, which thereby miss precious opportunities to earn incomes and accumulate professional experience. The latter argument applies particularly to rural road networks.

In Mozambique, the problem is actually aggravated by two circumstances. First, not only is the country sparsely populated, especially in its central and northern part, but its space is also physically divided by numerous rivers. The resulting fragmentation makes its spatial integration by means of communication infrastructure comparatively costly. Second, the southern, richer, part of Mozambique, in which the capital city (Maputo) is located, is close to a large and economically more dynamic country, namely South Africa. It is no exaggeration to say that Mozambique's south is much more tightly integrated with South Africa than with the central and southern parts of the national territory. This situation is a historical legacy of the colonial period, during which Mozambique was treated as a transit country. Since its transport infrastructure was built primarily to serve mining and farming activities in the much larger economies of South Africa and Rhodesia, the rail and road networks ran east–west, with little communication infrastructure to support north–south traffic.[4] Moreover, there were few rural roads linking farms to markets, and those that there were, were quite distant from each other.

The post-independence period did not bring any major change to the unbalanced distribution of communication links. Thus, large trunk roads in the east–west corridors were financed by donors whose priorities rested on estimates of internal rates of return, themselves narrowly dependent on vehicle operation costs. Furthermore, small rural roads and feeder roads received only a small share of the budget for the construction and maintenance of roads. After the first free elections were simultaneously held in Mozambique and South Africa in 1992 – no doubt a consequence of the end of the Cold War and the demise of the apartheid regime – borders and trade flows between the two countries were reopened, leading to increasing economic integration between southern Mozambique and South Africa. An important upshot of this is that Maputo, the capital city of Mozambique, where a modern urban elite and the country's middle class are concentrated, is much closer to the agricultural heartland of South Africa than to its own rich farmland in the central and northern provinces. Encouraged by low transportation costs (and also massive corruption in the customs services), the demand for agricultural and other consumer goods has been consistently directed towards South Africa.

Geographical factors and the absence of vigorous policies aimed at redressing the ensuing imbalances have therefore created a situation in which the interests of the domestic industrial and service sectors have been continuously disregarded. South African supermarket chains distributing South African and Asian products have thus expanded into all provincial capitals to cater to the needs of city dwellers in Mozambique, and even staple foods are imported in this way. In short, the urban middle class of the country has been de-linked from its own agriculture and this process of distorted integration is deepening over time. As a matter of fact, with infrastructure investments (especially around Maputo) concentrated at the starting point of a new corridor leading to Durban, the connection between southern Mozambique and South Africa will only become closer, at the expense of the central and southern regions. The consequence seems inescapable: inter-regional inequality is bound to grow and national integration to become increasingly difficult.

In this context, the question as to whether the recent discovery of massive reserves of natural gas in the Rovuma Basin off the coast of Cabo Delgado (in 2016) can be a game-changer appears highly critical. This external shock offers

---

[4] The changing locations of the capital city of Mozambique are interesting in this regard. It was first established in Ilha because of economic links with Goa (in India), which Portugal ruled for 451 years, until 1961. The declining importance of the Indian trade and the growing importance of South Africa, especially after gold was discovered in 1860, caused the southward movement of the capital city to Lourenço Marques, which is located near the southern end of the country and positioned within 120 km of the borders of South Africa and Eswatini (Swaziland). After independence, in 1976, Lourenço Marques was renamed Maputo.

a golden opportunity to redistribute income-earning and employment opportunities towards the northern part of the country, and thereby stop the national disintegration just described. At the same time, however, we know too well that golden opportunities of this kind can easily turn into a natural resource curse, as so many African countries in similar situations have experienced. Unfortunately, the omens are not good because escaping the curse requires a government that will take decisions driven by long-term considerations and by the general interests of the population, rather than by the selfish interests of an elite living in the southern part of the country. The recent insurrectionary events in Cabo Delgado suggest that at least part of the local population holds a pessimistic view that sees such a requirement as unlikely to be met. In order to make our own assessment, the next step is naturally to look at the way politics functions in Mozambique and, in particular, how it relates to business interests – and with what consequences.

D Politics and Business

As pointed out earlier, defining features of the post-independence political regime in Mozambique are: (i) the initial merging of the Frelimo party with the state; and (ii) the continuous domination of the same party even after multi-party elections were organised. As a result, an enduring one-party state has so far presided over the destiny of the country. In theory, this could help promote development by prompting the leadership to design and implement a unified long-term strategy of investment, growth, and social advancement. But the same conditions can also have the effect of undermining this capacity if the lack of political contestation prevents the correction of wrong-headed policies, or if they cause political rulers to be more concerned with tightening their grip on power and preserving the accompanying economic privileges than with increasing the well-being of the population. To look into this matter, we need to distinguish between the period when a socialist state was in place and the subsequent period of formal democracy.

When Frelimo acceded to political power at independence, it embarked on a programme of radical change based on Marxist-Leninist principles. Practically, this meant discouraging private initiative, adopting protectionist policies and the import substitution strategy, as well as transforming the agricultural sector into one based on large-scale mechanised farms. This approach rapidly proved to be a failure, which was officially recognised at the Fourth Party Congress in 1984. Because of the situation of war into which the country fell, however, there was no immediate effect of this reckoning. Policies were not re-orientated – in particular, the contemplated shift from socialist agriculture to a strategy centred on the development of small-scale peasant farming.

A more important turning point was reached in the 1990s when liberalisation and privatisation policies came about in the wake of the Structural Adjustment Programmes (SAPs) conceived by the World Bank and the

International Monetary Fund (IMF). The separation of economic and political powers, merged by design during the immediate post-independence period, was then on the cards. Yet, instead of being mitigated or suppressed, the interpenetration of business and politics was actually reinforced. Privatised enterprises were taken over by party members, civil servants, and army officers, thereby ensuring *de facto* continuity with the previous state of affairs. This strategy was justified by the almost total absence of an experienced and independent business class in the country, and by the need to prevent the return of foreign capitalists, foremost among whom were Portuguese and South African business firms or groups. Its effectiveness was nonetheless doubtful inasmuch as a fraction of the new private entrepreneurs went broke or quickly liquidated their assets, and it is revealing that other entrepreneurs who continued their activities struck deals with foreign partners who possess the required skills and capital.

Whichever is the case, it bears emphasis that most new firm owners, some of whom acquired the public assets at very low prices, benefitted from some sort of exclusivity (such as a licence, a quota, or a contract for supplies to the government). When they were not closed down, therefore, public companies were simply transformed into private monopolies that continued to depend on government protection for the preservation of their privileges. Profits were (and remain) especially high in trade in imported consumer goods and exports of primary products, tourism, and construction activities stimulated by land development and privatised real estate. The privatisation process was questionable in terms of efficiency but equally from the standpoint of equity. This is not only because the emerging group of private firm owners was overwhelmingly made up of government officials and public servants, but also because entrepreneurs with ties to the opposition were consistently excluded.

The pattern of business–politics relationships is thus one in which big business is organised by politicians, rather than the other way around (big business exerts a strong influence on politics by financing the campaigns of politicians). As there is no credible alternative political force, Frelimo is in a comfortable position that allows it to continuously lock in the political allegiance of the business community. Being deprived of the possibility of hedging their bets by financing the campaigns of multiple political parties, members of the business elite of Mozambique have their privileges narrowly tied to Frelimo's continuing in power. The Frelimo machine is oiled by their money, which includes donations by foreign business partners and associates, but that money itself is obtained thanks to egregious advantages dispensed by the party's top brass.

Why is it that Frelimo has enjoyed, and continues to enjoy, such a strong incumbency advantage? The answer is twofold. For one thing, Renamo, its main rival, has difficulties attracting many voters, especially the young, owing to excessive centralisation of its party machine. And, for another thing, elections tend to be manipulated through fabrication of the list of candidates and voters register, intimidation during campaigns and on the day of the election, as well as through manipulation of the results achieved by stuffing ballot boxes and tinkering with the final tabulations. The tampering with the democratic process is made easier by the limited access of independent (external) observers to the different stages of the elections. The end outcome is that elections in Mozambique are not free and fair, and most observers agree that the situation is not changing for the better.

Does the above account mean that there is no stiff competition in Mozambique's political arena and that, as a result, its political leadership is able to ensure the continuity of the country's development strategies? The answer is negative since, inside Frelimo, various factions fiercely fight for access to power positions. Financial strength being a key determinant of the ability to rise within the party's machine, this elite rivalry creates a fertile ground for the spread of money politics and influence peddling. Thus, if the control of the state allows privileged access to capital accumulation and juicy rents, it is conditioned by the control of Frelimo, as witnessed by the fact that the president of Frelimo almost automatically becomes the president of the republic, and the party's candidates for parliament are appointed on the basis of blocked party lists. There is no such thing as dynastic power, so that the struggle between different political barons, each with his own support network of business people and other allies, is a play for high stakes.

It is thus at the level of the primaries, which is an internal affair, that economic leaders choose which alliances they wish to enter into, hedging their bets with a view to reducing future risks for their businesses. On the other side of the bargain, those inside the party who want to stay in central party organs and obtain high offices in the government need to raise funds both to finance the party and to capture votes at the primaries. Vote-buying therefore lies at the heart of primary elections in Mozambique, and it has become common practice only because of the complicity of the courts, which shut their eyes to corruption and other illegal acts. A portentous upshot of the internal tensions inside Frelimo provides an answer to a question that was raised earlier: despite the existence of a *de facto* one-party state, there is no guarantee of policy continuity over time. The possibility of the instability of development strategies is illustrated by the difficult transition from President Guebuza to President Nyusi, who was not Guebuza's preferred candidate and had a different approach to policy and reform.

Clearly, the most important potential advantage of a regime founded on an overwhelmingly dominant party has not materialised in the case of Mozambique. Changes at the level of the presidency can cause significant shifts in development-related policies, can explain the piecemeal approach to policy formulation, as well as major rotations of personnel in government and leading positions in the public administration. Moreover, in the very logic of political patronage and crony capitalism, members of the government are inclined to view their ministry as their own fief: that is, they see it as a source of rents that should naturally accrue to them for personal appropriation and for redistribution to the network of their supporters, brokers, and financiers. In these conditions, strategic information-sharing and coordination between different parts of the executive tend to be obstructed, with the effect of seriously impairing the effectiveness of development policies. To this shortcoming of political patronage must be added another one, better known among economists: it fosters pork barrel projects, private transfers, and local public goods at the expense of public goods that are in the general interest, such as education and health.

Finally, it must be emphasised that the onset of extractive industries and, subsequently, the awarding to international companies of exclusive rights to explore and exploit oil and gas reserves in Cabo Delgado (in 2006), followed by the confirmation of the existence of plentiful reserves of natural gas (in 2010), have created new rent opportunities, real or anticipated, that have considerably raised the stakes involved in the struggle for political power and influence. It is probably no coincidence that the trend of an improvement in governance indicators was reversed after the occurrence of the aforementioned shocks to the economy. More specifically, it is hard to dissociate from the 'pre-boom curse syndrome' scandals such as the hidden debt scandal (2016), which has deeply affected both the economic and political climate in Mozambique and the country's relations with the international community. Corruption, cronyism, and money politics, which pose a genuine danger to the vitality and sustainability of the economy, are unlikely to recede in the new rent-prone environment. This is especially true because of the weakness of anti-corruption institutions and their lack of independence from political influence.[5]

E Institutional Diagnostic of Mozambique: A Compact View

Having expounded the critical elements of the diagnostic, we can now take a comprehensive view in which Mozambique's institutional weaknesses are traced back to deep and proximate causes, and their economic consequences are brought into relief (see Table 4.2). Bearing in mind the analysis presented in the three sections above, the factors featured in the table, as well as their chosen location, are almost self-explanatory.

The deep factors, which ultimately account for the key institutional weaknesses detected in Mozambique, can be distilled down to five. The first and second are the binding constraints born of the physical and human

---

[5] To be more precise, in the final years of Guebuza's second term, three semi-public entities took out over US$2 billion in loans from private foreign banks without submitting them to the Assembly for approval, even though they greatly exceeded the limit placed on government borrowing by the relevant annual budget appropriation bill. These three entities were owned and controlled by a very small group of individuals and were very closely linked to the security sector. When the existence of the loans became public, the IMF suspended its support to Mozambique, and much foreign aid, including all direct support to the state budget, was frozen or significantly reduced.

TABLE 4.2 *A synthetic ordering of the institutional factors impeding Mozambique's long-term development*

Deep factors	Proximate causes	Basic institutional weaknesses	Economic consequences
– Physical and human geography (1): low population density – Physical and human geography (2): proximity to a big and sophisticated economy – Colonial and geopolitical legacy: a one-party state, initially socialist, inheriting a situation of widespread poverty – Natural resources endowment: natural gas – Critical dependence on external finance: aid and foreign direct investment	– Large inter-regional disparities – Fusion of politics and business, with an upper hand for politics – Continuation of one-party state, with internal competitive clientelism – Weak policy continuity – Lack of separation between executive, legislative, and judiciary	– Weak national integration and strong centrifugal tendencies – Widespread corruption and cronyism, and lack of transparency and serious auditing – Low state capacity: poor coordination between departments and low administrative skills – Low state capacity: inability to implement announced plans and strategies – Lack of sufficient attention to critical public goods (e.g., education and health)	– Lack of an inclusive growth engine and lopsided development pattern – Slow poverty reduction and rising inequalities – Low level of domestic savings and inefficient financial sector – Low quality of education and health – Poor investment climate – Chronic aid dependence – Vulnerability to external shocks

geography of the country, consisting of low population density and proximity (on the southern border) to a big and more sophisticated neighbour. The third factor is the legacy coming from the colonial period, and the geopolitical situation of Mozambique. What we have essentially in mind here is the one-party state born of the liberation struggle, the socialist approach to growth and development that it initially took, and the context of Cold War tensions that it had to face. The fourth factor is the presence of rich natural resource endowments, mainly in the form of natural gas reserves, which have been discovered rather recently. And the last factor is the critical dependence of Mozambique on external finance for its continuation and development. Among the sources of external financing, aid occupied pride of place until the discovery of gas resources. From then on, foreign direct investment has assumed growing importance.

The way the chain of causation unfolds from these deep factors to lead to the economic liabilities which we observe today can be seen in the table and directly linked to the preceding discussion. It is nevertheless important to stress that if the proximate causes can be usefully explained in the light of the deep factors, they are not mechanically determined by them. If this were the case, there would be no ground for formulating policy implications as we do in the next and last section. Thus, for example, the adverse effects of low population density on remote areas could have been mitigated if the government had chosen to take steps towards countering them, instead of letting market forces freely operate. This would have allowed the populations inhabiting these areas to benefit from better services like education, health, and agricultural infrastructure and extension. To take another example, the fusion of politics and business in the framework of an overwhelmingly dominant party could have given way to a more genuinely democratic regime if the authorities had chosen to bring more competition into the political arena, instead of confining it to the internal space of Frelimo.

As a last illustration, we can cite the country's tight dependence on external finance. Here, the government could have decided to be more autonomous vis-à-vis external forces and international organisations and donors if it had chosen to tax its well-to-do people more effectively. Admittedly, such a step would have been difficult to take soon after independence, when Mozambique was in a formation state and in the midst of a nasty war that was not of its own making. At a later stage, however, the emergence of a prosperous group of rich businesspeople, state officials, and middle-class residents of big cities, such as Maputo, opened up the possibility of taxation and income redistribution to the benefit of the rest of the population, and the poor in particular. That this course was not followed can obviously not be blamed on deep factors.

F Policy Implications and Recommendations

An important policy implication of the diagnosis proposed is the need to correct the disequalising effects of market forces in the form of growing inter-regional disparities and increasing income inequality. Two lines of reforms spring to mind. First, infrastructural investments aimed at better connecting the poor central and northern parts of the country to its much more prosperous south should become a major plank of any comprehensive development strategy. There is a strong argument for creating a single Ministry of Infrastructure Development, which would be fully dedicated to a task that is presently split over separate ministries, such as Health, Education, Transport and Communications, Agriculture, Public Works, and Energy and Mineral Resources. Such a step would help bring forth a more coherent and unified approach to infrastructure development.

Second, a core element of any growth strategy should be the active support of small- and medium-scale agriculture and agro-processing activities in areas where land is of a sufficient quality. Moreover, special attention ought to be paid to the central and southern parts of the country, where such lands exist, so that both inter-regional and personal income inequalities, as well as poverty, are simultaneously reduced. To be effective, this strategic orientation requires the reinforcement of the institutions in charge of the delivery of agriculture services, including irrigation, credit, training, supply of modern inputs, and marketing outlets, of the support for the development of appropriate technologies used in the processing of agricultural products, and of the dissemination of more efficient storage and distribution technologies.

In terms of infrastructure, priority should be awarded to the construction and maintenance of farm-to-market and feeder roads, which are presently underdeveloped. Regarding credit to smallholders, the creation of a lower-risk agricultural bank, such as is found in many developing and developed countries, must be seriously contemplated. Loan guarantees are a pivotal issue here, and it is therefore essential to analyse it carefully. In particular, are the possession rights of Mozambican farmers sufficient to enable them to use their land as collateral to obtain credit? If not, is there any conceivable alternative collateral, such as standing crops, that could avoid the costly step of formalised land titles? Regarding agro-processing, focus must be on the transformation of products, such as fruits and vegetables (baby corn, green beans, citrus fruits, bananas, and mangos), cereals (maize and related products, sesame), and cut flowers.

All of the above requirements will not be met unless competent national and regional agencies for project identification and appraisal are put in place and receive the support of local bodies and NGOs with experience of grassroots development elsewhere in Africa. In this regard, two remarks deserve to be made. To begin with, it is important that public resources are not allocated based on a mechanical fixed-rates criterion. In Mozambique, debates about the budget shares to be allocated to different sectors are often reduced to references to various international declarations, such as the 2003 Maputo Declaration and the 2014 Malabo Declaration. According to these declarations, 10 pre cent of the total state budget should be allocated to agriculture (it was 5.7 per cent in 2018). Instead, the allocation of the budget should be based on explicit socioeconomic criteria and the ensuing analysis should demonstrate the ability to achieve targeted outcomes in line with established policy goals. This is a complex exercise since expenditures in education, health, energy, roads, bridges, transportation, communications, rural commercialisation, and many other sectors all interact with, and impact on, agriculture. For instance, the promotion of tourism and agro-tourism, the production of electricity from hydropower and natural gas plants, as well as transportation services, are activities that could easily be expanded in the wake of, or concomitantly with, agricultural growth. Finally, in a longer-term perspective, and given the risks of climate change for agricultural production, it is imperative to develop clear adaptation strategies and technologies that are environmentally friendly and resilient to climate shocks.

The second remark is related to the necessity to avoid a top-down approach. Effective development of smallholder agriculture will not be achieved unless rural communities are involved in more than perfunctory ways. More concretely, they should not only be consulted by specialised agencies in charge of agricultural development, they ought also to be key actors in the establishment and operation of local institutions intended to solve their most pressing problems, such as how to store and dispose of their harvests most profitably, how to ensure proper maintenance of local public goods (e.g., roads, irrigation and draining facilities, collective granaries), how to secure supplies of critical inputs, how to organise training in such a way that it does not disrupt their ordinary activities, and so on. It is at this low but essential level that the contribution of NGOs can prove most useful.

Besides the need to correct for growing inequalities, it is hard to see how the country's development potential could be better mobilised in the absence of serious measures aimed at combatting the most egregious dysfunction of the prevailing political system. This is the most difficult task and, obviously, it cannot be tackled upfront because any direct reforming attempt is certain to arouse the stubborn resistance of the entrenched ruling elite, whose interests would be unavoidably harmed. This said, even though it will be difficult to break the link between politics and business, the hope of mitigating its worst effects must be actively entertained. Below, we suggest some measures in this direction.

The effective separation of the executive, judicial, and legislative powers is an objective that should not be lost sight of. Limiting our attention to the judiciary, an important first step would be to create an additional post of president of the judiciary. Instead of being appointed by the president of the republic, the president of the judiciary should be elected by all judges, whose votes would have equal weight, so that no one would have special voting powers. He or she would be barred from fulfilling the standard jurisdictional function of the courts, and his or her mandate would be of limited duration (four to five years) and would not coincide with the years of presidential and parliamentary elections. A body for oversight and control could be elected for the same period as the president of the judicial power. Composed of judges acting collectively to approve the way the budget of the justice department is allocated and to manage complaints, its members would represent, in due proportions, different areas or courts, but not different categories of judge. Following this recommendation, the president of the Supreme Court would keep the position of *primus inter pares* but would not represent the judicial power.

As much as possible, laws should be enacted that prevent the use of public funds or resources for campaigning purposes. The best way to ensure proper law enforcement is to guarantee the freedom of the press and its right to exert pressure on the government and other public agencies for maximum transparency and accountability. This should also apply to other forms of regulation and contracts, in particular those that involve large sums of money. In this respect, it is advisable to establish a public company charged with the task of exploiting and extracting hydrocarbons on a large scale and in the general interest of the population. A competitive and transparent policy in line with best international practices should be developed to hire managers, engineers, and other professionals. Also, the public company should be managed in an autonomous manner, implying that it should be immune to any direct political interference. It should be supervised by an administrative board, which in turn operates under a transparent management system. The participation of new international companies competing in the exploration and production of hydrocarbons should be kept open.

Genuine decentralisation must be pursued on the basis of the approval by the parliament (April 2019) of three bills providing for the election of provincial governments and assemblies, and the creation of a secretary of state for each province. Since the stated goal of these initiatives is to further democratise and empower local levels, it is critical that these reforms do not end up in a situation where the position of provincial state secretary offsets the political power of provincial governors (who are locally elected).

Given the pivotal role of human capital accumulation for long-term development, efforts to improve education quality must not be spared. The present state of affairs is unsatisfactory, in part because pupils and students are too often allowed to graduate at higher levels while they do not actually satisfy the minimum standards officially required. Class and teacher attendance needs to be tightly monitored and mechanisms need to be created to allow for the denunciation of attempts to buy certificates. *Mutatis mutandis*, the same principles apply to the health sector where, in addition, the Ministry of Health (a normative and regulatory body) ought to be separated from the National Health Service (the implementing agency) to avoid evident conflicts of interest.

Our last point concerns the dependence of Mozambique on foreign aid. What we wish to stress is that the government must be able to assess and address the concerns of donors while taking into account the general interests of the country. This implies that it has the capacity to balance the conflicting interests of different foreign countries (as different as China and the USA) against Mozambique's long-term goals. The possibility must therefore be accepted that aid offers are rejected when they are not in line with national policy and plans. This has concrete implications. In particular, the Foreign Service should be strengthened so that all aspects of foreign policy can be brought to bear on relations with foreign countries. Furthermore, transparent rules of the game based on clear and objective criteria must be laid down for all foreign investments (public and private), and they should be duly implemented. Such measures will not achieve their purpose if there is no strong interface, chaired by the prime minister, between key coordinating ministries and sector ministries, such as the Ministry of Industry and Trade, the Ministry of Energy and Mineral Resources, and the Ministry of Agriculture and Rural Development.

APPENDIX: THE CAREER OF PATRICE TALON

Patrice Talon's business career started with the provision of inputs in the cotton sector, where he quickly acquired a dominant position. His control over the cotton industry was followed by the creation of ginning factories at the time the sector was liberalised in 1990, and later by the acquisition of the factories initially operated by the national company (SONATRA) at the time it was dismantled in 2008. The success of the former operation owed much to the support he brought in 1991 to the election of President Nicephore Soglo, previously a World Bank official, and the success of the latter to his shift of allegiance in favour of President Thomas Boni Yayi, a former governor of the West African Bank for Development. Since Yayi was opposed to Soglo in the 2006 presidential election, Talon's move amounted to a betrayal – the more so because he had close links with the Soglo family. His calculation was presumably that Yayi's chances of winning the election were higher, therefore providing a more secure way to expand his control over the cotton sector. The plan worked according to expectations, since several competitors (foremost among whom was Sefou Fagbohoun) were politically eliminated at the behest of the newly elected president.

In the meantime, Sébastien Ajavon, another outsized businessman who accumulated wealth in the cross-border trade with Nigeria, threw his weight behind Adrien Houngbédji, the local leader of the rich Ouémé region, who was defeated by Yayi. Ajavon nonetheless succeeded in becoming the president of the powerful employers' association (*Association du Patronat*), which transformed him into the most prominent rival of Talon. The next presidential campaign, in 2011, created the stage for a new but faked about-turn on the part of Talon. At stake seems to have been the management and control of the juicy rent opportunities opened up by the new Programme for the Inspection of Imports (*Programme de Vérification des Importations*, or PVI), an agency in charge of assessing the value of imported goods. Talon made approaches to Ajavon and Houngbédji, thus betraying his alliance with Yayi, at least upon a first reading of the event. His tactic was more subtle, though, as it consisted of playing Yayi off against Houngbédji in order to extract from the former the concession that he was seeking. Once more, his political stratagem paid off, since he was awarded the operating licence of Benin Control, the new private agency in charge of implementing the PVI, as well as other highly profitable business deals. The big loser was Ajavon, who was indicted by Yayi for alleged tax evasion. Surprisingly, only one year after the election, disagreements about how to share the spoils of state power drove Talon into a poisonous conflict with President Yayi (Yayi actually accused Talon of having attempted to poison him), following which he was forced into exile in France. In essence, Yayi found Talon to be too greedy. In this way, even though it was Talon who bankrolled two successful campaigns for Yayi, the two men became involved in what has been called 'one of the more bizarre fallouts in West African politics in recent years' (Corey-Boulet, 2019).

Talon did not give up, however. He clinched a deal with Dossou, a businessman with interests in the railways, and with his old enemy Ajavon. Determined to return to his country and to regain his business privileges, he discreetly prepared his campaign for the presidential election of 2016. This move disturbed Ajavon and Dossou, who considered it a violation of their tacit agreement according to which the supreme state power should remain in the hands of politicians. In reaction, Ajavon decided to apply himself as a candidate for the presidency. As a result, the two individuals with the highest net worth in Benin started to confront each other openly on the political terrain. The saga did not end there because, upon reflection, the two men understood that the priority lay in breaking Yayi's system. Talon took the lead over Ajavon but made serious concessions that included the reimbursement of all the state debts owed to Ajavon's commercial companies. Talon became president. However, he quickly came to the conclusion that the demands of his partner-rival were impossible to meet. Ajavon responded angrily and, in due course, became the number one enemy of the regime. Interestingly, Benin Control, whose operations had been suspended in 2012 as a result of public outrage over its bad performance and the excessive pricing of its services, was reinstated by the new government of Talon, who had also been the successful tenderer of the PVI in 2011. The opacity of the procedure that was followed, particularly regarding the new contract and the extent of fiscal exonerations provided, again raised a public outcry.

5

Directed Development with Big Conglomerates

South Korea

I INTRODUCTION

The objective of the following pages is not to provide yet another account of the Korean miracle.[1] In line with the preceding summary of the IDP and methodology, the main question asked is as follows: 'What would have been the conclusion of an institutional diagnostic of the development potential of South Korea conducted in the mid- or late-1970s, at a time when the country was still a low-income country, at roughly the same income level as the case studies in the IDP project?' Of course, the context and method of such an exercise would be different from the diagnostic exercises undertaken within the IDP project since it would rely exclusively on the existing literature on early Korea's development and on statistics available for that period rather than later on. In the 1960s or 1970s there were no institutional or governance indicators comparable to those existing in international databases today, no surveys were run about how people felt about the institutional context of economic development, and thus no thematic study could have been launched based on the information gathered from such surveys. Yet the abundant literature that exists on Korea's development permits us to partly fill in the holes and to formulate a diagnostic that is approximately comparable to those in the IDP project.

Such an undertaking has a twofold objective. On the one hand, it provides a kind of test of the general approach to diagnosing institutional weaknesses and strengths in connection with economic development features and challenges, as pursued in the IDP. On the other hand, and most importantly, it offers a benchmark for the diagnostic exercises undertaken on today's low-income countries. South Korea is undoubtedly a development success

---

[1] See for instance Chu (2018) or Schneidewind (2016). More oriented towards policy, see also Kong (2000).

story. Yet this was certainly not evident back in the early days of its take-off. It is thus particularly interesting to see what a diagnostic would have made of its institutional framework in terms of being a facilitator of, or an obstacle to, its future development at a time when the latter was still very uncertain, and what can be said a posteriori about the role of institutions in development achievements.

This abridged institutional diagnostic of South Korea during its take-off period is organised along the same lines as the institutional diagnostics completed within the IDP. Following this introduction, the next two sections summarise the geographical and historical context of South Korea's early phases of development. The fourth section deals with the main features of that development, the main challenges the country overcame, and those it was still facing around, say, the mid-1970s. The next section analyses the process by which key policy decisions were taken and implemented within the institutional framework that existed in those days. In view of that background, Section VI then presents an institutional diagnostic of South Korean development as we believe one could have been established more or less at the middle of the 1970s. A few general remarks are then offered in conclusion.

II GEOGRAPHICAL AND EARLY HISTORICAL CONTEXT
OF MODERN DEVELOPMENT IN SOUTH KOREA

The Korean peninsula is a stretch of land that forms a kind of bridge between the Asian continent, essentially China in the north and Japan in the southeast. This location explains much of the historical episodes that have shaped modern Korea. The eastern part of the peninsula is mountainous, although more in the north than in the south, whereas the western and southern parts consist of hills separated by narrow valleys and coastal plains. The climate is temperate, with rainfall concentrated in summer. The south is more suitable for farming, rice being the dominant crop. Historically, the south was thus more oriented towards agriculture, and had always been a net exporter of rice before World War II. By contrast, the north of the peninsula is very rich in mineral resources, including coal, iron ore, and a wide variety of non-ferrous metals and rare earths. Consequently, the north was more industrialised than the south after the splitting of the country.

Population density has always been high in Korea. However, the separation of the peninsula into two parts at the end of World War II introduced a strong asymmetry. Around the 1970s, the period we shall focus on here, South Korea sheltered 32 million people, with a density of 365 inhabitants per square kilometre. North Korea's population was half this size, spread over the same surface area. Already at this time, South Korea was the most densely populated middle-sized country in the world. Population growth was slightly below 2 per cent but was receding at a quick pace thanks to a fast drop in fertility – from around 6 children per woman in 1960 to 2.7 in 1980 (it was a little more than one in 2018). The demographic transition was just beginning: the population was still very young, with around half being below twenty-five. Historically, the Korean population has always been culturally and ethnically very homogeneous. This remains the case today within each of the two entities that share the peninsula, but much less so when comparing the two, in view of the markedly different paths they have followed since separation.

A major turning point in Korea's history before its separation into North and South was Japanese colonisation. It is thus convenient to divide the following brief account of Korea's history before the split according to that event.

A Korea until the Japanese Annexation

The history of the Korean peninsula goes back very far. In the Common Era, three epochs can be distinguished, up until the current period. The first extends throughout the first millennium and witnessed a constant rivalry between two or three kingdoms, some of them stretching at times far north into Manchuria and even Siberia, with repeated interventions by China and Japan within peninsular conflicts. The second covers the second millennium until the early twentieth century. One of the aforementioned kingdoms had become dominant and thus was able to rule over the whole peninsula. Two dynasties, the Goryeo and the Joseon, occupied the throne for almost 500 years each, but in both cases they were in a subservient position with respect to China for a large part of their rule. The third period witnessed the entry of Korea into the modern age, essentially through its being forced to end its isolationist policy and to open up to trade, first with Japan and then with the West. The influence of Meiji's Japan and its push to promote the modernisation of Korea grew during the last third of the nineteenth century, until the first Sino-Japanese war in 1894–5 freed Korea from China's suzerainty and saw it fall under Japanese control. Efforts to resist that pressure, notably by seeking support from Russia, failed, and Korea became a Japanese protectorate in 1905. Five years later, after the assassination of the Japanese resident general, the country became a Japanese colony.

B Japanese Rule

Japanese colonisation lasted forty years, until the defeat of Japan in World War II. It was particularly severe at the beginning of the period, as Japan sought to quickly impose its rule and way of life on Korean society, and again in the last ten years, as Japan first prepared for the war and then fought it, first against the Republic of China and then against the Allies. During these two episodes, particularly the last one, the coloniser engaged in the forced Japanification of the Korean population and its mobilisation for its own benefit and as part of the huge war effort. This went as far as forcing Koreans to adopt Japanese names and prohibiting the Korean language in schools. In between these two periods, however, life in Korea could be said to resemble the days of allegiance to the Chinese emperor, except that the Japanese suzerain was more severe – but also more modern and entrepreneurial. Moreover, with time, Korea acquired a kind of central place in the colonial power's strategy of expanding across the Asian continent, and benefited from the development of transport infrastructure and industrial hubs aimed at supplying military equipment for the Japanese troops and settlers in Manchuria – or Manchukuo as it was called under Japanese rule.

The jury is still out about how to evaluate Japanese colonial rule and its contribution to the foundation of modern Korea. The legacy of that period is complex, with both positive and negative elements. Some historians emphasise the fact that colonial rule coincided with the modernisation of the economy and suggest that the former facilitated the latter. This view, which refers to 'colonial modernity, has much in its favour.[2] Undeniably, Japanese rule brought huge investments in infrastructure (railroads, roads, and ports), industrialisation opportunities, initially for both local and Japanese markets and later for war equipment and weaponry provision, up-to-date technology, a modern schooling system, high standards of efficiency in business as well as in government matters, and the effective training of local bureaucrats. Even though it cannot be discarded that such an evolution would have taken place by mere replication of what could be seen across the strait that separates the peninsula from Japan, the latter's oversight may have accelerated and deepened this process by bringing its example closer to the Koreans and by providing opportunities for new developments.

Several of the aforementioned development factors were already in gestation before Japan's annexation. For instance, education had been flourishing in the last two decades of the Joseon dynasty. Private schools were increasing in number, and a public educational system was about to be created. If the Japanese introduced new schools and a new curriculum (although the latter was initially shorter for Korean students), unlicensed private traditional schools spread because of the limited space in the formal system, especially in rural areas. This appetite for education has undoubtedly been a characteristic of Korean society ever since. Likewise, some industries already existed before Japan's takeover, although apparently concentrated in the north. Moreover, this small group of entrepreneurs was able to take advantage of, and to learn from, collaboration with Japanese business, in particular the *zaibatsus* present in Korea (*zaibatsu* refers to large family-controlled and multi-firm conglomerates that developed in Japan after the Meiji Restoration of 1868). These large Japanese business conglomerates were later to inspire the Korean *chaebols*.

The benefits from this modernisation of the Korean society and economy went primarily to the coloniser. Korean workers were underpaid in comparison with Japanese workers, and landlords and farmers were dispossessed by Japanese settlers and firms, which acquired swathes of land and transformed

[2] See Kim, Kyu Hyun (2004).

a portion of farmers into tenants, tenants into landless workers, and workers into jobless migrants who moved to the cities. The traumatic experience of the war period, when Japanification became the watchword of the colonisers and Koreans were controlled based on the needs of the occupier, must also lie on the negative side of the balance, even though it is sometimes considered that this experience forged the national spirit that would later reveal itself in the postcolonial era. The tearing apart of families and communities through migration to various neighbouring countries, and the near-total breakdown of society, were aspects of this trauma.

Beyond these hardships, and beyond the economic legacy of Japanese colonisation, the model offered to the Korean population of Japanese state-directed economic development, first across the Korea Strait and then on its own territory, would later prove important in the post-war period and after the North–South separation. There is no doubt that key players in the modern history of Korea were very much influenced by this example.

Koreans rejoiced at the end of the war and the departure of the Japanese occupiers. They certainly thought that the trauma of war was behind them and immediately started to think about a new structure of government for the peninsula. They did not know that a still more dreadful tragedy was awaiting them.

III EARLY POST-INDEPENDENCE HISTORY

The origins of the division of the peninsula between North and South are not completely clear. At the end of World War II, a decision was taken to place liberated Korea under a trusteeship, headed by the victors, for a few years, until the economy and the society stabilised. It was resolved that the Soviet army would occupy the northern part of the peninsula and the US army the southern part, in order (it was said) to guarantee a smooth and peaceful return to normality. On both sides, the trusteeship and the division were bitterly contested by the population, but steps were taken to restart political life in a unified country as soon as possible. However, ideologies quickly differed between the two sides. Under the leadership of Kim Il Sung, Communists rapidly dominated in the North, supported by the Soviet Union, whereas liberals led the game in the South, under Syngman Rhee, a pillar of the independence and a strongly anti-Communist public personality who had spent the last years of Japanese rule in the United States.

The determination to reunify the country was strong in both the North and the South and early moves were made in this direction. The South proclaimed the Republic of Korea in August 1948, followed a month later by the North proclaiming the Democratic Popular Republic of Korea. Three months later, the General Assembly of the United Nations recognised the former as the sole legal government of Korea. This was seen as a provocation in the North and the peninsula was soon dragged into war.

A The Korean War

War broke out in June 1950. The North, militarily stronger than the South and counting on the support of unofficial volunteer forces from China and equipment from the USSR, saw the opportunity of unifying the country under its own rule. Its army crossed the 38th parallel demarcation line and invaded the South. After early successes, the Northern forces were repelled by the Southern army, powerfully backed by the US army and other United Nations allies. In turn, the Southern forces invaded the North, triggering a strong intervention by China, which could not accept the military presence of the United States near its border. With such support, the North succeeded in crossing the demarcation line again, only to be repelled once more a few months later. A stalemate around the line then settled in, lasting almost two years, while difficult armistice negotiations involving UN forces, China, and the Northern army took place. A conclusion was finally reached in July 1953, which ratified the division of the peninsula into two countries. However, the treaty was not signed by Syngman Rhee for the South and the North never fully dropped the idea of reunifying the peninsula, as was evident in its multiple attempts to intervene south of the 38th parallel demarcation line, which had become a 4-km-wide demilitarised zone.

The damage of the war was enormous. It is estimated that approximately three million Koreans, or 10 per cent of the population, lost their lives, two-thirds of them civilians killed in aerial bombings. Around ten million families were broken apart because of the war and the division of the country. Material losses amounted to roughly one year of GDP, approximately 30 per cent of all productive assets and infrastructure. Experts estimate that GNP in the first year after the war was 30 per cent below the pre-war level in North Korea and a little more than half this in South Korea.[3] Not only was the South less affected than the North, but its physical capital was also less damaged and numerous refugees from the North made up for the loss of population. The North had initially been more industrialised and richer, thanks to mineral natural resources, but it would take much more time to rebound. By contrast, the South was back to its pre-war income levels by 1953, although it is fair to say this was very much thanks to generous US aid.

B Post-War Politics

Three stages can be distinguished in the history of post-war South Korea: the reconstruction during the first normal years of democratic life until 1960, the dictatorship under Park Chung Hee and later Chun Doo-Hwan, and the definitive return to democracy in 1987 (which is outside our period of interest in the present analysis). Interestingly, this periodisation fits rather

---

[3] See Koh (1993).

well the main features of economic development and the strategies that were implemented during this period.

Post-war South Korea was to be dominated by the personality and authority of Syngman Rhee, who was president from 1948 onwards. Rhee was a rather rigid and authoritarian character, and had a very personal sense of the interest of the country. He headed the Liberal Party, which had no clear ideology other than seeking to enrich its most notable members. Very quickly, the issue arose of Rhee's serving a third four-year term, which required a modification of the constitution. The necessary amendment was passed (though it was one vote short of the two-thirds majority required). Rhee was re-elected in 1956, but with a much smaller lead than in the previous elections. Ageing, heading a deeply corrupt regime that was perceived as ineffective in pushing the economy forward and curbing poverty, his personal aura as a nationalist figure had started to fade by this time, whereas the opposition, regrouped within the Democratic Party, was gaining increasing support.

Rhee stood again as a candidate in 1960, together with a vice-president who it was supposed would be his successor if he had to resign because of his age. He won by a landslide thanks to flagrant vote-rigging, but his election triggered vigorous protests. Students organised a march towards the presidential residence and police fired on and killed 139 of them. Protests continued the following day, but the army refused to fire on demonstrators. Having clearly lost the little popular support that was left him, Rhee resigned. An interim government was then formed, which set out to write a new constitution that would reduce the power of the executive in favour of the parliament.

The government that came out of this process faced a difficult situation. The economic recovery process was slow, inflation was accelerating, the political context was essentially unstable due to the relatively inexperienced political parties and a constitution that reduced the power of the executive, workers were striking for higher wages, students were demonstrating almost uninterruptedly, while some voices were rising in favour of opening a dialogue with the North. It was in the middle of this chaos that some high-ranking army officers, concerned about the increasing climate of corruption, the incapacity of the politicians to re-establish order, and the danger of showing too much weakness in the face of the threat posed by Communist North Korea, organised a coup in May 1961. While General Park Chung Hee was placed at the head of the military junta that would govern the country for a few years, his rule was to last almost two decades in total.

C The Park Era

Park's career before the coup had been rather turbulent. Initially a schoolteacher, he went on to enrol in the Japanese army. After graduating from officer school in Manchukuo and spending some time as a foreign student at the Japanese Military Academy in Tokyo he served in the Manchurian

Infantry Corps. He was then twenty-seven, and this Japanese experience was to have a big influence on his later views about economic development and industrialisation. At independence, he entered the Korean Military Academy and was then assigned to the US–Korean force. Before reporting for duty, however, he was arrested because of his links with Communist movements within the Korean army. He eventually got himself out of trouble and was attached as a civilian to the intelligence unit at army headquarters. Two years later he was reinstated in the army at the outbreak of the Korean War. Amid strong suspicions regarding leftist attitudes within the South Korean army, it is remarkable that Park was not only reinstated but then pursued a brilliant military career, despite his past Communist record – not only during the war, when the army expanded massively, but also thereafter. This indicates an impressive personality, which appealed to his superiors, as well as a powerful friendship network within the army.

The political platform of the junta was unambiguous in its anti-Communist orientation and its aim of reinforcing links with the United States. It also had a revolutionary element, in its determination to root out corruption and to eradicate the misery of the masses. In addition to consolidating Park's control over the army, and the political system in general, the first years of the junta were devoted to establishing the administrative structure that would be able to achieve Park's ambitions. Especially important in this respect were the Korean Central Intelligence Agency (KCIA), a formidable organisation with observers in practically all business, academic, political, and social groups, and the Economic Planning Board (EPB), staffed with highly competent technocrats and responsible for designing and managing the country's economic growth strategies, starting with the first Five-Year Development Plan.

However, the junta did not last long. The US mission in Korea, which had remained powerful since the end of its de facto protectorate in the post-war years, if only through the huge aid it was providing to the economy, impressed upon Park the need to return to a civil regime. Somewhat reluctantly, Park accepted, and democratic rule was re-established. Park resigned from the army and, with the implicit support of the KCIA, created his own Democratic Republican Party. He was elected president in 1963, though by a relatively small margin. His tight, quasi-military control over the political system was maintained during his term, within the apparent limits imposed by democracy. Then, in the election in 1967, with satisfactory results on the economic front, Park easily won again.

The prospect of the 1971 election reopened the issue of a constitutional amendment that would allow Park to seek a third term. The opposition tried to resist this and several student demonstrations were organised to mobilise opinion against it. Yet the amendment was passed, although allegedly in a somewhat suspicious way. However, the newly re-elected president's position was much less secure than it had been previously. Soon after, Park declared a state of emergency, officially because of renewed threats from North Korea and geopolitical changes that were leading the United States to reduce its military presence. One year later, martial law was instated, the Assembly and political parties were dissolved, and the existing constitution was replaced by a new one, called the Yushin constitution, officially to permit South Korea to adjust more flexibly to the changing international security order.

Practically speaking, the new regime was a barely concealed dictatorship that empowered Park to rule without constraint and that sheltered him from legislative and judicial controls. He had become, to all intents and purposes, a life-long president, his re-election relying on a hand-picked National Congress for Unification. South Korea then entered a dark period of authoritarianism and ubiquitous repression, and in some cases elimination, of all political enemies of the president. At a later stage, Park even had to separate from old supporters he thought were becoming too ambitious as competitors. Amid mounting public discontent he became a more and more solitary ruler. The economic situation itself was becoming critical at the end of the 1970s, because of swelling domestic and foreign debt and the shocks caused by oil price booms. Had he lived, Park would probably have faced a difficult time, but he was shot in October 1979 by the KCIA director, a friend whose motivation for the assassination is still unclear.

The rest of the country's political history is of lesser importance for our purpose since we aim to adopt a perspective that corresponds to the early history and the situation of South Korea in the mid- or late-1970s – say, some time before Park's death. For the sake of completeness, however, some major events that took place in the next decade must be mentioned because they shed light on the state of South Korean society and the inherent difficulty it faced in those times as regards installing a stable democratic regime.

D The Chun Dictatorship and the Difficult Return to Democracy

For a brief period, Koreans thought they would return to a freer regime and the Yushin constitution would be abolished. A kind of caretaker government was appointed until a new constitution could be voted on and a new government elected. All parties prepared to compete, but in a kind of repeat of 1961, a group of generals organised a coup and took power. Chun Doo-Hwan, the new strong man, easily stepped into Park's shoes. Yet the coup aroused the ire of the public. Students protested the martial law, as well as the continuation of the Yushin constitution. One massive demonstration was repressed by the army, leading to 2,000 casualties. Although forever discredited in public opinion, Chun was able to consolidate his power and ruled until the end of his term, which he had pledged not to go beyond. Chun then tried to singlehandedly impose his protégé Roh Tae-Woo as the new president. Huge protests immediately took place, with a large part of the population, not only the students, taking to the streets and demanding a new constitution. Chun gave in, the constitution was amended, and – apparently fair – elections took place in

1987. It was eventually won by Roh. His five-year term was essentially transitional, but it represented a major turn in Korean society towards democracy.

The constitution, which had gone through no fewer than ten changes since the first republic in 1948, was not reformed again. Elections went on to be held every five years in a peaceful way, and with perfect regularity.

IV THE PACE AND STRUCTURE OF SOUTH KOREA'S ECONOMIC TAKE-OFF AND INDUSTRIALISATION[4]

The take-off of the South Korean economy in the two and a half decades between the end of the Korean War and shortly before Park's assassination was truly phenomenal. On average, the annual rate of growth of GDP was 8 per cent, with GDP increasing sevenfold. In the following pages, we give more details on this dazzling development, insisting first on the major structural transformation of the economy, which was both the cause and the consequence of that vibrant growth, which was essentially engineered by manufacturing exports. We then focus on how the impressive accumulation of capital and infrastructure needed for such development was made possible. We finally touch upon social aspects, including the fast progress in education and the inclusiveness of growth throughout this take-off period. The next subsection then turns to the main policy decisions and strategic orientations that contributed to such outstanding results.

A Growth and the Structural Transformation of the Economy

It took some time for the rate of growth of the South Korean economy to reach the stellar level that made it possible to later approach the ranks of the advanced economies. This progressive acceleration reflects the gradual rise of its main engine, the manufacturing sector. Until 1975, manufacturing value-added systematically grew at a rate roughly double of the rest of the economy, but its contribution to overall growth increased with its size: it was small in the late 1950s, when the manufacturing sector represented only 10 per cent of GDP (at current prices), but it was much more important when it approached 20 per cent ten years later – see Table 5.1.

Unsurprisingly, a major structural transformation of the economy accompanied this performance. As has been the case for practically all development experiences in history and across countries in the contemporary period, the share of agriculture fell rather regularly over time, on average by one percentage point of GDP every year. This drop in the agricultural share benefited both manufacturing and the rest of the economy, mostly the former until 1965 and both equally afterwards – at least when considering GDP at constant prices. In

---

[4] This section owes much to the excellent review of South Korea's economic development edited by Il and Ko (2010).

TABLE 5.1 *South Korea: growth, employment, productivity, and structural transformation, 1955–1985*

Year	1955		1960		1965		1970		1975		1980		1985	
GDP at factor cost (1970=100)	33		40.3		57.4		100		160.8		242.6		381	
Five-year average growth rate			4.1		7.3		11.8		10		8.6		9.4	
Population (1970=100)	69.9		79.5		90.7		100		109.8		118.6		128.1	
Gross national income (GNI) per capita at constant factor cost (1970=100)	47.1		50.7		63.3		100		146.4		204.5		297.4	
Five-year average growth rate			1.5		4.5		9.6		7.9		6.9		7.8	
Sector structure of GDP (market prices) (%) (current price and constant 2015 prices)	Curr.	Const.	Curr.	Const.	Curr.	Const.	Curr.	Const.	Curr.	Const.	Curr.	Const.	Curr.	Const.
Agriculture	42.3	31.7	38.6	27.6	34.4	26.8	27.1	17.2	23	13.9	15	8.7	10.4	7.8
Manufacturing	10.9	3.3	11.9	4.5	16.7	5.9	16.7	8.3	21.4	11.9	21.8	15.2	25.4	16.6
Other	46.8	65	49.5	68	48.9	67.3	56.2	74.5	55.6	74.2	63.2	76.1	64.2	75.5
Total employment (1970=100)					82.2		100		121.1		140.6		153.6	
Sectoral structure of employment (%)														
Agriculture					59.4		50.4		45.8		33.9		24.9	
Manufacturing					9.2		13.2		18.6		21.6		23.4	
Other					31.4		36.4		35.6		44.5		51.7	
Overall labour productivity (1970=100)					69.8		100		132.8		172.5		248	
Labour productivity by sector (1970 overall productivity = 100)														
Agriculture					31.5		34.2		40.3		44.3		77.8	
Manufacturing					45		62.9		85.3		121.5		176.4	
Other					149.2		204.6		276.7		295		362.4	
Decomposition of overall productivity gains														
Productivity gains							30.2		32.8		39.7		75.5	
Of which: structural change							8		0.4		23.5		20.9	
autonomous gain							22.2		32.5		16.2		54.6	

Source: Bank of Korea and Economic Statistics Yearbook for employment figures.

this respect, it may be noted that the relative price of manufactured products relative to that of other sectors tended to fall throughout the period, in line with the fact that productivity gains are faster in industry – partly thanks to a greater substitutability of labour by equipment – than in services. In the case of South Korea, this phenomenon was amplified by the outward orientation of the manufacturing sector and its exposure to foreign competition. The same cannot be said of the agricultural sector, even though it also produces a tradeable good.[5]

The structural transformation must also be considered from the point of view of employment. This is done in the second part of Table 5.1. Because employment data are not comparable before and after 1963,[6] the beginning of the period had to be ignored. Over the next fifteen years, however, the share of agriculture in total employment, which was initially close to 60 per cent, was halved. Given the progression of total employment, the volume of employment in the sector increased until the mid-1970s, but then decreased at a fast pace afterwards. Initially, the manufacturing sector was the main beneficiary of the net flow of workers leaving agriculture. In a later stage, however, this flow went to other sectors, among which services was the most important.

Sectoral changes in labour productivity underpin this bi-dimensional reallocation of output and labour. In this respect, it is interesting to observe that the first phase of South Korean development illustrates – but also somewhat contradicts – the familiar Lewis–Kuznets view in development theory. This theory holds that the structural transformation of the economy led by the movement of workers from rural informal production to modern industry and services is the main engine of growth in early phases of development. Capital accumulation takes place in the modern sector of the economy, which easily expands employment by drawing on under-employed workers, or surplus labour, in the informal or traditional agricultural sector. If the former is sufficiently dynamic and labour-intensive, there comes a moment at which the surplus labour disappears in the informal sector. A 'turning point' is thus reached at which labour earnings begin increasing in both sectors and the agricultural sector starts to modernise. Such a scenario fits well the development of South Korea until the early 1970s: labour productivity was approximately constant in agriculture, whereas labour flowed from agriculture to (mostly) the manufacturing sector.

Where South Korea fits the theory less well is in the observation that the structural reallocation of labour away from low-productivity agriculture to the rest of the economy did not contribute much to the overall productivity gain in

---

[5] The convergence between the constant and current price structure of GDP would have appeared more clearly in Table 5.1 if the constant price series had referred to a less recent base year than 2015, which is the base used in the Bank of Korea's historical database.

[6] See Koo (2013).

the economy. The latter amounted to a little less than a doubling in the decade after 1965. However, as can be seen at the bottom of Table 5.1, the main contribution to those gains was not so much the reallocation of labour away from agriculture – the row titled 'structural change' – as the autonomous productivity gain within manufacturing and other non-agricultural sectors. The reason for this is essentially that the labour reallocation took place mostly between agriculture and manufacturing, and the productivity gap between these two sectors was initially limited. The productivity gains within manufacturing and other sectors thus proved to be the dominant force behind the overall productivity gains. An explanation of this evolution within the Lewisian framework is that the composition of those sectors changed because of major policy choices and, most importantly, the deliberate export orientation of manufacturing, its necessary increase in international competitiveness, and the accompanying changes in supporting sectors. Later, things changed substantially, when the economy settled into this new regime and the productivity gap between agriculture and the rest of the economy was drastically amplified, especially with respect to the manufacturing sector – possibly because of the progressive shift there from light to heavy industry. Structural change was then the dominant contributor to overall productivity gains between 1975 and 1980, even though the average within-sector, or 'autonomous', productivity gains were still substantial.

The increasing productivity gap between agriculture and the rest of the economy in the early part of South Korea's take-off should be emphasised because it is somewhat original when compared to other successful development stories in Asia, particularly Japan and Taiwan.[7] In contrast to those countries, where initial major agricultural productivity gains permitted the development of the manufacturing sector, agricultural productivity in South Korea was low by international standards and stagnant. Such a state of affairs was due to the quality of the soil, the limited size of farms consequent upon a strongly egalitarian land reform, the low productivity of labour-intensive traditional farming techniques, and the lack of incentives and capacity to innovate in an over-populated rural sector. As a matter of fact, it is only when the development of the manufacturing and ancillary sectors had permitted absorption of the labour surplus in agriculture that productivity growth accelerated. The productivity figures in Table 5.1 suggest that this 'Lewisian turning point' could have been reached in the early 1970s,[8] and this seems to be confirmed by the fact that the volume of agricultural employment started to fall around the same time. Yet agricultural productivity and rural incomes continued to lag behind the rest of the economy, to such an extent that the government had to engage in a

---

[7] This paragraph relies on an excellent analysis of agricultural issues in the early phase of South Korean development by Brandt (1980).
[8] There was some discussion in those days about when this turn took place – see Sedjo (1976). With more hindsight, Ranis (2004) identified that this point was reached around 1973.

vigorous policy to support farmers' income, through infrastructure investment, ambitious agricultural extension programmes, and heavy price subsidies. Yet it was only after 1980, well after the South Korean economy had taken off, that agricultural productivity got off the ground.

A factor that is worth stressing – because it contributed to growth in income per capita that was faster than the growth in labour productivity – was the increase in the participation rate of the population to the labour force. This is due to two factors. On the one hand, the share of the population that was of working age tended to increase due to the fast reduction in fertility rates. On the other hand, an increase in the female participation rate was observed in the last 1960s, possibly because of the opening up of numerous female jobs in newly exporting factories.[9]

As a final comment on interpreting the figures shown in Table 5.1, it is important to stress that the contribution of the manufacturing sector to the overall growth of the economy went beyond its share in GDP times its growth rate. If it had not done so, then the contribution of manufacturing to South Korean growth in the earlier phases of its take-off would have been modest, despite its phenomenal growth rate. However, this argument ignores first that the expansion of a sector that was mostly oriented towards exports fed domestic demand, and therefore the growth of domestic-oriented, or non-tradeable, sectors and, second, the powerful backward and forward linkages between manufacturing and other sectors such as transport, communication, trade, and finance. On top of this, by making foreign exchange available, manufacturing exports contributed to facilitating imports of equipment and, through them, the diffusion of modern foreign technology throughout the economy. Unfortunately, no precise quantitative estimate of the actual contribution of the manufacturing engine of growth – beyond strict accounting practice – seems to be available.

B The Financing of Accumulation and Industrialisation

How was such a successful industrialisation take-off possible? The answer is through fast-growing investment that was largely funded by foreign sources, especially foreign aid in the first phases of the industrialisation process, quickly supplemented by growing domestic savings. Table 5.2 shows that the rate of fixed capital formation over GDP progressively increased from 11 per cent in the 1955s to more than 30 per cent by 1980, although the bulk of the increase really started only in the late 1960s. Given the limited initial stock of capital, even a low investment rate in these early years was able to generate a rapid increase in the equipment and infrastructure available for production. Young (1994, 1995) has estimated that the annual rate of growth of capital may have

---

[9] See Park (1990).

TABLE 5.2 *South Korea: expenditures out of GDP, foreign financing, composition of exports, 1955–1985 (current prices)*

	1955	1960	1965	1970	1975	1980	1985
Expenditures out of GDP (% of GDP)							
Private consumption	88.2	83.1	81.7	73.1	68.3	63.2	57.4
Government consumption	9.4	14	9.5	10.5	10.7	11.9	10.4
Gross fixed capital formation	11.1	11.6	17.1	27.1	28.5	30.5	29.9
of which: change in inventory	1.2	0.5	1.6	2.7	3.5	0.5	0.3
Exports	1.4	3.7	8.3	14.5	29.6	35.2	38.4
Imports	10.2	12.5	16.6	25.3	37	40.9	36.1
GDP	100	100	100	100	100	100	100
Net factor income from the rest of the world	1	0.8	1	0.5	−0.9	−2.6	−3.3
GNI	101	100.8	101	100.5	99.1	97.4	96.7
Financing of capital formation							
Domestic saving	2.4	2.9	8.8	16.4	21	24.9	32.1
Foreign saving	8.8	8.8	8.3	10.8	7.4	5.8	−2.2
of which: foreign aid	7	7.9	7	3	1.1	0.2	–
Composition of exports (% of total)							
Manufacturing		13	58.2	78.2	83.5	86.3	96
of which: miscellaneous		1	19.6	41.2	37.4	31.4	47.8
of which: clothing			11.9	32.5	22.9	17.9	25.4
Others		87	41.8	21.8	16.5	13.7	4

Source: Bank of Korea, Economic Statistics Yearbook, various years.
Note that all ratios refer to three-year averages around the year that heads the column, so as to smoothen short-run shocks – like oil prices in 1975 or 1980.

been above 16 per cent on average between 1965 and 1980 for the whole economy, excluding agriculture, contributing to a little less than half of the 11 per cent average annual GDP growth, the rest being almost all due to the growth of the labour force, after accounting for its increasing education level (on which more below), thus leaving a very limited role (roughly 1 per cent per year) of total factor productivity (TFP).[10] Early growth in South Korea was thus mostly guided by factor accumulation.

Capital accumulation in a low-income country requires savings and domestic currency to buy equipment, which is mostly imported. In the case of South Korea, both came from foreign savings and the deliberate export orientation of industrialisation throughout the period under analysis. Up to the mid-1960s, foreign aid, the bulk of which was provided by the United States, played a leading role, as it covered a major part of imports, including in the 1950s in the form of agricultural products. Things changed when the country approached

---

[10] Young (1994) considered this fact as contrary to the view that South Korean growth was predominantly the result of major TFP gain.

self-sufficiency in the 1970s and donors' assistance was progressively phased out, at which time foreign loans were used to finance the accumulation of capital that was not covered by domestic savings, even though the propensity to save was making huge progress – part of which was generated by the implicit taxation of depositors in a fully nationalised bank system.[11] Relying on foreign loans implied a rapid accumulation of debt. From an almost insignificant level in 1960, foreign debt grew to 40 per cent in the early 1970s. It then went down, only to surge again in the early 1980s during the global macroeconomic crisis that followed the second oil price boom. It is remarkable that the growth rate of GDP was little affected by debt. As a matter of fact, the investment rate kept increasing, reflecting a rather voluntaristic macroeconomic management.[12] As the domestic saving rate stayed on an upward trend, the country soon became autonomous in the financing of its investment operations.

Sustaining a high investment rate in a developing economy requires having enough foreign currency to buy goods that are not produced at home. Here lies South Korea's major achievement: its capacity to expand manufacturing exports, which became the true engine of growth, not only through their contribution to GDP but also through making foreign currency available for the import of equipment and foreign technology within the manufacturing sector itself, and also within the whole economy. Exports grew at an annual rate that was rarely below 15 per cent and was frequently above 30 per cent throughout the two decades from 1960 onwards, going from 4 per cent of GDP in 1960 to 30 per cent fifteen years later. Exports initially comprised chiefly food products, inedible oils, and crude materials, including various types of metal ores but during the 1960s the composition of exports drastically moved towards light manufactured goods – with clothing and footwear in the first place. As a result of an ambitious and resolute policy, however, they were then increasingly directed towards heavy and chemical industries (HCI) in the late 1970s, apparently against what had seemed to be the country's comparative advantage – that is, labour-intensive exports based on cheap and high-quality labour. It is the success of this bold policy that can be fairly termed the South Korean miracle.

The destination of exports also changed radically over time. The main client in the late 1950s was Japan and exports consisted of traditional products. Then destination countries were diversified, with the United States becoming the prime client at the expense of Japan, while exports concentrated on light manufacturing, mostly clothing and footwear. In the late 1970s, the composition of exports shifted again and started to include an increasing proportion of heavy industry, and clients comprised more developing and emerging countries.

[11] See Cho (1996).
[12] On debt see Collins and Park (1989), and on macroeconomic management in the 1970s see Amsden (1989: 93–108).

Back in the early 1970s, however, foreign currency sources had had three major origins. First, Japan's reparations payments for its forty-year colonial rule, after South Korea reconciled with its former coloniser; second, payments made by the United States in return for South Korea's participation in the Vietnam War; and, third, public works and building contracts in the Gulf countries after the first oil price boom – which, incidentally, provided Hyundai's founder, Chung Ju-Yung, with a leg up into big business. These last two items show another key feature of South Korean development: the capacity of its rulers and entrepreneurs to take advantage of all opportunities that might arise and that might be profitable for the country or for private business.

C Social Aspects: Education, Inequality, and Agriculture

The preceding tables and comments summarise in a very succinct way the first twenty-five years of South Korea's outstanding economic development. However, this picture would be incomplete without looking at their social counterpart. Here, too, the achievements were quite remarkable.

On the educational front, South Korea invested massively after its liberation from the Japanese coloniser, which had not done much in regard to the schooling of the indigenous population. Primary education was made a right in the 1948 constitution and the number of schools then mushroomed, despite a lack of resources in terms of teachers, school buildings, and textbooks. It has been said that student–teacher ratios were frequently as high as 100, and most schools operated two or three shifts a day. An important point is that this resulted as much from political will and policy decisions as from the fact that households themselves were eager to have their children educated so that they could qualify for good jobs – to such an extent that an author referred in those days to the 'widespread Korean obsession with learning'.[13] In many instances, however, the burden of providing schooling was on communities, with little help from local or central governments. Whatever the case, primary school enrolment was nearly universal by 1960, and the demand for secondary and tertiary schooling was also extremely high by international standards. On the other hand, the role of university students in the events that led to the resignation of Syngman Rhee in 1960, and later on in the country's political history, testifies to the importance of universities in the social and political life of the country already in those days.

This appetite for education never dwindled, so that fast progress was achieved at the level of the whole population. According to the Barro and Lee database, the average number of years of schooling in the working-age population increased from 4.5 in 1950 to 7.12 in 1975.[14] As a basis for comparison, the same figure is still below six in Bangladesh and Tanzania, forty-five years

---

[13] Likewise, Seth (2002) talks about an 'education fever'.
[14] See Barro and Lee (2018).

later. South Korea was also ahead of other late industrialisers – for example, Singapore, Brazil, and Turkey – on several key education indicators, such as secondary and post-secondary school enrolment, the number of tertiary students abroad, and the number of engineering students as a proportion of university students. As a sign of the strong demand by the population for good education, Amsden (1989) mentions the fact that teachers in South Korea were relatively well paid in comparison with army officers – at a time when the military were at the head of the whole society – or professionals and technicians.

Despite this clear quantitative advantage, several weaknesses affected the educational sector, including too generalist a curriculum, a poor vocational training programme, and, above all and for quite some time, a clear over-supply of educated workers for the existing demand. There were periods characterised by high levels of unemployment among highly educated people, and the preparation of the first Five-Year Plan in 1963 found an excess of high-level personnel in the bureaucracy. This issue was sufficiently serious for the Park administration to impose quotas to reduce college enrolment at a certain stage.

Another important social aspect of the early decades of South Korea's development concerns the moderate degree of inequality of the distribution of income, its stability over time, and its impact on the speed of poverty reduction. A side issue is that of the maintained income balance between the rural and the urban sector, where the engine of growth of the whole economy lay.

The relatively low level of inequality in comparison to many developing countries at the same income level is partly explained by the agricultural reform that was launched at independence, which redistributed land from Japanese and large domestic landowners to small farmers and former tenants, with a 3 hectares cap on each farm. The reform also abolished the tenant status. Given the importance of agriculture at that stage of the development process, the impact on the equality of the income distribution was substantial. This was reinforced by the relative equality in the distribution of educational levels in comparison with many developing countries.

To prevent an increase in inequality, the challenge was then to maintain a balance between the booming urban sector, led by manufacturing development, and the agricultural sector. As mentioned earlier, the balance initially moved against the latter. On the one hand, productivity was often low because farm size was too small.[15] On the other hand, grain production was rather heavily taxed, making life extremely difficult for small farmers. Average productivity was low – see Table 5.1 – and, if it increased somewhat during the 1960s, this was because of the flow of under-employed agricultural workers towards employment in the expanding industry. In the 1970s, the government's action to level off productivity and incomes across sectors yielded effective results. Especially important had been the reversal of the production tax into a subsidy through guaranteed prices that were above market level. Some of the support

---

[15] See Kim, S. (2021) on the distribution of land in post-land reform South Korea.

to agriculture went through the Saemaul programme, which was the first community-driven development experience in the world. This programme was as much social as economic, one of its goals being to achieve rice self-sufficiency.

With a roughly constant distribution of income – except for some short-run fluctuation episodes – the reduction of poverty followed the continuous increase in mean income per capita. The poverty headcount – the proportion of people below a certain income threshold defined as the 'poverty line' – cannot be computed for Korea before 1965, due to a lack of representative household income and consumption expenditure data. However, available estimates for the following fifteen years suggest that the poverty headcount declined rapidly, from 40.9 per cent in 1965 to 23.4 per cent in 1970, 9.8 per cent in 1980, and 4.5 per cent in 1984.[16] Thus, poverty was virtually eliminated within twenty years.

Such was the spectacular economic take-off achieved by South Korea in the twenty-five years or so after the end of the Korean War and the division of the peninsula that had led to it. It is now time to describe the way that such results were achieved, or, in other words, the strategies that were designed to that end, as well as the institutional framework within which they were elaborated and implemented

V THE DESIGN OF EARLY DEVELOPMENT
STRATEGY AND POLICY

Much has been written to explain the South Korean 'miracle'. The point here is not to offer an exhaustive summary of that huge literature, which, as a matter of fact, is often focused more on East Asia rather than the single South Korean case – as can be seen from the influential 1993 World Bank report on 'The East-Asian Miracle'. The goal of the following pages is more modest. It intends to list the main policy decisions and economic practices that led to Korea's stellar development from the mid-1950s to the 1980s, as well as the institutional framework within which these decisions were taken, and these practices developed.

Three periods are traditionally distinguished in the early development of South Korea: the 1950s under the presidency of Syngman Rhee and its import substitution strategy; the 1960s under the military rule of Park Chung Hee and the extremely fast development of light manufacturing exports; and the 1970s under the dictatorship of Park and the ambitious bet on the development of

---

[16] See Choo et al. (1996). A rough calculation suggests that the 120,000 won poverty line for a household of five persons in 1981 used in these estimates corresponds to US$3.6 per person and per day at 2017 international prices, which is a standard poverty line. The resulting poverty rate of 40.9 per cent for South Korea in 1965 seems an underestimation in comparison with today's lower-middle-income countries. Yet if the level is probably underestimated, the rate at which poverty fell seems correct.

heavy industry. We will follow that order. Yet, because of the similarity of economic policymaking in the last two periods, they will be dealt with together, whereas a third subsection will explicitly handle the way the decision was made regarding the heavy industry venture.

A The 1950s: Recovery, Import Substitution, and Corruption

It is not clear why this early period of South Korean development has been given the 'import substitution' label. It was, rather, a disorganised period of economic recovery after independence from Japan and the Korean war, which would better fit the expression 'everything goes'.[17] It is true that imports played a dominant role since the production capacity of the economy was limited. This explains the early formation of big trading businesses, which took advantage of the relationship with Rhee's government to obtain import rights in certain key areas. As a matter of fact, this is when the first big South Korean business groups (*chaebols*) appeared or expanded, as was the case for Samsung, which had engaged in trading activities since the period of Japanese rule, or LG, which was founded in 1958 to provide the local population with imported home appliances. Progressively, however, these trading companies got into local production, benefitting as they did from comfortable import barriers.

As was seen earlier, the generalised climate of corruption, including a government that maintained itself in power through bribery, vote-rigging, and intimidation, a flourishing black market in foodstuffs provided by the United States, and rents granted to a few business groups through import rights or high-level protection, severely undermined Syngman Rhee's regime. Student protests and accompanying turmoil pushed him out of the political arena. However, the democratic government that replaced him did not prove more effective in improving the country's economic prospects or in curbing corruption or political decay.

B The Economic Policy under the Military Junta and the Park-Led Civilian Government

As a matter of fact, there was little difference between the military and the civilian governments headed by General Park. However, several institutional reforms that were to have long-lasting implications were imposed by the military junta, which could probably not have been affected otherwise.

1 The Revolutionary Objectives of the Military Power

The junta that took power after the coup of May 1961 did so explicitly to end the previous era of economic and social disorder and to put an end to corruption. With General Park Chung Hee at its head, it presented itself and its

---

[17] Seth (2013) talks about an 'unpromising recovery' when analysing this period.

overall programme as a 'National Revolution'. The words are important here because, in many respects, the beginning of Park's era as ruler of South Korea was indeed a revolution from the point of view of politics, institutions, and economic policy. This state of affairs did not change much when the junta gave way to a civil regime, with Park as president, in 1963, as the army remained extremely powerful and military personnel continued to be strongly represented in most high- and middle-tier state decision-making units. The initial revolutionary impetus of the junta thus remained present for a long time under Park's leadership. Its main dimensions may be briefly described as follows.

First, the military in power drastically modified the way the country and the economy were run. The army had inherited a strong sense of discipline from the Japanese era. Once the power struggle about who would command the junta ended, a rigorous, well-qualified, and corruption-free administration was set up. The bureaucracy was reformed by introducing within it a military structure, especially a deep respect for the hierarchy and a strict observance of orders coming from superiors. The change from the rather disorganised management that was in place before was drastic. At the same time, a powerful intelligence unit was installed whose mission was to reinforce Park's grip on the whole political and economic system, including, in some cases, some army factions. The KCIA played a key role throughout Park's rule. In particular, it was the KCIA that managed the reorganisation of the bureaucracy along the preceding lines, notably through major purges and a drastic reduction in the number of bureaucrats, by getting rid of those who were found to be ineffective and/or rent seekers.

Second, the junta, and Park at its head, wanted to truly revolutionise the way the economy was run, which implied two big changes: (i) the introduction of serious economic planning; and (ii) fighting corruption. On the first account, a true 'planning' attitude and practice was introduced in policymaking. Planning was not new in South Korea, but it was previously ineffective. In 1962, the first Five-Year Economic and Development Plan was launched, essentially a top-down set of policies designed and executed by a highly able group of civil servants, the Economic Planning Bureau (EPB), whose head practically had prime minister rank.

In regard to corruption, the junta arrested all those who were taking undue advantage of the previous disorder within the economic system: 'illicit' profiteers of all types, tax evaders, 'hoodlums, as well as Communist sympathisers.

Of very special interest, and of key relevance for the forthcoming development of the country, was the initial threat issued to the owners of big businesses – that is, the so-called *chaebols* – who had built up huge rents under the previous regime, that they could be dispossessed of their wealth and could see their enterprises nationalised. In a celebrated encounter between Park and Yi Pyong Chol, the founder, owner, and manager of Samsung, then the most powerful group in South Korea, the latter suggested that instead of expropriating them, it might be better to have the *chaebols* work to advance the junta's policy, while maintaining the threat of full expropriation in the case of non-compliance or misconduct[18] – which occurred later in the case of Samsung, which was caught up in a corruption affair and which had to hand over its fertiliser company to the state. This general deal between Park and the *chaebols*, despite the general mistrust of the former and the army in regard to business, was to become the spearhead of South Korea's astonishing industrialisation process.

Third, as part of this fight against corruption and despite the *chaebols*' owner-managers being conditionally spared, all banks were nationalised so that credit operations could be under full central control. Other state-owned companies already existed at the time the junta took power, or were created shortly afterwards. In general, they produced basic commodities or utilities such as energy, water, and transport infrastructure. The most famous was the Pohang Iron and Steel Company (POSCO), created at the time the Park administration decided to launch its HCI programme.

Fourth, Park, as well as the army, were openly anti-Communist, an attitude that can be easily understood in view of the deep rivalry with North Korea. However, things went deeper than mere political divergences. Communist North Korea was a constant threat, which required permanent surveillance of its possible links with people in the South, as well as heavy military investment, especially when the US military presence started to weaken in the late 1970s. Park embarked on his heavy industry programme and on the creation of POSCO partly so that South Korea would be able to produce military equipment. Another aspect of the anti-Communist bias of the regime that succeeded to the junta was its repression of unions and labour movements.

To these basic changes brought about by the shift to a military regime, which were tightly maintained afterwards, it is crucial to add some of the key ideas held by the ruler and the small group of advisers around him. These ideas, indeed, inspired his policy during his twenty-year hold over South Korea's economy and society, and to a large extent explain the development achievements that could be observed at the time of his death in 1980.

2 Park's Views about South Korean Development

A few fundamental principles inspired Park's development policy from the first moment of his accession to power. One was a strict rejection of Communism as an economic system, despite his youthful flirtation with Communist movements before the Korean War. However, this did not mean for him relying

---

[18] Actually, the story is quite dramatic. Shortly after the coup most *chaebol* owners had been arrested and were about to be dispossessed. Their lives were threatened and, of course, their companies had stopped operating. The US representative in Korea is said to then have convinced Park that it would be bad policy to destroy the most dynamic business group in the country. Yi Pyong Chol, the head of Samsung, then negotiated this deal with Park according to which the *chaebols* would cooperate but would be dispossessed if they did not comply with Park's policy. See Kim Hyung-A (2011: 94–96).

blindly on market mechanisms: the state had to have its say in development orientations. A second principle had to do with the example of Japan, which he knew rather well and had been able to observe as a former student in Tokyo's Military Academy. He reportedly repeated throughout his leadership that his goal was to reach the development level of Japan in a 'single generation'. Another principle was well portrayed in his familiar saying, 'rich state, strong army', which he understood as implying a two-way causal relationship: a strong army would allow business to prosper while being sheltered from North Korean actions, and a prosperous state would be able to afford such a strong army. But building a strong army also required developing some heavy industrial capacity. A fourth principle that guided Park's action was highly diplomatic: it was the care he took to preserve peaceful collaboration with the US administration and its representatives in Seoul. This had not always been the case under the previous regime. Some tensions arose at times between Park and the US representatives, but it cannot be denied that, overall, the United States played a huge role in South Korean development, not only through its financial assistance but also through its economic advice. The US interest in such a collaboration must not be underestimated either. In the geopolitical context of those days, it was important for the Western superpower and its promotion of market capitalism that South Korea succeed and clearly overcome Communist North Korea.

With such principles, and given the rivalry with North Korea, which was able to live for a while on the strong industrial base it had inherited at the time of the separation, the economic goal of Park's regime could not be other than the pursuit of the fastest possible economic growth.

3 The Light Manufacturing Export Drive of the 1960s
This quest for fast growth relied on two pillars: the export orientation of the economy and heavy investments in infrastructure. On both fronts, success was quick and stellar thanks to original, voluntarist, and clever policies. Yet it is the phenomenal progress in exports that calls for the most detailed explanation.

The choice of export orientation as a strategy of development was based on an assessment of development limits experienced in the previous period and the relative failure of protection to produce fast import substitution-based growth. The analysis by Park and his advisers at the EPB was that such a policy would not succeed because the domestic market was too small and economies of scale could not be developed; hence the export orientation emphasis of the first Five-Year Development Plan. But an objective is nothing without the right instruments to achieve it. This is where South Korea was extremely innovative.

The key to the extraordinary South Korean export drive in the 1960s lay partly in the reform of the exchange rate, partly in the authoritarian management of Park's team, partly in an effective bureaucracy (both in key administrations and in the nationalised banking system), and very much in the dynamism

of private enterprises. There is indeed a notable difference between this pragmatic approach to export-led growth and both the neoclassical explanation
that is often given of the South Korean miracle as the mere result of moving to
a 'free-market' and 'free-trade' economic regime (Balassa, 1988), as well as the
heterodox view that South Korean success was essentially the result of inspired
stewardship which went as far as 'getting the prices wrong', to use the words
of Amsden (1992).

The civil government before the junta had rationalised the foreign exchange
market by eliminating a complex multiple exchange rate regime and adjusting
the official rate to the rate observed in the curbed market. The won had thus
been devalued by some 160 per cent in the space of two years, and foreign
exchange management had been made simpler.[19] This increased the profitability of exports. The second impetus to exports was given by several types
of incentives provided to exporters, which comprised: (i) tax incentives; (ii)
tariff exemptions and credit facilities on imported inputs; (iii) export credits at
subsidised interest rates; and (iv) foreign currency loans. Among them, interest
subsidies were probably the most important: by 1965 the subsidised rate to
exporters was 6.5 percentage points for an official lending rate of 26 per cent –
and a domestic inflation rate of 13.6 per cent, making the real borrowing rate
of exporters negative.[20] Most importantly, however, these subsidised credits
were granted by the nationalised banking system conditionally on comply-
ing with export targets set by the government for large trading companies in
charge of exporting the production of medium or large *chaebol* companies,
which would soon be at the head of a true global distribution network. This is
where a competent and non-corrupt administration and banking system were
crucial. On top of this, the export targets were changed over time, based on
the objective of the Five-Year Economic and Development Plans and based
on firms' views on what they could achieve from one year to the next. These
targets were set in negotiations with high-level government representatives, if
not with Park himself for the largest *chaebols*.

Even with such advantages, it took extremely dynamic entrepreneurs to penetrate foreign markets and then to increase their market share. This is where
the *chaebols* played a huge and crucial role. In a few years, between 1962 and
1971, exports of light manufacture – wigs, clothing, footwear, and plywood –
increased by US$700 million (7 per cent of 1971 GDP), essentially starting
from scratch. Such rapid progress is doubtless proof of the strong ability of
Korean entrepreneurs not only to seize the opportunities offered by export and
industrial policy incentives but also to make their way in foreign markets. At
the same time, huge economies of scale made them increasingly competitive,
which also suggests that, thanks to multiple export incentives, they accumulated solid rents that could be reinvested in other activities.

[19] See Yoo, Yungho (2017).
[20] See Cho (1996).

The economy grew rapidly. GDP was multiplied by 2.5 between 1962 and 1971. Could it have continued to expand at the same pace, based on the same line of exports? Korea's world export share in clothing trade was only 4.4 per cent at that time, but, of course, was much less if the world market, including national production for domestic consumption, is used as the reference. Moreover, it turned out that clothing exports from South Korea would go on to increase by US$1,600 million between 1971 and 1976, when they amounted to 10 per cent of world exports. Why then did the Park regime decide to launch the HCI programme, deviating completely from successful labour-intensive manufacturing exports?

4 Park's Dictatorship, the Chaebols, and the Heavy Industry Venture of the 1970s

After the serious social turmoil surrounding Park's aspiration to a third mandate, which was contrary to the existing constitution, martial law was decreed, putting an end to all protest, and a new (Yushin) constitution was passed that gave Park nearly dictatorial power. He then bluntly pushed the economy towards heavy industry, despite the general opposition that had expressed itself before the promulgation of the new constitution, and against the wishes of several of his advisers and top experts in ministries and government agencies, who favoured the continuation of the light manufacturing export strategy. Park's motivation might have been his ambition to replicate the Japanese development model 'in a single generation', but he also had a firm conviction that, in the very long run, light industry, including in those days consumer electronics, was a dead end in the journey towards joining the club of rich countries.

The HCI strategy relied on two pillars. On the one hand, it was necessary to build a powerful steel industry that could provide the basic metallic inputs needed by lots of kinds of heavy manufacturing. The state-owned POSCO had already been included in the first Five-Year Development Plan as a strategic industry but had not been implemented due to a lack of resources. It was maintained in the second Five-Year Plan, despite the opposition not only of a large part of the civil society and the bureaucracy but also of the World Bank, which had turned down a loan request, and of the US representative. Funding was finally available thanks to the US$500 million reparations payment made by the Japanese government in the late 1960s. Construction of the steel complex started in 1970 and the first POSCO mill became operational in 1973, with a capacity that was apparently among the highest in the world.[21]

The second pillar of the HCI strategy relied on the *chaebols*, from which Park required extended efforts to make their way in heavy industry exports, always with the same strategy of offering huge advantages of various sorts and making them compete against each other in the pursuit of an export

[21] On POSCO see Rhyu and Lew (2011).

breakthrough in a specific industry. This kind of tournament rule of the game, plus the risk of bankruptcy in the case of failure, was indeed a clever way of making sure that competitors would do their absolute best to succeed.[22]

One of the best examples of that strategy was the launch of an export-oriented shipbuilding industry. South Korea was already producing small fishing ships, but it did not have the capacity to produce huge vessels of the type increasingly demanded by marine transporters and oil producers. Park invited three *chaebols* to get into that business – Hyundai, Daewoo, and Samsung – providing them with the same types of incentives as had been provided for light manufacturing exports but also with particularly import-ant subsidised credits from domestic banks, as well as publicly guaranteed foreign loans, and promising nice rewards to the winners. It was obviously a hugely risky bet for a country that was renowned for wigs, apparel, and footwear exports to get into this kind of heavy business. Hyundai won the race, with a rather daring gamble involving two simultaneous contracts: one for two tankers to be delivered to a Greek company, and another for the purchase of a shipyard design and shipyard equipment from the Japanese Mitsubishi. The tankers were built at the same time as the shipyard was con-structed. Both Samsung and Daewoo were also operational and active in that line of business a year later. Quite remarkably, South Korea soon became a major global actor in shipbuilding.

Not all industrial ventures under the HCI project did so well. Moreover, they were not always devoid of political machinations involving Park and close collaborators competing to succeed him. It was thus not uncommon for gener-ous state advantages to be provided to a *chaebol* for some industrial venture in return for funding political campaigns or other political expenses. The whole manufacturing export drive strategy launched in the 1960s progressively evolved towards crony capitalism due to the growing economic power of the *chaebols* and the financing needs of the political game played by the small team in power.

The car industry, an important component of the HCI programme, which finally produced Hyundai's Pony for the domestic market and then Latin America, is a good example of the intertwining of *chaebols*, Park and his close collaborators, powerful state executives in key positions, politicians, and for-eign multinational companies.

The story starts in the 1960s, when car assembling companies were launched as a substitute to car imports. Various *chaebols* were present at this time, supported by a particular political faction and associated with foreign constructors. According to the competition model imposed by Park, three *chaebols* competed in the domestic market, which was much too small to exploit economies of scale. Even so, protection made the business highly

---

[22] The following paragraph on the *chaebols* owes much to Kim and Park (2011), whereas the part that deals with the automotive industry relies greatly on Lee Nae-Young (2011).

profitable and fed both the *chaebols* and the political factions behind them. The EPB then imposed an increase in the number of locally produced parts and, a little later, requested the creation of a local engine plant for the whole industry, which would benefit from generous subsidised credit and access to guaranteed foreign loans. Competition then took place between a *chaebol*, Sinjin, partnering with General Motors, and Hyundai, initially associated with Ford and later with Mitsubishi. Because Hyundai intended to produce not only a local engine but a full car, it finally won the deal and benefited from additional help from Park's cabinet, drawing on the newly created National Investment Fund, based on compulsory deposits of savings collected by non-bank financial institutions. The Pony car was launched in 1975 in the domestic market, while Sinjin continued to assemble General Motors cars, which were now much less popular than the national brand. Other assemblers went bankrupt in the process.

The provisional end of the story is that Hyundai almost immediately sought to export the Pony to gain in economies of scale. The car was shipped to the Central American market. Yet, despite its record low price – in large part thanks to the huge subsidies received from the state – the car was of bad quality and exports failed to pick up. Advanced countries' markets were inaccessible because high marketing barriers and the low quality of the Pony. It took several years and the mediation of Japanese companies for Hyundai to enter the low end of the US market around 1985.

Even before the assassination of Park in 1979, the central government had lost its hold over the *chaebols*. They had become 'too big to fail' and enjoyed extensive freedom with respect to the government. Some of them had incurred big losses in several failed ventures and could not repay their huge debts. Yet they controlled too many activities and employed too many people to allow them to go bankrupt. They were generally bailed out by the nationalised banking system. It was only after the death of Park, and with a lot of difficulty, that the fabric of the *chaebols* could be rationalised through mergers in order to reduce this kind of risk.

Meanwhile, the state-owned steel company POSCO, heavily subsidised throughout its first years of existence, had been able to achieve international competitiveness, in large part thanks to Japanese technological support. By 1981, it was supplying not only the domestic market but also the Japanese market.

It is difficult to evaluate the exact contribution of the HCI drive to South Korean development. Judging from the following decades of industrialisation it looks like a resounding success. Yet, as suggested by the preceding examples, it was costly, not only in terms of the various business failures it produced, by the cronyism it triggered, and the economic inefficiency it generated when various *chaebols* competed in markets that were too small for them, but also the damage it caused to the rest of the economy, especially to the SMEs that were unable to obtain resources in a banking system almost entirely devoted to the *chaebols* and SOEs. Yet success was undeniably there. Exports increased by

US$18 billion – representing a stunning rate of annual increase of 22 per cent in volume – between 1970 and 1980, with a large and increasing contribution of heavy manufacturing and with the positive effects seen above on the whole economy. The lingering question, however, is whether the same result could have been obtained with another strategy that would have extended the light manufacturing drive, which had been so successful in the 1960s and continued to be so in the 1970s progressively towards more capital-intensive activities instead of this abrupt dive into heavy industry.

VI AN INSTITUTIONAL DIAGNOSTIC OF SOUTH KOREA IN THE MID-1970S

It is a challenge to produce a diagnostic of a country that did so well on both the economic and social fronts as South Korea, even when considering the country at a time when its development level was comparable to that of contemporaneous lower-middle-income countries. It is indeed tempting to say that the country got everything right. Looking at it from the standpoint of the late 1970s, however, the feeling might have been somewhat mixed. Analysts in those days would have been looking at a country that had taken off thanks to a specific set of institutions, initial conditions, and a strong will to access prosperity after half a century of privation, a country that took its chances as a labour-intensive manufacturing exporter with phenomenal discipline and effectiveness. However, they would also have noticed some late changes in the way the country and the economy fared. Success was still as phenomenal as it had been before, but the governance of the country had changed somewhat, with an omni-president running the country together with huge business groups about to become multinational corporations and intending to push the country forwards in a kind of breakneck race. As a matter of fact, a setback was not far off when Park was assassinated. The 1979 oil price boom revealed major weaknesses in the South Korean economy inherited from the heavy industry programme that had been pursued in the preceding years: a huge foreign debt, a high rate of inflation, a nationalised banking sector crippled by non-performing loans (NPLs), some major *chaebols* that were near bankruptcy (with potentially explosive effects on the whole economy), and possibly a change under way in the international trade order, with the second doubling of oil prices in a few years.

In view of such a situation, it seems logical to articulate an institutional diagnostic of South Korea in the late 1970s in two parts: one relating to the institutions built since the creation of the Republic of Korea, and the causes of their success in setting its remarkable export-led growth path; and another focusing on the changes that are perceptible when looking more carefully at the 1970s.

The 'diagnostic table' (Table 5.3) has been developed following the same principles as those used in the case studies of the IDP project, with a central column listing readily observable institutional strengths and weaknesses,

TABLE 5.3 *Institutional diagnostic table for the three periods of South Korean development until 1979*

Deep factors	Proximate causes	Institutional strengths and weaknesses	Economic consequences
		First and Second Republics (1953–1961)	
Education level	Reconstruction period	Imprecise long-run strategy	Slow growth
	Weak political regime	Rent-seeking and corruption	Weak macro policy (over-valuation of the currency, inflation)
Homogeneity		Land reform	Key role of imports
		Junta and Third Republic (Park civilian regime): 1962–1971	
War legacy	Military-style National Revolution	Effective planning cum market system	Explosive labour-intensive export-led growth
Northern threat	Japanese development template	Control of the financial system	Fast structural transformation
	Foreign aid	Efficient and disciplined bureaucracy	Contained inequality
		Clever export-led industrialisation incentive system	Foreign lending/debt
Difficult democratic learning process		Presidential control of big business	Increasing concentration of business sector
		Crony oligopolistic capitalism	Infrastructure development
		Repression of social movements	
		Fourth Republic (Park authoritarian regime, 1972–1979)	
Foreign influence Japan	Park's HCI objective	Centralisation of decisions around Park (bypassing planning design)	Move towards heavy industry exports (HCI)
US	Signs of elite capture	Autonomisation of *chaebols* ('too big to fail')	Booming exports and GDP growth
		Further concentration of production apparatus	Successful major industrial projects (POSCO)
		Excessive distortion of market mechanisms	Further development of infrastructure
			Mounting foreign debt
			Critical situation of some *chaebols*

a column to its right listing the main economic consequences, a column to its left listing their major proximate causes, and, finally, an additional column on the left-hand side listing the deep factors behind those causes. Note that, for the sake of conciseness and simplicity, no representation has been made of the causality relationships between the various items in each column for a given period. In effect, causality applies among whole sets of items in the various columns, rather than among items on the same row.

The originality of this table for South Korea is that it is broken down into three periods – the same periods that were used to organise the discussion in the preceding pages. The reason for this lies in the deep differences in the way institutions functioned in South Korea during the post-war period, during the period of the junta and the first Park terms, and the period after the Yushin constitution, which gave quasi-dictatorial powers to Park. Sticking to the strict diagnostic exercise announced at the beginning of this chapter, it might have been sufficient to focus on the last period. Enlarging the lens allows us to see the evolving nature of institutions and how the way they were defined and worked in a given period affected how they would perform in the next period. For instance, the 1961 military coup in South Korea and the type of institutions set up by the military junta and then by Park's administration cannot be understood without some knowledge of the previous period. Likewise, the situation in the late 1970s, which is the core subject of our inquiry, can only be apprehended by reference to the institutional setting and economic success of the preceding period.

The various entries in the table for the first two periods, as well as the list of 'deep factors', have been discussed at some length in the preceding pages and do not need further comments. The table essentially summarises what factors explain South Korea's remarkable development throughout the 1960s. Yet those entries will be helpful below in producing a diagnostic of the last period.

Examining South Korea in say 1978, at the time when its income level was roughly comparable to that of Bangladesh, Benin, Mozambique, and Tanzania in 2020,[23] and scrutinising it in the same way as we did for those four countries, what would be our conclusion?

The first conclusion is obviously that in the span of a few years South Korea had developed an institutional setting that was particularly effective for development purposes. While its income level was perhaps comparable to the IDP case study countries today, it could count on huge advantages in terms of the educational level of its population, an effective and competent bureaucracy, and major infrastructure capital. It could also rely on an effective economic policy machinery, based on a planning bureau populated by high-level

---

[23] It will be seen in Chapter 7 that the comparability holds mostly for Bangladesh. Rigorously speaking, income per capita in 2018 in Tanzania is equivalent to South Korea in 1970, while the correct reference would be 1965 for Benin and 1955 for Mozambique.

experts and a network of correspondents in the presidency, the ministries, state agencies, and nationalised banks.

Even though it was also set to evolve, this institutional setting was an enormous asset for future development. It was itself the joint result of various factors: (i) an ethnically homogeneous population eager to get out of dire poverty after forty years of Japanese rule and three years of a deadly war, and frustrated by an ineffective and highly corrupt government; (ii) an army that, implicitly siding with the population, had carried out a coup and installed a junta willing to operate a radical change in the way the economy worked; (iii) the Japanese model of development, which was well known to the leaders of the junta, that could be used as a template; (iv) a well-trained elite and a sufficiently educated population that could form a competent bureaucracy; (v) the rivalry with North Korea; (vi) the support of the United States; and (vii) a gifted, clever, ambitious, and patriotic leader. In a few years, and based on a vigorous export-led strategy, the South Korean economy had taken off.

Signs did exist in the 1970s that the machinery was evolving. First, centralisation had strengthened, and the planning entity had lost some power in favour of the president's office, in an effort by the latter to impose the HCI programme, which was far from consensual among top experts in the planning bureau and other administrative entities. Park's obsession with the HCI programme had much to do with some of the 'deep factors' listed in the diagnostic table. The hostile relationship with the Northern neighbour would at some stage make armament production necessary in the South, which would require massive heavy industry inputs, steel in the first place. Also, North Korea boasted a steel industry, which caused South Koreans to feel somewhat ashamed of their apparel, wig, and footwear exports. Finally, was it not the case that the steel industry had been a key factor in Japan's development and its military power?

Park's strong will to move on with the HCI programme to intensify industrialisation and to continue with hypergrowth was also behind the constitutional change that gave him quasi-dictatorial power (on top of the more obvious objective of muting the opposition and democratic forces). Yet this move towards heavy industry exports entailed changes in the relationship between the president and the *chaebols*, which were the spearheads of this new strategy. They had already acquired considerable economic power in the previous period. The intensification of industrialisation, which could not rely on medium-sized enterprises, gave them still more power. At the same time, because of their earlier success in international markets, they had acquired considerable autonomy with respect to the central power, through their size, the holding structure they adopted to control a batch of very diverse activities, and through their links with multinational corporations in domestic and foreign markets. Given the huge financing facilities granted to them by the central power, they were able to keep expanding, sometimes in extremely risky ventures, following their own strategies. Paradoxically, the centralisation of economic power in the presidency came with some loss of control over the *chaebols*. In addition, the *chaebols* were also important in providing resources that allowed Park to pursue political objectives at a time when the opposition, labour unions, and civil society were gaining vigour, in part as a result of the astounding economic progress of the past fifteen years or so.

More autonomous, because more economically powerful, and essential for the continuation of fast economic growth, the *chaebols* apparently did not enter the political game. Thus, it would be an exaggeration to refer to elite capture. What seems certain is that they implicitly had a say in regard to economic policy, which had not been the case a few years before. In effect, by the late 1970s South Korea was converging with those modern societies where captains of industry or CEOs of major companies are at the same time the vectors of economic activity and progress as well as major interlocutors – and in some cases economic guides to governments. Such an evolution was not necessarily negative, even though it did not fit well with an authoritarian regime.

Another consequence of the huge advantages given to the *chaebols* to enable them to perform their breakthrough in heavy industrial exports was a deeply distorted financial market, where state-owned banks could not fully play their role of efficient resource allocation agents because of the huge funding requirements needed for the *chaebols'* ventures and, in some cases, for bailing them out. Such financial repression by the central power could have been very effective in the 1960s at the time when the manufacturing export engine needed to be kickstarted, but it was not adapted to an economy whose volume had quadrupled and whose citizens were now three times richer.

The years after Park's death were difficult ones, not least because of the second oil price boom, which severely affected the heavy industry due to its energy needs, but which also revealed weaknesses in the economic fabric woven by the *chaebols*. Under Chun's dictatorship, several years were needed to put an end to the 'everything goes' attitude that had prevailed during the last years of Park's era, and to restructure the *chaebols* into a sustainable but still fantastically effective driver of industrialisation and development, thus ensuring the final success of Park's risky HCI bet.

VII CONCLUSION

Retrospectively, General Park's leadership was decisive in setting South Korea on a development trajectory that led the country from lower-income country status in the early 1960s to being admitted to the OECD club of rich countries less than forty years later. There was still a long way to go when he was assassinated, and the path has not always been an easy one. Without the vigorous take-off of the 1960s under Park, however, it is unlikely that South Koreans would have attained the prosperity they enjoy 60 years later.

The development of South Korea in the 1960s should indeed be an example for least advanced countries (LACs) today. As poor as some LACs are today, South Korea was very much disorganised after passing through a major conflict, was without natural resources, had no clear development strategy, and was home to a corrupt regime, but a radical turn towards a labour-intensive manufacturing export strategy was taken in two or three years and propelled the economy on a rocket-speed development trajectory. Its key assets on that journey were a capable and disciplined bureaucracy, a dynamic entrepreneurial class, a population eager to learn, and effective and smart (although authoritarian) stewardship.

The debate will probably still last quite some time about whether the authoritarian nature of that leadership should be considered as another favourable asset in the early development of South Korea. From an economic point of view, however, the point may not be so much the nature of the political regime but rather the stability that it brought, in contrast to what had been observed in the previous post-war period.

With the Japanese development model in mind, but short of funds, South Korea was able to exploit all opportunities that arose to increase the resources that could be invested in its development. But it is certainly in its management of the business sector and the attribution of what could be called 'conditional rents' that the country was most innovative and successful. Providing heavily subsidised funds and other advantages to light manufacturing exporters conditionally on reaching predefined objectives proved highly effective. The same can be said of the competition imposed later on *chaebol* conglomerates in the conquest of foreign markets in heavy manufacturing. Yet this strategy would not have succeeded without a skilled and transparent bureaucracy that was able to tightly monitor business. Even though it was successful, however, it must be recognised that this strategy was a real bet. It could have failed, which would have had dramatic consequences for development.

It also bears emphasis that the South Korean economy was not devoid of corruption. Business was also often asked to contribute to the campaigns of top politicians, including Park himself, to such an extent that towards the end of his era the *chaebols* had acquired real leverage over the government, which made regulating them less effective. As a matter of fact, this culture of corruption has not completely disappeared, as can be seen from the numerous scandals that continue to tarnish South Korean political life. In the case of South Korea, however, this might appear more the consequence of a successful development strategy based on the relationship between the state and business than as a handicap for the implementation of such a strategy. This does not mean it is costless, of course.

A last lesson of South Korea's early development for today's LACs concerns the distribution of income and the accumulation of human capital. Not only was the degree of inequality moderate by developing country standards, but it was remarkably constant. This low level of inequality is to be related in part to the land reform that was implemented upon the departure of the Japanese colonisers, but also to the homogeneous progress of education within the population throughout this period. In addition, there was a constant concern on the part of the leadership to avoid mounting imbalances between the rural sector and the highly dynamic manufacturing sector and ancillary activities in urban areas. This relative stability of the distribution of income permitted economic growth to translate immediately and effectively into the reduction of poverty. At the same time, it did not prevent democratic movements forcefully expressing their discontent whenever possible in the face of essentially autocratic regimes – until democracy finally prevailed.

6

Directed Development with Mixed Firm Types

Taiwan

I INTRODUCTION

There are several reasons why development scholars should be interested in the case of Taiwan. As one author has written: 'It once had a single dominant party following the Leninist model; it now has a competitive multiparty system. It was once a classic economic dependency relying on the sale of primary products (sugar and rice); it is today a leading exporter of manufactures. Its Land-to-the-Tiller programme offers one of the most successful examples of creating a foundation for social equity and balanced growth' (Chan, 2002: 174–5).

The achievements of Taiwan are so varied and impressive that it is justified to talk about 'Taiwan's development miracle'. After presenting some of the most salient achievements we will search for explanations behind them; thereafter, we will raise the key issue of their replicability in different contexts. Important indicators of Taiwan's success are as follows:[1]

a. Fast economic growth: The gross national product (GNP) grew at an average of 8.8 per cent between 1953 and 1986, and per capita GNP at 6.2 per cent during the same period. As a result, the relative gap in per capita income between Taiwan and most advanced economies was narrowed down at an amazing speed. Thus, while in 1971 the per capita income in Taiwan represented hardly more than 8 per cent of the per capita income in the United States, its share rose to a staggering 39 per cent twenty years later (in 1991). In the early 1990s, per capita income in Taiwan exceeded that of Greece and Portugal but was smaller than

---

[1] We make ample use of the data provided in Wade (1990a: 38–41, 64. See also the appendix tables in Li (1995).

that of Spain. In the 2020s, Taiwan occupies the fifteenth position in the ranking of the world's countries in terms of gross domestic product (GDP) per capita.

b. Fast economic growth, accompanied by unusually equal income distribution: Incomes in Taiwan are much more equally distributed than in the typical developing country and more equally distributed than in some rich advanced countries, such as the United States and Japan (and South Korea).

c. Rapid improvements in material welfare: In 1982, already, almost all households in the country had electricity, televisions, refrigerators, and motorcycles, while two-thirds had piped water, telephones, and washing machines.

d. Remarkable speed of the demographic transition: The rate of population growth decreased from 3.5 per cent in 1953–62 to 2.9 per cent in 1963–72, 1.9 per cent in 1973–82, and 1.2 per cent in 1986 – that is, a two-thirds fall within about thirty years.

e. Rapid increase in life expectancy, school enrolment, and literacy: Between 1960 and 1977, Taiwan, together with Hong Kong, performed better in both life expectancy and literacy than all other cases in a sample of 100 developing countries, both market and non-market (Communist) countries. By 1982 life expectancy at birth was seventy-five years for women and seventy years for men. Moreover, virtually all primary school-aged children went to school, almost all of them went on to junior high school, and 80 per cent of senior high school graduates went on to schools of higher education.

f. Rapid increase in earnings from manufacturing industries: Real earnings in manufacturing increased at a rate of 15 per cent a year between 1960 and 1980, a period during which Taiwan embarked on industrialisation.

g. Strong competitiveness in international trade: Taiwan is one of the most trade-dependent countries in the world (behind Hong Kong, Singapore, and some small petroleum exporters), and from being a leading exporter of agricultural products it has become a leading exporter of increasingly sophisticated manufactured products (most noticeably, TSMC, from Taiwan, is one of the world's leading chipmakers in the 2020s). While in 1955, 85 per cent of Taiwanese exports consisted of agricultural or processed agricultural products, based mostly on rice and sugar, industrial products made up no less than 90 per cent of total exports around 1990.

h. Taiwan's economic transformation happened within a short time period of twenty-five years in a context of remarkable macroeconomic stability, without inflation and without recession. A milestone in Taiwan's development was its relaxation of stringent foreign exchange controls that had been in place for four decades and which had made Taiwan's foreign exchange reserves the world's biggest after Japan (by 1987).

i. Political liberalisation and the democratisation of the country was initiated by the one-party state itself, and proved to be effective and sustainable.

These stunning aspects of Taiwan's performance have been achieved despite a number of adverse initial conditions. Let us mention the most important of these. First, the newly independent Republic of China had to accommodate a massive influx of immigrants from mainland China who relocated to Taiwan after the defeat of the nationalists against the Communists.[2] (In this respect, the situation of Taiwan closely resembles that of newly independent Pakistan, where immigrants from India settled in big cities and initially dominated politics.) The process did not go smoothly, and an ethnic conflict broke out which was caused by the seizure of political power by the mainlanders. This was despite the fact that the islanders had originally come from China two or three centuries before (Wade, 1990a: 232). Riots quickly erupted and a harsh repression followed, which saw 30,000 Taiwanese people killed in early 1947. In 1949, martial law was declared by the Kuomintang (KMT), the party of the Nationalist immigrants from China, which was to last for thirty-eight years and was used as a way to suppress the political opposition during the years it was active. During the White Terror, as the period is known, 140,000 people were imprisoned or executed for being perceived as anti-KMT or pro-Communist. Many citizens were arrested, tortured, imprisoned, and executed for their real or perceived link to the Chinese Communist Party. Since these people were mainly from the intellectual and social elite, an entire generation of political and social leaders was decimated. On the other side of the coin, a large number of the migrating mainlanders were trained and experienced professionals.

The second adverse initial condition faced by Taiwan is the fact that although the country is comparable in size to Belgium or the Netherlands, it has much less arable land and many more people to feed. The first feature is the result of the fact that two-thirds of the country is mountainous. To make things worse, not only does Taiwan have a rugged topography, but many of its agricultural soils are also of rather poor quality. As for the second feature, Taiwan started with a high population density that was partly attributable to the massive immigration from mainland China. This exceeded 230 people per square kilometre in the early 1950s (reaching 572 people per square kilometre in the early 1990s), which translated into a very high level of effective land pressure given the aforementioned soil characteristics. Finally, the country is endowed with few mineral resources and small quantities of natural gas.

How did Taiwan succeed in overcoming these adverse conditions to engender a continuous and rapid development process that has been considered

---

[2] In 1946, Taiwan's population was slightly more than 6 million, to which the flight from the mainland around 1949 added some 1.6 million people. By 1964, the population had doubled (Li, 1995: 132).

almost miraculous? To what extent can we attribute the country's success to other initial conditions that were favourable: in particular, the broadly impressive Japanese colonial legacy, and the massive financial and technical aid received from the US government, which in the 1950s equalled 43 per cent of gross investment (Chang, 1965: 152)? And to what extent is the success traceable to efficient institutions and policies? It is impossible to answer these questions since the specific contributions of these factors cannot be adequately disentangled. What can be convincingly argued, however, is that Taiwan has successfully exploited the available opportunities and the advantages it had at its disposal at the start of its development process. As will become clearer in this chapter, both the strategic and institutional choices made by the Taiwanese government, whether helped by US advisers and the Japanese legacy or not, displayed a remarkable degree of pragmatic wisdom and consistency. Moreover, they were backed by strong political resolve and a highly competent administrative machinery. In the following sections, we start by looking at the deep transformation of agriculture and the rural economy initiated in Taiwan after independence. Thereafter, we will try to understand in what ways the Taiwanese state has been a developmental state, a mixture of relation-based authoritarianism, a devoted and competent bureaucracy, and a state apparatus immune from pressures from private interests.

II TRANSFORMING THE RURAL LANDSCAPE

A Taking Stock of Impressive Achievements

One of the great challenges of development, as seen by Ragnar Nurkse (1953) and Arthur Lewis (1954), is how and how fast the surplus labour existing in a large low-productivity sector, whether it consists of agricultural or other informal economic activities, can be absorbed in a modern or formal high-productivity sector, typically industry (and associated services). What Lewis has called the 'turning point' or the 'commercialisation point' is the threshold beyond which the two sectors start competing with each other on an equal footing: that is, the high-productivity sector must be ready to raise its wages to be able to attract labour from the low-productivity sector. At this point, there is no more excess labour in the latter and labour productivity increases in both sectors. Development is under way. Another related way of defining the turning point is when the absolute size of the agricultural labour force starts declining in absolute terms despite a positive natural growth rate of the rural population.

What do we find for Taiwan? Although an ever-increasing number of farmers left agriculture to live and work in growing urban areas, the population pressure on farmland was severe, especially during the early 1950s (Fei et al., 1979: 46–7). Thus, the agricultural population increased by one-third between 1952 and 1964 (from 4.26 to 5.65 million people) and, since the total farmed area stayed more or less constant, this meant that the average farm size fell to about 1 hectare (from 1.3 hectares in 1952). A few years later, however, the size of the absolute population engaged in agriculture reached a peak of 6.15 million (in 1969), from which point it started to decrease sharply – in particular, until 1975, when it was only 5.3 million (Thorbecke, 1979: 185). The labour slack that had prevailed during the years 1950–65 had gradually become exhausted: thus, total worker-days of labour in agriculture dropped from a maximum of 306 million in the years 1966–8 to about 285 million in 1973–5. This was the combined effect of a reduction in the number of worker-days per average worker and of the total number of agricultural workers.

The occurrence of the Lewisian turning point in the second half of the 1960s is confirmed by the rise in the same period of the agricultural wage compared to that of factory workers (Thorbecke, 1979: Thorbecke, 1979: 185–6). Moreover, labour costs became the fastest growth component among all agricultural inputs and, as expected in these conditions, the multiple cropping index (i.e., the ratio of planted area to cultivated area), after reaching a peak of 187 per cent in 1965–9, decreased steadily to 139 per cent in 1985–9 (Wu Huang, 1993: 51). Logically, the drop in the share of the agricultural population in the total population fell even more dramatically than the absolute number of agriculturalists, namely from more than 52 per cent in 1952 to hardly more than 15 per cent in 1985–9 (Wu Huang, 1993: 51).

What did Taiwan do to bring about the advent of the turning point in such an exceptionally short period of hardly more than fifteen years? Did the transformation process conform to the Lewis (and Nurkse) model, in which the expansion of a modern (and urban) sector gradually absorbs the surplus labour released by a stagnant traditional (and rural) sector? In sum, the answer to the first question lies in the conjunction of rapid technological progress in agriculture and an unwavering drive towards rural industrialisation – two engines of change supported by purposeful policies and strong institutions. While the former force led to increases in land productivity followed by increases in labour productivity, the latter gave rise to a steady expansion of off-farm employment opportunities. The same factors are behind the answers to the second question and imply that the Taiwanese pattern of development does not strictly confirm the predictions of the Lewisian model.

The socioeconomic environment in which the structural changes occurred had itself been deeply transformed by an ambitious land reform programme which Taiwan's government embarked upon soon after independence, and which produced one of the most effective land redistribution schemes seen in the whole developing world after World War II. Its initial motivation was mainly political: the government, dominated by Chinese mainlanders and strongly authoritarian, wanted to buttress its legitimacy by winning widespread support among the rural masses of the island. Giving the bulk of rural dwellers making up the island's population, a stake in the new regime was the way that was chosen to achieve this result (Wade, 1990a: 241). It also helped a great deal that the KMT's 'catastrophic learning experience' on the mainland convinced its leadership that failure to carry out land reform in (mainland) China had been a crucial mistake that must not be repeated in Taiwan. In the specific context of the latter country, land reform was the easier to implement as the social status and prestige of the local landlord class had been irretrievably dented by their active collaboration with the Japanese colonial authorities (1895–1945).[3] Moreover, strong opposition by Taiwanese landlords was not feared by the new government because these landlords had been greatly intimidated by the violent suppression of dissent during the chaotic interregnum of 1945–7, and they knew that the regime was not beholden to their interests (Park and Johnston, 1995: 197–8). The undertaking turned out to be a major success, both in terms of its political objective and in terms of reducing inequality and boosting economic performance. The rural inhabitants thus became staunch and obedient supporters of the regime, at least during the first decades, while the landlords were forced out of agriculture. Rural inequality was dramatically reduced.

Regarding economic achievements, it is admittedly impossible to say whether the route chosen was more or less conducive to growth and development than what a hypothetical modernisation process based on the extant feudal structure would have been. What can be confidently asserted, however, is that given the path chosen, maximum effectiveness was probably attained by means of the policy and institutional strategies followed to emancipate small cultivators. Going one step further, a long tradition of development economists argues that small farms are more efficient than large farms under conditions of land scarcity and labour surplus (see Mill, 1848; Sen, 1960, 1966; Schultz, 1964; Chayanov, 1966; Berry and Cline, 1979; Feder, 1985; and, for a survey, Ray, 1998: 446–55).[4] For them, the idea that an alternative policy anchored in big feudal farms could have yielded better economic results just makes no sense. This is especially so because rice is traditionally the main staple food in Taiwan, and is a labour-intensive crop that, moreover, requires much care (i.e., not only the quantity but also the quality of labour matters). It is therefore particularly suited for small-scale agriculture in which the cultivator is the residual claimant. Revealingly, already in the 1920s and 1930s, when Taiwanese farmers adopted the high-yielding *ponlai* rice varieties, large landowners found it advantageous to rent out land to them in small parcels to be farmed intensively (Park and Johnston, 1995: 199).

---

[3] In 1895, China had to cede the island of Taiwan to Japan following its military defeat in the China–Japan war (1894–5).

[4] Thus, John Stuart Mill wrote in the mid-nineteenth century that 'The peasant proprietor is of all cultivators the one who gets most from the soil', and 'the land nowhere occupies, and feeds amply without becoming exhausted, so many inhabitants as where they are [small] proprietors' (Mill, 1848, II.VI.2: 259–60; and I.IX.4: 149. For a detailed discussion of Mill's contribution on this point, see Platteau, 1983: 441–5).

On the other hand, rice being regarded as a wage good, a sufficient supply was necessary for economic stability and as a hedge against inflation. These objectives were of paramount importance given the bitter experiences of the food shortages and hyperinflation of the 1940s, which contributed to the loss of the Chinese mainland. As one author has written: 'Against this historical background, Taiwan's agricultural policy gave the highest priority to price stability and food production for basic foodstuffs, especially rice' (Wu Huang, 1993: 54).

We can now proceed by examining the Taiwanese strategy for rural development in more detail.

B Radical Land Reform

The land reform process was implemented quickly but in three gradual stages: rent reduction, public land sales, and the Land-to-the-Tiller Programme. These three steps had the drastic effect of converting in a very short period a landlord-tenant system to owner-cultivator agriculture based on small farms (see Koo, 1971; Thorbecke, 1979: 172–6). Initiated in 1949, the rent reduction programme limited farm rents to a maximum of 37.5 per cent of the annual yield of the major crop. This ceiling was significantly below the 50 per cent level historically practised in the more fertile areas. The immediate effect of this measure was to improve the lot of the tenants, while correspondingly reducing the incomes of the landlords and land values. The second stage of the reform consisted of the sale of public land that had been acquired after World War II from the Japanese colonisers. This land was made available for purchase by farming families and, to encourage the 'equalisation' of land ownership, the quantities that could be acquired by a single family were strictly limited.

Finally, the third and most important step in the land reform process was the Land-to-the-Tiller Programme, promulgated in 1953. It provided that any land in excess of 2.9 hectares was to be confiscated by the government and redistributed. The effect was to practically eliminate the upper tail of land distribution and to drastically reduce the proportion of tenants.[5] In the absence of a sizeable landless class, the transformation of non-owners of land into peasant owners did not cause the average farm size to be unviable. As for the landlords, they were compensated in two ways: they received commodity bonds carrying an interest rate much smaller than the market rate, and shares of stock in four big industrial firms. The monetary value of the compensation was calculated as the equivalent of 2.5 times the annual yield of the major crop, which was considerably below the average market value of paddy

---

[5] Between 1949 and 1961, the proportion of owner-cultivated land in the country's total agricultural area increased from 59 per cent to 90 per cent, while the proportion of tenant-operated land was correspondingly brought down from 41 per cent to 10 per cent (Chang, 1965: 157).

fields. Ho (1978: 271–4) estimated that the resulting wealth redistribution effect represented approximately 13 per cent of Taiwan's GDP in 1952. He also calculated that the increase in the income of the average tenant between 1948 and 1959 (the year in which he would become an owner-cultivator) was about 6.5 times higher than what it would have been had he remained a tenant benefiting only from the rent reduction measure (increases of 107 per cent and 16 per cent, respectively). Because landlords promptly sold their industrial stocks at prices far below value, and because a large portion of the proceeds went to consumption, the majority of them ended up being not much better off than the new owner-cultivators (Yang, 1970, cited from Fei et al., 1979: 43).

As we have learned from numerous disappointing experiences of land reform across the world, a redistribution of land can achieve its objectives only if effective accompanying measures are set in place as early as possible to raise farm incomes through increased land productivity (see, for example, Kikuchi and Hayami, 1978). On this level, too, Taiwan was remarkably successful. The complementary measures were not only designed and implemented almost immediately after land had been redistributed, but they were also comprehensive and supported by strong institutions, resulting in continued output growth during the transitional period and later. During the 1952–64 period, the net agricultural output grew by an impressive 80 per cent (5 per cent a year): that is, at a much more rapid pace than the agricultural population, which increased by about one-third (Fei et al., 1979: 47–8). This included infrastructural investments, such as in irrigation and feeder roads; the provision of credit and extensive services; the organisation of input delivery (chemical fertilisers, high-yielding seed varieties adapted to local soil conditions, water pumps for drainage, etc.) and output marketing; price stabilisation; and, last but not least, the strengthening and transformation of the farmers' associations inherited from the Japanese colonial period (Cheng, 2001: 21). Also noteworthy are the considerable resources put into agricultural research. Thus in 1960 Taiwan had 79 agricultural research workers for every 100,000 persons active in agriculture, compared with 60 in Japan, 4.7 in Thailand, 1.6 in the Philippines, and 1.2 in India (Fei et al., 1979: 49).[6]

Agricultural development in Taiwan did not only result from well-thought-out policies but also from strong support organisations. The Chinese–American Joint Commission on Rural Reconstruction (JCRR), which was almost totally financed through US aid funds, played a critical role in agricultural research, extension, and innovation, as well as in the planning and implementation of Taiwan's strategy for agricultural growth. The JCRR was a major catalyst for harnessing resources and ensuring their best use within the perspective of an owner-cultivator model of rural

---

[6] Foremost among the dedicated establishments were the Taiwan Agricultural Research Institute and the District Agricultural Improvement Stations.

development. Since it was insulated from the daily political and bureaucratic pressures of the relevant ministry or administration, the JCRR could take a long-run view of the whole process (Thorbecke, 1979: 201–2). In this respect, the importance of the international context, and the Cold War in particular, cannot be overestimated. Whereas the United States helped to introduce radical social and economic reforms in its Cold War allies in East Asia, it tended to be a conservative influence working against such changes in Latin America (Chan, 2002: 183). This differential approach is explained by the presence of a serious threat from Communism in the latter region, and its near absence in the former.

In addition, as pointed out by Eric Thorbecke (1979: 181): 'Perhaps the most noteworthy feature of agricultural planning in Taiwan has been the attempt at local participation. Starting with the First Plan, government agencies were required to specify goals on a county-by-county basis in consultation with local people and taking local conditions into account'. Whereas the farmers' associations and credit cooperatives set up by the Japanese to facilitate agricultural extension were top-down institutions dominated by landlords and merchants, the Taiwanese government and the JCRR decided to organise farmers into multipurpose farmers' associations whose membership was restricted to cultivators, to serve their exclusive interests. These were gradually expanded to include not only irrigation associations but also a credit department, which not only granted loans to farmers but also accepted deposits from them, and to provide facilities for purchasing, marketing, warehousing, and processing. In the words of John Fei and co-authors (1979): 'The associations thus became clearing houses for farmers, who controlled and maintained them and viewed them as their own creatures' (p. 45). At the same time as these associations grew in importance, credit became available to farmers from the JCRR, government-owned banks, and government agencies catering to the needs of farmers. That their entry into the rural credit business was effective is attested to by the fact that farm loans provided by the official channel and formal institutions soon came to represent the lion's share of the total (Ho, 1978: 179–80). The close relationship between farmers and their local multipurpose associations thus played a major role in promoting agricultural development by reducing liquidity constraints and transaction costs (Park and Johnston, 1995: 200).

If it is true that the farmers' associations were tightly controlled by the Nationalist party in power, it is equally true that the party was eager to involve the farmers in order to best meet their needs. Additional functions serving the same purpose were also fulfilled by so-called public service centres, of which there was one for each township. Staffed by full-time party officials whose job was to ensure that things evolved in line with the party's interests and recommendations, they included an extension section that organised farming study groups, training courses, and demonstrations (Wade, 1990a: 242; Park and Johnston, 1995: 200).

C Rapid Technological Change in Agriculture

The problem of land pressure was overcome in three ways: through substantial increases in land productivity at the intensive margin; through the diversification of agricultural production into more profitable crops; and through the part-time reallocation of labour to off-farm activities. In this subsection we deal with the first two points while the third one is deferred to the next subsection.

Increases in agricultural production stemmed from two sources: increased yields in traditional crops, such as rice and sugar, and the introduction of new crops. The first result was obtained thanks to a combination of factors. One of these consisted of the expansion of fixed capital, which increased by one-third during the years 1952–64, mainly as a consequence of investment in irrigation and flood control facilities and of the introduction of small tillers to replace water buffalo, and other small mechanical devices. Moreover, and thanks to the adequate supply of credit, working capital grew even more dramatically than fixed capital (by as much as 140 per cent during the same period), reflecting the continuous introduction of new seed varieties, chemical fertilisers, pesticides, insecticides, and commercial feeds. What bears emphasis is that the technological change was generally of the labour-intensive and land-and-capital-saving type. This effect was reinforced by the shift to more labour-intensive crops, such as vegetables, some of which – for instance, mushrooms and asparagus – require considerable amounts of labour per land unit (Fei et al., 1979: 48–50; see also Lee and Chen, 1979).[7]

Finally, thanks to the considerable attention given to agricultural growth and development, substantial savings could be transferred from agriculture. The net real capital outflow from the agricultural sector in the form of rents, interest payments, taxes, and others was positive throughout the pre-turning point period. More specifically, the compulsory purchase scheme for rice, and the rice-for-fertiliser barter programme, were implicit taxes that exceeded the total income tax of the whole economy almost every year before 1963 (Kuo, 1975: 161).

A major lesson to keep in mind is that, during the critical period which preceded the reaching of the Lewisian turning point, when agricultural population continued to increase (although at a reduced pace), the number of working days per worker steadily increased while the number of working days per hectare of land rose even more dramatically (from 170 in 1948–50 to about 260 in 1963–5).[8] This being said, the smaller farms remained unable to generate sufficient income, or to keep the entire family workforce fully employed, and, for them in particular, the availability of off-farm income-earning opportunities

---

[7] Thus, the cultivation of one hectare of asparagus required 2,900 times the labour input of the cultivation of one hectare of rice (Fei et al., 1979: 50).

[8] The number of worker-days increased by 17 per cent between 1952 and 1964, which is more than the rate of increase in the number of persons employed in agriculture (12 per cent).

was of great consequence. Since the average farm size more than halved between 1940 and 1970, it was also helpful for many other farming households. In 1970, 44 per cent of Taiwanese farms contained less than 0.5 hectares of cultivated land (Ho, 1979: 88).

D Rural Industrialisation

Equally remarkable was the success achieved by the government's rural industrialisation programme, which really started after the mid-1950s. Between 1956 and 1966, manufacturing employment increased at a yearly rate of 7.2 per cent in rural Taiwan, substantially faster than the rate of increase in urban areas. Paradoxically, therefore, the share of the rural sector in the country's manufacturing output increased during that pivotal transitional period leading up to the turning point. In 1966, agriculture employed just 54 per cent of the rural labour force while manufacturing employed 10 per cent (as compared to 20 per cent for urban Taiwan). Thanks to the decentralised industrialisation drive, an increasing number of farm households were able to combine farming with part-time or full-time employment in non-farm activities, thereby easing the pressure of the population on the land and reducing their incentive to migrate to cities.

In 1970, full-time farm households (those whose income was entirely obtained from agricultural activities) comprised only 30 per cent of all farm households (compared with 45 per cent ten years earlier), while those who earned more income from side-line activities worked out at 29 per cent (compared with 23 per cent ten years earlier). In addition, the proportion of family farm workers engaged in off-farm activities (for at least thirty days a year) increased from about 25 per cent to more than 31 per cent during the years 1960–70 (Ho, 1979: 88–9). The sector-wise distribution of farm household members who worked off their farms indicates that while one-third of them were engaged in activities associated with agriculture, fishing, and forestry (foremost among which were working as hired hands on other people's farms, and fish culture), as many as 26.5 per cent were found in manufacturing and mining (with 11.7 per cent in commerce; 5.8 per cent in home handicrafts; and 5.6 per cent in public administration and education). Five industries represented the bulk of rural manufacturing employment: food, textiles and apparel, metal products, chemicals, and machinery and equipment. The rural areas absorbed the largest shares of the increase in employment between 1956 and 1966 in textiles and apparel (55 per cent), food (57 per cent), wood products (including furniture) (41 per cent), and non-metallic mineral products (63 per cent). Note that, as expected, rural industrial establishments had an average size smaller than their urban counterparts and they were also more labour-intensive (Ho, 1979: 83, 88–89, 95).[9]

---

[9] Fixed assets per person employed in rural areas were about half those in urban Taiwan. There were two exceptions to the rule of higher labour intensity in rural areas: in the food, and in the pulp and paper industries, the capital intensity was higher in rural than in urban areas (Ho, 1979: 85).

The growing contribution of off-farm employment to farm household income is evident from the following evidence. From 1952 to 1972, the real income of an average farm household more than doubled, with the larger part of this increase being attributable to the very rapid growth in income from off-farm activities (a minor part was caused by rising agricultural productivity). More precisely, an average farm household earned 13 per cent of its income from off-farm sources in 1952, 25 per cent in 1962, 34 per cent in 1972, and 43 per cent in 1975. Revealingly, the income of farm families was strongly correlated with the share of their income obtained from non-agricultural sources. Access to sources of non-agricultural income was thus a key determinant of household welfare, especially for small farms which relied more on these sources than larger farms. Partly because of this inverse relationship between farm size and resorting to off-farm employment, the distribution of income among farm families became increasingly equal (Ho, 1979: 77, 90–2).

Two other interesting features deserve mentioning. First, a large number of farm household members obtained clerical jobs, an achievement that would have been impossible if the rural population had not been reasonably well educated. Second, a large share of those employed in full-time off-farm jobs were women (about 40 per cent in 1970). They were found in large numbers not only in home handicrafts activities but also in manufacturing and mining, where they comprised 42 per cent of the total number of household members employed full-time (Ho, 1979: 89).

The question naturally arises as to what enabled Taiwan to successfully implement a decentralised model of industrialisation. An array of factors were at play (see Ho, 1979: 93–5). To begin with, on the demand side, rural industrialisation was facilitated by the presence of a highly commercialised and productive agricultural sector, which provided an expanding demand for all sorts of non-food consumer goods and services, as well as for material inputs and capital goods used in agriculture. Being location-specific, most services demanded by farm households were locally provided. As for goods, those with relatively high-income elasticities, such as furniture, household utensils and furnishings, and clothing were produced in small to medium-sized firms operating in rural areas. In addition to a high level of agricultural commercialisation and technological development, two factors came to play a determining role in stimulating demand for industrial products. First, increasing rural incomes was a central policy goal of the Taiwanese government and it achieved a remarkable degree of success as early as the 1960s, despite consistent extraction of resources from the agricultural sector. Second, Taiwan enjoyed a low degree of income inequality (even before the 1949–53 land reform), thereby ensuring a large base for the expansion of demand linkages (Park and Johnston, 1995: 184–9).

Alongside this demand-side force, a series of supply-side factors must be mentioned. First, the government decided to continue the colonial Japanese policy of promoting large-scale agro-industrial firms in the countryside (in the colonial period, these were mainly sugar refineries). When the sugar industry went into decline (after Taiwan lost the protected market of Japan), efforts were directed towards the development of new food-processing industries, particularly the canning of vegetables and fruits, the entire production of which was exported. Second, the rural areas of Taiwan were blessed with effective infrastructure. For one thing, the rugged mountain chain that runs from the north-eastern corner of the country to its southern tip forced farms and the rural population to concentrate in the western part, an area endowed with a particularly well-developed transport system. As a result of massive public investments made by the government, combined with the infrastructure inherited from the Japanese, Taiwan came to enjoy not only a trunk road and a rail track connecting its two main port and industrial cities (Taipei in the north and Kaohsiung in the south), but also a very dense network of paved roads and highways, feeder roads, and railroads in its western portion.[10] For another thing, rural electrification, which began early in Taiwan, had reached 70 per cent of its farm households by 1960.

Last but not least, Taiwan had human capital that was ready to support rural industrialisation. Here again the country benefited from the Japanese legacy. In the 1930s the colonial power had embarked on an intensive programme to educate the islander population, with a special focus on primary education in rural areas. After independence, this effort was actively pursued by the new authorities, so much so that, when rural industrialisation was initiated, a highly literate workforce was available all across the country (nearly 90 per cent of the total population over the age of six was literate).[11] In addition, two-thirds of the farm population had some formal education. A lack of semi-skilled labour was thus not an obstacle to the growth of rural industry. On the contrary, 'a plentiful stock of disciplined, literate, and highly adaptable rural labour' constituted the most valuable resource of the country and 'an important nexus of agricultural-industrial interactions' (Park and Johnston, 1995: 189–91). Also worth stressing is the important supply of industrial entrepreneurs, in rural areas particularly, who started their careers as agricultural workers, small agents, or traders for agricultural products, and as owners of small workshops (e.g., metalworking for simple agricultural tools), or who were the children of those occupying such positions (pp. 192–5). This echoes the way modern entrepreneurship historically developed in Japan and other Southeast Asian countries (Smith, 1959; Hayami and Kikuchi, 1982). It seems that over time many farmers became

---

[10] The density of paved highway and feeder roads was 76.4 km per 1,000 sq. km in 1962 and 214.5 in 1972, which was very high in comparison with other developing countries.

[11] The employments share of workers with primary or no education, secondary education, and higher education went from 90, 8.8, and 1.2 per cent, respectively, in 1952, to 46.8, 41.7, and 11.5 per cent, respectively, in 1981 (Park and Johnston, 1995: 191).

experienced users of markets, and acquired a good understanding of the functioning even of export markets.[12]

In the same connection, it bears emphasis that during the years 1952–86, the growth of domestic market demand was much more important than export growth in regard to labour absorption. In a dynamic context in which newly emerging sectors require time to gain experience and become internationally competitive, the importance of domestic demand as a predecessor of export demand appears to be critical.[13] As we are aptly reminded by Albert Park and Bruce Johnston (1995), significant export sectors for manufactured products, such as the textile sector in a first phase of industrial development, began as relatively inefficient producers for the domestic market (pp. 183–4).

E The Subsequent Stage of Agricultural Transformation

Taiwan's growth and development model clearly differs from the Lewis model. Whereas in the latter the rural sector is conceived as just a reservoir of labour that is underutilised in agricultural activities and is available for absorption in a dynamic urban industrial sector, in Taiwan growth was engineered simultaneously in the two sectors. In the rural sector, increasing income came not only from technological innovations and shifts in crop choice in agriculture, but also, and to an even greater extent, from the expansion of labour-intensive rural industries. As a result of these two forces, both land productivity and the productivity of household manpower grew steadily. Furthermore, with women's increasing participation in off-farm employment expansion came a declining trend in fertility rates and rural population growth: the crude birth rate for the whole of the island fell from 37.7 per 1,000 inhabitants in 1961 to 27.2 in 1975 and 23.0 in 1979, a large part of this decrease being attributable to a fall in marital fertility. This trend accelerated when the demand for a smaller family size among the Taiwanese population was matched by an active official policy of family planning.[14] Taiwan was thus unique in its capacity to reach,

---

[12] From personal interviews, Park and Johnston found that it was easy to come across entrepreneurs from peasant families who succeeded thanks to their ability to perceive market opportunities and to adopt upgraded technology (Park and Johnston, 1995: 194). They gradually climbed the steps of increasingly sophisticated products, such as when they moved from the manufacturing of simple agricultural tools to the production of spare parts, power tillers, fans, and other simple electrical equipment, and even electronic products (see also Johnston and Kilby, 1975).

[13] In Taiwan, farm exports accounted for more than 90 per cent of total exports as late as 1955 (Park and Johnston, 1995: 184).

[14] This had to wait until the Fourth Economic Development Plan (1965–68), which included family planning as part of its public health plan, and the medical care programme as part of its manpower plan (Li, 1995: Chap. 4, 140, and Table 4.2 on p. 147, in particular). Yet, even before that date, the JCRR's Rural Health Division played a key role in the reduction in infant and child mortality and in the introduction of family planning programmes. According to Park and Johnston (1995: 200), these programmes achieved remarkable success in bringing down fertility rates and, hence, in contributing to slowing down the rise in the excess labour supply in rural areas.

in an amazingly short space of time, the point from which rural real incomes increased and the rural workforce decreased in absolute terms.

From then on, the same forces continued to operate. In particular, the proportion of full-time farm households fell from 49.3 per cent to 13.0 per cent between 1960 and 1990. Moreover, in the latter year 30.0 per cent of these households were aged farmers who largely lived on transfers received from relatives or other sources. On average, off-farm income represented 63.0 per cent of the total income of all farm families in the late 1980s, up from 40.7 per cent in 1965–69. On the other hand, the increase in the real cost of agricultural labour resulting from growing shortages of rural labour induced a fall in the multiple cropping index, measured by the ratio of planted area to cultivated area (Wu Huang, 1993: 51–2).[15]

Government policy quickly adapted to the new circumstances: thus, the agricultural programme of the Fifth Economic Plan (1969–72) called for the improvement of labour productivity instead of land productivity, with the objective of raising the farmers' income. This marked the end of the era of the so-called 'development of agriculture to foster industry, and the beginning of a new chapter of agricultural policy aimed at shifting from taxing to subsidising farmers. At the same time, there was acute awareness of the need to enlarge the size of farm operations so as to increase the use of mechanisation and thereby overcome the labour constraint. Under the farm mechanisation programme initiated in the 1970s, the government underwrote half of the cost of grain dryers, power tillers, and similar equipment, in an effort to free more labour for non-agricultural activities (Park and Johnston, 1995: 201). But it was only later, with the second phase of the farmland reform programme launched in 1983, that the government officially stated its intention to encourage the consolidation of farm plots into larger entities. Because it was reluctant to modify the existing land ownership structure, and continued to adhere to rigid land regulations that prevented the emergence of an open land market, the programme consisted of non-market initiatives, such as joint decision-making in specific operations, joint management, contract farming, and the promotion of specialised production areas. These measures were not sufficient to achieve the goal of farm size enlargement on a large scale. The fact of the matter is that the government did not want to lose the political support of the peasantry and confront the traditional attachment to land (Wu Huang, 1993: 55, 60).

What eventually aroused the opposition of farmers, especially after 1987, when rapid political liberalisation occurred, was another plank of the new agricultural policies, namely the move towards agricultural trade liberalisation. Initiated under the pressure of the United States towards the late 1970s, the policy was based on scheduled stage-by-stage reductions in tariffs and non-tariff barriers for agricultural goods. Agreed in exchange for US

---

[15] After reaching a peak of 187 per cent in 1965–9, the index value decreased steadily to 139 per cent in 1985–9 (Wu Huang, 1993: 51).

concessions on industrial products, these measures had the effect of transforming farmers from long-time obedient and staunch supporters of the regime into more independent actors ready to undertake rebellious actions against the government. The atmosphere was politically charged as fears of major disruptions were fuelled by the phasing out of sugar operations and the rapid decline of Taiwan's world-renowned canned food exports in the late 1980s.[16] But the opposition did not really succeed in changing the government's mind. In the subsequent plans, the authorities continued to assert their intention of transforming Taiwanese traditional agriculture into a modern sector open to foreign competition and based on internationally competitive products (Wu Huang, 1993: 55–9).

Similarly on the industrial front, growing labour scarcity persuaded the technocracy to encourage diversification into increasingly more sophisticated export products; and economic liberalisation, when it came, aroused the opposition of firms that were used to being sheltered from the full pressure of international competition (Cheng, 2001: 34–6).

III TAIWAN'S DEVELOPMENTAL STATE

Often dubbed a developmental state, the Taiwanese state proved remarkably effective in propelling the country on the path to sustained growth and development. Most important among its pro-development characteristics were its unified decision-making structure and its total dedication to long-term objectives, its autonomous bureaucracy, and its insulation from private interests and lobbies. In the following, we elaborate on these three attributes.

A A Nationalist One-Party System

To begin with, modern Taiwan was built on the basis of a one-party state system that, rather paradoxically, followed the Leninist model (Chan, 2002: 174). Until the political liberalisation that started in the mid-1970s, it was no doubt authoritarian, yet not totalitarian.[17] The Taiwanese regime during this period can best be defined as one of 'authoritarian corporatism' (Wade, 1990a: 27). To understand how this could be established in the country, it must be borne in mind that Taiwan 'had never been an independent state with its own indigenous bureaucracy and landed elite' (p. 231). For fifty years, the Japanese had imposed on the local population the rule of a strong colonial state which stood above and apart from a weak civil society. The colonial administrative

---

[16] Various export corporations for pineapple, mushrooms, and asparagus ceased operations in 1988 and 1989.

[17] In particular, there was a limited recourse to the development of a fully blown cult of the leader and to the massed politics of the street. Moreover, the nation was not presented as an extension of the family (Wade, 1990a: 249).

structure penetrated right down to the village level and ensured that no local formal organisation came into existence beyond kinship and residential groups. Furthermore, not only did the colonial authorities prevent wealth accumulation in the hands of their Taiwanese subjects, but they also kept them out of senior managerial positions in large-scale commercial and governmental organisations (they even prohibited the founding of religious institutions, such as Christian churches). It is therefore not surprising that when they were chased out, the Japanese left behind them a leadership and managerial vacuum (Wade, 1990a: 232).

Contrary to what was observed in many postcolonial countries, in Taiwan the vacuum was filled by the incoming mainlanders, from whom the islanders had been cut off during the years of Japanese occupation. The only 'legal' basis of legitimacy for political takeover by the former rested on their claim that they were the rightful government of the entire country of China. Coming to power as though it was occupying an unfriendly region, the mainlanders' party organisation, the KMT chose to impose strict controls on the population and was little inclined to bargain with established groups or organisations. Much as in the case of Japanese colonisation, the weakness of existing organisations and elites made the task rather easy (Wade, 1990a: 233–4). It is noteworthy that, in transplanting itself to Taiwan, the KMT succeeded in shaking off its predatory nature and in providing political space for technocrats to implement a series of industrialisation programmes and strategies (Cheng, 2001: 19).

The KMT landed in Taiwan equipped with a ready-made ideology defining the appropriate relations between state, party, and society. The central tenet was that, first, only a powerful military and a strong government could enable the island to regain control of mainland China, and, second, that this mission justified minimal commitments to existing social groups and limited the reliance on markets. Those two forces were indeed regarded as potential threats that could constrain state actions. As stressed by Robert Wade (1990a), the KMT's Nationalist ideology was of a special kind since the largest part of the nation lay outside the border. It could therefore afford to be more uncompromising in the sense of refusing all bargains or agreements that could jeopardise the goals of national development and reconquest (1990: 234–5). State control was very encompassing since the KMT had effective control over all social groups, via the incorporation into its party structure of sector-based associations, such as those for labour, state employees, women, students, intellectuals, and various professions. Its hand was so strong that it was able to direct and mediate the selection of leadership for these associations, thus operating according to the principle of democratic centralism. Needless to add, the outspoken local elite were either co-opted or suppressed (Chan and Chu, 2002: 198).

Because of its belief that its defeat by the Communists had partly been caused by what it considered party indiscipline, the KMT simultaneously set to tighten the party's organisation and to purge it of its unreliable elements. Factionalism within the party was bridled, with the effect of making the party state not only an omnipresent but also a coherent entity placed under the paramount leadership of general Chiang Kai-shek. In sum, the mainlander leaders saw themselves as being at war, thereby vindicating the creation of a one-party state and the promulgation of the longest-running period of martial law in the world (Wade 1990a: 235–7; Cheng and Chu, 2002: 198).

The issue then is how the new regime succeeded in infusing its ideology into the population. The answer lies in the significant efforts made by the government to create a common Chinese-ness amongst Taiwanese citizens, through the school system and intensive campaigns of 'ideological moulding'. These efforts were centred on the diffusion of the three central values of the nation, the family, and obedience to authority, rallied around the symbols of Sun Yat-sen, Chiang Kai-shek, and the national flag (Wade 1990a: 243–6). As we have seen earlier in the case of the rural population, however, the major way used by the authorities to establish their legitimacy consisted of economic development and more equal income redistribution.

Even aside from these formal, corporatist channels, many people had contacts with the political-economic establishment via their personal networks. As in South Korea, Taiwan's political regime was 'relation-based', implying a lack of separation between the legislative, executive, and judicial spheres; a decentralised system in which ministries and bureaus were in direct relation to networks and business firms; and the availability of *ex-post* renegotiation possibilities (in contrast to rules-based regimes), ensuring a good measure of flexibility about the ways to achieve the (inflexible) goals set by the central power. Relation-based authoritarianism is different from standard authoritarianism in the following sense: under the latter regime, private agents comply with government prescriptions because the government is omnipotent, whereas under the former they fear that non-compliance will entail the government's unfavourable treatment in the future (Okuno-Fujiwara, 1997: 378–80, 391–3). This mode of authoritarianism seems to be in tune with 'the East Asian tradition of a high degree of personalisation of government', in which 'benign neglect is not a politically feasible option' (Lau, 1997: 68–9).

B An Able and Cohesive Bureaucracy

When they attempt to characterise a political regime, social scientists, including economists, are typically interested in determining whether and to what extent the executive, legislative, and judicial powers are separated – seen from which standpoint, Taiwan's political regime clearly appears undemocratic. Seen from this angle, the state bureaucracy is viewed as an arm of the executive, so that the issue of the relationship between a government and its bureaucracy does not arise. This issue, however, is of the utmost importance since top bureaucrats occupy permanent positions and therefore stand as guarantors of policy continuity. Of course, a new government can decide to re-orient policies and the role of the bureaucrats is then to follow suit. The problem comes when bureaucrats are subject to continuous and arbitrary pressures from the executive, and when these pressures are not aimed at a better implementation of officially sanctioned policies. For reasons explained earlier, the Taiwanese bureaucracy was not subject to that risk: the state was fully committed to its objectives and the bureaucracy formed a cohesive entity that was fully devoted to the state and insulated from the political elite.

The Japanese colonial power bequeathed to Taiwan (and South Korea) a modern, meritocratic, and authoritative bureaucratic structure. Thanks to a long tradition of bureaucratic statecraft which drew its legitimacy from the claim that its civil servants were the best and the brightest elements of the society, the Taiwanese had no difficulty in adhering to Japanese doctrines (which Japan itself had imported from Prussia). It is therefore no surprise that all of the offices and a substantial portion of the personnel from the colonial era were carried forward into independence (Woo-Cumings, 1997: 328). The civil service continued to be 'merit-oriented in recruitment and promotion, lifelong in tenure and relatively uncorrupted by comparison to other developing countries' (p. 332).

With the arrival of the mainlanders, the quality of the Taiwanese bureaucracy was not affected, even though the jobs of state bureaucrats down to quite low levels were now occupied by the newcomers. Being an alien force, these bureaucrats 'had no choice but to identify their own interests with those of the state, their protector, making for an unusual merging of interests between state rulers and their officials' (Wade 1990a: 339). These were ideal conditions for the prevalence of clean and competent officials since the bureaucracy was 'neither caught between and penetrated by struggling interest groups nor subverted from above by the politics of rulers' survival' (p. 339). Moreover, the bureaucracy formed an elite civil service possessing a strong corporate identity and internal coherence, and, in no small measure, the presence of dense informal networks linking officials in different bureaus and ranks helped reinforce these two features.

There is another important reason why the bureaucracy achieved a high degree of internal coherence, and it can be traced back to a critical decision taken in mainland China in the early 1930s (see Wade 1990a: 246–8, on which our account is based). The Natural Resources Commission (NRC) was a sort of Economic Planning Bureau created by the Nationalist government of Chiang Kai-shek. In the 1920s and 1930s, however, responsibility for industrial policy was so diffused that no less than five ministries claimed to be in charge of its design and implementation. In addition, political connections determined appointments to leading economic policy positions. A critical moment came with the shock caused by Japan's conquest of Manchuria in 1931, and the sense of external threat that ensued. The political leadership responded to this challenge by recognising the urgent need to create a non-political (but patriotic) bureaucracy comprised of the best experts available. It is in this spirit that in 1932 the government thus founded the National

Planning Defence Commission, whose name was changed to the National Resources Commission a few years later (in 1935). The Commission was to work under the direct supervision of Chiang Kai-shek, and to act as a unique centre of command.

In conclusion, it was a sense of national emergency – the idea that the regime could not survive in the absence of a large cadre of experts in production and planning – which justified the replacement of a politicised and fragmented institution by a new technocratic and integrated one. This lesson was learned for good and was transplanted in due time to Taiwan, where a cohesive and competent bureaucracy prevailed – and continues to prevail to this date. Moreover, because the weakness of the Nationalist government, both against foreign aggression and the Chinese Communists, was attributed partly to the subjection of corrupt bureaucrats to powerful private lobbies, the KMT leaders wanted to endow China, and later Taiwan, with a bureaucracy that would also be autonomous in the sense of being immune from the pressures of the private sector. Their suspicion vis-à-vis the business elite, and their determination to subjugate them, was reinforced by the fact that, after the defeat of the Nationalists at the hands of the Communists, few big mainland capitalists chose to follow Chiang Kai-shek to Taiwan, preferring other destinations – the United States and Hong Kong in particular. Moreover, the few that went to Taiwan eschewed significant commitments of capital until a bilateral treaty between the United States and Taiwan guaranteed the latter's security (Woo-Cumings, 1997: 330–1).

C An Autonomous State System

1 *The State–Business Relationship until the Late 1980s*
The suspicion towards big (mainland Chinese) capitalists nurtured within the National Resources Commission explains why the Taiwanese policy network included hardly any representatives of private business, and why 'the government retained a striking degree of autonomy in setting the directions and details of policy' (Wade 1990a: 304). K. Y. Yin, although he went through several rounds of resignation and reinstatement, was the main architect of the country's economic development strategy (Cheng, 2001: 27). Contrary to what has been observed in other Southeast Asian countries, South Korea in particular, there was no intimate state–business relationships in Taiwan, and the KMT party state did not actually encourage the creation of big industrial concerns. On the other hand, because its official ideology was based on Sun Yat-sen's doctrine of 'people's livelihoods', which advocated the harmony of the interests of capitalists and workers, it was eager to regulate private business capital and instead promote the formation of state capitalism. In accordance with this principle, most industrial assets under the Japanese colonial administration, and most *zaibatsu*, were converted into SOEs. Whether in finance, public utilities, or the industrial sector, these types

of firms predominated until the drive for economic liberalisation gained momentum in the second half of the 1980s.

The enterprises taken over from the colonial administration covered a large number of manufacturing sectors – energy, fertilisers, sugar-refining, tobacco and wine, steel, shipbuilding, heavy machinery, construction, and defence-related industries – as well as a wide array of service-based sectors, such as public transportation, shipping, insurance, and non-banking finance. In most of these sectors, the private sector was either barred from entering or effectively crowded out (Cheng and Chu, 2002: 197, 199). When the state itself established new upstream industries, it either handed the factories over to selected private entrepreneurs (for example, in the sectors of glass, plastics, steel, and cement) or ran them as public enterprises (Wade 1990a: 78). In the former instance, the beneficiaries were typically loyalist mainlanders, members of a few politically well-connected native families known for their loyalty to the regime, or local county-level patrons with a stake in region-based oligopolies.[18] Whichever was the case, they were called on to run the new enterprise as a private firm or to participate in it as a shareholder (and manager) of a semi-public concern (Cheng and Chu, 2002: 202–3). What needs to be emphasised is that, as a rule, the KMT was always keen to maintain a system of competitive clientelism so as to keep rent-seeking activities in check. In practice, this meant that it typically cultivated at least two competing factions in a given county, thus preventing a single faction from reaching a position of political monopoly over the distribution of economic rents (Cheng and Chu, 2002: 208).

It also bears emphasis that, for fear of encouraging powerful groups that could one day challenge the state, the Taiwanese government consistently exhibited a preference against big businesses. Just to cite one example, when it decided to start promoting the petrochemical industry in the 1960s, when the private sector was still reluctant to participate, it allowed a public enterprise, China Petroleum Company (CPC), to undertake the most upstream naphtha cracking production. But the government was simultaneously responsible for the allocation of feedstock to undertake midstream production. At this level, an egalitarian approach was followed in the sense that the feedstock from the CPC's naphtha crackers was distributed among as many independent firms as possible. Moreover, when the Formosa Plastics Company, then the largest conglomerate in Taiwan, applied for a licence to build its own naphtha cracker, its request was repeatedly turned down, at least partly on the ground that monopolisation of upstream supplies had to be avoided to leave room for smaller firms (Chu, 1999: 18).

SMEs were no doubt a dynamic element of the Taiwanese economy, particularly in manufacturing exports, where their share peaked at 75 per cent in 1982 (Chu, 1999: 10). A distinctive feature of most SMEs is that they

---

[18] For sectors considered risky, such as plastics and synthetic fibre industries, the state often had to actually cajole private firms to take over the model plants it built (Cheng, 2001: 26).

were owned and run by islanders, and were typically of the family type. In addition, for their operations they typically rested on the informal horizontal networks that are characteristic of traditional south China society (Ho, 1980; Orru, 1991; Kao, 1991; Luo, 1997; Hamilton, 1997, 1998).[19] These networks, in which relationships are very functional, enabled the SMEs to get access to all the resources, financial and non-financial, necessary for their foundation and survival (Hattori and Sato, 1997: 353). Finally, many SMEs had quite flexible modes of organisation, including non-factory forms, such as the putting-out system for labour-intensive tasks, member units of a network of similar types of firms, and subcontracting to large firms involved in direct exports (Chu, 1999: 8–12).[20]

The aforementioned features of the SMEs explain why their social links with the government were 'tenuous at best, involving very few lineage bonds, marital links, school ties, or links due to a common social background. The formal channel of contact between the two sides was through industrial associations, which were shaped and managed by the party state. The important point is that, with a huge state sector inherited from the Japanese, the relocation of a continental-sized civil and military service to the island, and the strong political and financial support of the United States, the Nationalist regime did not need the political support of the business sector (Cheng and Chu, 2002: 197–8). This was especially true because there was no strong local business class, since the Japanese had gone and the islanders had been subdued by the colonial bureaucrats, who were adept at state-guided development (Woo-Cumings, 1997: 330–1).

Clearly, in the above-described political environment, economic technocrats operating mainly within the purview of the National Resource Commission had a wide latitude to manage development plans and projects, free from societal pressures. As pointed out by Tun-Jen Cheng and Yun-Han Chu (2002), they were answerable only to the party's top leadership, and were responsible mainly for the overall performance of the economy and the success of the targeted sectors. Their political fortunes hinged less on maintaining privileged ties with the business community than on their credibility in the eyes of the political leadership, and they naturally 'cautioned themselves against nurturing intimate ties with private businesses, be they natives or mainlanders' (p. 199). We have already stressed that the autonomy of the economic technocrats

---

[19] The so-called *guanxi* relationships, which are not confined to the family circle, are built up through gift exchanges typical of traditional village societies. Thus, when a person meets a potential partner with whom he has the right 'feeling, he does not use a contract to seal the deal; rather, he and his business partner reach an understanding that is sealed by exchanging small gifts, drinks, and banquets' (Hamilton, 1998: 66).

[20] Putting out was actually encouraged by the government, which even had a slogan for it ('the living room as the factory'). As regards the second form of organisation, the bicycle sector offers a vivid illustration: it was common to observe the formation of horizontal networks of bicycle assemblers and parts producers organised as SMEs.

vis-à-vis business was greatly enhanced by the existence of an economic base independent of the private sector. In effect, in addition to its monopoly or near-monopoly position in a vast number of manufacturing firms, it also directly controlled agricultural exports – the most important foreign exchange earner – and the entire banking sector.

As things happened, economic technocrats initially opted for a mixed strategy using both an import-substitution strategy based on SOEs, and privileging HCI, on the one hand, and an export strategy centred on agricultural and agro-processed products, on the other hand (export promotion efforts started as early as the early 1950s, with twenty exports singled out for government assistance). In a subsequent stage, as the role of SOEs shrank relative to the private sector in the 1960s, export-led industrialisation became the dominant plank of the national development strategy. But throughout the 1960s and 1970s, the SOEs continued to play their role of deepening and upgrading the industrial base while implementing anti-cyclical policies and supply-side management. They also served as a training ground and a reservoir for the economic bureaucracy, allowing the technocratic elite to incubate an army of satellite suppliers and downstream firms (Cheng and Chu, 2002: 199–200).[21]

To be the engine of export-oriented industrialisation was the central task assigned to the private sector, and to fulfil this objective its firms enjoyed a variety of policy incentives – tax benefits in particular. Noticeably, the use of highly distortionary measures, such as targeted lending, was consistently avoided by state bureaucrats (Wade, 1990a: 159–75; Park and Johnston, 1995: 196). The key point is that many of the industrial policy measures were product- or industry-specific, not firm-specific. Even more importantly, they did not discriminate against the SMEs. For instance, export loans and fiscal benefits were awarded to any firm that succeeded in receiving export orders.[22] This was the government's general line of conduct: rents awarded to private firms were performance-based and all the benefits and special privileges were of no value to new enterprises and of no cost to the government

---

[21] To give an idea of the economic importance of the SOEs in the Taiwanese economy, their total asset values were consistently several times bigger than those of the Taiwan's top 500 private companies (Cheng and Chu, 2002: 200).

[22] The domestic allocation of textile export quotas granted to Taiwan by the United States and the European Union provides a revealing example of the performance-based approach followed by the government. The quota-holders were thus allowed to retain only 80 per cent of their initial quotas. The remaining 20 per cent were to be returned to the government for reallocation through open competition on the basis of the highest unit value achieved on *bona fide* export orders. As stressed by Lawrence Lau (1997: 60), this competitive bidding system, which had the advantage of being transparent and independent of bureaucratic discretion, 'provides the incentive for manufacturers to innovate and to try to increase the added value of their products (and as a side benefit reduces the tendency for exporters to understate their export revenue in order to circumvent capital export and tax laws)'.

unless the new enterprises turned out to be profitable and generated taxable profits. This was particularly evident for incentive measures such as investment tax credits, accelerated depreciation, and tax holidays for *new* enterprises (Lau, 1997: 60).

Besides the aforementioned direct incentives, the SMEs benefited from the government's effort to persuade foreign corporations to invest in the country with the explicit aim of increasing local content in their assembly operations. This was a great boon for the SMEs, which mushroomed and prospered in the wake of foreign investments (Cheng and Chu, 2002: 200). Furthermore, already in the 1970s Taiwan set up a number of national research institutes, among which the Industrial Technology Research Institute played an important role in initiating or reviving several major manufacturing areas, such as bicycles, sporting goods, computers and computer peripherals, and semi-conductors (Lau, 1997: 63–4). Evidence nevertheless indicates that technical assistance from the state mainly benefited large-scale enterprises (Wade, 1990a). As for credit provided by commercial banks, this went primarily to large firms, while SMEs mostly relied on informal credit markets, especially rotating credit societies (*hui*) and the use of post-dated cheques (Park and Johnston, 1995: 196). At least, this was true until the 1970s, when the state decided to boost lending facilities for these firms in order to support the country's export drive (Cheng, 2001: 31; Chu, 1999: 19).

In the matter of education, both SMEs and big firms benefited greatly from governmental efforts. It is remarkable that, from early on, a two-track educational system was in place, which sent many primary and middle school graduates to vocational schools. By 1971, the country could thus rely on no less than 316 training institutes and, from that date, the number of students in vocational senior high schools exceeded the number of students in academic ones (Park and Johnston, 1995: 191). This is an exceptional state of affairs if we compare Taiwan to other Asian countries. Engineering was especially popular and about one-quarter of all university graduates since 1960 have been engineers. If they are clubbed together with science students, they accounted for over one-third of post-high school (junior college plus university) graduates during the 1960s, more than 40 per cent during the 1970s, and half by 1980 (Wade, 1990a: 64–5). Engineering studies were not only prestigious, a situation which already prevailed in China in the early twentieth century, but they were also considered a fast track to management positions in the industrial sector. Hence in 1971 Taiwan had more engineers per 1,000 people employed in manufacturing than any other of a sample of fourteen middle-income countries, with the exception of Singapore (p. 65). Since engineering skills are so essential for running industrial firms and improving technology and products, Taiwan's performance in the education sector comes out as a critical factor in its industrial success.

Did the ambitious plans of the planning technocrats lead to strong inflationary pressures? The answer is negative because their projects were severely held in check by a conservative central bank that enjoyed strong regulatory power over the banking sector. Interestingly, Taiwan's monetary discipline was initially motivated by the determination to prevent a replay of the disastrous hyperinflation and currency crisis of 1947–8, which had contributed to the defeat of the KMT leadership by the Communist regime in 1949. The consequence of the rigorous regulatory regime, which lasted for almost four decades, is that most private firms were only moderately leveraged, particularly in comparison to South Korea (Li, 1995: 103–9; Cheng and Chu, 2002: 201).

Finally, how state–business relationships were formally organised in Taiwan is a question which we have only slightly touched on so far. The state organised the private sector into a hierarchy of associations along the corporatist line. Membership was compulsory and associations covered every product line, every aspect of business activities, and every step of the production processes. Regrouped into three peak federations whose leaders were usually handpicked by the head of the state, they functioned as an arm of both the state economic bureaucracy and the Nationalist party. The purpose was to conduct industrial surveys, collect and disseminate business information, solicit policy inputs, and implement sectoral policy. As for the business representatives, they could use the regular meetings to convey their problems and present policy suggestions to the party and the government.

According to Cheng and Chu, (2002), however, the system of corporatist industrial associations did not work quite as intended. For one thing, the rule of compulsory membership was never effectively enforced, and many firms ultimately did not have licences to operate. And, for another thing, most business associations were barely functioning, owing to a lack of finance, or they were under the control of leading and politically active businessmen. As a matter of fact, the primary function of a large number of these associations was political co-option, 'as successful business elite would bid for organisational leadership first, and then political offices, all under the auspices of the KMT' (2002: 202). These imperfections should serve to qualify the somewhat idealised picture of state–business relations in Taiwan, in which a competent state negotiated on economic policies with representative business leaders (see, for example, Johnson, 1987).

In general, an important advantage of corporatist arrangements, whether they apply to business or other social groups, is that they allow the state to channel and restrain demands addressed to it as those demands arise and grow. This advantage is all the stronger where the arrangements are constructed before interest groups begin to gain strength, and where the demands emanate from encompassing organisations – two conditions which were rather well satisfied in the case of Taiwan (Wade, 1990a: 339).

2 The State–Business Relationship after the Advent of Democracy

We have seen above that combining the one-party state system based on the principle of central planning with considerable financial clout the KMT was able to overrule local factions and big business, not to speak of social organisations such as labour. In the mid-1980s, though, it began to initiate a series of political reforms (including the lifting of martial law in mid-1987) aimed at making stepwise progress towards a rule-of-law system (Wang, 2002). In the late 1980s, the sudden crisis that arose over the political succession to the regime's strongman, Chiang Ching-kuo, had the effect of accelerating the pace of political transition and economic liberalisation. These events provided the business elite with a golden opportunity to enhance their bargaining power, particularly their capacity to influence strategic decisions at the policymaking level. Full-scale national elections in the early 1990s broke the firewall between local and national politics, as a result of which candidate-centred campaign financing, political machine-based vote-buying, and pork-barrel politics were no longer confined to the local level. In these new circumstances, 'business groups became the most sought-after patrons of elective politicians and local factions, and when they had a well-delimited regional base, they did not hesitate to invest heavily in the election of the county magistrates and city mayors. Some groups even fielded their own family members as candidates instead of bankrolling their political agents' (Cheng and Chu, 2002: 203–4).

The same process was noticeable at the national level. The national legislature (the Yuan) progressively became 'an arena for horse trading among economic officials, party officials, and lawmakers who act as surrogates of special business interests' (Cheng and Chu, 2002: 204–5). As a consequence, the government had to bargain with lawmakers on the content of legislative proposals and the timetable for their implementation. Another effect of the change is that interpersonal connections between the KMT leadership and the business elite were accentuated and 'the economic policymaking process began to show signs of politicisation' (Cheng and Chu, 2002: 204–5). The democratic transition thus gave an impetus to policies of economic liberalisation that had been debated since the early 1980s. Business groups benefited most from the new policies (in particular, the removal of barriers to entry to a series of SOE- or parastatal-dominated sectors), denoting their rising political clout.

All this being reckoned, there is little doubt that the influence of the business community remained constrained both by its low internal cohesion and the immense wealth of the KMT. The former factor largely resulted from the heterogeneity of this community, made up of large-scale industrial groups coexisting with a host of family-owned firms that craved individual connections and preferred specific rewards for their political investment to the collective advantages of business associations. The rift between these two components was widened as economic officials succeeded in fostering a new crop of SMEs in high-tech industries. These firms, which acted as a link in the global production chain of Western firms, were destined to become the mainstay of Taiwan's industry and export sector, hence the strengthening of their bargaining position vis-à-vis rent-seeking big business. As for the latter factor, it must be borne in mind that the KMT controlled a huge party apparatus and a considerable economic empire. Thanks to these assets, the KMT continued to be the only power bloc in place. The implication is that it largely retained its ability to lock in the political allegiance of the business groups, to set limits on influence-peddling, money politics, and policy contestation, as well as to impose a hard budget constraint on rent-seekers. For example, the KMT was strong enough to deter the individual members of provincial assemblies from reckless requests for lending to their clients (Cheng and Chu, 2002: 205–9). In the words of Cheng and Chu, (2002): 207):

> Democratisation of the polity has not transfigured the KMT's power structure at the core. It has remained essentially a hierarchical structured constellation of entrenched state and party elite based permanently in the state and party apparatus. Its decision-making process continued to follow the principle of democratic centralism.

Up to this point, the process was under control and seemed to herald a protracted transition from authoritarianism to democracy, as described by Chan (2002). The presidential election of March 2000, however, disrupted this apparently smooth process and constituted a watershed in Taiwan's politics: the KMT was dislodged from power, thus marking the first transfer of political power in the history of post-war Taiwan. The state–business relationship was bound to be affected, especially because the downfall of the KMT meant a sizeable reduction in the political clout of most big business groups allied with it. These were denounced as part of a mafia state by the victorious opposition. At the same time, the economy was being gradually restructured, with business captains in the high-tech industries emerging as the new pivot of Taiwanese industry. Similar to the entrepreneurs of the traditional SMEs in the pre-democratic days, their inclination was towards political neutrality or even passivity. Interestingly, and providing evidence of the adaptability of the one-party state's economic strategizing, the newly emerging information sector, in which semi-conductor and computer firms featured prominently, had been actively promoted by KMT technocrats, who increasingly saw the role of the state as one of technology supporter, research coordinator, and supplier of human capital.[23] In this sense, it is correct to say that 'the developmental state in Taiwan [was] not unravelled, it [was] merely reconfigured' (Cheng and Chu, 2002: 209–11; see also Li, 1995).

IV CONCLUSION: A COMPACT INSTITUTIONAL DIAGNOSTIC OF TAIWAN

To end our analysis of the case of Taiwan, we lay out the diagnostic table in Table 6.1. This case poses an interesting challenge because some of its initial conditions at the time of independence were not *a priori* favourable, and yet

---

[23] This does not mean that state choices were always appropriate. Thus, if the policy of industrial upgrading pursued by the Taiwanese government proved very successful in the case of the information sector, and broadly successful in the case of the machine tool industry, it essentially failed in the case of the automotive industry (Cheng, 2001: 32–3).

TABLE 6.1 *A synthetic ordering of the institutional factors behind Taiwan's development*

Deep factors	Proximate causes	Institutional strengths and weaknesses	Economic and political consequences
Geography: a largely mountainous country *Demography*: a high pressure of population History and Japanese colonial legacy: * huge infrastructural investment; * educational effort; * rural industrialisation initiated; and * an authoritarian state History and mainland China: * authoritarian security-based regime; * strong suspicion vis-à-vis business elite; * a strong commitment to development; and * skilled administrators Foreign assistance: massive aid from the United States in Cold War context Bitter opposition between mainlanders and islanders	Political stability caused by one-party political system Clear sense of mission among the political leadership and big role of central planning Able and competent bureaucracy dominated by economic bureaucrats Remarkable use of well-designed, performance-based incentives Use of stepwise interventions rather than disruptive policies Key role of exports and export diversification Subjugation of private business interests and use of corporatist arrangements Commitment to equality, both at individual and spatial level: * radical land reform; * rural industrialisation; and * control of rent-seeking Great attention to human capital development, both general and technical	Developmental state backed by a strong Natural Resource Commission (economic planning agency) Strong state legitimacy anchored in economic growth with equity Strong state capacity with effective law enforcement and legal stability Regulation of key sectors dominated by big business Rent-seeking under control Incentive systems for small and medium-sized firms Availability of important public goods: education, electricity, communication, and transport Lack of accountability of key public agencies Limited property rights in relation to land	High quality of education, especially in engineering and science High sustainability of the growth pattern: dynamic industrial sector able to adjust to international competition Emergence of a new class of high-tech firms Swift emancipation from aid dependence Capacity of the political system to evolve towards democracy and economic liberalisation Erosion of corporatist arrangements Rising civil society Worrying vulnerability to takeover by mainland China

there is no doubt that characterising Taiwan as a development miracle is not an excess of language. Since the content of the table speaks of itself, discussion of its various elements is unwarranted. Three central lessons deserve to be drawn from the whole exercise.

First is the strong influence of historical legacy, coming both from colonial Japan and mainland China. For one thing, the Japanese contribution to Taiwan's development consisted of laying the basis of a dynamic smallholder agriculture; creating and expanding transportation, irrigation, and electrical power systems; improving education and sanitation; establishing financial institutions, agricultural parastatals, and farmers' associations; sparking agro-processing industries (centred on rice and sugar); and clarifying property rights so as to facilitate an effective system of tax collection (Cheng, 2001: 20–1).[24] For another thing, and rather surprisingly, although the Nationalist immigrants to Taiwan were staunch anti-Communists, the regime they established on the island was not only authoritarian but also gave such an important role to central planning and state-led economic guidance that it was considered as inspired by Lenin's principle of democratic centralism. The replicability of Taiwan's experience is evidently limited by the deep legacy bequeathed by the Japanese colonial officers and the Kuomintang.

Second, the growth pattern of the Taiwanese economy was anchored in the modernisation and commercialisation of smallholder agriculture and in the development of rural industries tied to the farming sector through numerous supply and demand linkages. These included the supply of labour, capital, and even industrial entrepreneurs, on the one hand, and the demand for intermediate inputs, agricultural equipment, and non-food consumption items, on the other hand. The power of this development model, in which the rural sector was considered as a full-fledged engine of growth from the very beginning, lay not only in its dynamic properties based on manifold interlinkages between sectors, but also in its strongly egalitarian tendencies.

Third, distinctive features of the developmental state of Taiwan proved critical for the country's successful performance on the economic and social fronts. In the critical stages of its growth and development process, the country (i) was led by a one-party state possessing a unified vision of the national future and endowed with a competent and cohesive bureaucracy; (ii) was able to prevent its capture by private interests; (iii) used a minimum of coercion and a maximum of performance-based incentives to align business interests with the general interest; (iv) proceeded in sequential steps rather than in big jumps; (v) invested large amounts of public money in infrastructure and in human capital; and (vi) gained its legitimacy, especially among the islanders, through its impressive achievements in terms of economic growth, equity, and multidimensional welfare. The resulting development model has turned out

---

[24] Cheng (2001: 24) goes so far as to say that 'The KMT regime only had to restore, not to create, education, public health, agricultural parastatals, market and financial institutions'.

to be extraordinarily resilient, as attested by Taiwan's ability to adapt to the challenges of globalisation, liberalisation, and democratisation, as well as its ability to weather the Asian regional financial crisis of the late 1990s. At the root of this resilience lies the implementation of an incentive scheme based on fiscal incentives, technological support through the sponsoring of research and development activities, participation in the formation of venture capital firms, and the provision of crucial public goods, rather than credit allocation and a loose monetary policy. Also critical has been the gradual emergence of a polymorphous industrial structure dominated by a great variety of SMEs, rather than by national champions susceptible of becoming too big to fail (Cheng, 2001: 32–6).

INSTITUTIONAL OBSTACLES TO
STRUCTURAL TRANSFORMATION

INTRODUCTION TO PART III

This last part of the volume puts together the lessons learned from the in-depth case studies undertaken within the Institutional Diagnostic Programme, and the more cursory analysis of the success development stories of South Korea and Taiwan at about the time when they were at a broadly similar level of development as our four case studies today. In doing so, the objective is to provide a kind of analytical list of potential institutional obstacles to development based on the conclusions reached in our analysis of the case study material at hand, whether those obstacles still prevail nowadays or have been removed in one way or another. We also rely on other development experiences, whenever links to them are suggested by our base material, in terms of either similarities or contrasts. Even though our knowledge of those additional country experiences is more superficial, it may still supply valuable insights that complement or enrich those obtained from our main analysis. In other words, from the institutional diagnostics established on Bangladesh, Benin, Mozambique, and Tanzania, as well as the central messages emerging from an institution-focused approach to the early development experiences of South Korea and Taiwan, we are able to extract a set of summary 'generic institutional issues'. Awareness of these issues should help us to better understand the nature of the most important institutional constraints on economic development in general, and to provide a guide to identifying the most binding constraints in the case of a particular country at a particular point in its development.

This list of critical institutional problem areas should assist experts and analysts in uncovering the factors which slow down the development of a country, and the deep institutional reasons behind them. By perusing these generic issues one by one, experts and analysts will have their attention drawn to *potentially* important impediments to growth and development, and should then reflect on how constraining they actually are in the particular country they are interested in. Even though several items in the list can apply to countries at varying levels of development, it should be borne in mind that the whole research programme on the basis of which these generic institutional issues have been established deals with low-income or lower middle-income countries. Other institutional issues might have to be considered at later stages of development.

The analysis we provide below is nevertheless more ambitious than simply listing generic institutional issues or obstacles. On the basis of our four (plus two) case studies, it also offers an in-depth analysis of their possible causes and economic consequences, and, most importantly, the political economy factors that spark resistance to reforms that could mitigate or remove their adverse effects. Beyond mere identification of institutional weaknesses, we thus aim to supply a framework that will enable analysts to reflect on these weaknesses by placing them in their own specific context and their own set of institutional interactions, including those linking formal and informal rules and organisations.

This last part of the volume is organised into three chapters. The first chapter (Chapter 7) focuses on the nature of the *economic* obstacles to development which may be found in a low-income country, with special attention to those that can only be surmounted if some institutional dysfunction is addressed. A key lesson from the case studies is that this inquiry must imperatively be based on an approach that views development as a process of structural transformation by which the great mass of poor people gets out of poverty by moving into decent formal jobs or accessing modern technology. This approach was formalised by the fathers of the discipline and is at the heart of the tradition initiated by the seminal works of Arthur Lewis (1955) and Simon Kuznets (1966), in particular. An aggregate approach in the spirit of Hausman, Rodrik, and Velasco (2005) is helpful in revealing problems in the way the economy works and, possibly, in shedding light on their institutional underpinnings. Yet it is bound to miss key sources of blockage located in the structural dimensions of development. Based on what we learned from the four IDP case studies and two East Asian success stories, the first part of our discussion thus summarises the various types of economic factors which may block, slow down, or accelerate the process of structural transformation, as well as the broad institutional domains involved.

The second part of our synthesis work is presented in the next two chapters. It delves into key institutional factors by following a conceptual approach that starts by regrouping them into generic institutional issues, as defined above, and then proceeds by probing each of them methodically. By conceptual approach we imply that, beyond a mere listing of these issues, we provide a framework of analysis that goes into the details of each institutional problem area in an orderly and meaningful manner, using concepts borrowed from the existing social sciences literature, and economics literature more particularly, as reviewed at the beginning of this volume. More fundamentally, in the light of our in-depth case studies, and the comparison between the latter and the successful early development experiences of South Korea and Taiwan, we intend to reflect on the proximate and deep causes of institutional dysfunctions, and on how they can be reformed. This concern about reforms makes it necessary to examine the political economy environment in which the country operates. Although the deep causes behind the generic institutional issues, and the directions for reform, inevitably include country-specific elements, care is taken to identify what may be of more general relevance for low-income or lower middle-income countries.

The above logic leads us to divide the strictly institutional part of the analysis into two chapters. The first one (Chapter 8) deals precisely with the role of institutional factors of a political nature, as well as politics per se, in interfering with the process of structural transformation. As for the second one (Chapter 9), it addresses the same issue from the more functional perspective of the capacity of the state to efficiently deliver public goods and services, and to regulate the private sector so as to make it compatible with the long-term interests of the country, including through the protection of property rights.

7

The Challenge of Modernising the Economic Structure

I INTRODUCTION

Whether in the four IDP case study countries or in the successful Asian development stories at the time these countries were at a comparable level of income per capita, development consists first of providing the great mass of poor people with either decent jobs or access to other income-generating facilities, which can help them to exit poverty. As an overwhelming majority of these poor people operate in the subsistence agricultural sector or other subsistence activities, a central issue of development is the structural transformation of the economy. Such a transformation may take the form of people moving out of agriculture and other low-productivity activities to higher-productivity jobs in metropolises, middle-sized cities, or even so-called cottage industries in the countryside. But it may also involve technological or organisational changes that progressively modify a subsistence agriculture into a market-integrated commercial farming sector exhibiting higher yields and incomes. This chapter summarises what the diagnostic exercises conducted in the four case study countries – Bangladesh, Benin, Mozambique, and Tanzania – reveal regarding the type of economic obstacles that hinder faster structural transformation, and the major institutional weaknesses involved.

A basis of comparison is needed to evaluate the nature and the strength of these obstacles in a particular country. In what follows, this is provided by the benchmark of two of the East Asian tigers, South Korea and Taiwan, considered as they were several decades ago in the 1960s, when the process of their startlingly rapid structural transformation was only just starting. The idea here is not to suggest that the path followed by those development champions could or should be imitated some forty or fifty years later by low-income or lower-middle-income countries as of the late 2010s. Rather, it is to allow for an easier evaluation of obstacles to, and facilitators of, structural transformation by comparing the present situation of the case study countries to the situation prevailing in the two tigers when they were taking off, or shortly thereafter.

With this objective in mind, we proceed in two steps. The first step (Section II) consists of reflecting on the conditions which surrounded the start and then the acceleration of the structural transformation and development in South Korea and Taiwan. One effective way to approach this question is by looking at their performance in the light of the canonical model of 'dual economy development' proposed by Arthur Lewis and amended or refined by other scholars. This approach is especially attractive because this model has been extensively used to analyse the mechanisms of structural transformation in the two countries. Owing to its relative simplicity, it provides an analytical framework which makes it somewhat easy to identify the contextual factors imping-ing on the structural transformation of a country. In a second step (Section III), we then consider the main economic obstacles on the path to structural trans-formation as we can ascertain them in the IDP case study countries, and we offer some first clues about their possible institutional causes.

II THE SOUTH KOREAN AND TAIWANESE 'MIRACLES' THROUGH THE LENS OF THE LEWISIAN FRAMEWORK

As just mentioned, we begin this brief review of the early development of Taiwan and South Korea by recalling the basic economic mechanisms under-lying the structural transformation process as modelled by Lewis and his followers in the 'dual economy' tradition.[1] In effect, an important part of the subsequent development literature used the South Korean and Taiwanese early development experiences as good illustrations of this line of develop-ment modelling, which then acquired in the development literature a rather universal connotation, very much undue.[2] By laying bare the basic structural transformation mechanisms, the Lewisian framework also supplies a help-ful analytical guide to diagnose potential obstacles to structural change in other countries.

A The Dual Economy Model of Arthur Lewis

The Lewisian representation of development is based on an observation that seems universal among countries in the early stages of development: the coexistence of a mass of poor people sharing the income of low-productivity

---

[1] Lewis's original paper dates back to 1954. Fei and Ranis's paper (1961) is probably the first and most well-known and influential paper to have extended Lewis's framework. For a review of the huge literature on the dual economy model see Kirkpatrick and Barrientos (2004) and, more recently, Gollin (2014).

[2] See the application of the Fei and Ranis theoretical model to Korea and Taiwan in Fei and Ranis (1975). Note that the relevance of the dual economy framework in explaining the development performance of these countries is not consensual – see the conclusion in Gollin (2014).

activities in subsistence agriculture or informal retail and handicraft occupation in rural or urban areas, on the one hand, and modern firms using more productive technologies and employing salaried workers at a higher level of earnings, on the other hand. The 'dual economy' model thus distinguishes between a modern or formal sector, essentially made up of firms organised according to a capitalist mode of production, and a traditional or informal sector, generally constituted by family farming or small family businesses in retail trade or handicrafts. Capital accumulation at the country level is taking place in the modern sector, which thus recruits an increasing number of workers at some given wage level. The marginal productivity of labour in the informal sector is assumed to be small, possibly zero if there is 'surplus labour' – meaning that the overall labour force may diminish in that sector without affecting the volume of production. Informal workers therefore receive earnings which, albeit low, are disconnected from the marginal productivity of labour. Various assumptions have been made about the level of these earnings. In Lewis, it is conveniently conceived as 'customary income', which remains roughly constant as long as the marginal productivity of labour in the informal sector is below that obtained in the formal sector.[3] More rigorously, competition in the labour market across the whole economy implies that the modern sector must pay a wage equal to, or somewhat above, earnings in the informal sector to attract workers, which modern firms can afford thanks to their capital-using technology. This assumption is of course the basis of the 'dualism' observed in many developing economies. Modern firms thus operate as if faced with what Lewis called, in his famous 1954 paper, an 'unlimited supply of labour'. In alternative specifications, the wage is exogenously fixed in the modern sector at a level above the average income in the informal sector, which is allowed to vary with the size of the labour force operating in this sector. Various justifications have been adduced for such an apparent absence of competition on the labour market, in particular efficiency wage setting[4] or the imposition of a legal minimum wage in the formal part of the economy.

Within such a framework, development involves a structural transformation of the economy. Through a process known as 'capital-widening', capital accumulation in the modern sector leads to proportionate increases in the demand for workers, which help to gradually reduce the pool of excess labourers pumped into the informal sector. If accumulation proceeds at a rate faster than population growth, the share of employment and output originating in

---

[3] Lewis (1968) offered reflections, fourteen years later, on the nature of the main assumptions adopted in his original model, suggesting that some of them were not necessary or had been misinterpreted by readers who considered them unrealistic.

[4] If the productivity of a worker increases with the wage received, it may be in the interest of formal employers to pay a wage higher than earnings observed in the informal sector. In the informal sector, absent formal capital and formal employers, labour earnings are generally assumed to result from income sharing among workers.

the informal sector falls with capital accumulation (in the modern sector). This process stops when there is no surplus labour left, or, roughly speaking, when the average productivity of labour in the informal sector has risen enough to catch up with the corresponding productivity in the formal sector. The reserve of labour becomes depleted and competition for workers forces the modern sector to raise its wage rate so as to remain able to attract additional labour force from the informal sector. It is then the case that earnings increase in both sectors, with the effect of prompting modern employers to use increasingly labour-saving and capital-using techniques, including in previously informal activities.[5] This process, called 'capital-deepening', succeeds the 'capital-widening' mechanism characteristic of the labour-surplus economy.

In this highly simplified description of the development process, the modern sector is the *engine of growth* of the economy and the structural transformation it generates is another way of describing the modernisation of the economy. Practically speaking, however, there are many ways in which this transformation process may be hindered or even halted. Let us mention a few of them. First, the accumulation rate in the modern sector may not be high enough, or population growth may be too fast, so that the volume of employment in the informal sector rises, even though its share in total employment may fall. Second, complementary production factors such as skilled labour or infrastructure may not be available or may grow too slowly. Third, the same may happen with imported inputs, such as key capital goods, if the capacity to export is insufficient or grows too slowly, unless foreign funds are available. Fourth, (unskilled) labour-saving technology imported from advanced countries may be so effective as to be technically efficient (or technically superior), so that it will be adopted by profit-maximising employers in spite of a relatively low cost of labour.[6] As a result, the labour absorption capacity of the modern sector is reduced.

---

[5] Alternatively, if wages are exogenously fixed in the modern sector and earnings in the informal sector are determined by the average productivity of labour, the latter will increase as soon as some workers start leaving this sector for the modern sector. The unlimited supply of labour will then vanish when the average product of labour in the informal sector reaches the exogenously fixed wage in the modern sector.

[6] A technology is technically efficient or superior when less capital and less labour are needed to produce the same level of output than with any available alternative technology, regardless of the ratio of input relative prices. Moreover, analogously with technologies, a product is technically efficient (or superior) if it exhibits the best performance in all the dimensions that matter to define its quality (for a car, for example, not only the speed at which it can move, but also the energy it uses up, the resistance of its body to bad roads, etc.). If the superior product is associated with a relatively capital-intensive technology, which is plausible if the product possesses a number of characteristics that make it suited for rich countries, firm managers in developing countries will also adopt the capital-using production process even though it does not match their resource endowments (for a discussion of the difference between the concepts of technical efficiency and economic efficiency, see Sen (1975: Chaps. 1–5); for an extension to products, see Stewart (1977: Chap. 1)).

In addition to structural transformation stalling for the preceding reasons, other complications may also arise in the simple dual model of development when amending it to accommodate different country contexts. An omitted factor in the model is land. As a matter of fact, Lewis stipulates that his theoretical framework is adapted to 'overpopulated' countries where land is scarce and fully used, so that labour in the agricultural subsistence sector is likely to be redundant. *A priori*, the situation is expected to be different in countries where land is abundant, which would still seem to be the case today south of Sahara. Yet, because of imperfect market integration caused by a deficient transport and communication infrastructure, lack of access to adequate technology or inputs, or the presence of institutional factors responsible for inefficient land allocation, farming may remain a low-income-earning activity in these countries in spite of its rich potential. Characteristically, such a situation will be reflected in the under-utilisation of both land and labour.[7] Structural transformation from low-productivity agriculture to higher-productivity sectors along the Lewisian mechanism would then remain a possible development strategy, but the promotion of a more efficient use of available land and a dynamic agriculture form another strategy for growth-cum-structural transformation. In the latter case, thanks to the removal of barriers to agricultural expansion, notably the physical isolation of remote areas, subsistence farming would progressively transform into a commercially integrated sector oriented towards domestic and/or foreign markets. As a matter of fact, the structural transformation would somehow be operated through informal production units being modernised or modern firms taking over traditional activities in rural areas. In the context of sparsely populated countries, because of the high per unit cost of connecting isolated areas in terms of providing not only transport and communication links but also social amenities, schools, health centres, and various agricultural support services, this second strategy may be deemed inferior to the Lewisian labour reallocation mechanism.[8] Yet it can certainly not be discarded *a priori*.

The simple model can be extended to take into account the demand side of the economy and the constraints that it may impose on growth and the structural transformation. In a closed economy, the expansion of the modern sector requires that the demand for its products expands at the same rate as it grows. If not, the relative price of modern products will fall, lowering the profitability of the whole sector. Capital will then tend to flee and the structural transformation to stall. This will also happen in an open economy if the modern sector is not able to compete with foreign produced goods in domestic and/or foreign

---

[7] On the way population density and population growth in land-abundant economies affect the nature of agricultural institutions, backwardness, and lack of commercial integration, and lead to economic dualism, see Binswanger and McIntire (1987) and Binswanger et al. (1989).

[8] For an extensive discussion of this vicious circle, see Platteau (2000: Chap. 2) (see also Delgado, 1992).

markets. Even if effectively protected from foreign competition domestically, a point will be reached at which domestic demand will be saturated, so that any further extension of the modern sector will require operating on export markets, which will not be possible if it is not internationally competitive. To be sustainable, the structural transformation thus necessitates not only capital accumulation at some minimum pace but also competitiveness gains that will allow the modern sector to effectively compete with foreign producers in some product lines.

These product lines depend on the comparative advantage of the country. They may consist of labour-intensive manufactured goods, agro-industrial products – which require that the modern sector operates in agriculture or sources its inputs in traditional farms – or services such as tourism. What matters for the structural transformation to keep going is that no demand constraint bears on the expansion of the modern sector, even if this means a constantly evolving product mix.

This diversification of production may be uneasy because the external competitiveness of the modern sector is restricted to a narrow set of products, typically agro-industrial, or mineral and energy natural resources. The extraction of the latter employs little labour so that it does not directly contribute to structural change. It does it indirectly, however, thanks to the domestic demand that it generates through the income it brings to local agents, including the state, and the outlets it provides to the rest of the modern sector. Without export diversification, or possibly import substitution at some early stage, the pace of development of the economy is thus determined by the growth of primary commodity export net receipts, which may be lower than desired.

Despite its apparent simplicity, the Lewisian framework, as well as its extensions or variations in the development theory literature, offers a most useful guide to the understanding of a development process viewed through the lens of the structural transformation of the economy and the constraints weighing on it. This of course requires that the framework is sufficiently enlarged to fit the specific features of the country examined. As will now be seen, it is quite remarkable that the general dynamics of the model, suitably adapted to the context, has proven to be appropriate to describe the successful early development of East Asian countries such as South Korea and Taiwan between the mid-1950s and the mid-1970s, a period during which both countries would have been classified as low- or middle-income according to today's international income scale. Differences between the two countries stem from the initial conditions, the pattern of structural transformation, and some major policy orientations associated with this pattern.

Back in the early to mid-1950s both countries had a level of real GDP per capita around US$1,400 at international 2017 prices – see Table 7.1. Taiwan had a slightly higher level of income than South Korea, and its share of GDP originating in agriculture, generally considered in the development literature as the main component of the informal sector and the reserve of surplus labour in the dual economy model, was then lower. Both on the aggregate and from a structural development point of view, Taiwan was thus slightly more advanced. In the two countries, however, the structural transformation in the following twenty years was astounding. The GDP share of agriculture went down by 25 percentage points in both South Korea and Taiwan, while the GDP share of manufacturing increased by 25 percentage points in Taiwan and 15 per cent in South Korea. It is more difficult to conduct the same calculation for employment because available data are not comparable across the two countries.[9] Nonetheless, it has been estimated that, helped by a slowdown of population growth, both countries reached the Lewisian turning point – at which the absolute volume of employment in agriculture starts declining – at about the same moment, in the early 1970s. By 1980, the GDP share of the industrial sector was as high as 45 per cent in Taiwan and 33 per cent in South Korea – in both cases, a high level by today's standards. In the two countries, the dynamics of structural transformation by which low-productivity workers in agriculture and elsewhere in the economy were progressively absorbed into the growing modern sector of the economy, including manufacturing, thus appeared to work according to the Lewisian mechanisms set off by an extremely fast accumulation rate of capital in the latter sector. If the manufacturing export-driven expansion was a powerful engine of growth in the two countries, however, there were clear differences in the way it was activated and then sustained, and, as a matter of fact, in the way the Lewisian logic unfolded.

B Taiwan

In the case of Taiwan, the expansion of the manufacturing sector relied on a dynamic group of small and medium-sized enterprises (SME), a sizeable proportion of them being located in the rural sector and functioning symbiotically with an agricultural sector that was stimulated by a radical land reform and vigorous accompanying policies (see Park and Johnston, 1995). The early emphasis on, and dynamism of, the agricultural sector in Taiwan are worth emphasising as they constitute a departure from the straight structural transformation model where overall productivity gains result from the mere sectoral shift of labour from agriculture to industry. Here, productivity gains within agriculture contributed to the aggregate gain, too. In any case, both in rural and urban areas, the SMEs provided rising employment opportunities to surplus agricultural workers, who were absorbed in labour-intensive manufacturing activities directed towards the domestic market, under tariff protection in a first stage, and then increasingly towards foreign markets.

The SMEs were incentivised to export by a set of policies which included a favourable exchange rate reform – a 60 per cent devaluation between 1958 and 1961 – and tariff relief for imported equipment and other inputs. The whole

<hr>

[9] The preceding figures are drawn from Chen (2001).

sector was highly competitive and financially autonomous in the sense that it could rely on internally generated savings and a small-scale private credit market, rather than on state bank credit (see Chu, 1999). Quickly, a whole integrated network was formed, made up of SMEs buying and selling from each other in a highly efficient way. On the other hand, large firms, which were inherited from the era of Japanese colonisation and then nationalised, also contributed to the production and export of manufactured goods. Yet they proved less dynamic than the private sector and the expanding network of SMEs.

At the macro level, it must be reckoned that US assistance played a huge role in the early stage of Taiwan's development, covering as much as about 25 per cent of public expenditures in the 1950s. However, as the Taipei government faced huge defence expenditures during that period, it is not clear how much foreign aid contributed to bridging the trade balance gap. What is certain, however, is that the trade balance regained an equilibrium position as early as 1963, and non-military US aid fell drastically after 1965.[10] The price stability achieved during these two decades, and later, is another achievement that needs to be stressed.

In short, the dramatic structural transformation of Taiwan from the mid-1950s to the mid-1970s relied on a powerful industrial export growth engine, itself based on the dynamism of a network of SMEs enjoying various favourable conditions: a stable macroeconomic context, undistorted prices and competitive market mechanisms, and a sound regulatory policy. The SMEs were also helped by several initial conditions: (i) an efficient agricultural sector made up of small and medium-sized farms and prior export experience in agricultural products, obtained during the colonial period; (ii) a dense transportation network, again inherited from the Japanese colonisers; (iii) a literate labour force and a population eager to achieve educational progress, so that an increasing supply of skilled labour became available when it was needed later on in the development process; and (iv) a relative advantage in gaining access to the US and Japanese markets. From the network of SMEs, progressively emerged larger companies which would take on the next stage of industrialisation with more capital- and technology-intensive lines of production and exports.

In twenty years, Taiwan was able to multiply its income per capita by three, thanks to an average growth rate close to 6 per cent. What is remarkable, moreover, is the fact that this fast growth and a drastic structural transformation of the economy could be achieved with apparently no change, and possibly a drop, in the degree of inequality of the distribution of income. In other words, all people saw their living standards grow in the same proportion, and possibly those at the bottom of the distribution more than others.

As a final observation, it should be noted that if Taiwan's process of development followed the Lewisian pattern of a rapidly growing, self-financing labour-intensive modern sector that absorbed low-productivity workers from

---

[10] For details on US aid in the 1950s and early 1960s, see Chang (1965).

agriculture, it differed from it in one major respect. Instead of being confined to the passive role of a provider of cheap (excess) labour to the modern urban sector, the traditional informal sector, here equated to the rural sector, itself actively participated in labour surplus absorption, capital accumulation, and productivity growth. This was the result of an early modernisation of agriculture, both in terms of techniques and crop choices, and of a uniquely successful programme of rural industrialisation (unique, if we except Japan). In short, dualism in Taiwan was reduced rather rapidly both through productivity gains of the lagging sector and the rising employment share of industry.

Another point which deserves attention yet tends to be underplayed in the dual economy literature, is the export orientation of Taiwanese development, without which, most plausibly, the country could not have undergone the drastic structural transformation it experienced. This feature prevented domestic demand, the size of which was limited because of the low income of the population, from forming an obstacle to the exploitation of scale economies and the growth of the manufacturing sector. For this to be possible, the economy had to quickly become internationally competitive in a few lines of products.

Reflecting on the institutional features of the Taiwan of the 1950s, it makes little doubt that its dramatic transformation is first of all the result from a well-thought centrally elaborated strategy, which largely rested on decentralised private incentives and was implemented by an able bureaucracy. In short, at the heart of Taiwan's success lay a successful combination of central planning and market mechanisms. It appears to owe much to the past history of the Chinese Nationalist leadership that settled in Taiwan after losing the war against the communists on the mainland.

C South Korea

The same structural transformation engine operated in South Korea, where several initial conditions were shared with Taiwan, some of which originated in their common past as Japanese colonies. These included a competent and disciplined bureaucracy, an early progressive land reform made possible by decolonisation, a relatively advanced educational system, and a population eager to learn and to acquire advanced skills. However, compared to Taiwan, South Korea had less developed infrastructure, partly because the core of economic activity before separation was located in the north of the peninsula. What deserves to be underlined is that the patterns of the structural transformation and the policies mobilised to activate the industrial export engine were substantially different in South Korea from those used in Taiwan. If the development path was similar, the engine was somewhat different, and it was activated later.

The real start of the South Korean structural transformation can be dated back to 1961, and it was after a chaotic period of slow growth and intense rent-seeking activity. It was under the leadership of General Park and his team of experts that the export-led manufacturing strategy was launched. In their vision, there was no future for development based on import substitution because this was bound to be constrained by a domestic market of limited size, due to the low (initial) income of the population. By contrast, a labour-intensive manufacturing export strategy could expand the size of the market, provided that domestic producers succeeded in becoming internationally competitive. Similar to Taiwan, this could be achieved through a favourable exchange rate and duty-free imports of equipment and intermediated goods. In contrast to Taiwan, however, the strategy also included generous credit allocation at a liberally subsidised interest rate and state-guaranteed foreign loans. To make these incentives effective, they were granted conditionally to exporters who complied with targets set in agreement with the ministries or state agencies in charge of the export strategy and in conformity with the Development Plan. The various export ventures were undertaken mostly by business groups that emerged in the previous period. This strategy also required complete control of bank credit, which had been made possible by the early nationalisation of the entire banking system. The strength of the industrial export engine thus depended not only on the dynamism of business groups but also on the volume of resources made available to them, the nature of their conditionality, and their effective and rigorous monitoring by a competent and non-corrupt bureaucracy.

Since the saving capacity of the country was initially very limited, accumulation at the aggregate level had to rely on foreign funding. Most resources were initially provided by US official assistance. Yet domestic savings increased rapidly, partly through forced savings policies. However, because accumulation was accelerating too, foreign funding was still needed. After 1965, this consisted mostly of foreign loans so that the external debt of the country started to rise. Yet because of the fast rate of GDP growth, it was possible to maintain the debt-to-GDP ratio at sustainable levels. Within the country, moreover, the expansion of credit facilities to exporters was responsible for a high level of money creation and a high rate of inflation. The financing of export business ventures and heavy public investments in infrastructure were thus implicitly secured through an inflationary tax on households.

The strategy worked well. South Korea grew very quickly from the early 1960s onwards, while the manufacturing sector and its forward and backward linkages absorbed an increasing proportion of surplus agricultural workers in a typically Lewisian manner. In contrast to Taiwan, however, the agricultural sector was rather passive in the initial stages of development. It was only in a second stage, and in view of the growing development asymmetry between the rural and urban sectors, that specific efforts were made in favour of agriculture and rural areas, through extension services, building infrastructure, and the creation of special industrial zones in rural regions.

It would have been possible to pursue this labour-intensive manufacturing export strategy and, as a matter of fact, exports of clothes, wigs, footwear, and plywood continued to increase at a fast pace and to diversify for an additional decade or so. Yet Park thought that the prospects of such a growth path were limited and that, like in Japan, investment in heavy industry should take over from light manufacturing without waiting any longer. To a large extent against the advice of experts and advisers, he then embarked on the so-called 'heavy and chemicals industry' (HCI) programme. At the same time, and possibly linked to that controversial decision, he strengthened his grip on South Korean civil society by imposing a new constitution that granted him quasi-dictatorial powers.

The HCI programme was implemented through two channels. First, a state-owned enterprise (SOE) was created, which would be responsible for creating a giant steel production unit. This strategy was similar to the one followed in Taiwan, where, as a legacy of Japanese colonisation, a group of nationalised enterprises were specialised in heavy industrial production, but it was to some extent bolder in South Korea because of the lack of experience of the country in this line of production and the huge size of the planned venture. Second, big business groups, known as *chaebols*, which had emerged in the previous phase of the export-led growth strategy, were tasked with undertaking heavy manufacturing export ventures. Towards that purpose, they benefited from considerably enlarged incentives, notably in terms of subsidised credit allocation and foreign borrowing, when compared to those offered to light manufacturing exporters.

Against the expectations of many observers, and possibly because of the rigorous control exercised over the *chaebols*, Park's HCI gamble succeeded. Among the most daring successes was the setting up of shipyards able to build tankers and other heavy vessels for foreign marine transport companies as soon as in 1974. Meanwhile, the steel producing SOE started operations in 1972.

The achievement of the production and export targets of the HCI programme entailed a high social cost, however. Not only were the incentives provided to *chaebols* especially important, but also investment failures were not infrequent: against the rules initially set, some *chaebols* had to be bailed out by the state, essentially because they were 'too big to fail'. There was thus a double burden on the national budget, and foreign debt rapidly increased. When the second oil price boom hit in 1979, the year President Park was assassinated, the macroeconomic situation became critical. The government nevertheless succeeded in surmounting the crisis, and in restructuring the *chaebol* network so as to put them on sounder financial grounds. At that time, the structural transformation of the country was complete, and South Korea was quickly advancing on the path to becoming an industrial country.

Institutionally, the South-Korean take-off experience shares with Taiwan the reliance on centrally designed strategies resting mostly on private business, except for key activities such as steel production, and under the close control of an effective and competent bureaucracy, including, in the case of South Korea, the direct involvement of central leadership. Again, the successful combination of authoritarian economic management, market mechanisms and business incentives was the key to success. In South Korea, the export targets set by the planning commission, the state control of banks as a way of allocating credit and rewarding successful chaebols through generously subsidised interest rates, or the direct bargaining between the president and *chaebol* owners about export targets and the provision of resources came clearly under central planning. On the other hand, exporting firms operated in a strict market environment both at home and abroad.

Both the Taiwanese and South Korean take-off experience are good illustrations of the Lewisian transformation at work: an extremely dynamic modern sector absorbed the surplus labour in the traditional part of the economy in a little more than a decade. In both cases, the potential limitation arising from domestic demand has been overcome through the successful export orientation of the domestic production apparatus. Such a strategy was initially facilitated by an easy access to the US and Japanese markets and, at least in South Korea, by generous export subsidies and powerful incentives. If the South Korean case fits the Lewisian model of a single growth engine that pulls the whole economy forward by progressively absorbing its lagging segments, the process has been slightly different in Taiwan. There, the traditional sector, assimilated to agriculture, has shown an impressive internal dynamism which allowed it to be modernised and to increase the earnings of the workers who remained in it.

Such were the early development experiences of the two East Asian tigers, South Korea and Taiwan, at a time when their income levels and their formal-informal structures were comparable to those presently found in the low-income or lower-middle-income countries that we selected for intensive study. Relying on our previous analysis, we now set off on the following exercise: to summarise the features specific to those latter countries that could either enable them to pursue a similar path towards structural transformation, possibly at a different pace and according to somewhat different patterns, or derail their development process and perhaps drive them into a deadlock.

III OBSTACLES TO AND ENABLERS OF STRUCTURAL
TRANSFORMATION IN THE FOUR CASE STUDY COUNTRIES

Equipped with a flexible analytical model of structural transformation and with two major historical Asian benchmarks, we now review the experience of the four case study countries of the Institutional Diagnostic Project. The main question asked is that of the nature of the obstacles that prevent structural transformation from taking place or proceeding faster, and what kind of policy could overcome them.

A comparison of the four IDP case studies with the two benchmark countries is offered in Table 7.1. The situation of each case study today is compared to that of both South Korea and Taiwan at a period where the latter had a

TABLE 7.1 *Comparing the development and sectoral economic structures at equivalent levels of GDP per capita of the four IDP case studies and the Southeast Asian tigers*

	Mozambique	Taiwan	South Korea	Benin	Taiwan	South Korea	Tanzania	Taiwan	South Korea	Bangladesh	Taiwan	South Korea
Year	2018	1950	1955	2018	1960	1965	2018	1965	1970	2018	1970	1975
Income per capita[a]	1133	1460	1410	2160	2160	1920	2870	2880	2970	4020	4040	4360
Growth rate (ten-year average)	3	5.3	2.3	1.4	4.3	6.7	3.1	6.5	8.6	5.3	6.9	7.4
GDP shares (%)												
Agriculture	24.6	36	42.3	27.1	28.5	34.4	27.9	22	27.1	13.1	15.5	23
Industry	23.6	15.6		14.6	26.9		29.5	31.8		28.5	36.8	
Including: manufacturing	8.7		10.9	9.7		16.7	9.1		16.7	17.9		21
Others (incl. services)	51.8	48.4		58.3	44.6		42.6	46.2		58.4	47.7	56
Employment shares (%)												
Agriculture	70.6	56		39.1	50.2	59.4	69.7	43	50.4	40.1	36.7	45.8
Industry	8.2	16.9		18.3	20.5	9.2	9.2	24.2	13.2	20.5	28	
Including: manufacturing										14.2		18.6
Others (incl. services)	21.2	27.1		42.6	29.3		21.1	32.8		39.4	35.3	

[a] In US$ at 2017 purchasing power parity.

Source: World Development Indicators, ILO statistics for the sectoral structure for employment, Statistical Yearbooks of various ears for Taiwan and South Korea

level of income per capita roughly comparable, that is in the 1950s or 1970s depending on the country. In each case, the table shows the level of income per capita, its growth trend, and then the sectoral structure of both total GDP and employment, even though data for early periods are scarce regarding the latter.

What is striking is that both the structure of GDP and employment differs, in some cases radically, between the case study countries and the Asian benchmarks, even though they are observed at a comparable level of development. The only common fact is the higher share of manufacturing among the Asian tigers than among IDP countries both in terms of employment and output. The shares of other sectors may be quite different, which may partly be due to statistical problems in defining them, but also reflect strongly different initial conditions or institutional settings. The conditions for the structural transformation to proceed successfully in the IDP countries differ from what they were in the Asian benchmarks. This is what we intend to analyse in the rest of this chapter, relying on country studies in the other volumes of the IDP project, and their summaries presented in previous chapters.

A Bangladesh: Sustainability of Structural Transformation under Threat

In comparison with most developing countries today, Bangladesh may be considered as a success story. Since 2000, its income per capita has been multiplied by a little less than three and poverty has fallen by two thirds. The country has recently graduated from the low-income status in the World Bank classification. Its debt is at a manageable level, and it boasts a rather stable macroeconomic situation over the last three decades.

It is evident from Table 7.1 that, as of 2018 Bangladesh was coming rather close to Taiwan and South Korea in the 1970s: the level of GDP per capita and the sectoral structure of GDP and employment are roughly the same. It also shares with these countries several important historical, geographic, and economic features: a violent nation-building war, an egalitarian land reform, a high population density implying an acute land scarcity, and, today, a powerful labour-intensive Ready-Made Garment (RMG) export growth engine. Yet growth proceeds in Bangladesh at a slower pace than during the take-off of the Asian tigers, and the manufacturing sector is significantly smaller in relative terms.

Structural transformation in Bangladesh has also progressed at an impressive speed. If surplus or low-productivity labour is assumed to be essentially located in the agricultural sector, then Bangladesh would seem to have passed the so-called Lewisian turning point where the absolute number of workers in the agricultural sector starts falling and surplus, or low-productivity labour starts vanishing around the turn of the millennium. As a matter of fact, agricultural employment has been declining by 2 million people over the last three decades, especially during the 2000s. Accounting for demographic growth in rural areas, we can estimate that some 12 million people have left the agricultural sector in the last two decades.

Yet it would be wrong to believe that all these people went to work in the rest of the economy. To assess the structural transformation capacity of the Bangladeshi economy, the role of temporary migration must be brought to the fore. An estimated 10 million Bangladeshis were working abroad in 2019. Judging from the evolution of remittances, the total net outflow of migrant workers may have summed up to 9 million people over the last three decades. This is much more than the observed drop in agricultural employment, so that, absent migration, agricultural employment would have been increasing throughout that period. This remains true even if we assume that, say, half the migrants came from non-agricultural sectors. In short, the growth of the modern sector, driven by manufacturing, does not appear to have been fast enough to absorb the agricultural surplus labour defined as agricultural workers with the lowest productivity.

Of course, migration also contributed to economic growth via worker foreign currency remittances and induced demand effects on the domestic economy. If the overall growth of the Bangladeshi economy has been rather satisfactory over the last three decades, at close to 6 per cent a year and 4.4 per cent per capita, it has partly stemmed from the increasing flow of migrant remittances. It was estimated that remittances contributed to approximately a fourth of GDP per capita growth (see Raihan et al., 2023). Yet this observation about the significant role of remittances as a source of national growth raises several issues. Should the sending of a sizeable portion of a country's population to work abroad be considered as a valid development strategy or as a second-best policy aimed at compensating for the possibly temporary failure of the domestic modern sector to create enough jobs? To what extent is such migration-based development strategy sustainable in the long run? Relatedly, there is a social cost in migration, even when it is temporary, and this should be accounted for in evaluating development.

Even imputing migrants to the agricultural sector, the outflow of workers towards the rest of the economy would still amount to at least 5 million people over the last twenty years. Were all these workers, plus those resulting from the growth of the non-agricultural labour force, absorbed by the modern sector, the RMG export sector in particular? Or did they go to work in informal non-agricultural activities with a labour status and an income level little different from those prevailing in the informal agricultural sector? The answer is provided by the following estimate: 87 per cent of the labour force was informal in 2010 and this share has apparently not changed much since then.[11] These are high proportions, which might suggest that the structural

---

[11] Most recent statistics (2017) are not comparable to the 2010 data – they would moreover point to an increase in informality. The 2013 Labour Force Survey is more comparable and does not suggest any significant change.

transformation was less pronounced than it would appear on the basis of a simple agricultural/non-agricultural dichotomy.

A large part of the urban informal sector may be considered as complementary to the modern sector of the economy. However, its mode of operation follows a different pattern with self-employment or micro-firms as the dominant type of production organisation. Somehow, that part of the urban informal sector may be thought as a subsector of the modern part of the economy, whose informality is mostly motivated by the possibility it offers of evading taxes and labour regulation. It is difficult to say which portion of the informal urban sector must be thus assimilated to the modern sector. There is, indeed, some ambiguity about how to measure structural transformation, or, equivalently, about how the type of jobs and the levels of earnings within the non-agricultural sector should be accounted for. In any case, this does not lessen the transformative importance of the huge shift of labour away from agriculture that took place in Bangladesh during the last decades.

As in South Korea and Taiwan at the time of their take-off, the main growth engine behind the structural transformation in Bangladesh's economy over the last three decades has been the labour-intensive manufacturing export sector, mostly ready-made garments (RMG). It grew at an annual rate of 11 per cent since 1990 and created a little more than 2 two million jobs, close to 10 per cent of the whole increment in the labour force. Bangladesh is now the second global RMG exporter after China. Directly or indirectly, through backward and forward linkages as well as foreign currency receipts, the RMG sector contributed in a major way to the growth of GDP and living standards. Its overall contribution to GDP growth has been estimated to be as high as 40 per cent (by Raihan et al., 2023). Its transformative impact, most notably on and through female employment, has also been substantial. Yet, if it had not been for outmigration, this would not have been enough to absorb the surplus labour present in the agricultural sector. To the extent that there is uncertainty about future migration opportunities (India's present political regime is hostile to Muslim migrants, which hurts Bangladeshi migration), sustaining the structural transformation at its current pace, may thus prove difficult.

There is also some uncertainty about the future development of the RMG sector. Technological change seems likely to drastically reduce its relative labour intensity and the comparative advantage it draws from particularly cheap and repressed labour, whereas exports will soon lose their Least Developed Countries preferential trade status in advanced countries because of the recent graduation of Bangladesh to (lower) middle-income country status. As a matter of fact, such a slowdown can already be observed in the volume of exports – since the 2008 crisis and particularly the 2013 Rana Plaza accident where 1,100 workers died when their factory collapsed. The slowdown in employment growth is even more pronounced.

If the Bangladesh economy seems to share many features and follow the same path as the Southeast Asian newly industrialised countries at the time of their take-off, there is a risk that its growth rate decelerates and even that its structural transformation dynamic gets jammed. At the same stage of development in the benchmark countries, the manufacturing sector was larger and was growing faster. In short, the growth engine was more powerful. Moreover, it was gaining more power still through diversification, both within their initial area of excellence (RMG and other labour-intensive exports) and without. On the contrary, manufacturing exports in Bangladesh tend to concentrate everyday more on RMG products, and within RMG, on a limited set of product lines.

This issue of the diversification of labour-intensive manufacturing exports is the main challenge that Bangladesh will soon face in trying to sustain its rates of growth. This has been recognised, now for quite some time, by observers and policymakers. On several occasions and in several official documents, the government has committed to adopting such a strategy. But no tangible results were delivered yet, even though the continuation and the needed acceleration of the structural transformation depends on this diversification. From the point of view of the relationship between development and institutions prioritised in this volume, the question is: what is the institutional cause of this apparent blockage of measures that would benefit the national community?

Various factors can be mentioned, including the endemic lack of a clear development strategy and implementing capacity, a culture of business-government informal 'deals', a notoriously corrupt public and private financial system, and very limited public resources due to an exceptionally low average tax rate. In that context, a major impediment to a strategy of diversification seems to be the size of the RMG sector and its critical importance, up to now, in the overall development of the country. As a result, the leverage that it can bring to bear on the government is particularly strong, leading to the pre-emption of the development of other sectors of the economy and the monopolisation of public support and credit. On the other hand, the lack of diversification within the RMG sector itself seems to result from a strong specialisation in those product lines that make most use of exceptionally low labour costs.

In summary, there is a risk that, even though it has been rather effective over the last two or three decades, the growth engine that feeds the structural transformation of the Bangladeshi economy will slow down in the close future. There are some signs that this has already started, especially with respect to job creation. Remedying that situation would require the RMG to increase its global market share by expanding the scope of its activity or supplementing it by other lines of labour-intensive manufacturing exports. The first option would require a substantial improvement of the competitiveness of the RMG sector, which has relied until now mostly on the low cost of labour and poor working conditions imposed through the co-option of trade unions. Enhanced RMG competitiveness or diversification of the export manufacturing sector also requires progress to be made in various areas: (i) better production infrastructure in a country where land is particularly scarce – a

priority that is acknowledged by the present government; (ii) a more educated
and skilled labour force, not only in quantity but also in quality terms, which
requires significant progress on the latter; (iii) the laying down of clear and
well-thought-out development policies, and the setting of an effective bureaucracy apparatus to implement them, rather than the reliance on informal
deals that essentially favour dominant economic actors; and (iv) an efficient
and non-corrupt financial system. It is not clear, at this stage, that all these
requirements for the pursuit of an autonomous and fast structural transformation of the economy and the society, possibly one that is less reliant on
migration, will soon be met.

B Tanzania: An Uncertain Growth Engine

After a difficult transition from a socialist development experiment to a market economy, growth has proceeded at a rather satisfactory rate of 6 per cent
annually over the last two or three last decades in Tanzania. But population
growth has curtailed that rate by a little less than half when considering GDP
per capita. Since the turn of the millennium, living standards have approximately doubled and poverty has fallen, although at a slower pace lately. The
structure of the economy has also changed with the GDP-share of agriculture
falling in favour of services and, to a lesser extent manufacturing. The share
of agriculture in employment has fallen too, but it is still high at 70 per cent.
Somewhat surprisingly, however, labour was reallocated primarily towards
the construction sector, retail trade and hospitality services with a noticeable
fall in labour productivity in the latter two sectors.

Such an evolution is hardly consistent with a powerful engine of growth
moving low-productivity agricultural workers to higher-productivity jobs in
the rest of the economy. It resembles more a process of demand-driven growth
where income gains, partly stemming from the expansion of mining (gold) and
favourable changes in the terms of trade, are spent on domestic production,
including construction investments and services.

Although limited, the relative increase in the output and employment shares
of the manufacturing sector sends a positive signal. That it has come with a
significant expansion of labour-intensive manufacturing exports is especially
encouraging. But it is still too slow, and the sector is too small to have a major
impact overall. There was also some promising progress in tourism before the
COVID-19 pandemic struck.

The fall in the employment share of the agricultural sector conceals a limited
reallocation of labour to the rest of the economy and, because of population
growth, an absolute increase in the size of the agricultural sector. There were
10 million workers in the agricultural sector in 2000 – 82 per cent of the
whole labour force. Demographic growth would have raised this figure to 17
million by 2018, but because of net migration to other sectors or to foreign
countries, they were only 15 million. Discounting foreign outmigration, the

absorption capacity of the non-agricultural part of the economy was thus quite limited. Somehow, the structural transformation worked backwards since population growth, at the rate of 2.8 per cent annually, overcame job creation in the dynamic part of the economy. Things would even look worse if part of the observed increase in the employment share of urban informal sectors were considered as participating in the accumulation of surplus labour in the non-agricultural part of the economy.

The preceding argument needs to be seriously qualified, though. As already pointed out, the Lewisian model presupposes the full utilisation of land in the context of densely populated countries, and it is in this specific context that the concept of an unlimited labour supply in the rest of the economy makes sense. In most African countries, including Tanzania, Benin, and Mozambique in the present project, this condition does not seem to be satisfied, so that the rural population may grow without labour productivity falling. If it did so, the low absorption capacity of the non-agricultural sector would not be a problem, and the economy's structural transformation could rest not only on the growth of the non-agricultural sector but also on an extension of the agricultural sector and on agro-industrial development.

It turns out that the Tanzanian agricultural labour productivity has been increasing during the period under analysis without it being possible to distinguish autonomous gains in yields per hectare and changes in the cultivated area. In any case, the average labour productivity in agriculture remained much lower than in the rest of the economy – the gap even slightly increased – which means that the structural transformation argument above remains correct in the sense that absorbing agricultural labour contributes to growth and to the reduction of agricultural low-productivity pockets. From that point of view, it remains the case that the absorption capacity of the non-agricultural sector was limited, and Tanzanian development has been little transformative. On the other hand, this discussion, and the evidence on productivity in agriculture suggest that this sector holds development opportunities that may presently be underexploited.

The situation of Tanzania today clearly differs from that of Taiwan or South Korea when those countries were at the same level of real income per capita – see Table 7.1. If the GDP share of agriculture is of the same order, the employment share is much higher in Tanzania, whereas the share of manufacturing in GDP and in employment are substantially smaller. These contrasts imply that differences in labour productivity between agriculture and other sectors are more pronounced in Tanzania, this being particularly true for the industrial or manufacturing sectors. This suggests that the structural transformation was already more advanced among the Asian tigers when they were at the same level of GDP per capita as Tanzania today. Of course, this advantage essentially reflects their higher level of industrialisation and the various circumstances and conditions that made it possible, including the accumulation of physical and human capital or their institutional setting.

The above type of transhistorical comparative exercise should obviously be interpreted with caution. There is no reason to expect history to repeat itself across countries or regions and it would be naïve to believe that the only pathway to development and structural transformation is the one followed some fifty years ago by the two East Asian countries. This being acknowledged, the above comparison provides diagnostic insights that can be helpful in gauging, almost mechanically, the development potential of Tanzania, and in highlighting the consequences of a missing engine of long-run growth.

Even with continuing favourable terms of trade, and possibly with the benefit of rents accruing from presently untapped reserves of natural gas, Tanzania's known natural resources are not sufficient to ensure the future prosperity of the country. Moreover, the labour content of such a strategy would be limited. To be effective and sustainable, especially in view of the fast population growth expected for still a few decades ahead, the structural transformation must additionally rely on a solid growth engine based upon the production of labour-intensive goods and services, the demand of which is not constrained by the size of the domestic economy. Obvious candidates are labour-intensive manufacturing exports, agroindustry, and tourism, the two latter corresponding to clear comparative advantages of Tanzania. As a matter of fact, the last three administrations committed to pursue a development strategy based upon industrialisation and export diversification. Yet, as of the late 2010s, results have been quite modest.

What can explain the limited success of this industrialisation strategy? Many factors should be mentioned. The most important one seems to be the difficulty of disciplining business. The big business sector is highly monopolistic, and, because of the fractionalisation of power within the dominant party, it had, until recently, a powerful leverage on state decisions that would go against their short- or medium-run interest. Things may have changed with the Magufuli administration in the late 2010s but, even then, the relationship between state and business was a difficult one. In theory, appropriate incentives, duly conditioned on results should permit to align business interests with the government's strategy. Such incentivising policies may infringe international WTO trade rules, which did not exist at the time of the East Asian industrialisation. Yet the subsidisation of credit at the firm level, duty exoneration on inputs, or the provision of critical infrastructure, are perfectly legal, and may help Tanzanian firms to become competitive on foreign markets where they are not present. However, managing such incentives and their conditionality on results requires a skilled and uncorrupted administrative apparatus, which may not be up to the task in Tanzania.

Other factors that hinder the diversification of exports include the limited public resources arising from a low overall level of taxation, the slow accumulation of soft capital – progress has been made in enrolling nearly all children of schooling age, but learning outcomes remain disappointing – and the slow rate of infrastructure building – until recently, Tanzania was a laggard in energy production and distribution, ports, roads, and rail transport facilities. With respect to the agroindustry, the complexity and ineffectiveness of the law governing land user rights is also often cited as a major impediment to commercial production and exports.

Moreover, excessive financial dependency on foreign countries or organisations may be considered as a source of uncertainty for future development. Foreign assistance has continued to account for 5–8 per cent of GDP since the late 2000s. One can therefore worry about what would happen to public investments if the volume of aid were to fall in line with the recent announcements made by several donors.

In summary, Tanzania's growth performance since the turn of the new millennium provides reasons to celebrate, although optimism must be tempered. Tanzania is still in the middle of the dualistic stage of development and the problem is whether it has the potential to reach in the foreseeable future the next stage of the structural transformation where the cross-sectoral labour productivity gap starts narrowing down. The evidence suggests that it lacks a clearly identifiable engine of sustainable long-run growth, and, more worryingly, an institutional setup appropriate to develop such an engine and meet the challenges ahead. More will be said about these institutional aspects in Chapters 8 and 9.

C Benin: Informal Growth as a Delusory Development Strategy

Benin's development over the last few decades has been characterised by modest growth performance and a rather atypical sectoral structure of employment. Although some acceleration has been observed during the last five years, the average annual GDP growth rate has been slightly below 5 per cent since 2000. With an almost 3 per cent rate of growth of the population, income per capita has grown rather slowly, and in any case at a slower pace than in the rest of the continent. Concerning the sectoral structure of the economy, it can be seen in Table 7.1 that the share of agriculture is of the same order as in South Korea and Taiwan when those economies were at the same level of income, but also that the share of the manufacturing sector is well below that of these Asian tigers. Benin's sectoral structure of GDP is close to that of Tanzania and, as a matter of fact, that of most sub-Saharan low-income or lower-middle-income countries. Where Benin is atypical relative to both sub-Saharan countries and the Asian comparator countries, however, is in the structure of employment. It exhibits a substantially smaller proportion of the labour force employed in agriculture – and therefore a higher proportion in other sectors – and a somewhat higher average labour productivity in that sector relative to the whole economy. The latter is partly the consequence of the importance of cotton production and exports in the Beninese economy, even though productivity in this activity has gone through sharp cycles since the turn of the century.

The modest rate of growth of the Beninese economy has its roots in an investment rate which has been below 20 per cent over the 1995–2017 period, except in the very last years of that period. As a matter of fact, the overall growth of GDP owes more to the movement of labour out of low- productivity agriculture than to sectoral productivity gains, except perhaps in agriculture, which benefits from a rather weak population pressure on available land. In effect, productivity has gone down in all non-agricultural sectors due to population growth, limited investment, and the inflow of labour coming from agriculture.

Despite the slow rate of growth, the structural transformation of the Beninese labour force has been substantial, but in a direction and according to patterns that are quite peculiar. In the decade from 2006 to 2015, it is estimated that 30 per cent of the agricultural labour force went to work in other sectors. As population growth was slightly higher, the total volume of agricultural employment went slightly down. What makes this restructuring so particular, however, is that, instead of going to work predominantly in the modern part of the economy, most workers went to the commerce and service sectors, which are the lowest productivity sectors outside agriculture. In commerce, new entries caused such a significant decrease in the mean income that it became hardly higher than in the agricultural sector.

There is ground to believe that the transfer of informal employment from agriculture to the rest of the economy has been caused by the largely informal cross-border trade (ICBT) with Nigeria rather than by the growth of the informal non-agricultural sector in tandem with the development of the formal sector (as observed elsewhere). This is a major specificity of the Beninese economy and the consequence, as well as a possible cause, of slow formal development. ICBT was first encouraged by differences in tariff and non-tariff barriers between Nigeria and Benin, which, as a member of the West African Economic and Monetary Union (WAEMU), applies the Union's rules. These differences create arbitrage opportunities for products legally imported into Benin and re-exported to Nigeria, where they enter illegally, and vice-versa for certain products smuggled illegally from Nigeria, where they are cheaper, into Benin. Such informal, and mostly illegal, trade activity is estimated to account for a little more than 10 per cent of GDP, only slightly less than official cotton exports, and to employ directly at least 2 per cent of the labour force, but much more indirectly. Both figures are thought to have sizeably increased over the last ten years.

By itself and through its upward and downward linkages, ICBT has huge effects on the Beninese economy and society. First, it contributes to increasing the incidence of informality and to nurturing a culture of corruption. Informality follows from the illegal nature of the activity, while corruption is used to buy the complicity of state executives and bureaucrats at various levels of the administration (including customs officers), and to obtain credit facilities from banks. This is particularly true for the large-scale smuggling of gas and other materials from Nigeria. Second, ICBT displaces some formal activities and diverts entrepreneurs from potentially more socially profitable lines of formal business. Several smuggled products outcompete domestic producers, most notably in gas distribution and cement production. Third, the failure of the state to curb this illegal activity entails a loss of intervention capacity in other areas indirectly affected by the cross-border trade. For instance, incentives to develop other activities are rendered inoperative, despite the presence of a dynamic entrepreneurial class. Fourth, at the macro level, illegal trade with Nigeria makes Benin dependent on the former's oil revenues and subject to oil price fluctuations in international markets. The macroeconomic shortcomings of this dependence are well known, especially for a country, which being a member of the WAEMU has adopted a fixed exchange rate system.

Cross-border trade with Nigeria is a revenue-generating opportunity and it is natural that some entrepreneurs have been eager to seize it. Yet its overall contribution to development may end up being negative, because of the informality and the culture of corruption that it has brought about, the uncontrolled smuggling that it has triggered, its unsustainability, and the marked dependence that it has created vis-à-vis Nigeria's trade policy. In effect, the ICBT activity has very much expanded between 2005 and 2014, due to the high price of oil. Yet GDP has not grown much faster during that period and poverty has changed little.

The fact that Nigeria recently decided to close its border with Benin, and has effectively stuck to that decision, is a sore reminder of the high economic dependency of Benin on its giant oil-exporting neighbour.

As mentioned earlier, cotton is the main formal activity in Benin, representing 12 per cent of GDP, and providing most of the country's formal export revenues. The organisation of the whole sector, and the respective roles of the private and public sectors, have gone through several changes over time, with direct effects on production and exports. Except for farming, the whole chain of production is structured as a monopoly and has been very much under the control of a single business group, headed by Patrice Talon, an entrepreneur who was elected president of the Republic several years ago and has just been re-elected. The monopolistic structure of the cotton sector necessarily entails significant efficiency costs. It is fair to recognise, however, that the sector has done rather well since its organisation has been stabilised, and this despite the monopolistic organisation of input provision, ginning, and commercialisation.

Since cotton exports or cross-border trade can hardly be conceived as powerful and sustainable vectors of development, it must be acknowledged that there is no engine of growth nor any real structural transformation process presently at work in the Beninese economy. For a while, it may have been the case that one could earn more by selling bottles of smuggled gas on roadsides than by working in the family farm, but this is not what development is about and such a restructuring is essentially unstable. More seriously, it is not clear that an effective growth engine able to trigger genuine structural change is about to be developed.

Benin has clear comparative advantages in agriculture, not least because there is plentiful land available, particularly in the northern part of the country, which has been largely neglected by successive governments in Cotonou. Developing agro-industrial exports is a real possibility as some encouraging starts are attesting. However, to push these further and to create an impetus that can spread to other areas and other lines of products requires a better provision of public goods, including a competent and non-corrupt bureaucracy, better infrastructure, more investments in quality schooling, and, most importantly, a clear and consistent development strategy.

The economic diagnosis about the stalled structural transformation – and about the kind of wrong-headed change that has taken place – is evident. The nature of the development strategy that should be pursued, whether on the agricultural side, by looking for complements to cotton, or possibly on the manufacturing side, by substituting domestic production for smuggled goods, is equally clear. The issue is why no such strategy had been implemented.

The answer must be found in the governance of the country, at least until Talon became president. There were then two major sources of rents, cotton exports and ICBT with Nigeria, and a rent-sharing agreement had been reached between the oligarchs who controlled these two sectors, including Talon, and those in power. Here is a perfect case of state capture. The equilibrium between the main players of that rent-sharing game got disrupted at some point, which led the oligarchs to compete for political power. One of them won. Precisely because political and economic power are now in the same hands, the nature of the equilibrium has changed, and new development strategies may emerge.

Although controversial, the present administration seems to be making progress in that direction. But there is still a long way to go before a genuine structural transformation and a definitive dent on poverty can take place in the country.

D Mozambique: Natural Resource Curse or Structural Transformation?

In comparison with other case study countries and a fortiori with South Korea and Taiwan, the combination of development advantages and shortcomings in Mozambique is quite specific. First, both its geography and ethnic composition are extremely fragmented. The country extends over 2,300 km from north to south and its population includes ten main ethnic groups, rather clearly differentiated by geographic region. From the latter point of view, Mozambique is comparable to Benin, except that the groups are physically more distant from each other, their isolation being amplified by a limited development of transport infrastructure. Second, the country obtained its independence much later than other African countries – as a matter of fact, not long after Bangladesh in 1975 – but it fell quickly into a long civil conflict which paralysed economic development for fifteen years. Third, similar to other case study countries in the Institutional Diagnostic Project (IDP) project, Mozambique adopted a socialist approach to development at independence, which delivered poor results, especially in the context of the domestic conflict. A transition towards a market economic system was made under the supervision of the international financial institutions, yet it proved more difficult and painful than elsewhere because it was launched at a time when the conflict was still ongoing.

Despite these hindrances, and largely thanks to an unusually high level of foreign development assistance, the Mozambican economy was able to grow at a fast rate until a few years ago. Growth was first triggered by the recovery from the civil war, and it then proceeded via more standard economic mechanisms. GDP per capita has thus grown at a little more than 4 per cent annually since the turn of the new millennium, and until 2016 when a major economic crisis struck for reasons which are detailed below.

Focusing on the last two decades, when the economy and the population have fully recovered from the civil conflict, two very different structural growth regimes were observed. Both the sectoral structures of GDP and employment varied little during the 2000s, except for some progress of the manufacturing sector. Overall growth originated in labour productivity gains across the board, including in agriculture. Things then changed radically during the 2010s: aggregate growth resulted essentially from a major sectoral restructuring away from agriculture, both in terms of GDP and employment, and in favour of non-agricultural sectors, except manufacturing.

This structural transformation has indeed been significant. During the six-year period from 2009 to 2015, just before the recent crisis, 1.5 million workers left agriculture to go to work in the rest of the economy. They represent 16 per cent of what would have been the agricultural labour force at the end of the period. This outmigration from agriculture has been so large that it overcame population growth and total agricultural employment fell. Yet the difference with the Southeast Asian countries and Bangladesh, and to a lesser extent Tanzania, is that the main sector of destination for those workers leaving agriculture was not manufacturing but private services, a sector where informal low-productivity jobs coexist with formal high- or median-productivity jobs. The issue then arises of the type of job taken up by agricultural workers, whether belonging to the former or to the latter category.

That labour productivity fell drastically in the private service sector suggests that employment increased for both types of job, probably more in the subsector based on informal low-productivity jobs. Yet the average labour productivity in the private service sector remained much above that in agriculture, so that the structural transformation mechanism kept working even though with some uncertainty about the exact nature of the process.

The manufacturing sector that came to represent 14 per cent of GDP in the 2000s did not contribute to the absorption of low-productivity labour in agriculture. This is not surprising given its lines of production. A major part of its initial growth has actually come from the production of aluminium made possible by the availability of cheap hydroelectric power on the Zambezi

River. But this activity, very much akin to the exportation of natural resources, employs only a small number of workers and has limited linkages with the rest of the economy. Moreover, its capacity stopped expanding around 2008, and since few other lines of manufacturing activity have developed afterwards, the GDP share of the manufacturing sector has fallen continuously since then. Over the last decade, the dynamic part of the Mozambican economy has been the extraction of coal and natural gas. The latter is expected to expand drastically in the future when the huge reserves discovered in 2010 will enter into full exploitation. Together with aluminium and electricity sales to neighbouring countries, coal and natural gas represent today some 70 per cent of total exports and their share of GDP may be estimated at around 12 per cent.

It is thus fair to say that Mozambique has become an exporter of natural resources and has tended to live on the related rent over the last few years. This explains why slow progress has lately been made in the production of tradeable goods, since the largest part of domestic growth has been accommodating the rent-based increase in the aggregate demand for non-tradeables, including private services. Quite telling in this respect is the fact that both agricultural and manufacturing output per capita have stagnated since 2010, and even somewhat earlier for manufacturing.

A possible reason for the lack of dynamism of the manufacturing sector is the absence of an entrepreneurial class in Mozambique. After independence, a period characterised by central planning, bureaucrats came to oversee the production apparatus, as Portuguese entrepreneurs had left the country. When the transition to a market economy took place a little before the end of the civil conflict, production units were privatised in favour of political personnel with little or no business experience and relying more on political connections and rent creation than commercial flair. Now that the country can live on the rent arising from natural resources, incentives for the appearance of an ambitious class of industrial entrepreneurs are weak and might become even weaker in the future. The demand arising from the rent will be mostly addressed to domestically oriented sectors such as services and construction and, presumably, it will mostly benefit the urban part of the country, and Maputo, the capital city, in particular.

The prospect of huge rents related to the future exploitation of natural gas has also exacerbated the appetite of rent-seekers and revealed the extent of corruption in Mozambique, at the same time as the ineffectiveness of the state apparatus to control it. A major scandal struck in 2016 about a US$2 billion embezzlement involving senior officials. It led donors to cancel foreign assistance payments, which plunged Mozambique into a deep financial and economic crisis. Yet the worst damage was created by the surging awareness of the pervasiveness of rent-seeking and corrupt practices, and their prevalence over entrepreneurship and bureaucratic effectiveness.[12]

---

[12] Accordingly, Governance Indicators plunged as was seen in Chapter 2.

Finally, we need to turn our attention to the agricultural sector and the issue of poverty, which affects more than 60 per cent of the population and is concentrated in rural areas. Given that the present and future engine of growth lies in natural resources whose exploitation is based on capital-intensive techniques, there is little hope for a quick absorption of low-productivity agricultural labour by the exporting sector, and for rapid advances on the poverty front. Can we witness a repetition of the structural transformation scenario that was observed in the early 2010s when a huge outflow of agricultural workers towards the service sector was observed? There is great uncertainty in this respect. Moreover, it was seen above that there was some ambiguity about the productivity of the jobs created in the service sector. Given the present size of the agricultural labour force, its low level of incomes and the absence of an autonomous labour-intensive growth engine outside agriculture, any reasonable development strategy must include an agricultural component.

An important challenge that Mozambique will face in the future thus lies in its capacity to use its forthcoming rents from gas exports to boost the traditional agricultural sector. This alternative to industrial development as the main engine of structural transformation, which befits land-abundant countries, must find its way into the minds of Mozambican policymakers if they want to make a real dent in poverty and establish a broader base for the country's development. However, agricultural or rural development in Mozambique is made more difficult than in most other countries by the geographic stretch and the ethnic fragmentation of the country. Combined with largely insufficient and inefficient transport infrastructure, both factors reduce labour mobility and limit the gains that could be obtained from inter-regional trade. Agricultural productivity increased at the same pace as the rest of the economy in the first decade of this century, when the recovery from civil war times was most likely completed. Its pace slowed down since then. Efforts should be made to revive this earlier period, possibly accelerating productivity gains while avoiding Dutch disease phenomena, which will unavoidably manifest themselves as natural resource exports increase.

In summary, the key development issue in Mozambique is whether existing institutions and the structure of political power will allow a structural transformation of the country that will simultaneously absorb part of rural labour, increase agricultural productivity, and expand local markets through a deeper physical integration of the country. The recent evolution of the economy and the reappearance of social and political tensions, including recent terrorist attacks in the coastal area facing the offshore gas fields, are worrying in this regard.

IV CONCLUSION

Several general conclusions can be drawn from the preceding brief diagnostic of economic impediments to long-run structural transformation in the countries covered by the IDP project and their comparison with Taiwan and South Korea at the time of their take-off.

First, the diversity of national experiences bears emphasis. It originates in different geo-economic contexts and initial conditions across countries. In all cases, a structural transformation has accompanied economic growth in the sense of a declining share of agriculture in GDP and total employment, and therefore a relative fall in the share of agricultural low-productivity labour reserves. In some cases, the process went far enough for the volume of agricultural employment to start getting smaller, as expected in Lewis's model. In others, the structural transformation was not strong enough to reach that result, but the question then arises as to whether this should be an absolute objective in countries where the land availability constraint is not binding, and agricultural labour productivity is increasing despite rising employment. In some countries, the engine of structural transformation is the manufacturing sector, or in effect manufacturing exports. In other countries, workers who leave agriculture find jobs in other sectors of the non-agricultural economy, including in the informal urban sector. This still contributes to overall growth and less poverty provided that the labour marginal productivity gap between agriculture and the sector of destination is large enough. But, of course, the impact of structural change may be limited if the domestic labour reallocation flow is between informal agricultural and informal urban production units.

Second, the nature of the 'growth engine' able to push the structural transformation forward is essential. South Korea and Taiwan's take-off stemmed from a growth engine operating in labour-intensive manufacturing exports. Bangladesh has followed the same path, even though the engine there was proved less powerful. Without the help of outmigration, it would not have been able to achieve the structural transformation that has been observed and is still far from being completed. By contrast, there has been some significant growth in Tanzania over the last decades, yet without a clearly identified growth engine, except perhaps a modest one in manufacturing exports. Instead, growth over the last two decades seems to have been mostly the result of the economy responding to the increasing domestic demand arising from favourable terms of trade, rising rents from natural resources and large inflows of foreign capital. The same can be said of Mozambique over the last decade when it started exploiting more intensely its natural resources, and of Benin which took advantage of its proximity with Nigeria. In all cases, there is much uncertainty about the sustainability of such growth regimes. Comparatively, there is less risk, more autonomy, more direct labour absorption capacity and more positive externalities on the rest of the economy in a growth pattern grounded in the exports of labour-intensive goods whose prices are more stable and global demand unlimited for relatively small economies.

Exports need not be exclusively composed of manufacturing goods. Land abundant countries may have some comparative advantage in agro-industrial exports – or import substitution in some cases – provided the adequate infrastructure, especially of transport, is available.

Third, the identification, and then the sparking and the maintenance of a growth engine require the designing and effective implementation of a clear state-managed development strategy. The provision of essential public goods and services for business activity is an absolute necessity. But it is unlikely to be sufficient. The presence of numerous market failures, of scale economies – which cannot be exploited in domestic markets – or of sunk costs – which slow down the adoption of new technologies or the opening to foreign markets – require more than such a minimal approach. In this respect, the industrial policy followed by the Asian tigers and the strong incentives they provided to manufacturing exporters are telling, as is the strong support brought by the state to the RMG sector in Bangladesh. They contrast with what is observed in the other countries. To be sure, 'development plans' are ubiquitous in the developing world, but they are not always well and realistically designed, and their implementation is often ineffective.

The design and implementation of such state-led development strategies require well-functioning institutions, and this is where serious institutional obstacles are likely to appear. They will be analysed in depth in the next two chapters, but it is hard to deny that a competent, honest and dedicated bureaucracy have been crucial assets in the success of East Asian development strategies. They often have been, and still are, in many instances, liabilities in the development of the four IDP case study countries.

Fourth, the need for well-thought strategies should not conceal the critical role of infrastructure, both hard and soft, in structural transformation. After all, it is because it could rely on a competent and effective bureaucracy, a population with a middle educational level, a dense transport network and power plants – inherited from the Japanese colonial era – that the KMT was able to launch an ambitious development strategy in Taiwan in the early 1950s, despite the country being then almost as poor as Mozambique is today. In South Korea, Park seized power in 1961 in the context of an economy which was as poor, inefficient, and corrupt as several low-income or lower-middle-income countries today. However, he could count on a strong bureaucratic apparatus and a sufficient number of highly skilled people to permit the quick elaboration and the rigorous implementation of a bold development strategy. Investments in this kind of soft infrastructure and education are necessary to establish basic initial conditions without which valuable opportunities cannot be seized when they arise.

Developing these instruments also calls for institutional prerequisites. The identification of the main obstacles to effective state capacity and the exploration of the role of politics in establishing and implementing structural change in developing economies are the two central issues addressed in the subsequent chapters.

8

Behind the Veil of Institutions Where Politics Matters

As is evident from our accounts, Taiwan and South Korea represent clear model cases of structural transformation and sustainable development. This does not mean that their experiences are easily replicable, but that they are inspiring in the following sense: they draw our attention to pivotal dimensions of the development process and to critical problems that a country willing to develop must face and solve as satisfactorily as it can. It is with respect to these generic issues that the confrontation between the experiences of Southeast Asian tigers and our four case study countries can prove illuminating and insightful. That replicability is necessarily limited already becomes evident when we look at the initial conditions that Taiwan and South Korea enjoyed at the time of their independence, be they historical, geographical, or socio-political.

It is essential to realise the existence of significant differences in initial conditions between these two countries and many others (including Bangladesh, Benin, Mozambique, and Tanzania), if only to help us mitigate our expectations regarding the scope and timing of development achievements in the latter. In the subsequent discussion, we therefore start by taking stock of initial conditions before addressing the generic issues that our institutional diagnostic approach has highlighted. In this chapter, the focus is on issues that involve politics. More specifically, we look at the role of political leadership and state autonomy in development. The institutions involved determine the quality of governance in a country, but they are not the only ones to have this effect. Institutions influencing state capacity constitute a second type of governance-related institutions. In order to keep the size of the present chapter within a reasonable range, however, we have decided to deal with state capacity issues in the next chapter.

That we devote a full chapter to the role of politics reflects the huge importance of political forces in shaping or constraining development. This is probably the most salient lesson to draw from our six case studies, and also the most original insofar as this dimension is largely neglected or under-estimated by many institutional analyses. Especially worthy of attention is the type of relationships that exist between state authority and business interests, with the possibility that the latter capture the former. Incidentally, the empirical relevance of political factors confirms the importance of the political economy approach to institutions that we have discussed in Chapter 1. In this regard, it is interesting to bear in mind that when the East Asian miracle was retaining the attention of the economics profession in the 1960s and 1970s, the key controversy was centred on the question of the respective roles of the state and the market in economic development.

With few exceptions, the arguments were about the advisability of an approach stressing the need for a developmental state to guide the market, and of an industrial policy in particular. Doubts about not only the capacity but also the readiness of the state to take up such a role were rarely expressed. In the following, fully informed by the trend of the growth and development literature that emphasises the critical influence of political economy constraints, we set off to revisit the comparison between East Asia and presently developing countries. The perspective that our contribution adopts is thus very much the same as the one used by Robert Wade (1988, 1990a, 1990b), a political scientist, in his seminal works devoted to the role of institutions in development.

I INITIAL CONDITIONS

Taiwan and South Korea were colonised by the Japanese, not by European powers. In the case of Taiwan this is reflected in a unique combination of strong central (colonial) power and decentralised development based on the modernisation of agriculture and the creation of rural industries, in sugar-processing in particular. Foundations for the physical and institutional infrastructures required for the purpose were laid in the colonial period and it is therefore no exaggeration to say that the development path of Taiwan (and, to a lesser extent, South Korea) was born in this period. Unsurprisingly, this path resembles the Japanese approach to development, which was initiated during the Meiji era and which T. C. Smith (1959) so vividly and accurately described.

Moreover, after the defeat of the Japanese in World War II and the subsequent advent of independence, US development assistance came in a big way to both Taiwan and South Korea. In the case of Taiwan, the US government was ready not only to go along the colonial path of comprehensive rural development but also to support, financially and through technical advising, the most radical land reform that the non-communist developing world has ever successfully implemented (from then to the present day). Its main component, the Land-to-the-Tiller Program, practically eliminated the upper tail of land distribution. The United States adopted the same policy line for South Korea where at independence land was redistributed from Japanese and domestic landowners to small farmers and tenants whose status was abolished. The apparent paradox of such a policy, which contrasted so strikingly with the approach adopted for other countries in Africa and Latin America, is unveiled as soon as we bear the geopolitical position of the above two countries in mind. Indeed, the central objective of US foreign policy, of which development cooperation policy was a part, consisted primarily of countering the communist influence from mainland China. This implied the need to help Taiwan and South Korea become an alternative model of rapid growth-cum-equity. The egalitarian approach was all the easier to adopt as the indigenous landlord class had collaborated with the Japanese colonial authorities and was therefore not seen as an ally whose interests had to be protected.

These exceptional circumstances contrast with those prevailing in most developing countries whose sheer existence was effectively guaranteed by the charter of the United Nations, and which did not feel such a direct challenge from communism as Taiwan and South Korea. Yet the latter were not the only countries that occupied a key geopolitical position during the Cold War era, and thus benefited from abundant development assistance from the United States. In particular, Egypt and Pakistan were also privileged recipients of foreign aid and yet their development performances have not been anything near those achieved by the two East Asian tigers.

With respect to geophysical conditions, mixed conditions prevailed in Taiwan. The mountainous terrain in a large chunk of the country has caused concentration of the population along a North–Southeastern axis, thereby easing connectivity throughout its inhabited portion. The other side of the coin is a strong population pressure on land resources, itself enhanced by the relatively poor fertility of many agricultural soils. South Korea was also characterised by high population pressure on land resources.

We are now ready to turn to the issue at the heart of the present chapter, namely the role of politics. As it is argued below, a relatively high degree of state autonomy and a high-quality political leadership are critical conditions conducive to effective and sustainable structural transformation and development of poor countries.

II QUALITY OF POLITICAL LEADERSHIP AND STATE AUTONOMY: TWO POLAR SITUATIONS

It is almost trivial to say that promising development prospects are conditioned by the quality of a country's political leadership. There can be no development without a developmental state that is led by a mission-driven leadership with a clear view of long-term objectives, a competent assessment of realistic ways of achieving them, and sufficient autonomy to implement its policies and reforms. This condition is especially important in an international catch-up environment in which development latecomers feel a strong pressure to bridge the gap with development leaders or pioneers, if only because national autonomy and external weight would be jeopardised by relative economic and technological stagnation. When a high-quality leadership is available from the beginning and is sustained over a sufficiently long period of time, the omen are good.

And they are still better if the political elite or the ruler benefits from a strong measure of initial legitimacy, so that sacrifices and discipline are more easily accepted by the population. Yet the condition of strong initial legitimacy is not necessarily fulfilled, as epitomised by the cases of Taiwan and South Korea.

A The Successful Experiences of Taiwan and South Korea

There are historical examples of enlightened elites or rulers enjoying a strong initial legitimacy and using this advantageous position to build a modern state, foster the emergence of a nucleus of industrial capitalists, transform traditional institutions, regulate the market, and harness the country's resources for the long-term advantages. Think of the Meiji elite in Japan (made of lower-level samurai and the intelligentsia), or of Atatürk and the Kemalists in Turkey. Having gained a lot of prestige from his military victory against Greek troops in the battle of the Dardanelles, Atatürk was in a position to embark upon radical reforms aimed at educating the people, removing the hold of religion on their minds, and totally transforming the Turkish legal system, even though a large part of the population was still immersed in a traditional Muslim culture (Kuru, 2009: 214–15; Zürcher, 2012: 136, 214). In the Middle East, this approach was later adopted by President Bourguiba in Tunisia, who was not supported by an army but by a strong single political party (Platteau, 2017, 2022). Even more recently, in the People's Republic of China, the far-reaching market-oriented reforms initiated under the paramount leadership of Deng Xiaoping in 1978 marked a critical turnaround for a country just emerging from a radical left-wing deviation and the ensuing chaos of the Cultural Revolution. They played a decisive role in launching China on a path of rapid catching-up with the advanced countries of the Western world (see, e.g., Wu, 2005).

The case of Taiwan illustrates a somewhat different situation: here, an enlightened elite from the KMT, the ruling party defeated by Mao's communists, settled down in Taiwan with the firm idea of one day reconquering continental China. On the island, it did not initially enjoy strong legitimacy because, unlike a common view that sees all (Han) Chinese people as forming a homogeneous group, its seizure of political power was considered with a lot of suspicion by the indigenous inhabitants, most of whom left China during the last centuries, starting in the seventeenth century (To this date, around 90 per cent of Taiwan's inhabitants are Han Chinese).[1] Bloody riots quickly

---

[1] These circumstances partly evoke those prevailing at the birth of Pakistan when a massive wave of Muslim migrants from India settled in the newly formed country. Here, homogeneity was supposed to arise from the common religion of the vast majority of inhabitants (Islam) yet, in reality, a great measure of heterogeneity prevailed as attested not only by the tensions between the immigrants from India (the Mohajirs) and the local population in the Sindh province, but also by the considerable cultural and historical differences between Balouchistan, the North-West Frontier Province, the Punjab and the Sindh provinces.

erupted which were harshly put down by an authoritarian KMT-dominated regime. However, thanks to impressive economic achievements and to effective dissemination of a national ideology, the same regime succeeded in overturning the situation by becoming much more popular than it was at the beginning of independence. Development success was obtained on the basis of a strong one-party state system, which can be described as one of 'authoritarian corporatism' and, paradoxically enough, had adopted important features of a central planning system. Convinced by the importance of its mission (regaining control of mainland China), it did not hesitate to impose strict controls on the population and was little inclined to bargain with established groups or organisations. Since the latter were rather weak, the task of the new masters of the country was relatively easy, much like the task of the Japanese colonisers had been before. Still, although the regime cannot be described as totalitarian, it was under martial law until 1987.

There were at least two main lessons drawn by the KMT from its failure to stay in power in China: the defeat was caused by both party indiscipline and business capture of the nationalist government. To solve the first problem, the party's organisation was tightened and purged of all unreliable elements. As a result, factionalism inside the party was bridled and the party state became a coherent entity placed under the paramount leadership of general Chiang Kaishek (1949–75) and, later, Chiang Ching-kuo (1975–88). As for the second problem, the regime was determined to keep all business groups on a short leash, treating them like all other social groups. Again, this was all the easier to do as almost all the established business firms from mainland China had chosen to migrate to the United States and Hong Kong rather than to Taiwan. It is thus revealing that the Taiwanese policy network hardly included representatives of private business, allowing the government to retain a striking degree of autonomy in setting the directions and details of policy. As a matter of fact, the powerful economic technocrats were largely free from societal pressures, being answerable only to the party's top leadership and responsible mainly for the overall performance of the economy and the success of the targeted sectors.

There were thus no intimate state–business relationships, and the KMT party state did not actually encourage the creation of big private industrial concerns. In fact, most industrial assets under the Japanese colonial administration and most *zaibatsu* were converted into SOEs, implying that key sectors of basic industry (power, cement, steel, heavy machinery, shipbuilding, defence-related industries, etc.) were under state control. Elements of political patronage were clearly present since political loyalty was a major consideration behind the choice of managers of state firms. Moreover, when state firms were allowed to go private or to be transformed into semi-public concerns, or when the state itself created new upstream undertakings, choice of owners was based on the same considerations: priority was given to loyalist mainlanders, members of a few politically well-connected native families known for their loyalty to the regime, or local county-level patrons with a stake in region-based oligopolies. Therefore, recruitment was not unambiguously based on competence under the KMT regime. The central principle was rather that only once political loyalty is assured can selection be made primarily on the basis of competence criteria. In other words, obedience to the top political leadership and compliance with its prescriptions were the most highly praised virtues. Because rules were strict and corruption was put severely under check, the system did not degenerate into widespread and uncontrolled cronyism.

Finally, the Taiwanese economy has a dual structure: coexisting with relatively large firms are SMEs, most of which are family firms located in both urban and rural areas, and largely owned and run by islanders. Institutionally, it is through industrial associations shaped and managed by the party state that the latter communicated its regulations and that performance-based incentives for investment, production, and export were negotiated. The overall picture is therefore one in which the state was largely autonomous vis-à-vis social groups and business interests, in particular. It was thus able to orient the destiny of the country, devising and implementing effective development policies, the success of which served as a sound basis for the emergence of an integrated economy, society, and polity. If clientelism was allowed, it was essentially of a competitive kind because the party state was eager to keep rent-seeking activities under tight control. In practice, this meant that it typically cultivated at least two competing factions in a given county, thus preventing a single faction from reaching a position of political monopoly over the distribution of economic rents.

Like Taiwan, South Korea could rely on an autonomous state. Yet the beginnings were more laborious. The first autocrat, Syngman Rhee, had no vision for the future of his nation and was more preoccupied with enriching himself and his ruling clique. His deeply corrupt and ineffective regime was heavily contested, particularly when students organised themselves toward that purpose, and he was forced to resign when he lost the support of the army. Convinced that civilian politicians would be unable to end the prevailing mayhem, re-establish order, and root out corruption, the army eventually came forward with another candidate who was to prove much more enlightened and long-lasting (two decades) than his predecessor, General Park Chung Hee. In order to achieve its objectives of fighting against corruption, poverty, and public sector ineffectiveness, he equipped himself with two powerful organisations: the Korean intelligence services (the KCIA) and the EPB. While the former's function consisted of controlling all segments of the civil society and ensuring law and order, the latter's role was to design and manage growth strategies based on development planning. To enable the EPB to fulfil its mission, Park staffed it with highly competent technocrats, and did not hesitate to grant its head a rank practically equivalent to that of prime minister.

Park's rule was no doubt harshly repressive and deeply authoritarian, and military personnel operated in most high- and medium-level tiers of state decision units. However, it is under his regime that South Korea embarked on a remarkably successful growth strategy. Having inherited a strong sense of discipline from the Japanese army doubled with a national patriotism reinforced by the threat of communist North Korea, the South Korean military, and the KCIA in particular, were able to build a rigorous, corruption-free administration where competence and discipline were the predominating virtues. In order to finance development along the priorities set by the EPB, and to eradicate corruption, all banks were nationalised. In addition, SOEs were created or strengthened in strategic sectors, such as energy, water, and transport infrastructure. Simultaneously, big private concerns, known as the *chaebols*, were brought to heel.

Because of its critical importance for the country's development, the relationship between state authorities and the *chaebols* deserves a few more words. Under Rhee's regime, when imports played a dominant role in the South Korean economy following the end of the Korean War and the demise of Japanese rule, big trading businesses were consolidated (e.g., Samsung, which was born under Japanese rule) or formed, which benefited egregiously from their privileged connections to the state. Privileges were obtained in the form of exclusive import licences in some key sectors. Progressively, and again under privileged conditions – in this case, high import barriers – these big trading companies started to expand their activities into local production. Collecting huge rents, the *chaebols* became dominant players in a political economy pervaded by bribery, vote rigging, and intimidation. A major turning point came with the advent of Park to supreme power. To avoid being nationalised outright, the heads of these firms accepted a deal according to which they would fully cooperate with the new authoritarian regime lest they should be expropriated. That the threat was credible was soon proven true when Samsung was caught in a corruption affair and immediately punished by being coerced to transfer its fertiliser company to the state. From then on, the *chaebols* became the main instrument of the state to push development in the direction set at the highest political level.

The South Korean model was born, which combines a mix of state-guided development centred on the task of coordination in macro resource allocation, on the one hand, and coordination in micro-corporate strategies managed by big private companies, on the other hand. While the former task aims at coaxing private economic activities so that they help move the economy in a certain direction, the latter is intended to improve the internal strategies of the private firms (product and process innovation, marketing, quality control, product standardisation, etc.) with the purpose of enhancing their efficiency (Okuno-Fujiwara, 1997). It is nonetheless interesting to notice that, on the occasion of the heavy industry programme launched by Park, the *chaebols* increased their bargaining power tremendously, to the point of challenging the state authority. It was actually in the logic of export incentives that they would raise the leverage of exporters since a major incentive to drive firms to enter the new heavy industry sector was the provision of credit at highly subsidised interests (which tended to be significantly negative in real terms) and state-guaranteed foreign loans. It was then unavoidable that some failures, sometimes major ones, occurred. What was unanticipated, though, is that because they had become 'too big to fail' as a result of a considerable expansion of their investments and operations, several *chaebols* had to be bailed out by the state against the terms of the contract struck between the two parties. *Chaebols* had acquired a real but ominous autonomy vis-à-vis the executive and the EPB. Still, the macroeconomic crisis that followed, itself accentuated by the second oil price boom, allowed the government to impose restructuring measures aimed at putting the *chaebols* on a sounder financial footing.

From the political economy standpoint adopted above, it is easy to imagine circumstances susceptible of derailing the development process. Two of them retain our attention here: (i) a leader enjoying strong initial legitimacy and authority makes flawed economic policy choices that cause the erosion of his/her political capital; and (ii) a leader who does not enjoy strong initial legitimacy and authority or prestige, and cannot be accused of having followed inept economic policies, is unable to resist the pressures and influences of powerful business interests. Strong initial legitimacy, it may be noted, means that a ruler is in a good position to achieve national integration, an objective especially challenging in the case of countries abruptly emerging from colonialism and comprised of disparate populations. It could be argued that inefficient economic policies are the price to pay for the building of a new nation, implying the existence of a trade-off between economic and political objectives. But this is not the sort of situation we have in mind under scenario (i), where economic policies and development strategies involve costs that could have been avoided, not costs justified by the need of national integration or political stability.

The ensuing discussion follows three successive steps. In the first step, pursued in the next subsection, we illustrate the possibility of faulty economics as understood under scenario (i). In the second step, pursued in Section III, we consider a number of important trade-offs between economic efficiency and political stability or social harmony, whether they arise from the challenge of nation-building or not. Finally, in the third step, pursued in Section IV, we address the pivotal issue of state capture by business interests, which corresponds to scenario (ii).

B Faulty Economics

A common feature of most faulty economic development policies is their excessive reliance on central planning and ignorance of the role of individual incentives. We begin with the regime of Julius Nyerere in Tanzania. Head of the party which led to the country's independence struggle, Nyerere soon became prime minister (in 1961) and then president of the newly formed country in 1964. Endowed with the considerable prestige and authority of the 'father of the nation', he embarked upon an ambitious development programme

announced in his famous Arusha Declaration in 1967. The ideological orientation was clearly socialist as it provided for the state control of the means of
production and exchange, implying the nationalisation of a major part of the
non-agricultural sector. As for the agricultural sector, a top priority under the
programme, a major approach to its modernisation consisted of exploiting
scale economies through the regrouping of dispersed subsistence farms into the
so-called Ujamaa villages. Lastly, Nyerere aimed at rapidly expanding education and health among the masses, as well as increasing equality and participation in public decision making.

Things did not go according to plan, though. For one thing, nationalised
enterprises were inefficient as a result of bureaucratic mismanagement, constant
meddling of politicians in the running of state firms, and mounting corruption among the managers themselves. For another thing, agricultural reforms
yielded so disastrous results that Tanzania shifted from being a net exporter to
a net importer of food crops in just a few years. Major problems arose from
the coercive displacement of rural populations, which were attached to their
traditional land location, and from the collectivisation of agricultural services,
including the marketing of crops that were traditionally disposed of through
rather effective networks of small and medium-scale merchants. Although
Nyerere initially resisted the pressure exerted by international donors and
organisations to modify his socialist strategy, he had eventually to give in
and accept both a stand-by agreement with the IMF in 1985 and a Structural
Adjustment Programme with the World Bank. That his over-confidence in the
guiding role of an all-powerful state and his consequent denial of the potential
role of market forces in the economy were misplaced and doomed to failure
became evident when the income per capita of the Tanzanians started to fall
after 1976. At the time of Nyerere's retirement (in 1985), Tanzania was actually among the poorest countries in the world.

This being reckoned, it bears emphasis that, if Nyerere thus lost the control of economic development policies, his political capital was not completely
wasted because of his indisputable achievement as the builder of the Tanzanian
nation. He succeeded not only in disbanding the multiple traditional chiefdoms
existing in the country, but also in bringing cohesion and national unity to the
country. Furthermore, this successful national integration drive was fostered
and complemented by major social investments in literacy, education, and
health, all areas in which Tanzania appeared as a rather exceptional performer
on the scale of sub-Saharan Africa. Finally, Nyerere has been a major factor
behind the country's political stability, a feat that owed much to his personal
integrity and his respect of constitutional rules. The latter became plain when
he decided not to run for a new presidential mandate, preferring to let his successors manage the transition to a market economy.

In Benin (then known as Dahomey), the long-lasting regime of Lieutenant-
General Mathieu Kérékou (1972–90) bears some similarities with Nyerere's
regime. Even though his ascent to power came as the result of a military coup

(the sixth one in succession since independence), Kérékou wanted to lead his country to a new destiny by undertaking a Marxist-Leninist revolution. This came at a time when, understandably, people aspired to more political stability without which development is impossible to achieve. Kérékou thus started his political career with a good measure of popular support, yet mainly in the north from where he originated. Therefore, his nationwide legitimacy was not as strongly established as that enjoyed by Nyerere (or Nkrumah in Ghana). His regime, inspired by the same 'socialist' vision, ended calamitously.

His leftist revolution involved the creation of a one-party state and single workers' and youth organisations, the nationalisation of production units and the development of collectivism. Democratic centralism and state economic interventionism became the new watchwords. The former principle implied restrictions of fundamental freedoms while the latter was to be applied with special vigour to agriculture where massive investments were contemplated to attain food self-sufficiency. Hopes were soon shattered as the poor economic performance of the new regime were coupled with its propensity to nurture corruption and rent-seeking. Top-down corruption and widespread inefficiency were noticeable in virtually all parastatal organisations, which turned out to be highly bureaucratic and hierarchical, as well as full of employees who, besides being corrupt, were in many cases unqualified or ill-qualified, and tended to be idle, undisciplined, and arrogant. Growing frustrations about the suppression of freedoms, corruption, months of salary arrears, and deteriorating living conditions resulted in street protests and general expressions of anger against the ruling clique by teachers, civil servants, workers, and church groups, in particular.

Mozambique's experiment with Marxist economics yielded basically the same results as those highlighted above. It was carried out by the Frelimo, the party which came out victorious of the independence struggle and many of whose members were opposed to private sector development. It is in 1977, three years after independence from Portugal, that Frelimo declared itself a Marxist-Leninist vanguard party in charge of establishing state farms, imposing agricultural mechanisation, and forcefully resetting important population groups, among other things. As could be easily anticipated, support for the regime among the peasantry sank as a result of these policies, and Frelimo was forced to quickly backtrack. The opposition party, the Renamo, which was historically supported by Apartheid South Africa and Rhodesia, did not miss the opportunity to exploit people's frustrations. Its base was enlarged from people with roots in the central part of the country and who had serious grievances, ethnic and religious, against the regime, to people who had become increasingly critical of its top-down orientation. And even though Renamo did not succeed in displacing Frelimo from power, probably due at least in part to electoral manipulation, there is no doubt that the nation-building efforts of the latter party were undermined by its misguided economic policies.

There are two important differences between Nyerere's regime, on the one hand, and the regimes of Kérékou and the Frelimo (in the socialist period), on the other hand. The first difference lies in the widespread corruption which characterised the latter regimes but not the former. Second, the success of the nation-building project of Nyerere contrasts strikingly with the fragmentation of Benin and Mozambique along ethno-regionalist lines. Under Kérékou, in particular, state rents disproportionately favoured his own region and network of supporters. Let us now delve into this second issue, which affects many developing countries, especially but not exclusively in sub-Saharan Africa.

III QUALITY OF POLITICAL LEADERSHIP AND STATE AUTONOMY: THE ISSUE OF NATION-BUILDING

To gain a proper understanding of the institutional constraints on development, we must reckon that political forces are frequently at work that hamper economic efficiency in a significant way. This is particularly evident when politics intrudes because of the need to build a cohesive nation and a viable polity, but other trade-offs may also be present which are related or not to the nation-building imperative. In the following, we start by highlighting the main challenge behind nation-building. We then proceed by referring to different situations involving a clear trade-off between economic efficiency and political stability or social harmony.

A The Challenge of Nation-Building

As Clifford Geertz (1973: 239) has pointed out a long time ago, the formative stage of nationalism essentially consists of 'confronting the dense assemblage of cultural, racial, local, and linguistic categories of self-identification and social loyalty that centuries of uninstructed history had produced with a simple, abstract, deliberately constructed, and almost painfully self-conscious concept of political ethnicity – a proper "nationality" in the modern manner'. In any nation-building process, therefore, the new states, or their leaders, must contain or domesticate primordial attachments instead of wishing them out of existence or belittling them. They must be able to reconcile them 'with the unfolding civil order by divesting them of their legitimizing force with respect to governmental authority, by neutralizing the apparatus of the state in relationship to them, and by channelling discontent arising out of their dislocation into properly political rather than para-political forms of expression' (1973: 277). Clearly, a nation-building effort can succeed only if a sustainable compromise can be struck between the need of a country to modernise its social, political, and economic structures so as to adapt to the world environment, on the one hand, and the need to win a mass-based legitimacy and to involve traditional interests that play upon primordial attachments, on the other hand.

In other words, there is a need to somehow overcome the severe horizontal cleavages inherited from the past, and which Basil Davidson (1992) called 'the black man's burden'.

Whereas in Taiwan and South Korea, the adoption of an effective and inclusive development model that did not ignore agriculture and the rural sector helped integrate the nation at a rapid pace, in most of sub-Saharan Africa, the daunting task pointed out by Geertz has only been partly accomplished and, in some countries or regions (e.g., Somalia and the Democratic Republic of Congo), it has not even started to be seriously addressed. If, at the supra-territorial level, pan-African ideologies and pan-African political movements (such as the National Congress of British West Africa, with branches in the Gold Coast, Nigeria, Sierra Leone, and the Gambia) had gained currency toward the end of the colonial period, 'tribal patriotism' (Iliffe's words) generally prevailed at the infra-territorial level, resulting in the spawning of innumerable local associations of traders, commercial farmers, teachers, clerks, and clergymen. Although their official purpose was to promote the development of the country, in actual practice they defended particularistic interests and did not hesitate to foster tribal identities to better achieve their objective. Nationalism was often a veil behind which many parochial interests concealed themselves. In the words of Iliffe (2007: 258), 'as predominantly local people, most Africans saw nationalism in part as a new idiom for ancient political contests'.

In sum, nationalist movements were frequently plagued by factional conflicts that put local issues in the forefront while minimising the importance of national party affiliations. The fact of the matter is that 'nationalism only partially aroused many of Africa's deepest political forces', and that 'responses to it depended on local circumstances' (Iliffe, 2007: 257). It is thus revealing that the political driver of many African insurgencies during the colonial period, such as the Mau-Mau rebellion in Kenya and the Teso rebellion in Uganda, was 'parochial rather than regional in orientation' (Jones, 2009: 50). Instead of being directed at district and regional officers, grievances typically originated in local conflicts between rival ethnic groups and clans, between different age groups (often youngsters against elders), or between ordinary people and traditional chiefs or village council chairmen. And they often turned around land issues (see Platteau, 2014: 190–6, for more details). Precisely because it was thus absorbed into local political rivalries, the nationalist movement was able to gather the support needed to remove the colonial rule. Yet it is for the same reason that after independence people continued to perceive national issues in terms of local interests and to judge their representatives and the state on the basis of their contributions to local advancement (Iliffe, 2007: 258, 267). As pointed out by Basil Davidson (1992: 112): 'From being instruments of pressure against foreign rulers, the new parties *at once* became instruments of rivalry within the nation-statist political arena', implying that the competing interests of the elites 'took primacy over the combined interests of the masses' (our emphasis).

When put in this broader perspective, Tanzania's success appears quite remarkable. A careful examination of the history of its nationalist movement sheds interesting light on the reasons behind this success. At the same time, it provides another illustration of the importance of initial conditions. The first thing to point out is that many African countries did not obtain independence after a protracted anti-colonial struggle (think of South and Southeast Asia by way of comparison), as the abdication of colonial power came rather abruptly and unexpectedly.[2] With the notable exception of Portuguese colonies, their nationalist movements were therefore of rather recent origin at the time of national emancipation. A direct consequence of this situation is that the African elites were confronted with the hard challenge of *abruptly* shifting from the comparatively easy task of claiming national freedom and sovereignty by uniting against an external power to the much more complex task of building a modern nation endowed with sufficient cohesion.

In this regard, Tanzania occupied a relatively enviable position because of the exceptionally widespread support enjoyed by the nationalist TANU party thanks to its use of the widely spoken Swahili language and the absence of strong tribal politics, conditions largely inherited from Tanganyika's nineteenth-century experience (Iliffe, 2005, 2007: 256).[3] The nationalist movement was also helped by the existence of multiple ethnic groups of comparatively equal strength – a feature at variance with the situation of many African colonies where the presence of a few dominant ethnic groups created a fertile ground for polarised conflicts. As a result, leading political figures functioned 'as companions rather than as rivals', in contrast to, say, Nigeria where they went at each other's throat for the spoils of office (Davidson, 1992: 112). Inside TANU, moreover, the radical and activist faction represented by the Youth League was remarkably effective in constructing a nationalist discourse, and defining the content of a national identity and common destiny. In pursuing its aim of gaining independence swiftly, it did not hesitate to openly blame the ruling clans for protecting unqualified officeholders and denying positions to educated individuals, for preventing appeals against the decisions of the chiefs' courts, and for perpetuating inefficiency, nepotism, and corruption (Giblin, 2005b: 143–4; Monson, 2005: 109–10).

These historical antecedents do not diminish the important role of Nyerere who, thanks to his outstanding leadership qualities, was able to give a decisive

---

[2] In the words of the winner of the 2021 Nobel Prize in literature, the departure of the colonial authorities in Africa 'was so sudden, so hurried that it somehow looked as though it was decided impulsively' (Gurnah, 2002 – our own translation from the French version published in 2021).

[3] TANU was thus denying the vitriolic denunciation of its claim to erect a new nation by Colonial Governor Twining: 'Tanganyika does not exist because of any natural unity, but only by the accident of events over which its peoples have exercised no control .... There is no language nor tradition nor interest in common, except what has been lightly overlaid by little more than half a century of alien authority' (cited from Iliffe, 2005: 177).

impetus to the process of Tanzania's nation-building after independence. Still, a balanced account must also acknowledge the influence of the Youth League on the leader, as well as the pre-independence dynamic of a strong and strictly disciplined nationalist movement.

B Trade-offs between Economic Efficiency and Political Stability

The social cost incurred as the result of the wrong-headed economic policies followed by Nyerere in Tanzania cannot be considered as the necessary price to pay for advancing the nation-building project: they represented a sheer waste of scarce resources. The same actually applies to another outstanding figure of a 'father of the nation' in Africa, Kwame Nkrumah in Ghana. Interestingly, the latter entered into a vivid controversy on precisely this kind of issues with his special economic adviser and Nobel Prize winner in economics, Arthur Lewis (see Tignor, 2006, for a detailed review). Indeed, Nkrumah argued that politics should have primacy over economics, and therefore refused the idea that his actions can be rated in terms of economic efficiency yardsticks since their objective was political. Lewis was particularly disturbed by the fact that Nkrumah was ready to justify some expensive and inefficient policies by the need to crush the opposition and put an elite political party in the position of the supreme authority of the country (Lewis, 1965: 30).[4]

It is nevertheless possible to look at the issue in a way more charitable to Nkrumah's standpoint (Kanbur, 2017). As hinted at above, we would then stress that building a new nation is hard in societies riven by intersections of horizontal cleavages of region, ethnic group, language, and religion. In such contexts, adopting policies that cut across the most important group divides in a nation may well be justified even though they involve efficiency losses from a conventional economic standpoint. In other words, reaching political compromises and maintaining a proper horizontal balance can be a top priority, especially at the early stages of state formation. In the following, we elaborate on this proposition by referring to four different issues, the last of which will deserve a rather detailed illustrative discussion.

Examples 1 and 2. Coming to mind here are (temporary) positive discriminatory policies in societies polarised between elite immigrant groups and the mass of native residents, or between elite and subject castes, or between historically favoured and traditionally backward regions (think of positive

---

[4] An important challenge to nation-building in Ghana (then, the Gold Coast) came from the determined opposition of the Ashanti kingdom to the rising pro-independence party of Nkrumah (the Convention People's Party, or CPP). Riddled with court intrigues and a host of dues euphemistically called 'gifts', the kingdom was ruled by a rigid hierarchy with the Asantehene at the top and customary chiefs at the lowest level. Educated people had no voice in such a system and therefore tended to join the CPP, the ideological platform of which better corresponded to their aspirations for emancipation (see Busia, 2020).

discrimination in Malaysia, India, and South Africa, as examples). Such policies are not first-best efficient, since they erode incentives to effort for both categories of people, yet they are arguably constrained-efficient in societies suffering from strong horizontal cleavages and lacking a minimum level of cohesion. Land and family laws are other policies or rules that reflect a trade-off between economic efficiency and political stability in societies fraught with horizontal cleavages. It is often the case, indeed, that the lawmakers willingly forsake the benefits of uniformisation and standardisation of local norms and informal rules in order to avoid head-on conflicts with local communities and their cultures (more on this in Chapter 9).

This is especially evident when states choose to accept and even institutionalise the coexistence of modern laws and their associated courts, on the one hand, and traditional norms and practices and their informal conflict-settlement mechanisms, on the other hand. Known as legal pluralism, this system has been implemented with remarkably positive effects on social and political stability in a country such as Indonesia where it dates back to the post-independence secular military regime of Suharto (see Bowen, 2003; Platteau, 2017). In that country, the same pluralistic principle has been followed in matters of schooling, since madrasas (formal religious schools) have been allowed not only to survive but also to expand side by side with secular public schools (see Marx et al., 2020). In such instances, inter-cultural harmony and social cohesion have clearly been prime objectives dominating economic efficiency concerns.

Example 3. Along the same line, a valuable insight is suggested by an analysis of the demand for wealth redistribution in the presence of 'communities', when the latter are conceived as so many social networks or informal organisations that provide local public goods specifically targeted to their membership.[5] The idea is that, if these public goods are largely funded by rich members, the poorer ones may not demand a reduction of the former's wealth, even when they directly benefit from the ensuing transfers. The reason is that they would then lose access to local public goods, which they value. In such a setup, Dasgupta and Kanbur (2007) show that in societies with multiple communities, each with its own exclusive public goods, pro-poor income growth would dampen or eliminate incentives to demand radical wealth redistribution whereas pro-rich income growth would have the opposite effect of generating incentives for the poor to support cross-community redistributive alliances along class lines. Moreover, pro-rich growth can turn opponents of redistribution in the middle class into its supporters. A possible lesson to draw from

---

[5] As group-specific public goods, one can think of those which serve the function of constructing and maintaining group identities (religious schools, places of worship and activities, community rituals and festivals, leisure amenities, etc.), or local physical infrastructures, such as feeder roads, irrigation systems, recreational facilities, and the like (Dasgupta and Kanbur, 2007: 1817).

this analysis is that a government eager to avoid the turbulence arising from demands for radical wealth redistribution has an interest in opting for pro-poor growth, even if it means that capital accumulation may be slowed down and that informal agencies beyond the grasp of the state will continue to play an important role in maintaining social order. Otherwise, pro-rich growth may be its preferred choice of development strategy.

A serious problem with the pro-poor growth solution, however, is that communities are and remain separated in the sense that the members of a given community do not have access to, or do not value the activity (or public good) constitutive of another community's identity. In these conditions, they have an incentive to support the expropriation of other communities, thereby creating a fertile ground for sectarian political platforms and communal strife. Fortunately, such a forbidding state of affairs can be potentially avoided if, rather realistically, some individuals are ready to relate to other communities or have multiple identities. Even more promisingly, they may want to contribute to a public good that transcends communal divisions and incorporates a 'meta-communal' element to their self-identity, assuming that such a good exists or can be created. In a two-community framework in which intra-community wealth differences (i.e., vertical inequality) are abstracted away, Dasgupta and Kanbur (2005) show that the two communities will contribute to the meta-public good provided that the wealth gap between them (i.e., horizontal inequality) is relatively small. In addition, while they remain separated at the level of their own specific public good, no individual has any incentive to support expropriation of the other community. The reason is that the capacity of the latter to contribute to the meta-public good, which both communities value, would then be reduced.

By contrast, a wide wealth gap implies that only individuals in the richer community will contribute to the meta-public good, an outcome that entails the risk of communal tension. In this instance, what happens is that 'even non-communal forms of identity, such as nation, class or language, would become identified with the dominant community, and would not have the capacity to hold distributive conflicts in check' (Dasgupta and Kanbur, 2005: 160).[6] Illustrative of this possibility is Indonesia (and, we could add, Myanmar) where, despite attempts at developing a national identity, ethnic tensions have remained strong because of persisting inter-community wealth disparities (2005: 164). Malaysia offers a better picture, probably thanks to the afore-mentioned positive discrimination policies, which have helped mitigate wealth inequalities between the Bumiputera and the Chinese communities. The central message is therefore the simultaneous importance of a meta-communal public good, which is essentially tantamount to a nation-building project, and

---

[6] Note that if some members of a community are allowed to contribute to the public good constitutive of the other community, large wealth disparities will generally create a situation in which no individual in either community will seize upon this opportunity.

a moderate inter-community inequality in wealth. Deliberate efforts to create these two conditions, even if they involve significant losses of economic efficiency, hold the key to communal harmony in societies fraught with deep divisions of race, ethnicity, religion, or language (2005: 164).

Example 4. Concessions which a civilian ruler or regime makes to the military with a view to preventing them from seizing power through a coup, and following their own vision of the country's destiny, provide yet another illustration of how economic efficiency may be sacrificed to maintain political stability. In most instances, such concessions take the form of allowing the military to participate in lucrative business activities on terms that are generally very generous. Bangladesh is a case in point: since 2009, after a short and disastrous return to the forefront of politics, the army retreated to its barracks and agreed to support the civilian government, yet not without becoming a major beneficiary of contracts for large-scale infrastructure projects, in particular.[7] Involvement of the military in business is even more massive in countries such as Pakistan, Myanmar, Syria, Egypt, and Sudan (see Siddiqa, 2017; Sayigh, 2019). Because contracts, licences, monopoly rights, and other advantages are typically granted to the army as political favours, implying that they are unaccompanied by performance-based conditions, and because the beneficiaries have been selected for their status in the military hierarchy and not for their management qualities, losses of economic efficiency are unavoidable. Often revealed as time delays, cost overruns, and poor quality of the works supplied, they are actually the price which the civilian regime is willing to pay in order to co-opt the men in uniform and keep them inside their barracks or on the backseat of politics.

In reality, the political game is more complex than what has been suggested above. As theorised by Auriol, Platteau, and Verdier (2021), and explained in Chapter 1, the political game played out in countries where radical religious movements are present is a triangular game between the ruler, the military, and religious clerics. An important implication of this more complete perspective is that in order to stabilise his power and avoid a state coup, a ruler may choose to reduce the strength of the military and simultaneously co-opt religious leaders. This strategy of double co-option is likely to involve even higher efficiency costs than the strategy of exclusive military co-option because religious authorities are typically opposed to key institutional reforms that would encroach on their traditional prerogatives. Such reforms include those aimed at removing land access rules which hamper efficiency or maintain many people under feudal shackles; at emancipating individuals from the sway of communal or collective prescriptions; at replacing rules emphasising status or loyalty by

---

[7] In Bangladesh, when the military were actually in charge of running the economy during the years 2007–2008 (they were the real actors behind the smokescreen of an interim civilian government), the results proved so disastrous that they lost much of their credibility as economic managers.

merit-based selection; or at combating forms of social discrimination, against women and low caste members in particular.

The cost of religious co-option is particularly evident in the case of Pakistan, a country founded on the idea of a Muslim identity distinct from the Hindus of India. Unsurprisingly, Muslim movements and organisations of a conservative puritan kind (the Deobandi school of Islam) were active from the beginning, pressuring successive governments to decide how far they would go in the direction of creating a Muslim state. On the other hand, because of its geopolitical situation and, more specifically, because it has borders not only with India but also with Iran, China, and Afghanistan, Pakistan has attracted a lot of attention from the United States. Economic cooperation and, above all, military assistance, have thus been willingly provided by the US superpower, which had the effect of reinforcing the influence of the Pakistani military (Haqqani, 2005; Shah, 2014). Interestingly, and in broadly similar geo-political circumstances, General Ayub Khan (1958–69) pursued a course that seemed to replicate the regimes of Chiang Kai-shek in Taiwan and Park Chung-hee in South Korea. He thus pursued active industrialisation policies that made the country's economy the fastest growing one in Asia, and major infrastructural projects (hydroelectric stations, dams, and reservoirs) were completed under his watch. In addition, he cracked down on religious hardliners, banned the Jamaat-e-Islamic fundamentalist party, and checked the political influence of Sufi orders. This allowed him to enact remarkably progressive family laws. Lastly, he inherited a colonial legacy of strong bureaucratic state and weak representative institutions: elected politicians only had an advisory role and were effectively subordinated to an executive rule where the military and the civilian bureaucrats called the shots. A combination of circumstances caused his downfall: corruption of his family and the clique around him, accusations of vote rigging and political murders, an unpopular peace treaty with India, popular uprisings in East Pakistan (today's Bangladesh), and food demonstrations (Abbas, 2005: 37–54; Wilder, 2009).

A major turning point happened somewhat later, under the regime of another general, Zia ul-Haq (1978–88). In the wake of his predecessor, Zulfikar Ali Bhutto, Zia reinforced the subordination of the bureaucracy to elected politicians, so much so that the latter acquired the power to suspend and transfer uncooperative civil servants and gained unprecedented access to district officials inside strategic departments. Under his watch, the administration thus became highly politicised. Also worth singling out are Zia's pandering to emerging business elites constituted as political families ready to play by the new rules of the political game, as well as the Islamisation at his behest of the administration, the army (and the intelligence services), the judiciary, and the education sector (Malik et al., 2022). All these steps meant that, in spite of indisputable economic accomplishments – he oversaw the highest GDP growth in the country's history – Zia deeply undermined key Pakistani institutions with ominous long-term consequences (Cheema et al., 2005; Platteau, 2017: 217–23). The country's change of direction brought about by Zia led Pakistan astray, as none of his successors, including not only General Musharaff but also civilian presidents (Benazir Bhutto, Nawaz Sharif, Imran Khan), would really dare question the new orientation chosen for the country, namely a model based on a close military-religious alliance.

Since Zia, Islamist clerics have been systematically instrumentalised by the army and the intelligence services (known as the ISI) for the purpose of serving their foreign policy objectives, particularly in Kashmir and Afghanistan. In their view, indeed, India has always constituted a serious threat to the very existence of the Pakistani nation whose defining feature is Islam. To counter this presumed, and in fact much exaggerated threat, it was deemed important to intervene in neighbouring countries with a view to stirring up trouble or promote the interests of Pakistan. It is for such tasks that extremist militias acting as surrogates in the defence of national identity confounded with the Muslim faith proved highly convenient. However, if radical religious clerics trespass the limits set by the army, they are quickly called to order, as has been recently demonstrated by the repressive military campaign along the Afghan border (in North-West Frontier Province). In the end, it is the prominent role of the army (and the ISI) as the carrier of the national project, and its continuous manipulation of Islamist movements, that have forced the civilian authorities of Pakistan to grant egregious privileges to the men in uniform and to let radical clerics wield an outsize political influence (Platteau, 2017: 209–22). The long-term efficiency costs have been considerable.

When Bangladesh, then East Pakistan, seceded from (West) Pakistan, Islamist movements, the Jamaat-e-Islami in particular, took sides with the central government against the pro-independence fighters backed by India. Being considered as traitors and even war criminals, they invited the opprobrium of a large part of the population and wielded much less power than their counterparts in Pakistan.[8] And, yet, because authoritarian rulers chose to cynically court them in a way reminiscent of Zia's strategy in Pakistan, they were able to gain unexpected political influence. Whereas under Sheikh Mujibur Rahman (1972–5) the new nation was constitutionally defined as *Bangali*, that is, alongside an ethno-linguistic secular dimension, Generals Ziaur Rahman (1977–81) and Ershad (1983–90) opted for transforming 'Bangladesh identity from ethno-linguistic Bengali culture and secular polity to religious-cultural Muslim Bangladeshi identity and Islamic polity' (Sheikh and Ahmed, 2019: 11–12). Such a move, as stressed by the same two authors, was part of a tactic consisting of portraying political rivals as intended to make Bangladesh into

---

[8] It must be noted that even in Pakistan popular support for Islamist movements is limited: moderate Muslims consider their ideology as coarse and their tenets as poor exemplars of Islamic scholarship (compared to the great schools of Islamic thought that were found in India at the time of the partition, in Delhi and Hyderabad in particular). The power wielded by Islamists, so our argument runs, is largely decided by secular political actors whose strategies may be partly based on their instrumentalisation (see Platteau, 2017 for a detailed elaboration of this thesis).

a satellite state of Hindu India, and of reviving an Islam-oriented Bangladeshi nationalism susceptible of gaining the support of religious and conservative parties. In the same move, Ziaur Rahman created the BNP, a party which was also joined by many members of left-leaning political parties with links to China and anti-India sentiment.

It is thus by presenting the secular Bengali identity as pro-Indian or pro-Hindu in a context where Indian domination was resented by popular masses, that the regimes of Ziaur Rahman and Ershad attempted to obtain their legitimacy. Despite successfully gaining public support, the former was nevertheless unable to ensure the backing of the armed forces and he was eventually assassinated by a group of army officers, thereby replicating the tragic fate of the nation's founder himself.[9] What deserves to be stressed, however, is that in stark contrast to Zia's regime in Pakistan, the use of Islam under Ziaur Rahman and Ershad was more a matter of ostensible symbols than real substance. It rested on displays of Quranic verses and Prophet's sayings on posters hanging in government offices, telecasting of principles of Shariah on radio and television, frequent visits of mosques and Islamic shrines by high-level officials, regular attendance by the same to religious festivals and events, establishment of a new Islamic university and provision of generous grants to religious institutions, promotion of Islamic learning, and the like (Sheikh and Ahmed, 2019: 13).

After a prolonged period of authoritarian rule with generals at the helm of the country, Bangladeshi politics became essentially the arena for contest between two major political parties, the BNP and the AL, led by two dynastic figureheads (the so-called begums), Khaleda Zia and Sheikh Hasina, respectively. Even though in 2013 the Jamaat-e-Islami was banned from registering and contesting in elections (by a High Court order), twenty-two Jamaati candidates obtained tickets to run under the BNP banner. A lot of turmoil ensued, and the BNP eventually decided to boycott the 2014 elections. The AL won an easy victory and a few years later, in 2018, Sheikh Hasina threw her rival begum in jail. There then began an era of uncontested political dominance of the AL, backed by the army and the intelligence services, duly purged of all BNP elements and properly remunerated for their support (see above).[10] As for the Jamaati leaders, they were not only excluded from politics but also sued for crimes committed during the independence war.

---

[9] It is revealing that, in the chain of events that preceded the assassination of Sheikh Mujibur Rahman by a group of renegade officers, a key turn was his conciliatory stance towards Islamic groups combined with his distancing from his left-wing allies. In 1973, for example, he released thousands of Islamists from jail while ignoring virtually all his imprisoned allies from the left. After the assassination of Sheikh Mujib and much of his family, a martial law government was proclaimed. Thanks are due to Umar Salam who pointed this fact to us.

[10] Close to the security services and the police is a paramilitary force known as the Rapid Action Battalion (RAB). In addition to its official function of arresting drug gangsters and terrorists, this genuine thugocracy is often used to settle political scores and hound members of the political opposition, not hesitating to kill them with total impunity (Economist, 2022a: 47).

As can be seen from our examples, Example 4 in particular, efficiency losses may result not only from the pursuance of political objectives such as the imperative of nation-building, but also from the possibility that the strategy designed toward that purpose is misguided or unnecessarily costly. In this matter, unfortunately, it is practically impossible to make out whether a specific strategy is constrained-efficient in the sense of minimising efficiency losses given the need to attain a certain political objective. Quality of available leadership and the international environment are critical determining factors and are essentially exogenous. Nonetheless, a central lesson from the experiences of Taiwan and South Korea must be borne in mind: to a non-negligible extent, nation-building can be achieved gradually as the consequence of successful long-term development strategies. In short, nation-building is partly endogenous to sound development policies. To carry out these policies, however, there is still need for minimum state capacity and a strong commitment of the country's leadership to the idea of development as a lengthy process embodying structural transformation and deep societal change. The former condition, state capacity, will be examined in detail in Chapter 9. As for the latter condition, commitment to development, it implies that the interests of business oligarchs or Big Men are kept at bay so that they do not intrude on the domain of policymaking. Unfortunately, as argued in the rest of the present chapter, it is often the case that the state is captured by powerful private interests.

IV QUALITY OF POLITICAL LEADERSHIP AND STATE AUTONOMY: THE RISK OF BUSINESS CAPTURE OF THE STATE

State capture by business interests, as we have found out, is a critical and much neglected obstacle to structural transformation and development. To present our findings effectively, we have opted for a two-step approach. First, in the light of the successful experiences of our two comparator countries of East Asia, we propose a general framework enabling us to shed light on the conditions under which business interests can be tamed for the benefit of general development. Second, we examine the way state–business relations work and impede development in Benin, Tanzania, Bangladesh, and Mozambique in that order.

A Sketching a General Framework

We now turn our attention to the first task, which amounts to highlighting what is perhaps the most critical institutional difference between Taiwan and South Korea, on the one hand, and many poor developing countries, on the other hand. To recall, the state in the two Southeast Asian tigers has been effectively insulated against potential pressures from private sector interests. In this sense, there were strong states, able to impose a coherent and sustained direction on the economy and the society. Because their leaders did not initially enjoy great popular legitimacy, their power had to rest on authoritarian rule whose effectiveness depended on the support of a powerful organisation such as a political party (the KMT in the case of Taiwan), the army, or the police and intelligence services. And it is only after the regime's economic and social achievements became largely visible that its legitimacy was gradually building up, thereby making relaxation of restrictions on freedoms, political liberties in particular, eventually feasible.

In many poor developing countries, rulers with relatively low initial legitimacy and no strong supporting organisation at hand were forced to seek access to political power through elections of some sort, whether in the open space of the whole nation or in the restricted arena of a single party. If, indeed, there is no strong ruler or autocrat at the top of the state and the dominant (single) party, competition for the leading position inside this party is typically stiff. In such conditions, and particularly on the occasion of elections, ambitious politicians need to court wealthy individuals or Big Men (men with deep pockets) to finance their political campaigns and the distribution of perks to the heads of their voting blocs and their clientelistic networks between election rounds. In return for their financial support, the Big Men demand advantages and privileges which only politicians can provide, such as import, trading or manufacturing licences, public procurement arrangements and direct adjudication of juicy government contracts, privileged access to on-sale state assets, tax exemptions, licences, special land grants, favourable labour laws, interference in the settlement of judicial and administrative cases, and so on.

When open electoral contests take place in the above-described context, a major feature of political parties is that they are not organisations articulated around a clearly defined programme, but rather loose setups based on the strong personality of the leader and whose main role is to establish electoral alliances for the purpose of winning the forthcoming election. They are single-purpose vehicles designed solely to catapult their leaders to power (*Economist*, April 2, 2022b 36). Not surprisingly, party switching is a common phenomenon, sometimes called 'turncoatism' (in the Philippines, for example), and electoral alliances made in every legislature are essentially opportunistic (for illustrations, see Qerubin, 2012, 2016, for the Philippines; Malik et al., 2022a, 2022b, for Pakistan). Just take the example of the three most important politicians of Kenya: Mr Odinga has belonged to six political parties, Mr Ruto to five, and President Kenyatta to four. Moreover, in February 2022, Kenyatta endorsed Mr Odinga, once his bitterest rival, and denounced Mr Ruto, his deputy for the past ten years. Politics in Kenya, as in many other countries, such as Benin and Tanzania in our sample (see details later in this chapter), is thus like looking through a kaleidoscope: 'the bits are still the same but every time you shake it they form different patterns' (Economist, 2022b: 36).

The outcome of this personalised and non-programmatic political system, in which politics is pervaded by clientelistic practices and electoral strategies are focused on contingent political exchange such as patronage and vote-buying, is the loss of autonomy of the state and its consequent inability to guide the country on a path of sustained development compatible with the general interest. In addition, there is the deleterious effect of corruption and sleaze inherent in crony capitalism: public trust in public institutions such as the judiciary, tax authorities, and customs service is gradually eroded while perceptions that the country's political economy is rigged in favour of Big Men and their political associates inexorably undermine support for the regime.

An important determinant of the Big Men's bargaining power is the relative demand for politics money, that is, the ratio of politicians seeking to reach top-level positions to the number of business people susceptible of financing their ambitions. An immediate implication is that the more fractionalised the political space – the higher the number of political candidates – the greater the ability of business oligarchs to dictate their conditions on these candidates. And, conversely, when the political arena is less competitive, either because political parties or groupings are rather few or because the number of factions within the dominant party is rather low, we expect the bargaining strength of the business oligarchs to be relatively weak. The relationship between the relative number of political candidates and the scope for business capture is not monotonous, however. As a matter of fact, if the number of these candidates is high compared to the number of business oligarchs, the latter will be unwilling to finance the former because the probability of their being elected is then too small. This incentive dilution mechanism can be overcome only by driving politicians to regroup and form coalitions for the purpose of elections, an outcome which they should quickly understand is in their own interests. If that does not work, powerful business people may be tempted to run for elections themselves, a last resort solution which they are typically eager to avoid, especially if they belong to foreign communities. As we are soon going to verify, Beninese politics aptly illustrates the two possibilities, political regrouping and the move of oligarchs to the forefront of politics.

For reasons easy to understand, the endogamous relationships between state and business are intrinsically opaque. Lack of transparency is especially valued by businesspeople belonging to ethnic minorities, such as Chinese entrepreneurs in Malaysia and Indonesia, Indian entrepreneurs in Tanzania, Kenya, Uganda, and South-Africa, or Lebanese traders and businessmen in West Africa. Being vulnerable to xenophobic attacks when they are economically successful, they are eager to act behind the stage, believing rightly that the more occult their power and their influence the more effective they will be. Deviating from this strategy can be extremely costly, as recently epitomised by the sudden flight of the Gupta brothers from South Africa, where they publicly appeared as the financial arm and the policymaking brain of the highly corrupt President Jacob Zuma. It is only under exceptional conditions of political uncertainty that Big Men – typically not members of ethnic minorities – can consider it rewarding to personally claim the supreme position of political power. President Talon of Benin vividly illustrates this possibility.

Table 8.1 schematically presents and illustrates the political regimes that arise under different combinations of initial conditions and effectiveness of social and economic development policies. Two types of initial conditions are considered: the initial level of legitimacy of the ruler and whether the latter could rely on a strong supporting organisation when starting his/her rule. By strong organisation, we mean an organisation, such as a single party, an army, or police and intelligence services, which meets the following requirements: (i) it fulfils a public function and does not enjoy an electoral mandate; (ii) it possesses a unified internal structure; and (iii) it is not subservient to particularistic interests, business interests in particular, whether domestic or foreign. Thus, an army or a political party lacking a strong leadership and fraught with factionalism, or an army at loggerheads with the intelligence services or the police, or a puppet army at the beck and call of foreign interests, are all examples of weak organisations according to our definition.

We distinguish between two types of policies, developmentally sound or developmentally flawed or, equivalently, enlightened and non-enlightened. Developmentally sound policies have four characteristics that must be simultaneously observed, although to varying degrees: (i) they rely on private initiative and the associated individual incentives, meaning that the market mechanism is allowed to operate and static efficiency considerations are given due attention; (ii) they create the physical infrastructure needed to make private initiative profitable; (iii) they provide for human capital accumulation, thereby laying the basis of dynamic efficiency; and (iv) they ensure that income inequalities are held in check, so that whatever national integration exists is reinforced rather than eroded.

Developmentally flawed policies are those that fail to satisfy at least one of the above four conditions. For instance, economic and other policies driven by dogmatic ideologies rather than by pragmatic considerations cannot meet requirement (i), even though they may well satisfy some or all of the remaining requirements, sometimes to an admirable extent. The ideology guiding economic policymaking is political when a government rigidly adopts socialist policies of central planning, which repress the market mechanism and give pride of place to a bossy state. This situation is observed in most so-called socialist regimes, including states bent on social achievements and emancipation at the expense of competitiveness considerations (the state of Kerala in south India comes to mind here). Ideology is also political when a radical laissez-faire approach is advocated without due consideration to the need for redistribution and sufficient attention to the importance of collective goods, including human and physical capital. In these instances, objective (i) is pursued at the expense of all the other requirements. On the other hand, ideology is religious when rules and policies are governed by religious prescriptions and when recruitment or promotion (at least in public organisations) is based on profession of faith allegiance and not on competence criteria. Regimes that ground their policies in religion are likely to fail with respect to both conditions (i) and (iii).

TABLE 8.1 *A summary table of potential political regimes as per their initial conditions and effectiveness of development policies*

Initial conditions crossed with quality of development policies	Initial legitimacy			
	Strong		**Weak**	
	Supporting organisation: Strong	Supporting organisation: Weak	Supporting organisation: Strong	Supporting organisation: Weak
Developmentally sound policies	Atatürk (Turkey, 1923–38) Habib Bourguiba (Tunisia, 1957–87) Deng Xiaoping (People's Republic of China, 1982–7) Xi Jinping (People's Republic of China, 2012–)	Ellen Johnson Sirleaf (Liberia, 2006–16) Pravind Jugnauth (Mauritius, 1983–)	Chiang Kai-shek and Chiang Ching-kuo (Taiwan, 1950–75 and 1975–88) Park Chung-hee (South Korea, 1962–79) Ayub Khan (Pakistan, 1958–69) Paul Kagame (Rwanda, 2000–)	Patrice Talon ? (Benin, 2016–) John Magufuli ??(Tanzania, 2015–21)
Developmentally flawed policies	Julius Nyerere (Tanzania, 1964–85) Kwame Nkrumah (Ghana, 1952–66) Frelimo (Mozambique, 1975–) Gamal Abdel Nasser (Egypt, 1952–70) Houari Boumediene (Algeria, 1967–78)	Zulfikar Ali Bhutto (Pakistan, 1971–8) CCM post-Nyerere (Tanzania, 1985–)	Mathieu Kérékou (Benin, 1996–2006) Anwar al-Sadat (Egypt, 1970–81) Zia ul-Haq (Pakistan; 1978–88) Omar al-Bashir (Sudan, 1993–2019)	Failed states: Somalia Post-Gaddafi (Lybia, 2011–) Haiti

Finally, regimes dominated by big business interests, often referred to as crony capitalism, may be lacking not only with respect to (i) – since market competition is then throttled – but also, possibly, with respect to (iii) and (iv).[11]

Before looking at country-specific lessons, two important remarks are in order. First, the actual effectiveness of enlightened or developmentally sound policies depends on the existence of an enabling international environment in the form of economically advanced countries allowing poor developing countries to temporarily gain special access to their markets and shield their domestic industries from the effects of foreign competition. Second, the question of democracy has been deliberately eluded, the main reason being that development has often been pursued in contexts where individual liberties were initially restricted. The historical experiences of Taiwan and South Korea, as well as the contemporary examples of communist China and Vietnam, are cases in point. Whether the trampling upon individual liberties is justified by long-term development objectives is an immensely complex issue that clearly lies beyond the scope of the present book.

Clinging to our dichotomous categorisation, there are eight possible regime configurations. For the sake of illustrating all of them, we provide examples drawn not only from our four case studies but also from other regime/country experiences. It turns out that endogamous state–business relationships have created serious obstacles to stable and sound development in all our country case studies. Benin is particularly worthy of attention not only because of the aforementioned exceptional feature (the rise of an oligarch to the presidency), but also because it has been analysed in comparatively great depth. We therefore start our discussion by telling the Beninese story. Thereafter, our attention will be turned to Tanzania, Mozambique, and Bangladesh in that order.

B Benin

Until recently, Beninese politics has been characterised by a profusion of political parties: their number thus reached the astronomical figure of 250 during the 2010s. Considerably exceeding the number of ethnic groups in the country, these parties were designed as true vehicles for power by ambitious politicians backed by wealthy businessmen forming factions inside ethno-regional groups. Obeying a clientelistic logic, they do not confront each other on the level of programmes and policies based on varying visions of the country's future. Instead, inter-party competition is really a struggle for power conceived as a zero-sum game, the payoffs of which consist of the huge rents associated with state control. Opportunistic coalitions made before presidential elections ensure that the contest is actually limited to a few Big Men or oligarchs. Besides

---

[11] Under crony capitalism, or cronyism, businesses thrive not as a result of free initiative and risk-taking, but rather as a result of egregious advantages obtained from the political class to which they have a privileged access.

causing important allocative and dynamic inefficiencies as well as encouraging all sorts of malpractices, this system has created a lot of political instability underpinned by regular shifts of alliances and acts of personal treason vis-à-vis political allies. It is therefore not surprising that the country's press has been rife with accusations of embezzlement and rent capture related not only to prestigious construction projects but also to pro-poor programmes and the delivery of essential local public goods (water, electricity, and other vital infrastructure projects).

The business career and political role of Patrice Talon, the present president of Benin, is illustrative in this respect. By betting on the right presidential candidate at each critical stage of his personal capital accumulation process, even when this implied dropping support for the incumbent in favour of another candidate deemed to have better chances of winning the subsequent contest, Talon succeeded in gradually gaining control of the main sectors of the Beninese economy, including the customs service. Of course, maintaining control is as important as gaining it, hence his continuing interest in politics. In a major turning point, however, Talon decided to eventually run for presidency himself (in 2016). Political instability and increasing uncertainty about results in an atmosphere fraught with extremely tense interpersonal rivalries between a few oligarchs persuaded him that the usual tactics of pushing frontmen onto the political stage to represent one's interests had become far too risky. To exert direct control over the state apparatus appeared as the only reliable solution, and one justified by the need to bring back law and order, fight against corruption, and end instability.

Talon's winning gamble caused the defeat of the old political elite, and the question then arises as to whether this major political change can be a game changer. On the one hand, because Talon has succeeded in consolidating his power and taking a firm control of the polity and the economy of Benin, democracy has suffered. This has caused a major stir in a country where freedom of expression is highly valued and where free elections and changes of incumbents had become a regular feature of the political scene during the last decades. On the other hand, precisely because he holds key decision-making levers in his hands, he might perhaps become an enlightened autocrat eager to promote his fame and reputation as the man who rescued his country from stagnation and pervasive corruption. This is actually the image of himself that he is keen to project, as he declares that his role model for leadership is Paul Kagame, the authoritarian but effective president of Rwanda. In contrast to Kagame, however, Talon is an oligarch, which raises serious doubts about his ability to design enlightened policies oriented toward the general interest of the Beninese people. It could nevertheless be retorted that precisely because he exerts a large control over the economy, and has now become immensely rich, he does not need to bother any more about wealth accumulation. Therefore, he can devote all his energies to a high-order mission susceptible of bringing him superior satisfaction. It is of course too early to form a judgement on such a thorny issue, but the forthcoming future will be particularly interesting to watch.

So far, the signs are rather good. Surrounded with a team of highly competent technical collaborators – many of them assembled in a special office directly attached to the presidency, somehow in the manner adopted in Taiwan and South Korea – Talon has established sound priorities for reforms that address key constraints on the country's economic development. They include reforms of the education system (with emphasis on the creation of technical schools and training institutions), plans for infrastructure expansion (including the improvement of the generation and distribution of electricity), and measures aimed at diversifying the economy and adding value to agricultural and raw material (e.g., cotton) products. Moreover, Talon has made efforts to keep the streets clean and clear the rubble in big cities such as Cotonou. Even more importantly, he has declared war against corruption. In just a few years, the petty corruption that was so extensively observed under all the previous regimes appears to have been significantly reduced as a result of drastic sanctions imposed by his government. Since day-to-day extraction of bribes by officials (the police, in particular) hits poor and ordinary people especially hard, energetic steps to combat this practice is bound to earn him popular support. What remains to be seen, however, is how a president-cum-oligarch will be able to surmount the serious conflicts of interests inherent in his double capacity (hence the question mark in the cell of Table 8.1 where Talon's regime is featured).[12]

C Tanzania

Tanzania offers an interesting contrast to Benin in the sense that, instead of proliferating political parties representing micro ethno-regional groups, a single party (the CCM, formerly TANU) has largely dominated national politics since independence.[13] The central lesson, though, is that this setup has not prevented the same clientelistic logic as in Benin from operating inside this party: in this restricted arena, bitter struggles oppose faction leaders backed by different businessmen, foremost among whom are big entrepreneurs from the Indian community (and, at a later stage, from the Arab trading community).[14] Because it is essential to maintain the unity of the party at election times, the head of CCM refrains from expelling powerful party members who

[12] For example, how can a man who privately controls the customs end corruption in that vital part of the revenue collection system? How can his monopoly position in key sectors of the economy (including the retail distribution of petroleum products) be made to work for the general good? And how can one be assured that tax avoidance by members of his business entourage will be actively fought against?

[13] Although the single party system was abolished in the post-Nyerere period, and opposition parties started to play a significant role in the political debate, the CCM party, into which TANU had morphed after the union with Zanzibar, remained the major political force in the country.

[14] To this date, there is only one African Tanzanian name in the list of the twelve richest businessmen in the country.

illegally trade business money against undue privileges. This is a game with a bad corruption equilibrium where, given his belief about how other party members behave, no player has an incentive to play a clean move. Some members make illegal deals while others refuse to sanction bad behaviour, and the head of the party does not have the power to break this equilibrium owing to his fear of causing its dissolution in the transition to a new equilibrium. Incidentally, this situation resembles that observed in Malaysia where, as the dominant party (the United Malays National Organisation, UMNO) became increasingly fractionalised, the financial support of Chinese businessmen became more crucial for political campaigns (Jomo and Gomez, 1997: 364). This is in line with our earlier prediction that fractionalisation of the political space helps to enhance the power of big business interests vis-à-vis the state.

Even across parties, political clientelism prevails. This is illustrated by the 2015 presidential election for which the CCM nominated John Magufuli as its candidate instead of former prime minister Edward Lowassa. The latter was actually the front-runner but had been displaced after his involvement in a big corruption scandal was made public. Revealingly, rather than withdrawing from politics, Lowassa defected to the main opposition party who selected him as its candidate for the presidential race. This choice attests how much the opposition plays the same game of political clientelism and cronyism as the incumbent party. By contrast, the CCM's choice of Magufuli was vindicated by his anti-corruption image acquired while minister of public works in the previous government. This decision was probably not a reflection of a genuine desire for changing the rules of the political game, but a rather opportunistic defensive move. As a matter of fact, the party had been badly discredited by a wave of resounding corruption affairs, especially toward the second term of Kikwete (Magufuli's predecessor), which led donors with a pivotal role in the funding and designing of Tanzania's development strategy to suspend their aid programmes. As in many countries emerging from a socialist planning regime, news about corruption scandals actually started to proliferate after the process of transition to the market economy was initiated (that is, in the post-Nyerere period).

Because of his premature death from COVID, Magufuli's mandate at the helm of the country was dramatically shortened. There is no doubt that his rule was deeply authoritarian, and his methods echoed those used by Kagame in Rwanda: intimidation and disappearances of critical journalists, jailing of political opponents, and so on. Yet, at the same time, Magufuli was bent on stamping out corruption, stopping the internal disunion inside the CCM, and imposing a strict discipline on its leaders. His idea was apparently to re-establish full control of the party in the hands of its president (implying a return to Nyerere's system), to terminate the practices of political clientelism, and to reduce the influence of the oligarchs by prohibiting deals with private firms. This last strategy led him to be especially tough with both domestic and foreign business concerns. Moreover, he launched a vigorous anti-corruption campaign for which some success was beginning to show during his shortened mandate. Similarly for Talon, therefore, we put a question mark in the corresponding cell of Table 8.1.

D Mozambique

The Frelimo in Mozambique, which also benefited from strong initial legitimacy as a successful anticolonial movement, occupies about the same dominant position as the CCM in Tanzania. And, most relevant for our discussion, its internal politics is also dominated by fierce struggles for access to power. Financial strength being a key determinant of the ability to rise within the party's machine, this intra-party elite rivalry creates a fertile ground for the spread of money politics and influence peddling. The interpenetration of business and politics was reinforced after the liberalisation and privatisation drives imposed by the IMF and the World Bank in the 1990s. What happened was sheer political capture of the privatisation process itself. Thus, privatised firms were taken over by party members, civil servants, and army officers, thereby ensuring de facto continuity with the previous state of affairs.[15] As for entrepreneurs with ties to the opposition, they were systematically excluded. Given its overwhelmingly dominant position, whose persistence is partly caused by its ability to manipulate elections, the Frelimo was in a position to effectively rein in the country's business community, since the latter was deprived of any credible alternative to protect its interests. In the quid pro quo at the heart of a circular and self-reproducing patronage system, the Frelimo machine was thus oiled by the money obtained from the rents it itself awarded to supporters-turned-businesspeople. In other words, the corruption money and equivalent in-kind advantages flow up and down the ladder of political clientelism and, as long as the gives and takes are predictable, a corruption equilibrium is well established.

The rent-awarding process is based on internal competition. It takes place at the level of presidential primaries in which business leaders seek political frontmen with whom to forge an alliance while party insiders willing to stay in central organs and obtain high offices in the government reciprocally look for men with money to achieve their ends. The winner of the internal political contest becomes the president of the Frelimo, who automatically becomes the president of the Republic. Precisely because of the logic of competitive

---

[15] The same situation has been observed in many other countries transitioning from central planning to a more market-oriented system. In Malaysia, for instance, we learn that cronies of the national executive were best placed to capture the most lucrative opportunities arising from the privatisation drive encouraged by multilateral financial agencies in the early 1980s. Not only have well-connected businessmen from the dominant ethnic group (the Bumiputeras) gained priority over others, but many privatisations 'have not even involved the formality of an open tender system, and thus many beneficiaries have been chosen solely on the basis of political and personal connections' (Jomo and Gomez, 1997: 366).

clientelism prevailing inside the Frelimo, its de facto character of a single party state offers no guarantee of intertemporal policy continuity.[16]

What bears most emphasis is that things could have evolved differently. At the beginning of the reform process initiated at the behest of external forces (international organisations), the Frelimo was in a strong bargaining position reminding us of KMT's position in Taiwan. It held the most important cards in its hands and was apparently able to manipulate election results in its favour. It could therefore have chosen to use party discipline and its leverage on the nascent business community to launch the country on a consistent development path. In contrast to the KMT, however, it chose not to follow that line and instead promoted a system of crony capitalism based on a competitive clientelistic system from which transient leaders would emerge. In the end, it is perhaps the lack of a strong and enlightened leadership at the head of the party that best explains why the option of a developmental state was ignored.

The discovery of oil and gas reserves in Cabo Delgado (during the years 2006–10) did not help. The existence of these valuable resources created new rent opportunities, real or anticipated, that considerably raised the stakes involved in the struggle for political power and influence. In this context, it is not surprising that the trend towards improvement of governance indicators was reversed, and that huge scandals came to the surface, such as the hidden debt scandal in 2016, which deeply affected the country's economic and political climate and its relations with the international community.[17] Given the weakness of anti-corruption institutions and their lack of independence from political influence, it is hard to think of significant improvements of this situation in the near future.

E Bangladesh

In Bangladesh, two political parties, the AL and the BNP, have dominated national politics since the end of the military dictatorship of General Ershad in 1990: they correspond to two groups with unclear ideological differences but neatly differentiated identities defined by strong leaders known as the two begums. The stands of these two parties have always reflected the deep personal antagonisms between Sheikh Hasina (the daughter of Sheikh Mujib,

---

[16] A vivid illustration is provided by the difficult transition from President Guebuza to President Nyusi, who was not Guebuza's preferred candidate and had a different approach to policy and reform.

[17] To be more precise, in the final years of Guebuza's second term, three semi-public entities, owned and controlled by a very small group of individuals and closely linked to the security sector, took out over US$2 billion in loans from private foreign banks without submitting them to the Assembly for approval. Upon learning about the existence of these loans, the IMF suspended its support to Mozambique and much foreign aid, including all direct support to the state budget, was frozen or significantly reduced.

the founder of the nation) and Khaleda Zia (the widow of General Zia), and their winner-takes-all approach to politics. The year 2008 witnessed the end of regular rotation of these two parties in power as the AL was able to take full political control of the country. What our study of Bangladesh reveals about state–business governance is the important political leverage of the textile business sector. This sector is no doubt one of the main drivers of economic growth and exports in the country. It is nevertheless striking that the textile business elite, thanks to their intimate connections with influential politicians, has been able to extract enormous advantages in a variety of forms: tax exemptions (textile exporters are exempted from import duties on intermediate products), export performance benefits, subsidies of various kinds, export guarantee schemes, and lax labour laws condoning low wages, long working hours, absence of regular contracts, and poor working conditions (as epitomised by the Rana Plaza disaster, in which more than 1,000 workers died when their factory building collapsed). With trade unions suppressed and union organisers intimidated, workers' rights have no chance of being properly protected.

It can be argued that, since they are part and parcel of an industrial policy and this policy has proven to be remarkably successful, the above measures evoke those adopted by the governments of Taiwan and South Korea to encourage economic development and manufacturing growth in particular. Two remarks are nevertheless worth making here. First, and in contrast to Taiwan and South Korea, the government support for the textile sector has been rather exclusive in the sense that it has not been justified as a component of a comprehensive economic development strategy aimed at the diversification of manufacturing and export activities. There is therefore a legitimate suspicion that the favourable treatment of the textile sector and the relative neglect of other sectors have been the outcome of the disproportionate political influence of the textile lobby. Second, it is even harder to understand why the well-being of the labour force operating in the favoured sector has been so much ignored by the authorities, hence reinforcing the suspicion that politicians serve the interests of the textile firm owners rather than the whole sector. The compliance of the former is explained by the regular donations they receive from the latter for their political campaigns and other purposes.

V CONCLUSION

In the foregoing analysis, primary attention has been given to the oft-observed predicament of state capture by business interests and the conditions under which it is likely to occur. An important and thought-provoking proposition is that, other things being equal, the extent of state capture is larger when political competition is fiercer in the sense that the number of contenders is higher. By implication, a change of political regime that opens up the political space and sparks political competition may have the paradoxical effect of increasing the capture of the state by powerful business people. And to the extent that their private interests are at odds with the collective good, their capture of the state is susceptible to throwing the country on a development trajectory that gives precedence to rents over social efficiency.

On the other hand, the experiences of Taiwan and South Korea, as well as those of the People's Republic of China and Vietnam, testify that a state immune to capture by business interests and able to devise and implement enlightened development policies can acquire legitimacy over time and thereby contribute to reinforce national integration. Conversely, a charismatic leader enjoying a good measure of initial legitimacy may waste it if he adopts misguided policies, which ignore long-term objectives, the necessary role of individual incentives, and the need to strengthen national cohesion through income redistribution, poverty reduction, and the building of strong physical and social infrastructures.

As illustrated by the lives of Nyerere and Nkrumah – yet not Kérékou and so many other autocratic rulers – strong leaders can retain some popularity thanks to the aura they gained as 'father of the nation', if they achieved positive results on the social and political fronts. Progress in health and education, and immunity to corruption, are examples of the former and the latter, respectively. The fact remains that the dire economic situation of the country resulting from their disastrous economic policies creates a difficult challenge for their successors who do not have their charisma and pedigree as founder of the new nation.

Leaving aside extreme cases of economic disaster following policy experiments of centralised planning, we must admit the existence of potential trade-offs between economic and political objectives. In particular, the nation-building project may arguably impose constraints on the extent to which efficient economic policies can be pursued. This is especially true at the critical time when varied population groups with particularistic interests need to be morphed into a national entity with sufficient cohesion. This being reckoned, there is solid ground to believe that, over the long run, national integration and the legitimacy of a regime depend foremost on the implementation of viable and effective development strategies.

Consisting of heterogeneous elements in spite of a common language and ethnic origin, the Taiwanese nation was not 'a given'. As in Pakistan, it was the result of the mixing of immigrants and indigenous population groups: Han Chinese from mainland China and (mostly) Han Chinese from Taiwan in the case of Taiwan, and Muslims from India and Muslims from the Pakistani provinces in Pakistan. In contrast to Pakistan, however, the KMT regime of Taiwan succeeded in gradually building up a strong nation thanks to an effective pattern of egalitarian and rapid development led by an autonomous state. By contrast, Pakistani politics has been continuously dominated by self-centred political dynasties and reactionary forces, foremost among which are puritan religious movements. The latter have been instrumentalised by the military (and the intelligence services) to counter overdone external threats. Beset by political clientelism, the pressure of Islamists and greedy, power-hungry army officers, the nation-building process went astray, and the country was never set on an effective development path.

Bangladesh was also plagued by reactionary religious movements and entrenched political dynasties, although the latter are not rooted in rural areas as they are in Pakistan, and although the influence of the former has been much more superficial. Its government did not miss profitable external trade opportunities when they emerged, and this eventually allowed it to kickstart the country's industrialisation process. The challenge, here, is double: how to rein in the influence of powerful textile business lobbies so that economic diversification can take place and the working population can obtain a higher share of the growth proceeds; and how to reduce the country's dependence on foreign funds, remittances in particular?

Politics does not only influence a country's development trajectory through leadership quality and the degree of autonomy of the state vis-à-vis business interests in particular. It also produces effects through the type of operating bureaucracy and the way property rights are established or enforced. Yet these two aspects of state capacity cannot be exclusively reduced to a political problem, hence the wider perspective that their analysis requires. This will become clearer as we proceed with our investigation in the next chapter.

Before embarking on this chapter, a question that comes to mind is what happens to countries that have proven unable to build a sufficiently strong state and a sufficiently integrated nation? It is here that the analysis of Charles Tilly (1985) provides valuable insights. His central point is that the end of World War II marked an important turning point in the sense that the independence of all sovereign nations became guaranteed by the newly formed United Nations. An immediate consequence is that failed or weak states are no more allowed to disappear, get absorbed by a stronger neighbour, or split into several parts, under the action of external forces, military or political. Neither are they compelled to transform themselves with a view to improving their performances and their capacity to withstand such forces, preserve their integrity, and simply survive. Countries which would have dissolved in the times preceding World War II may now persist, however woefully, thanks to internationally protected borders and to foreign assistance. In other words, evolutionary changes of the Darwinian kind, or adaptive transformations imposed by necessity (in the manner suggested by Arnold Toynbee), cannot be set off to spark institutional reforms as they could do in modern European history, for example.

9

State Capacity and Property Rights

After having examined the role of politics in spurring or slowing down structural transformation and development, we are now ready to probe into issues of state capacity, a theme which has received growing attention among economists during the last decades (see, e.g., Levy, 2007; Besley and Persson, 2009, 2010; Bourguignon and Verdier, 2012; Dincecco, 2017; Dincecco and Katz, 2016; Khemani, 2019; Wilson, 2019). This will complete our discussion of the role of governance-related institutions. In a second step, we then look at the second generic type of institutions deemed crucial for development, namely property rights.

I WEAK STATE CAPACITY

The following presentation is articulated around three major issues: bureaucratic failures; inadequate incentives and professional norms (as illustrated by the education sector); and ineffectiveness of the judiciary. They are discussed in this order.

A Bureaucratic Failures

As we have done in the preceding chapter, we start by considering the successful experiences of Taiwan and South Korea before attempting to understand the sources of bureaucratic failures in three in-depth case study countries. We follow a general approach to the problem of state capacity wherein it is seen as a problem of incentives and norms rooted in politics. In the words of Stuti Khemani (2019: 2–3):

Politics fundamentally shapes the culture of bureaucracy all the way to the frontlines of service delivery. Processes or platforms of political contestation, and the leaders it produces, from those at humble local levels, such as in a village, to those occupying the national seats of power, have implications well beyond elections and politicians, through how they influence the incentives, beliefs and norms (or expectations of how others are behaving) of state personnel and thus, the day-to-day functioning of myriad agencies within the bureaucracy.

1 Positive Lessons from Taiwan and South Korea

Taiwan and South Korea have not only been endowed with determined and enlightened top leadership but also with an effective bureaucracy. In this respect, they were fortunate to inherit from the Japanese colonial power a modern, meritocratic, and authoritative bureaucratic structure that fitted well with the nature of the new regime. Recruitment and promotion criteria in the civil service thus continued to be based on merit, state employees received lifelong tenure, professional norms were strong, and corruption was limited. In Taiwan, moreover, the jobs of state bureaucrats down to quite low levels were now occupied by newcomers from mainland China, which automatically ensured political loyalty. Being an alien force, the new bureaucrats developed a corporate identity which was all the stronger as they had to identify their own interests with those of the state, their protector. These were obviously ideal conditions for a clean, cohesive, and competent bureaucracy. Another favourable factor consisted of the overarching responsibility of the NRC, the agency in charge of the country's industrial policy. Made of the best experts available, it acted as a unique centre of command under the direct supervision of the supreme leader. Here, too, historical circumstances played a key role since the Taiwanese leadership learned bitter lessons from their defeat at the hands of Mao's communists in China. Foremost among the causes identified was the existence of fragmented and politicised bureaucracy which, moreover, was too compliant with the requests of the private interests of powerful business lobbies.

There is yet another, less well-known aspect of state capacity in Taiwan, namely the administration's approach to SMEs. Since the operation of these firms was deeply anchored in traditional, horizontal networks relying on informal contract enforcement mechanisms where interpersonal trust played a major role, the willingness of the Taiwanese authorities to allow varied forms of production organisations to prosper and to actually support SMEs without unduly interfering with their specific mode of operation, is a good example of a successful interaction between formal and informal institutions. The pivotal contribution of SMEs to the country's growth and manufacturing exports is solid proof that this flexible approach of the government was fully justified.

In South Korea, as we have seen earlier, the commanding responsibility for economic development rested in the EPB, and the external threat posed by the close presence of the communist regime of North Korea, which benefited from an early industrial base which South Korea did not possess, was a powerful incentive to proceed fast and with maximum coherence and efficiency.

Characteristically, both the NRC in Taiwan and the EPB in South Korea were modelled on the famous MITI (Ministry of International Trade and Industry) of post-war Japan. Filled with high quality and highly motivated bureaucrats – a legacy of high morals inherited from the classic bureaucrats of the pre-war period – this agency applied administrative guidance in order to push growth in a desired direction and 'managed' competition accordingly.[1]

Bureaucratic effectiveness in both Taiwan and South Korea stemmed from an additional source that deserves special mention: the top layers of their bureaucracies struck clever, incentive-based deals with private business firms, as though they had understood the basics of modern contract theory. Their general approach thus provided that special advantages granted to these firms (licences and permits, export loans, tax exemptions, subsidies) were conditional on their demonstrated ability to reach the objectives assigned to them (export targets, for example), and to become profitable within a reasonable span of time. Targets could be modified to allow for changes in the economic environment. Moreover, instead of awarding monopolistic positions, they tended to impose competition on the private sector so as to bring the discipline of the market to bear on its firms. In short, the stimulus of internal competition was systematically added to the stimulus of external competition. In South Korea, incentives to comply with production and export targets in heavy industry were reinforced by tournaments organised among *chaebols*. The government was thus able to overcome the information asymmetry which, in fully new export ventures, prevents the effective monitoring of firm performances by the executive and other state entities. For two *chaebols* committed to some new industrial export target, the tournament formula made it suboptimal for both not to do their best to reach their target. This is because they were keen to avoid the prospect of failure, and of practically going bankrupt, while the rival company would succeed.

Outside the industrial sector, and in line with the approach of inclusive development, careful attention was devoted to the creation of wisely conceived

---

[1] In the terminology of Okuno-Fujiwara (1997), the Japanese model, which had its roots in the tightly regulated and controlled economic system that developed during the war, is of the *relation-based government* type. The difference between such a system and *authoritarian government*, such as found in Taiwan and South Korea, lies in the degree of centralisation of the market's administrative guidance: while bureaucrats are tightly controlled by those in power in an authoritarian government, they have a stake in the power structure of the ministry for which they work in the jurisdictionally decentralised government of a relation-based system. Under the latter, since career bureaucrats of the ministries have relatively large influence over decision-making, the challenge for the government is to achieve proper coordination between different ministries and bureaus. This is typically done through negotiation (pp. 393–402). The expression 'relation-based' is derived from the fact that, because bureaucrats have less power when not backed by an authoritarian and centralised regime, they rely on long-duration relationships with agents (business owners or managers, for example), and the associated reputation effects, to obtain compliance.

institutional vehicles for the active support of agricultural and rural development (training institutes, cooperatives, promotion of innovation, etc.). Worth noting here is the fact that bureaucrats carefully avoided substituting themselves for private middlemen, letting competition percolate down to local levels. At the same time, producer cooperatives were encouraged to benefit from scale economies in modern input procurement, output transport and marketing, veterinary services, training and adoption of new technologies.

It is also remarkable that the move toward economic liberalisation (and even political liberalisation in the case of Taiwan) was authoritatively imposed by the state itself. This radical policy reform was initially opposed by important sections of the population, the business community in particular. It is only at a later stage, when the benefits became more and more manifest, that trade liberalisation was gradually accepted by important group coalitions, and that the prescient decision of the state authorities was largely praised. Incidentally, this example has been used by Fernandez and Rodrik (1991) to illustrate their argument that, when there is uncertainty about the distribution of the costs and benefits of a reform, a radical move from above may well be justified.

2 Key Aspects of Bureaucratic Failures in Bangladesh, Benin and Tanzania

That the experiences of Taiwan and South Korea were rather exceptional is borne out by our case study material. A major institutional deficiency appears to be a serious lack of coordination between different ministries, resulting in confused, overlapping, and poorly enforced regulations. This problem is often ascribed to poor information-sharing, itself caused by the absence of good communication equipment. Here, we want to stress another aspect more in line with a political economy approach. In the very logic of political patronage, members of the government are inclined to view their ministry as their own fief, that is, they see it as a source of rents which should naturally accrue to them for personal appropriation and for redistribution to the network of their supporters and brokers. Combined with funds obtained from state budgets and from business oligarchs (see Chapter 8), rents extracted from the bureaucracy through appropriate channelling up help politicians to meet the costs of electoral competition and nurse a constituency between elections.[2]

---

[2] The mechanics of redistribution may vary from one context to another. One context in which it has been precisely unravelled concerns the centralised bureaucracies of India (Wade, 1985). Bribes are extracted by frontline workers from users of public services – which is rather easy to do for ministries or departments such as the Interior (the police department, in particular), Agriculture, Land Planning, Finance, Public Works – and then channelled up the hierarchy to more senior officers and politicians. For instance, irrigation engineers may raise vast amounts of illicit revenue from the distribution of water to farmers and the awarding of contracts to building entrepreneurs (Wade, 1982). The channelling up takes the form of successive cuts at the different levels of the bureaucratic machinery. But there exists another widespread mechanism,

Under these conditions, the sharing of information and any form of cooperation between different parts of the executive tend to be obstructed with the effect of seriously undermining the coherence and the effectiveness of development policies. These problems of coordination come on top of the costs potentially arising from the fact that the generation of illicit income may conflict with economic efficiency.[3]

Land laws and their implementation in Benin are an example that comes to mind here. Reforms of land tenure have proven unbelievably complex, volatile, and non-monotonous, and one important reason is to be found in the assignment of responsibility for land regulation to multiple agencies and the continuous shifts of missions between these agencies. The Ministry of Agriculture, the Ministry of Town Planning, and the Ministry of Finance have been the main contenders for playing a major role in dealing with land matters. At a lower level, rural municipalities have strongly resisted against attempts to reduce their own land prerogatives. For example, thanks to their efforts, missions that belonged to the National Agency for Land Administration under a law were shifted to them under a subsequent law. They also successfully opposed the officialisation of rural land transactions, which would have implied the end of sale conventions of which they were in charge. In the same way as the customs service and the tax administration, the land administration is the object of fierce political struggles because of the huge rents that its control can potentially create. Decisions in these strategic public sectors represent high stakes for powerful groups – such as traders and businessmen for the former two, and notaries, barristers, architects, and land surveyors for the latter – which are therefore ready to pay for obtaining decisions to their liking. Payments are direct when they are made in the form of bribes to officials in charge, or indirect if they consist of donations to the political party that is in control of the administration or the service concerned.

When elections are won by different parties, or by different factions belonging to the same (dominant) party, time-varying allocations of key ministries or public agencies will not bring an end to corruption as long as the political

which Robert Wade calls transfer sales, whereby a desirable administrative post (or location) is purchased by an officer who recoups his/her outlay through the sale of the posts of subordinate ranks. This chainlike payment system, which starts at the lowest levels, goes up to the chief of the administration and the Minister. To distinguish it from 'parochial corruption' (Scott, 1972), it is labelled 'market corruption' by Wade. Whereas under the former, ties of kinship, affection, caste, and so forth determine access to the favours of the powerholders, under the latter advantages are granted to those who pay the most, regardless of who they are (Wade, 1985: 468). It is rather ironical, writes Wade, that relatively frequent transfers inside the state machinery, which are now part of the corruption mechanism, were a deliberate strategy of the British colonial administration to combat corruption (1985: 488).

[3] Thus, in the case of irrigation investigated by Wade, engineers have an incentive to make water supply more insecure (in the short term) to increase the rents extractable from the farmers while, on the side of maintenance, their interest is in providing low quality maintenance despite their official duty to ensure proper maintenance of the system (Wade, 1982: 314).

game continues to be played according to the rules of clientelistic politics. What may change, however, are the laws and regulations enacted by the ruling government. And this is a serious problem to the extent that changing laws and regulations are susceptible of causing uncertainty, itself a source of disincentives to invest. This possibility is again illustrated by land legislation in Benin where new laws involved backtracking on previous ones, or introduced additional confusion.

Another reason why land laws are unenforced in Benin lies in a misalignment between the law and state capacity: this happens when a complex law is enacted for which the state does not have the administrative resources required for effective implementation. Politics may also play a role here if complicated laws are enacted in the full knowledge that their implementation will be difficult, or if they serve to satisfy contradictory interest groups without much concern for the actual enforceability of the legal compromise. The latter possibility is especially likely when formal rules aimed at uniformising and simplifying the diverse customary practices and norms found on the ground run counter to informal and local power structures. The difficulty to reconcile the two points of view illustrates one key issue of nation-building as mentioned in Chapter 8. It not only concerns land matters but also family and other spheres of everyday life. Conflicts thus easily erupt when formal laws are guided by international norms borrowed from advanced Western countries, which exert direct and indirect pressures on poor countries for their adoption.

As examples, we can think of all the laws that confront deep-rooted informal or customary practices, such as laws that prohibit early age marriage or polygamy (as in many West African countries), and laws that prohibit rural land sales above a certain (low) threshold, impose official authorisation for the purpose of buying rural lands, or mandate the owner of an uncultivated landholding to rent it out (as in Benin). In these instances, institutional dysfunction at the state level arises not from sleaze and rent-seeking but from ideological motives or external pressures to adopt laws which, being ill-conceived and out of touch with reality, are almost doomed to be unenforceable. Bureaucrats in charge of their implementation face an impossible task, or they are compelled to resort to brutal force which people will try their best to circumvent through various stratagems. In these instances, prescriptions emanating from international organisations and foreign donors are doomed to yield disappointing effects. The root cause lies in a lack of political economy perspective.

In Tanzania, coordination failures at the level of the administration bear strong similarities to those noted for Benin. In land matters, for example, laws are even more complex and confusing than in Benin, which is partly due to unresolved tensions and swinging moves between two objectives: protecting small and medium landholders and encouraging investment by large agro-processing export companies. Such tensions are institutionally reflected in the existence of a dual tenure system that will be explained later. Institutional overlaps are found at the levels of both the land administration and the land dispute settlement systems. To illustrate the former, while land officers in the local government authorities are paid by, and report to, superiors in the Ministry of Land, Housing, and Human Settlement Development (MLHHSD), they simultaneously execute functions for local governments, which are themselves under the responsibility of the President's Office. As for the latter, at the lower level the village land councils and the ward tribunals are under the responsibility of the local government authority, but right above, the District Land and Housing Tribunals (DLHT) are governed by the Ministry, and at the top, the High Court (Land Division) and the Court of Appeal are under the judiciary. By contravening the principle of separation of powers, this institutional set-up creates serious problems of accountability.

Examples of multiplicity and overlap of institutions are easily found in other parts of public administration, too. Thus, the National Land Use Planning Commission is largely redundant with the Direction of Urban and Rural Affairs in the Ministry of Agriculture. There is a clear lack of cooperation between the Tanzanian Revenue Authority, responsible for tax collection, and the Minister of Finance, which lays out the tax schedules. Furthermore, the production and distribution of electricity is managed by a public monopoly, Tanesco, but is regulated in parallel by the Ministry of Mining and a regulatory agency (Ewura), the missions of which are overlapping. As a last example, the demarcation between the mandates of local government executives and those of officers appointed by the central government is often blurred, while the relationships between local government authorities, the prime minister's office, the Minister of Finance and various other ministries are extremely intricate. If it is sometimes hard to retrace the origins of these dysfunctions, the effects are almost always negative. Thus, Ewura may have its recommendations – for instance, about the pricing of electricity – overturned by a President fiat although they had been grounded in serious work performed by excellent experts. And firm managers do not tire of complaining that they must obtain approval from an abnormally large number of government agencies before they can market a new product or service.

Turning now to Bangladesh, we find a country plagued by essentially the same problems as those discussed above. To illustrate, the education sector is riddled with confusing and sometimes conflicting divisions of responsibility between multiple actors. Thus, with respect to primary schools, overall ministerial control lacks effectiveness because three main ministries and several smaller authorities are entrusted with management roles. Added to this dysfunction are tensions and contradictions arising from the devolution of responsibility across central, regional, and local authorities. In these conditions, chains of responsibility and accountability are unclear.

It is typically because the multiplication of ill-coordinated agencies, departments or services obeys the need to create and entrench niches where rents can be earned by state agents that reforming the public administration faces stiff resistance. Thus, in spite of two Public Service Reform Programmes, no clear sign of consistent progress has been detected. The culture of recruitment of personnel on other grounds than ability and skills, or of promotion based on seniority or partisan links rather than merit, has largely persisted. In addition, shirking behaviour, embezzlement of state resources, and bribe-taking remain widespread. Poor peer monitoring and absent or perfunctory supervision are the most immediate causes of this predicament.

Besides a lack of coordination between different ministries and administrative units (which is again particularly evident in land matters), pervasive corruption at all levels of the civil service, and low transparency of decision processes, an additional problem undermining state capacity is the frequent meddling of the highest state authority in administrative decisions, such as we have seen for Ewura in Tanzania's electricity sector. The financial sector, which is severely dysfunctional, epitomises the adverse effect of this last factor. In particular, the lack of even formal autonomy of the central bank is perhaps the most egregious example of institutional impediments to development in Bangladesh. The governor of the Bangladesh Bank is thus in a clearly subordinate position vis-à-vis the government and the president and, given the tight links between state and business, vis-à-vis private bankers as well. Subservience to private interests has become even more pronounced as the Bangladesh Association of (private sector) Banks, the BAB, has recently gained increasing political influence. As a consequence, regulation of the whole banking sector is essentially ad hoc and typically unable to control the numerous malpractices committed by the country's commercial banks. The dual authority ruling over the banking system – state-owned banks are governed by the Banking Division of the Ministry of Finance while private banks are under the purview of the central bank, itself under the thumb of the presidency – is an additional factor causing ineffectiveness in the regulation of the whole sector.

In the light of these major institutional failures, it is not surprising that the banking sector in Bangladesh, despite its undeniable role in financing the expansion of the textile industry, has shown very poor management performance. In 2017, Bangladesh thus occupied a miserable 147th position out of 179 countries according to the international Z-score, an indicator of the probability of default of the entire banking system. Its Z-score was also the lowest among South Asian countries. The main factor responsible for this disastrous situation is the low quality of the sector's lending operations, which is itself the result of regulatory and policy capture: bankers are subject to political pressures to grant unproductive loans, or loans which they know will never be repaid by the borrowers. In addition, cases of embezzlement through legal insider lending – that is, to the bank's owners or their family – have been reported. In such an unhealthy environment, NPLs is a major concern: while representing 25 per cent of outstanding loans in the early 1990s, their proportion shot up to an astronomical 41 per cent in 2000.

Effective reform measures were then taken, in part under the pressure of the IMF, but also as part of an anti-corruption policy led at that time by the BNP government. As a result, the ratio was successfully brought down to a reassuringly low figure of 6 per cent by the late 2000s. However, because the root cause of the problem, which lies in the political system of patronage prevailing in the country, was left untouched, the downward trend was soon reversed as the proportion of NPLs practically doubled during the following decade. Even more worryingly, while NPLs tended to be initially concentrated in state-owned banks, they have soon started to spread to private commercial banks too. Besides negatively affecting the banks' prudential ratios, these bad loans have forced the banks to raise their borrower rates, thus discouraging private investments outside the privileged sectors (the textile industry, in particular), which have continuously enjoyed exceptionally favourable terms. To this shortcoming, we must add the frequent need for monetary injection in state-owned banks or in the bailouts of private banks.

B The Role of Incentives and Norms: The Example of Education

Education is a key factor of development, and it is even more true today for poor countries in need of production niches in high-value-added products and services. It is undeniable that enrolment rates at various levels of the education sector have significantly increased in many of these countries during the last decades. However, the achievement of high rates of enrolment and completion of different cycles is a smokescreen if the level of skills acquired in the education process remains low. In blatant contrast to South Korea and Taiwan, where education has been remarkably performing at low, medium, and high levels and in technical and scientific fields in particular, our sample of four poor countries exhibit dismal education records if we judge by learning outcomes. Especially worrying are the indicators measuring literacy, numeracy, and writing skills for children who have completed primary school. This situation, sometimes termed as one of 'learning crisis', is not exceptional since similar results have been found for other countries, particularly in India and Pakistan, which are close neighbours of Bangladesh. The latter country will receive special attention in a later subsection.

In what follows, we discuss the causes of poor performances in education under three different headings: weak state capacity, absenteeism, and low teacher quality. Before addressing this task, it is worth stressing that in all these respects, Taiwan and South Korea have done very well. In particular, from the beginning of the development process, education has been considered a top priority by the political rulers. Moreover, an effective and coherent administration was put in place to manage it and monitor its progress. Equally noteworthy is the strong demand for education among Taiwanese and Korean citizens, whose preferences are highly skewed toward their children's training. This implies that, as in many East Asian countries, parents, and even poor parents, are ready to incur substantial sacrifices in order that their children can get proper education and raise their income prospects in life. Given the foregoing characteristics, it is not surprising that both the quality and the social status of teachers in this region of the world are remarkably high, and that teachers and school directors exert great efforts toward fulfilling their duties.

1 Weak State Capacity and Institutional Dysfunction

The education sector is typically an area where it is uneasy to disentangle institutional dysfunction from limited state capacity (*stricto sensu*). Still, a useful distinction is between input amounts and the efficiency in their use. In many developing countries, including our sample countries, because of insufficient state budgets allocated to this sector, input indicators reflect a situation plainly unfavourable to education quality: very high pupil-teacher ratios, a very high number of pupils per classroom, shortage of teaching material, a low number of schools forcing many children to travel long distances, and so on. Except when the country is too poor to finance a vibrant education sector, and therefore needs external assistance, deficient funding of the school system is attributable to low public spending, as a result of low general taxation and/or the low ranking of education in the list of government priorities. While Mozambique, where international donors provide key financial support for education, offers a good illustration of the former situation, Bangladesh comes to mind as a striking example of the latter. In Bangladesh, indeed, not only is general taxation exceptionally low as a percentage of GDP, so strong are the pressures of powerful business lobbies on the government to limit taxes, but the country also devotes comparatively small amounts of public money to education, primary education in particular. The consequence of these two features combined is that Bangladesh has one of the lowest ratios of public expenditure on primary education to GDP in the world (significantly less than 1 per cent). Interestingly, major actors in the country formally agree that this situation ought to be remedied and taxes significantly increased. Yet, in practice, everyone behaves as though they are satisfied with the present equilibrium characterised by low taxes and low public expenditures. This is because, as in a prisoner's dilemma, everyone would like the other actors to bear the brunt of higher taxes while benefiting from better public goods.

The institutional dimension of the human capital problem lies in the effectiveness with which inputs, however small or large, are used in the education process. Institutional dysfunction generally arises from deficient incentives, absent or weak professional norms, and the power structure. In the following, we illustrate these three possibilities under the headings of two major problems: absenteeism of teachers and school directors, and poor teacher quality and training.

2 Absenteeism of Teachers and School Directors

A recurrent and distressing cause of low education performances is the pervasive absenteeism of teachers and school directors, as well as their lack of
punctuality. While the rate of teacher absenteeism in the primary schools was
relatively low in Bangladesh in 2006 (16 per cent compared to 25 per cent in
India), it was estimated to be as high as 31 per cent in a survey of Tanzania's
schools in 2014. The latter figure is of the same order as the rate of 27 per cent
observed in Uganda, but in 2006 (Chaudhury et al., 2006). In Mozambique,
the situation is even worse, with a rate of around 45 per cent for both primary
school teachers and directors in the same year. In addition to being frequently
absent, teachers in these schools have a bad habit of arriving late, or leaving
early, so that many pupils in the country are losing more than 50 per cent
of the learning time they are entitled to, as a result of late start times, early
closing, and extended recesses. These are astronomical figures, and the question immediately arises as to what are the reasons behind such widespread
non-compliance with contractual obligations on the part of frontline agents of
the education system. Note that the situation appears significantly grimmer in
the heath sector: the rates of absenteeism estimated for primary health centres
in 2006 are thus much higher than in primary schools, implying rates reaching
40 per cent in India and Indonesia, 37 per cent in Uganda, and 35 per cent in
Bangladesh (Chaudhury et al., 2006).

A first possible cause is low, or irregularly paid salaries, which compel these
agents to take up side jobs that distract them from their first duties. But this
cannot be a complete explanation since the phenomenon can be observed in
situations where the teacher salaries are well above the average local earnings.
A second explanation is the absence of professional norms ensuring that the
agent is internally punished when not fulfilling duties, say, by feeling guilt or
shame in front of peers, parents, and others. In this respect, there are obvious
differences between South Asia, Africa, and some countries of Latin America,
on the one hand, and East Asia where education is highly prized, on the other
hand.

A third explanation is the absence of effective monitoring, which entails
the consequence that defaulting agents cannot be externally punished, thus
encouraging them to act with impunity. This mechanism is likely to be inter-
linked with the previous one in the following sense: adequate social norms
are prevented from emerging if a dutiful teacher who starts by abiding by the
contract gets discouraged by seeing that others around him/her are not sanctioned upon violation of the terms of the contract. In game-theoretic terms,
agents follow a behaviour of conditional reciprocity, and the bad equilibrium
in which everybody feels free to act according to own selfish interests comes
into existence.

A fourth way to understand school dysfunction rests on individually rational behaviour. Thus, if many people do not perceive significant returns to education for their children – typically because they live in a region where there

are no job prospects in the formal sector of the economy – they will not send them regularly to school, especially so if they can employ them at home and/ or teachers are badly trained and, hence, of low quality (see the next subsection). As a consequence, parents may not consider teachers as socially useful specialists, and the latter lose their own motivation to regularly attend to their duties. In these conditions, professional norms of regular attendance fail to get established. In other words, a link is likely to exist between the formation (and maintenance) of norms and the intensity of the demand for education.

Finally, contract-breakers may feel protected by locally powerful people who can even be the instigator of the fraud. The existence of so-called 'ghost schools' and 'ghost teachers' in Pakistan, from which Bangladesh actually seceded in 1971, illustrates this possibility, showing that not only may education fail to be a priority, but it may also be actively opposed by local strongmen. The latter need not be necessarily religious leaders opposed to secular education and favouring religious teaching in madrasas (Malik et al., 2021). They may also be traditional landlords eager to prevent the emancipation of their dependents lest they should develop 'unrealistic expectations' and cause a shortage of cheap agricultural labour (Martin, 2016: 87). In such instances, school dysfunction is not (necessarily) caused by a lack of spontaneous demand for education, but by deliberate attempts by powerful people to repress it.

When they act as political leaders or brokers, reactionary landlords may go as far as diverting school buildings from their intended function by using them as cowsheds, farm buildings, accommodation for some relatives, and the like (Martin, 2016: 133).[4] Teachers themselves are then 'ghost teachers' who rarely turn up for their duty, and place false entries into the attendance registers (2016: 88). Their time and energies are diverted to other uses that serve the interests of their patrons who protect them from disciplinary action (see Zahab, 2020: 82, and Gazdar, 2000, for quantitative evidence). In some cases, primary school teacher posts are sold by politicians and officials for large amounts of money, thus inducing the beneficiaries to take side jobs to repay their loans (Hasnain, 2008: 137). Also, it may happen that teachers surrender as much as half their salaries in order to escape the duty of attending school because they are essentially happy with the reward consisting of the lumpsum pension of 2–3 lakhs which they receive at the end of their careers (Martin, 2016: 80).

In the presence of flawed monitoring by state authorities (school inspectors), a frequently proposed solution consists for schools to be monitored by stakeholders comprising parents of the pupils, in particular. Nowadays, this solution is promoted by many scholars, including economists. In Mozambique, for example, school councils (CEs) have been set up to precisely supervise school activities and denounce failures. And, yet, the results have fallen short

---

[4] Moreover, schools are often of poor quality because of commissions given to contractors.

of expectations. The underlying reasons are several, but two deserve special mention in the context of the present discussion. To begin with, members of CEs may lose their motivations to attend CE sessions because they do not derive any material gain, typically in the form of per diems, from their participation. This type of behaviour would be largely unthinkable in East Asia and in Western advanced countries, because members of school committees are either intrinsically motivated or attach a high value to improvements from which their own children will benefit. Next is typically a power-related problem: CEs frequently complain that children may suffer from reprisals by teachers and school managers if they point to unjustified absences, lack of punctuality, and abuses of power or to non-transparency in the use of school funds. As a result, the CEs risk being pseudo-participative institutions whose members are coaxed to accept what is decided by the school board, thus being reduced to a simple role of rubber stamping. In the same logic, school directors may exert their power and influence to bring a compliant person to the CE presidency.

3 Low Teacher Quality and Training

To a large extent, teacher quality depends on recruitment procedures and training (in addition to decent salaries). That these determinants are often distorted is starkly testified by the experience of Bangladesh. There, the recruitment of teachers is often biased by the leakage of the written exams on the basis of which selection is made. Moreover, the payment of bribes may decide which teachers will be transferred to Dhaka, the capital city, which is equivalent to a big promotion. In many poor countries, teacher training is strongly deficient with the consequence that the level of skills of, say, primary school teachers, is hardly higher than among the pupils. The reasons for this sorry state of affairs may vary. In countries such as Mexico, the main culprit is the teacher trade union, which staunchly opposes the skill upgrading of the profession. Being politically well connected, it is able to block or derail training reforms although they are manifestly in the general interest. The backtracking on these reforms by the present president, Lopez Obrador, who is himself close to the teacher trade union, attests to the possible influence of politics on teacher quality.

In another scenario, teacher training is undermined by severe budget cuts, which reflects the low priority that education quality receives at central state level or even among international donors. Thus, in Mozambique, the fast-track teacher training model, which abruptly reduced the number of years of training for primary teachers from three to just one, was seen as a way to increase the number of teachers in a short span of time without raising the burden of salary expenses (since salaries are calculated according to the length of the training period). If it helped contain the increase in pupil–teacher ratios, the reform had the devastating effect of supplying teachers with insufficient skills in reading, writing, and arithmetic. In Benin, within the framework of the Structural

Adjustment Programme of the years 1989–92, the imposed downsizing of the public sector led to a severe reduction of the education budget. This caused, inter alia, a doubling of the pupil–teacher ratios in the poor, northern part of the country with catastrophic effects on teaching quality.

4 An Inspiring Experience

An inspiring experience to which we want to draw attention in concluding our discussion of education problems is taken from an innovative approach adopted in the city of Sobral in Brazil's poor, north-eastern state of Ceara. Before the start of the programme, only about half of children could read by the time they finished primary school. After its completion, twelve Cearan school systems ranked among Brazil's twenty best. The key elements of success are: (i) the ending of the practice whereby city governments appointed their friends and political allies to serve as school principals, and its replacement by selection procedures exclusively based on merit (as assessed in interviews and tests); (ii) the priority given to enhancing teacher training with, in particular, the strictly enforced obligation for every teacher to spend a day per month in training; (iii) the systematic application of city-wide tests in math and Portuguese for all grades by local professionals, and the payment of bonuses to teachers who succeeded in hitting minimum targets; (iv) the setting of the absolute requirement that children must master basic literacy before they can enter the third grade (when they are aged eight or nine); (v) the devolution to cities of greater power to run their own schools; and, finally, (vi) the linking of a (small) part of the budget allocated to each city to improvements achieved in school results.

Perhaps even more decisive was an element of the policy environment. Sobral benefited from its unusually stable politics: the same political team has run the city for twenty-five years, and education was kept a priority during this whole period (*Economist*, 2021: 33–4). This condition sharply contrasts with the constant changes of education policy in a country such as Mozambique, particularly in matters of teacher training. The main lesson to draw from the Ceara experience is that success in improving educational performances very much depends on a bundle of conditions rather than a single factor. This is negatively confirmed by a recent randomised control trial which found no effect on student outcomes and teacher attendance of a scheme allowing high-performing teachers to receive their preferred posting in Uganda (Cohen et al., 2021).

C Lack of Independence and Effectiveness of the Judiciary

Since the judiciary is a critical part of the law enforcement mechanism, its functioning must play an important role in any assessment of a country's state capacity. Another issue is the degree of independence of the judiciary. Clearly, in Taiwan and South Korea the authoritarian nature of the regime meant that the judiciary was not independent of the executive, at least in matters involving freedom of expression, political organisation, and human rights. On the other hand, rights and obligations pertaining to the economic and the family spheres were effectively enforced, and this proved to be important for the smooth running of the economy and the harmonious life of the society. An independent judiciary in the full sense of the term was to wait until later, after the basis for sustainable growth and development had been built. Almost by definition, 'developmentalism' places higher priority on the modern transformation of the economy than on full democratisation of the society; the idea being that successful modernisation would naturally lead to the democratisation of a society, while the reverse does not necessarily follow (Okuno-Fujiwara, 1997: 403).

In two in-depth case studies that we conducted, Tanzania and Bangladesh, special attention has been devoted to the functioning of the judiciary system. The analysis reveals that not only is this system highly dysfunctional, but also its flaws go beyond problems of insufficient staffing, out-of-date equipment, archaic procedures, huge backlogs of pending cases, and poor communication of information. In evidence is the pervasive presence of corrupt practices and the meddling of powerful actors in the treatment of judiciary affairs, including day-to-day matters pertaining to the civilian and commercial domains of the law. It is therefore not surprising that there is such a strong distrust in judiciary institutions and the magistrates in many poor countries: people tend to believe that judicial decisions are biased in favour of those who are well connected to politicians or rich enough to afford paying bribes.

Expeditiousness of the judiciary system is low in Tanzania, at least if we judge from the situation of land dispute settlements. Backlog of cases and delay in settlement of land disputes are among the problems most often mentioned in relation to land administration. What needs to be stressed is that, in land and other matters, slowness of public decision making feeds corruption, as bribes are often demanded by officials on the ground that they know ways of speeding up delivery. In countries such as Tanzania and Benin, practices of bribe-taking persist in spite of the display of public notices in offices, warning that such practices are strictly forbidden (which we could verify by ourselves), and in spite of official anti-corruption campaigns.

As attested by testimonies in relation to Bangladesh, the situation may even be worse in the sense that lengthy procedures and various other tricks may be part of a delaying tactics intended for extracting illegal payments from both plaintiffs and defendants. Clerks, advocates, and judges are those whose strategic positions allow them to demand additional payments allegedly meant to 'accelerate' the resolution of the case. There is thus widespread suspicion that actors along the enforcement chain often indulge in practices evoking piracy: they artificially create the problem which they then pretend to be able to solve against illegal dues. The difference with the aforementioned situations where slowness of delivery of public goods or services feeds corruption is that in the present case corruption is born of calculated prevarication or fabricated administrative problems; that is, it is the result of malevolent manipulation.

Another salient dysfunction of the judiciary is caused by the meddling of powerful people in judiciary decisions. Bribes are not necessarily involved since political interventions may be part of an implicit contract of political patronage. This is attested by evidence collected in Pakistan. Thus, Lyon (2019) argues that one important reason why a Pakistani landlord may decide to engage in politics is to get a serious land conflict settled in his favour with the help of powerful politicians at district level. As for Martin (2016) and Mohmand (2019), they cite meaningful anecdotal evidence attesting that a political patronage system anchored at the village level enables landowners connected to a political machine to secure the recognition of their perceived rights, at the cost of bribing or intimidating judges if needed. This is especially true of the entrenched dynastic elite, which lord over hierarchically organised patron-client networks that they use as trustworthy voting blocs to endorse their favoured politicians (Malik et al., 2021).

What bears special emphasis is the deleterious effect of political interventions on professional norms inside the judiciary system. If Big Men can influence judicial decisions and derive direct or indirect advantages from their action, why should even low-ranking officials refrain from drawing small perks from their position? The situation is even worse when the appointment and/or the promotion of judges are the outcome of political and politicised decisions. In Bangladesh, this is true at the highest level of the judicial system since judges of the Supreme Court are nominated by the Ministry of Law, Justice and Parliamentary Affairs, itself vulnerable to high-level political pressures aimed at keeping political rivals at bay and buttressing the ruling political regime.

Delving deeper into the case of Bangladesh, it is possible to figure out how, based on perceptions and opinions of a sample of respondents, this country performs in comparative terms. Assessment of judiciary fairness relies on three indicators extracted from the Rule of Law Index of the World Justice Project (2019): while the first two measure the extent of inequality in access to the courts and in the treatment of the cases, respectively, the third one tries to capture the degree of corruption and bribery of the judges. Essentially, they converge to show that Bangladesh does not fare very well along the three dimensions considered. Where it performs especially poorly (with a rank of 115 among 126 countries) is in regard of the second indicator (measuring the degree of discrimination in case treatment) for which it nevertheless does slightly better than its two big South Asian neighbours, India (ranked 117) and Pakistan (ranked 118).

When the expeditiousness of the judicial procedures is measured by the backlog of pending cases, the picture which emerges is rather dismal. Civil court cases resolved during a recent year (2018) represent a significantly smaller number than the total number of cases received and filed, implying an increase in the backlog. This is clearly not a new or transient phenomenon since at the end of the year 2018, more than one-fourth of the total backlog of civil cases consisted of cases that had been pending for more than five years. A similar deterioration is observed when considering the total number of civil and criminal cases, and, interestingly, case backlogging is especially important in the three most prosperous administrative divisions of the country. Among the chief reasons behind this worrying situation are the shortage of judges and the ineffectiveness of the judicial procedures which continue to be based on manual paperwork and even require the judges to write by hand the statements of witnesses.

The lack of independence of the judiciary vis-à-vis the executive is harder to estimate, and evidence is unavoidably piecemeal. A rare exception is nevertheless the detailed and rather unique study of Mehmood and Seror (2019) for Pakistan.[5] They argue that meddling of the executive in judicial matters does not mean that all types of judgments are biased. Decisions most liable to be influenced by such interference concern cases where resources valuable to politicians are directly or indirectly at stake (think of expropriation of private property by government agencies, for example). They thus show that the rise of religious landowning elites, taken as a proxy of democratic regression, has increased the incidence of court rulings in favour of the government for cases involving land disputes with the government, and for cases involving violation of human rights. In contrast, no effect is detected for ordinary criminal cases such as thefts. Moreover, democratic regression has reduced the quality of judicial decisions as measured by case delay (the difference between the year of the case decision and the filing year) and by merit, as proxied by a dummy indicating whether the decision was based on evidence rather than technical or procedural grounds.

Unfortunately, there are no systematic data available to explore the influence of politicians on judicial decisions for civil cases. As argued above, we expect civil judgments to be biased toward the clients of powerful local politicians in contexts dominated by political patronage. Are reforms showing promising results? In Bangladesh, the mode of appointment of the judges, which is critical for their independence, has apparently improved since this prerogative has been taken away from the Public Service Commission, and actual implementation seems to have occurred in 2007. Yet there is lingering doubt about the extent to which in actual practice the judges are appointed for their competence and experience rather than their political loyalty. If we go by the reform experience of Pakistan, however, it is possible to entertain hope for progress: an important reform consisting in the appointment of judges by peers rather than the executive appears to have produced significant effects in the form of more expeditious and less skewed decisions (Mehmood and Seror, 2019).

<hr />

[5] Another exception is the recent study of the judiciary in India where the authors show that, against expectation, judicial decisions are not biased against the Muslim minority (Siddiqi et al., 2021).

II UNCERTAIN AND AMBIGUOUS PROPERTY RIGHTS

A useful distinction here is between property rights over business assets and rights over land. Land tenure is especially important in countries where a significant portion of the population still depends on agriculture and related activities to eke out a livelihood.

A Rights over Business Assets

Together with governance failures, the weakness of property rights is the main generic institutional obstacle against development, which economists repeatedly point out in their writings on the subject. The central argument is that absent or fuzzy property rights impede investment and growth both because they cause uncertainty about who will benefit from the investment effort and because, by preventing asset collateralisation, they make access to credit difficult or impossible. Perhaps the most egregious example of such an adverse effect is the high risk of politically motivated expropriation following a change of ruler, or a change of mood of the present ruler, in autocratic regimes. There is ample historical and contemporary evidence of this possibility as attested by the many instances in which, on the spurious ground of tax evasion, oligarchs have been suddenly dispossessed of their wealth and even thrown into jail.[6] Examples run from the Ottoman empire – where reaching positions close to the sultan (the post of the sultan's treasurer, in particular) was a dangerous step that could be quickly followed by demotion, arrest, and execution – to today's countries of the ex-communist world (Russia, Georgia, and the Central Asian Republics, for example) or the developing world (India, China, Malaysia, South Africa, etc.).

The examples of Taiwan and South Korea nonetheless show that this is not a necessary attribute of autocratic regimes. Enlightened autocrats are indeed able to internalise the negative long-term effects of violations of private property rights on their country's development, and they therefore stand as their strong guarantor. It is true that expropriation or nationalisation of business assets was an impending threat in Taiwan and, even more so, in South Korea. However, the threat would be executed only if a breach of contract was clearly committed by the business owner in his dealings with the state authorities. In other words, the risk of expropriation was predictable. As far as land property rights are concerned, the creation of a cadastral survey was one the priorities set by the Japanese authorities, which early on during the colonial period wanted to boost tax revenue and facilitate land transactions (Cheng, 2001: 20; Chu, 1999: 15). On the occasion of the radical land reforms carried out by the independent governments of Taiwan and South Korea, these rights were duly revamped.

---

[6] When using the word spurious we do not mean that the accused oligarchs have not actually committed tax evasion, but only that it is not a distinctive behaviour that can be attributed to them: other oligarchs commit the same crime and yet they are not harassed or jailed.

In our small sample of country case studies, Benin and Bangladesh are clear cases where property rights of Big Men are uncertain. The logic is plain: their rights are secure as long as the right political ruler, the one whom they have supported, is in power. In Benin, Ajavon bitterly experienced this logic after his defeat against Talon, who himself had to go into exile after his defeat against President Boni. Diversifying political support is the obvious way of avoiding or mitigating the expropriation risk, yet this may be an impossible tactic in strongly polarised political universes. Just think of Bangladesh where, until recently, a person of importance was compelled to choose either of the two available political sides, the AL and the BNP. Accusations of treachery or duplicity were easily proffered against anyone who appeared to play a double game. The risk is equally high for businesspeople belonging to ethnic minorities, as testified by the aforementioned fate of the Gupta family in South Africa or the expulsion of all Indian entrepreneurs and merchants from Uganda under Idi Amin Dada.

It is therefore not surprising that wealthy Indian, Chinese, or Lebanese entrepreneurs tend to adopt cautious behaviour when they enter into the political game, which is almost inevitable in most countries. One frequently observed tactic consists of sharing ownership with powerful local politicians-cum-businessmen. In Malaysia, for example, many of the bigger Chinese business interests have chosen to co-opt influential politicians from the dominant party (UMNO), as well as former civil servants from the dominant ethnic group, as directors and shareholders of their companies (Jomo and Gomez, 1997: 364). In the specific case of Malaysia, this tactic was especially appropriate as the Industrial Coordination Act (ICA) of 1974–5 provided that the development of the manufacturing sector should be aligned with the ethnic redistributive policies that the Malay political elite demanded with a view to achieving interethnic economic parity. (Until then, Malay businessmen had been essentially concentrated in agriculture and the public sector.) As a result, 'both Chinese and foreign companies began to actively solicit business ties with politically influential Malays willing to lend their names for a price without taking on executive roles after becoming owners and directors of the companies' (Bowie, 1991: 103–4, as cited by Jomo and Gomez, 1997: 363).[7]

In South Africa, to take another example, Indian-born entrepreneurs, the Gupta brothers, befriended the highly corrupt President Zuma and went into business with his son, Duduzane.

---

[7] While Chinese entrepreneurs are tempted by risky ventures, members of the dominant ethnic group are awarded privileged access to rent-earning business opportunities in sectors sheltered from competition, the non-tradable and the import-substituting sectors in particular (Jomo and Gomez, 1997: 354–5, 368). Moreover, indigenous Malay enterprises are generally assured of favourable government treatment, through licences, contracts, and access to finance and information, especially if supported by influential politicians who themselves often become involved in business (1997: 362).

B Land Rights

Before delving into the intricacies of land laws, it is useful to describe the major types of land conflicts observed in our four in-depth case study countries, and to decipher their root causes.

1 *Types of Land Conflicts and Their Root Causes*

Another sector of property rights for which frequent complaints were made in the course of our discussions with national experts is land rights. This explains why this issue has received special attention in the cases of Tanzania, Benin, and Bangladesh. We have already mentioned the extremely complex and even confusing character of many land laws, hinting that such a feature is a result of the big stakes involved in the way land is allocated. What we had then in mind are the lands located in urban and peri-urban areas, which carry relatively high values. A key problem here is the uncertainty of property rights caused by fuzzy original rights, double sales, production of fake documents, and other malpractices. Disagreements around the 2013 land law in Benin have thus resulted from conflicts of interest between those who wanted maximum security through the provision of a five-year period during which rights could be verified, on the one hand, and those professionals, intermediaries, and public agents who rejected the idea of an authorisation period, on the other hand. The 2017 amendment actually cancelled the five-year authorisation period provided in the 2013 law, creating confusion and furore among certain circles.

Another type of insecurity may also happen in relation to rural lands, particularly when village lands are coveted by international plantation companies. Here, the issue arises when villagers grant a concession over their customary land in the absence of a full understanding of the contract signed, or when the deal with the plantation company is made secretly by the village chief or the elder council for own profit. The latter possibility exists because of the temptation to use local power positions to unduly appropriate the rents obtained from the awarding of uncultivated common lands. In this instance, as in the case of urban and peri-urban lands, it is because the value of the land has suddenly increased that unscrupulous people may try to lay dubious claims on it, exploiting informational advantages, abusing their power position, or both.

Rising land values or scarcity are caused not only by the growing commercialisation of land-based activities but also by sheer population pressure. These powerful forces tend to disrupt traditional practices and customary rules, particularly in high-population density countries. Two types of land conflicts deserve special mention here, and they are both in evidence in our case study material of Bangladesh. First, intra-family conflicts around land inheritance tend to multiply when land becomes scarcer. For example, as some children have internally migrated to take an urban job, those who have stayed behind and live on agriculture may lay claim on the customary bequest shares of their migrant siblings. As has been shown in the case of pre-genocide Rwanda (André and Platteau, 1998), such conflicts can be so pervasive and severe that they end up tearing asunder the village social fabric and the core institution of the family, setting not only members against cousins, in-laws, and more distant relatives, but also brothers against sisters, brothers against other brothers, and siblings against parents.

Relatedly, when some children have settled in a foreign country (say, India), and the duration of their foreign stay is indeterminate, there may be undue attempts to appropriate their land in the village, whether by close or distant relatives or by neighbours. Such attempts are typically made without informing the rightful landholder. When these conflicts, as well as others (for example, boundary conflicts about the precise delimitation of land plots), cannot be resolved by informal institutions, the plaintiffs tend to go to litigation. The question then arises as to which laws ought to govern or guide the decisions of the judges.

A second important source of land disputes arises when the village population is heterogeneous, say because migrant farmer families coexist with descendants of founding lineages, pressure on land generally prompts the latter to remind the former that they possess only use rights and these rights can be rescinded if native families need their landholdings. The same customary principle, according to which freeholder rights exclusively belong to long-term native residents considered as the 'sons of the soil', is also asserted in situations where sedentary agriculturalists and nomadic land users, typically pastoralists, have claims over the same land territory. Coexistence between farmers and pastoralists is a ubiquitous phenomenon in Africa, not a surprising feature given that until recently and in most parts of the continent, land was abundant and therefore used in extensive ways. Under land pressure, the customary rights of the herders are denied by the farmers who want to enclose their agricultural plots to avoid encroachments by wandering animals.

Obviously, the tense inter-group relationships which result from these troubled circumstances can easily degenerate into violent conflicts, as numerous examples testify. For the first situation of heterogeneity, the bloody confrontations between Ivorian and Burkinabe farmers in the Côte d'Ivoire, or those between Senegalese Toucouleurs and Moorish farmers in the Senegal river valley, come to mind. In these two cases, the occupation rights of the ethnic minority stretched over several generations so that its members perceived those rights as having been progressively upgraded into full freehold tenure, especially so because they had made significant land improvements. In other situations, it is migrants of a rather recent origin who settle in areas where future land scarcity is anticipated by the local population. This is illustrated by the situation of the Chittagong Hill Tracts (Bangladesh), where Bengali farmers, encouraged by the central government, have obtained access to land situated in the traditional territory of native communities of forest dwellers, gradually transformed into farmers. As for the second situation of heterogeneity, we can think of the genuine war which opposed non-Arab agriculturalists to Arab herders in the Darfur province of Sudan, or of the ongoing insurgencies of Tuareg and other groups of herders (Fulani, for example) in some Sahelian countries (most notably, in the northern parts of Burkina Faso and Mali), or elsewhere in sub-Saharan Africa (in northern Nigeria, in the rift valley in Kenya, etc.).

2 The Need to Sort Out the Maze of Land Laws

The above-described issues are obviously intricate, and they all require government intervention, yet not of the same kind and intensity. Let us start with the situation of land-scarce rural areas where the population is heterogeneous, particularly when excruciating conflicts need to be defused and traditional informal mechanisms of conflict settlement are unable to come up with a satisfactory solution. In these instances where land conflicts risk degenerating into a vicious circle of bloodsheds and retributive reactions, the full force of the law and the supreme authority of the state must obviously be brought to bear. In order to save the face of customary authorities, the state is well advised to seek some form of 'accommodation' terms with them (see our Chapter 1 typology of formal-informal interactions). A key problem here is that the state itself may fail to act as a benevolent ruler and side with one group against another for reasons of political opportunism or on the basis of identity considerations. This is clearly what was observed in the nasty Darfur conflict where the authorities in Khartoum backed the Arab herder groups (both antagonists are actually Muslim); in the Sahel and other areas of Africa where the rights of the herders have always been ignored or under-estimated; or in the Côte d'Ivoire where the native farmers enjoyed the support of Ivorian nationalists.

In the latter instance, however, and following a protracted period of troubles threatening the integrity of the nation, the Ivorian state eventually decided to confirm the rights of longstanding foreign farmers to stay on their land, based on certified long-term land leases. Since the latter concept is compatible with informal rules, the solution is of the 'accommodation' type. The point remains that, when there is an inter-ethnic dimension to land conflicts, politics – and partisan politics for that matter – necessarily intrudes into debates around land legislation. Because political compromises may then be hard to find, we discover a vivid illustration of why land laws may be complex and even contradictory when opposite interests are confronted with each other.

We can now grapple with the issue of relationships between customary landholders and large-scale investors. Evidence shows that problems on the ground have generally not been remedied satisfactorily by state legislation and intervention. In a nutshell, this is because large-scale allocation of land by the state is frequently undertaken with no genuine prior consultation of the rural communities concerned. As a consequence of the absence of their informed consent, frustrations are likely to surge up when they come to realise that they are enduring losses or that their expectations (e.g., in the form of new jobs) are not met. The top-down state approach to large-scale agricultural investments seems to be the main culprit: public authorities act as though they consider that rural communities do not possess useful knowledge or are unable to understand all the stakes involved. Not surprisingly, therefore, the formulae that work best are contract farming or out-grower schemes. Local people, then, are not dispossessed of their land and they receive valuable inputs, including seedlings and training in new techniques, as well as assured markets for their produce from the investing company with which they are directly in contact.

The dual tenure system prevailing in Tanzania is worth considering in some detail because its approach (yet not necessarily the details) is so characteristic of many other African countries. Under this system, most rural lands belong to the category of so-called village lands, which are placed under the jurisdiction of village councils. Land rights based on customary tenure, which are not mandatorily registrable but can be backed by certificates issued by the village council, are either individual or collective. This implies that the land can be used by individual occupiers or by the community and, in the former instance, individuals may apply to have their private parcels surveyed and registered. Because the president of the republic is the eminent owner (the custodian) of all Tanzanian lands, a remnant of the colonial period confirmed by the socialist regime of Nyerere, the holders of village certificates are not entitled to transmit them, through sales, donation, or bequest, to somebody outside the village community without the approval of the village council. The intent is clearly to prevent land of a village from ending up being controlled by people alien to the village community. Inside the village community, however, rights acquired through bequests and purchases are valid, so that not all land is allocated by village councils. But land reserved for future use can be allocated by these councils to needy applicants, whether villagers or non-villagers. In all their operations, village councils are required to sanction customary practices only as long as they do not go against the fundamental principles stated in the written law, such as equal treatment of men and women.

The Land Acts resulting from the National Land Policy (1995–9) provide that the status of some village lands can be changed by shifting them to the category of so-called general land. Formal titles of long-term occupancy (for a maximum of ninety-nine years) are then granted by the state to both citizens and non-citizens, whether in rural or urban and peri-urban areas. If the land had occupiers, a process of compensation is initiated. The important point is that external investors cannot get village land unless it has been first converted into general land. Persuaded that many village communities have plenty of unoccupied or unused lands, the government of Tanzania intended to transfer a significant portion of the village land area to the general land category. In actual practice, the dual tenure system, in which centralised control coexists with devolution to customary law at village level, has given rise to deep discontent on the sides of both rural communities and external investors. Major reasons are the long and cumbersome procedures of approval (for areas exceeding 20 ha), which themselves create rent-seeking opportunities, inadequate compensations paid to the villagers, and considerable delays in their disbursement. An additional difficulty arises when, as often happens, there is no proof of ownership for parts of the village lands which, although deemed unoccupied, are actually used by the community as common lands or kept in reserve for the needs of future generations (in conditions of population growth).

Finally, it must be remarked that, despite the intentions of the lawmaker, the intricate land legislation of Tanzania does not actually prevent illegal land speculation. A habit has thus developed whereby separate villagers allow 'investors' to come in and buy land parcels that do not individually exceed the legal threshold of 20 ha. Once these purchases are aggregated, though, they exceed the statutory limit. Worse, they violate the spirit of the law insofar as, instead of developing the land, the buyer uses it as a collateral to borrow money from banks, and afterward sell it by surveying and creating plots.

What about the regulation of land problems that occur in situations of extreme land scarcity and hit the core of community and family life? These are the hardest to solve and, here, there is no escape from economic solutions consisting of enhancing labour absorption in agriculture and agriculture-related activities, and of expanding non-farm employment, whether in rural or urban areas. Therefore, institutions that enable these economic transformations, such as those put in place by Taiwan and South Korea, matter even more than land institutions. As attested by the experiences of many poor countries in Asia and Africa, legal inheritance norms, imposition of minimum viable farm size (below which any sale of land is prohibited), and similar measures produce weak or no effects. This being reckoned, it is in conditions of great scarcity that land titles, based on sound surveying and adjudication procedures, are most needed. Two major problems must nevertheless be overcome. First, titles cannot achieve their objective if land dispute settlement institutions are not effective and if judges are corruptible. (As one Kenyan farmer put it to one of us, 'a title is worth less than a bribe to the judge'.) Second, for titles to become widespread enough, an effective land administration must exist capable of not only surveying, registering and formalising land rights, but also of updating land registries systematically.

Evidence is not reassuring if one judges by the situation observed in many countries of Asia (Bangladesh and India, for example) and Africa. In Tanzania, where land is rather abundant, very few rural residents hold occupancy certificates (the Certificates of Customary Rights of Occupancy, or CCROs) aimed at securing their individual land parcels. One key problem is that the village land must be properly surveyed, and its land boundaries duly demarcated, before the ministry for land affairs can approve its regularisation and issuance of individual land certificates by the village council can proceed. The whole procedure takes several years to complete. In addition, only a small proportion of Tanzanian villages have land use plans, a precondition for transferring land to the general category. And, finally, only a minority of land records are found in the land registers with the consequence that cases of multiple titles for the same piece of land are not uncommon.

In Benin, another country where land is rather abundant, the initial approach to the formalisation of land rights was more decentralised and progressive than in Tanzania. It opted for a scheme, known as the *Plan Foncier Rural*, in which land demarcation is based on the community and undertaken on demand: only those villages which feel the need for a survey of village lands and their certification are eligible, and in each of them a committee is tasked with identifying and demarcating all parcels situated on the village territory.[8] Thereafter, customary land ownership is formally and legally documented in the form of transferable and collateralisable land certificates which, as in Tanzania, may be individual or collective. A clear advantage of this scheme is that it supplied convenient and fast services for obtaining legal proof of landholding rights and for carrying out land transactions. Yet it was soon to be called into question and telescoped under the pressure of external forces combined by the preference for centralisation of some politicians. A reform was thus initiated (in 2004–5) under the impulse and with the support of the Millennium Challenge Corporation (MCC), with the explicit purpose of ending legal dualism and streamlining and centralising the administration of land rights. Responsibility for implementation of a new Land Code (the *Code Domanial et Foncier*) was vested in a newly created agency (the ANDF), the central idea being to transform rural land certificates and urban residence permits into full-fledged titles. Aware that the issuance of titles is a time-consuming process, the lawmaker authorised the issuance of a new, temporary *attestation de détention coutumière* to replace the previous *certificat de propriété foncière*. Land sales continued to be permitted through conventions or through officially sanctioned contracts.

What is worthy of note is that only a minority of villages demanded the demarcation of their lands under the initial scheme and, even in those in which demarcation took place, the proportion of land certificates to the total number of parcels surveyed was typically low. The only exception comes from villages where migrants form a significant portion of the local population, thus confirming the idea that local demand for land documents varies greatly depending upon the specific context of rural communities, and that their heterogeneity is an important variable (together with population density). It barely needs to be added that the subsequent reform was unsuccessful.

Further confirmation comes from a recent study (Broka et al., 2021) conducted in the pineapple development scheme in one of the richest parts of the country, not far from the two main commercial cities in the south (Cotonou and Porto Novo), which shows that rural land markets are quite active despite

---

[8] This operation includes the mapping of customary ownership in the form of a full land survey.

the fact that most producers have no land certificate. Thus, a significant proportion of the plots owned have been acquired through outright purchase rather than through inheritance or gifts.[9] Looking at all the pineapple plots under cultivation, more than a third of them have been rented in by the possessor, and if traditional land loans are included, the proportions are much higher.[10] Even more strikingly, most land transactions have been made through strictly informal channels. Regarding the land rental market specifically, barely 60 per cent of the deals made by men rest on a written piece of paper while the proportion goes down to barely 45 per cent for women in couple. In these cases, moreover, the great majority of the land deals (about 85 per cent) are attested by a simple paper carrying the signatures of the two transactors and their witnesses (in the remaining cases, there is no witness). Hardly anyone has therefore followed the prescribed legalisation procedure before the competent court. And yet land disputes seem to be rather rare.

Compared to Tanzania and Benin, Bangladesh, as in neighbouring India, is in a radically different situation: population pressure on land resources is so high that land titling is necessary. However, as stressed earlier, land titling is not of much use if land records are not regularly updated, and the judiciary cannot rely on proper registry evidence. This is, unfortunately, the grim situation observed in South Asia, and, in these conditions, it is no coincidence that citizens distrust the land dispute settlement procedures even though there are other reasons behind their poor performances. Together with the noxious presence of corrupt and opaque practices, with which land acquisition and compensation procedures are riddled, particularly in relation to the creation of SEZs, the failure to keep valid records of land transactions is probably the most severe institutional dysfunction of land administration in Bangladesh and the whole region.

The lesson seems to be the following. In land matters and for rural areas particularly, a great deal of flexibility, decentralisation, and respect for informal arrangements is desirable. In the context of multi-ethnic societies governed by a plurality of norms, the ambition of the state to regulate land tenure rights in a top-down and uniform manner, without due consideration for the role of local agencies and semi-formalised mechanisms, is doomed to end in disappointment and failure. The main reason for involving communities in any process of land rights formalisation is that land issues are intimately related to other aspects of the village social life, so that mishandling them can have major consequences beyond the strict domain of land-related management and activities.

---

[9] Exact figures are: 40 per cent for men, 52 per cent for women whose husband is absent, and 29 per cent for women living alone.

[10] Exact figures are: 39 per cent for men, 48 per cent for women in a relationship, 35 per cent for women whose husband is absent, and 32 per cent for single women. If traditional land loans are included, the proportions rise to 48 per cent, 64 per cent, 45 per cent, and 46 per cent, respectively.

Evidence suggests that, as long as communities can function on the basis of informal rules, which they themselves devise and enforce, the state should not intrude into their land institutions or, if it does, it should do it with caution and restraint. It is to the special situations which require its intervention, and which have been identified above, that it should devote much of its attention and its formalisation efforts. In terms of the terminology used in Chapter 1, formal institutions or rules should substitute for informal ones in extreme situations while they should complement them in more ordinary circumstances.

III CONCLUSION

Politics has an enormous influence on state capacity. When the regime is rooted in political clientelism and cronyism, the money needed to mobilise and maintain support is obtained not only from donations made by big business leaders and from embezzled state budgets, but also from kickbacks extracted by low-level officers and channelled up the bureaucratic hierarchy. As substantiated by evidence from India, Pakistan, and Bangladesh, sales of desirable posts and locations in the administration, through appointments, promotions and transfers, are a pivotal mechanism of rent appropriation ultimately intended to grease the oil of the political machinery. Insofar as frontline officers are induced to take decisions that maximise rent extraction and these decisions run counter to the citizen's interests, the socially harmful effects of this mechanism can be substantial. Ghost teachers and ghost schools are an extreme example of the immense social cost that may result from rent-generating policies.

Political capture of the bureaucracy can yield another, less well-known undesirable effect: because in the logic of this capture, administrative departments operate as feudal fiefs under the control of political bigwigs, coordination between them is made intrinsically difficult, thereby hampering the effectiveness of development policies. In fact, the problem may be worse than just poor coordination if it consists of fierce struggles about gaining control of lucrative rent opportunities embedded in some key ministries or departments (police, customs, tax administration, land planning, to cite the most important).

Lacking state capacity may also stem from factors that have nothing to do with politics, however. Thus, if bad educational performances may arise from policy neglect reflected in small budgets and poor monitoring, from reactionary rural landlords working to undermine schooling efforts at local level, from bureaucratic dysfunction and/or the lobbying corporatist pressures exerted by trade unions, they may also be caused by a lack of professional norms leading to teacher and school director absenteeism. In turn, absent norms may ultimately appear to be the consequence of a low demand for education in areas deprived of job opportunities where returns to schooling can show up.

Turning to property rights, and land rights in particular, their uncertainty and ambiguity may be traced not only to undue meddling of politicians on behalf of influential people or to malpractices at the level of the state bureaucracy (land surveyors, architects, and the like), but also to unenforceable laws that prescribe unrealistic procedures or unattainable standards. The root of the problem may then lie in an incorrect appraisal of the genuine demands of the people, a lack of consultation with them (such as is typically the case with investments by large foreign plantation companies), unnecessarily slow and cumbersome procedures, or inappropriate attempts at systematisation and uniformisation of enduring informal rules and practices. Ill-advised external pressures by donor organisations informed by their own Western standards may actually be responsible for the latter type of dysfunction.

Finally, malfunctioning of the judiciary may originate in a variety of causes, which go beyond illicit political interference and corruptibility of judges and magistrates: poor equipment and staffing resulting in slow treatment of the cases, low quality of the personnel, imprecise or non-enforceable laws (see above), outdated working procedures, and unreliable documentary sources (e.g., land registries).

10

Conclusion

In this chapter, we begin by summarising the central contributions and the main lessons of our whole exercise. We then address the question of their possible implications for development assistance.

I MAJOR LESSONS

Three important contributions have resulted from the present endeavour. First, we have proposed a methodology aimed at enabling us to navigate one's way through the data and information that need to be collected to form a sound institutional diagnosis. Clearly, the approach proposed consists of two major phases: an exploratory phase during which international databases are mobilised and local expert opinions collected, and an in-depth analysis phase intended to probe into strategic sectors or domains where institutional obstacles appear to be especially salient. This meso-level institutional analysis is itself preceded by an economic diagnostic based on the twin concepts of growth engine and structural transformation, the latter being itself rooted in the dual economy framework initially proposed by Arthur Lewis. As we have found, poor countries tend to be characterised by the absence of a clearly identifiable growth engine (Tanzania), an artificial or unsustainable engine (Benin), a misleading engine based on resource rents (Mozambique), or a working engine at risk of misfiring (Bangladesh).

Our second contribution consists of the lessons learned from the institutional analysis: if institutional hurdles and the sectors of the economy where they manifest themselves are not necessarily identical between countries, behind them stand generic issues or problem areas. The identification of these issues provides us with a privileged instrument to penetrate into the institutional territory of a country, more particularly into its parts that matter for long-term development. Our attention has thus been drawn to institutional aspects that have been largely bypassed or generally under-estimated by economists and international experts to this date: the role of initial conditions with special attention to geographic and demographic conditions; the quality of political leadership and state autonomy; state capacity (including property rights, and land rights in particular); the nature of state-business relationships; the functioning of the judiciary; bureaucratic failures with special attention to coordination problems between its various parts; and the role of informal exchanges, including those mobilised for illegal transactions.

Moreover, crucial interlinkages between some of these core problems have been brought to light. For example, state capacity failures are often better understood when they are explicitly related to the political regime. This is typically the case when teacher absenteeism is caused by a political system of clientelism dominated by quasi-feudal local elites. Or, poor coordination between key administrative departments is more likely to be serious and difficult to remedy in contexts where these departments are viewed as political fiefs by the incumbent ministers and their close circles. To take a final example, formal property rights cannot be effectively enforced if the judiciary system is dysfunctional and, in particular, if magistrates and judges are prone to corruption. In the latter instance, indeed, cash notes carry more value than a land title.

As our third contribution, we have proposed the early development experiences of two East Asian tiger countries, South Korea and Taiwan, as useful benchmarks for putting the findings emerging from our four case studies in a broader perspective. The idea was not to use South Korea and Taiwan as models to be replicated but, more realistically, as guides susceptible of attracting our attention to important institutional dimensions of development. The generic issues of the role of initial conditions, the quality of political leadership and state autonomy, and state capacity have thus come out as key entry points into the Taiwanese and South Korean experiences of successful development. Furthermore, the critical importance of state-business relationships, which came out of our four intensive country case studies, has been fully confirmed by our review of South Korea and Taiwan at the time they were more or less at the same development level as these four countries.

There are several important and more specific lessons to draw from the comparison of the development experiences of our 4+2 countries.

Countries may have their own path to development. The fact that countries as apparently similar as Taiwan and South Korea, two showcases of developmental states, exhibited some significant differences in their mode of structural transformation, further reinforces this point. In particular, while South Korea's growth has largely rested on the dynamism of large firms, small and medium-scale enterprises have played a significant role in the economic development of Taiwan. On the other hand, if the comparison is made between these two countries and Western Europe, we can confirm the idea of Gerschenkron (1962), according to which the role of the state increases with the distance

between the take-off time of a country and the take-off time of pioneer countries. Relatedly, authoritarian regimes have been, and continue to be, a frequent
occurrence in presently developing countries, whether in Africa, Asia, or Latin
America. It is therefore not surprising that we have found them repeatedly
in our small sample of countries (Kérékou and Talon in Benin, Nyerere and
Magufuli in Tanzania, the Frelimo in Mozambique, Ershad, Ziaur Rahman,
and the two begums in Bangladesh).

In most cases, however, strong leaders have not been to the task, essentially
because they failed to see the critical role of private incentives in development
and, in some cases, to check corruption in the ruling clique. Those criticisms
cannot be levelled against South Korea and Taiwan. In spite of their having
many trappings of a socialist state, including economic planning and the centralisation of politics in the form of a single party rule, their political leaders
understood that sustained growth cannot be achieved if sufficient space is not
created for market forces to exert their competitive pressures. On the contrary,
they have exhibited great skills in mobilising private initiative and devising
performance-based contracts in their relations to the private sector. It is probably not coincidental, therefore, that East Asian past leaders have inspired the
present regimes of Presidents Kagame in Rwanda and Talon in Benin, although
in the latter instance the profile of the autocrat somewhat differs from those
of his counterparts in Taiwan and South Korea at the time of independence.
The short-lived regime of President Magufuli in Tanzania comes as another
possible illustration of the authoritarian way to development.

The quality of political leadership is clearly a major factor of successful
long-term development. A developing country needs effective leaders able to
conduct its destiny with the help of a team of technocrats in charge of setting economic priorities. This implies the existence of an autonomous state
immune to pressures from private lobbies and to large-scale corruption, as
well as its backing by an efficient bureaucracy. Moreover, it is essential that
such leaders prevail over the whole critical period during which the basis of
the economy's structural transformation is laid, which implies that the 'good'
leader remains a sufficiently long time in power or is followed by successors
endowed with similar qualities. This condition has been fulfilled in Taiwan
and in South Korea, although in the latter case the country had to wait for the
demise of the corrupt leader who seized power at the time of independence. In
some other instances, the inverse, less favourable scenario unfolded with 'bad'
leaders succeeding 'good' ones. Thus, in Pakistan, the early rule of Ayub Khan
held the promise of an effective state-directed development, yet was succeeded
by regimes which, starting with Bhutto and continuing with Zia ul-Haq and
Pervez Musharaff, reformed the country's institutions in a way that deeply
changed the rules of the political game. In short, they destroyed the autonomy of the state and the independence of the bureaucracy by encouraging
the politicisation of the administration and the subordination of civil servants
to elected politicians. Less calamitous is the experience of Indonesia where

President Suharto, a strongman who abolished politics and co-opted the army, gave a powerful and consistent impulse to the modernisation of the country during the long period of his rule (no less than three decades). It is on the basis of clear priorities decided at the top that business cronies were allowed to carry out the national plan. By contrast, President Joko Widodo (popularly known as Jokowi), who did not hail from the army or the country's elites, ended up frustrating the many hopes that his election raised among ordinary citizens. Mostly adept at entrenching his power through vast co-option of potential rivals, he let his cronies set the priorities. Damage has been more limited than in Pakistan because the engine of sustainable growth had been set into motion before his advent to power.

As we also learn from the East Asian experience, including post-1978 mainland China, an effective state-directed development is grounded not only in a successful industrial policy but also in sizeable investments intended for rapidly expanding the country's infrastructure and its human capital. In doing so, major attention needs to be paid to quality factors. This is especially evident in the case of education where performance must be measured not so much by admission or graduation rates as by learning outcomes.

II IMPLICATIONS FOR DEVELOPMENT ASSISTANCE

Our review of the four countries selected for intensive study has revealed that lack of insulation of the state from private business interests, faulty economics, and poor state capacity have largely contributed to disappointing development performances. Foreign assistance can help enhance the quality of the bureaucracy and to better manage the economy, but only in so far as bureaucratic effectiveness and quality of economic management do not depend on political factors. In reality, however, many institutional failures are traceable to the way political forces in a country play out.

Because almost all country diagnoses have so far ignored this basic truth, it is no surprise that hopes placed by Western donors in the development prospects of particular countries have been frequently dashed. Upon careful look, disappointment has been caused not so much by the sheer ignorance of politics as by the influence of rather naïve views underestimating the complexity of political economy mechanisms. This has been recently testified by the disastrous experiences of Western aid in countries such as Haiti, Somalia, Libya, Iraq, and Afghanistan. Moreover, because political patterns are influenced by the historical path of a country, its geopolitical situation, and particular aspects of its social fabric and culture (think of the role of clans and other traditional entities, of immigrant entrepreneurs, religious movements, regional and ethnic divisions, and so forth), any political economy analysis needs to be country specific. This does not mean that there are no common features between certain countries, but they should not be assumed a priori on the basis of superficial examination, and specific features should be investigated.

A first lesson is therefore that donors need to have a good knowledge of the countries it deals with, particularly with respect to the dimensions that our study has shed light on. Examples abound where interventions were made without sufficient information about potential backlash effects, without proper cognisance of impinging informal institutions (e.g., land tenure rules, contract enforcement mechanisms, exchange and credit relations) and their resilience, or without due awareness of the complex interests at stake. Second, since politics strongly affects development results, a donor cannot ignore the role of governance, and this implies that aid allocation decisions must necessarily be made on the basis of a needs-governance trade-off. In addition, the donor must decide whether the aid awarded is going to be effectively monitored with inevitable sanctions when fraud is detected. We have seen that in some cases, donors have shown a lot of laxity in the presence of a series of well-published scandals, presumably because stopping aid also involves costs for the donor country (due to fixed costs of establishing the aid link, to the harm caused to geopolitical interests, or to the ensuing losses for its own business firms). Also, their readiness to use ad hoc measures to bypass the implications of governance indicators is to be questioned.

As shown in Bourguignon and Platteau (2021a, 2021b), the advantage of using donor monitoring is that it increases the chance of poor and badly governed countries to be eligible for aid, provided, however, that the initial gap between their governance quality and the quality observed in other poor but better-governed countries is not too large. Budget aid, grounded in the idea of partnership between donor and recipient, is evidently not recommended when conditionality needs to be imposed by the former on the latter. When a donor deals with poor and badly governed countries whose populations cry for external assistance, project aid, and to a lesser extent programme aid, seem advisable. The reason is that such aid modalities are more easily monitored, in part because they may be implemented by NGOs or private companies contracted by the donors. An extreme case is the mode of intervention favoured by China when financing and building infrastructural facilities in Africa. Since monitoring intensity may be tailored to the specific governance situation of each recipient country, recourse to project aid need not be systematic: appropriate for so-called fragile countries, it may be largely dispensed with in poor and better-governed countries.

Devarajan and Khemani (2016: 21) make the point that, when government failures are the result of politics, priority ought to be given to aid modalities for which citizens' ability to hold the state to account is maximised. In short, aid should primarily aim at promoting citizen engagement and transparency (2016: 21). In the same line, Wade (1985: 488) stresses the need to strengthen the rules of public disclosure or accountability to curtail corruption. This prescription raises the moot question as to whether aid should aim to improve governance directly or, rather, to lay out the infrastructural basis of long-term growth, promote better education, health and technical training, and reduce poverty. We submit that the latter option should be followed but strict conditions and rigorous monitoring should be attached to the disbursement of aid so as to make it as effective as possible: in this way, aid-related governance rather than general governance can be improved. Moreover, whenever people's participation and self-assertion are an important prerequisite of success, as in many rural development programmes, the donors must encourage the underlying processes. In many cases, this may require that on-the-ground interventions are entrusted to non-government organisations, or similar types of associations, both local and international.

We thus believe that general governance in recipient countries is not susceptible to being exogenously modified, whether by demanding public transparency or otherwise. Placing great hope in the ability of foreign actors to initiate changes in governance is bound to lead to disillusionment, and it may even happen that such attempts will spark nasty backlash effects. As already suggested, the more realistic solution consists of applying aid allocation rules based on comparative country performances weighed down by considerations of intensity of needs and coupled with a serious monitoring of the aid use. On the other hand, as the Taiwanese historical experience testifies, improvements in state accountability and the promotion of a civil society evolve gradually and are the outcome of development rather than its prerequisite. Furthermore, if economic liberalisation was largely undertaken under foreign pressures, political liberalisation was to a great extent an endogenous process, in which even the authorities eventually participated. The problem is of course more complicated when political leadership is lacking, say because the clique in power is corrupt or the ruler has unrealistic views regarding the country's growth potential. It is in this sort of especially hard circumstances, however, that effectiveness in aid use should arguably be a major preoccupation of the donor community.

There is a snag, however. Endogenous or co-evolving progress toward political liberalisation is more difficult today than it was at the time Taiwan and South Korea developed. The reason is that globalisation and the accompanying exposure of elites and middle-class people to modes of living and values in developed countries, including democratic aspirations, cause their preferences to change more quickly than ever before. As a result, restrictions to freedoms have become less acceptable to people, the educated classes in particular, thereby requiring a greater measure of people's indoctrination, internal repression and isolation from international influences. The examples of Russia and China come to mind here. This reality thus points to a tragic dilemma for which no satisfactory resolution seems to exist. And ominous consequences for the international order also follow.

References

Abbas, H. (2005). *Pakistan's Drift into Extremism – Allah, the Army, and America's War on Terror*, M.E. Sharpe, New York and London.

Acemoglu, D. (2003). Why not a political Coase theorem? Social conflict, commitment, and politics, *Journal of Comparative Economics* 31, pp. 620–52.

Acemoglu, D., and Johnson, S. (2005). Unbundling institutions. *Journal of Political Economy*, 113(5), pp. 949–95.

Acemoglu, D., and Robinson, J. A. (2000). Political losers as a barrier to economic development, *American Economic Review* 90, pp. 126–30.

Acemoglu, D., and Robinson, J. A. (2006a). *Economic Origins of Dictatorship and Democracy*, Cambridge University Press, Cambridge.

Acemoglu, D., and Robinson, J. A. (2006b). Economic backwardness in political perspective, *American Political Science Review* 100(1), pp. 115–31.

Acemoglu, D., and Robinson, J. A. (2008a). Persistence of power, elites, and institutions, *American Economic Review* 98(1), pp. 267–93.

Acemoglu, D., and Robinson, J. A. (2008b). The persistence and change of institutions in the Americas, *Southern Economic Journal* 75(2), pp. 282–99.

Acemoglu, D., and Robinson, J. A. (2012). *Why Nations Fail: The Origins of Power, Prosperity and Poverty*, Profile Books, London.

Acemoglu, D., Johnson, S., and Robinson, J. A. (2001). The colonial origins of comparative development: An empirical investigation, *American Economic Review* 91(5), pp. 1369–401.

Akerlof, G. (1976). The economics of caste and of the rat race and other woeful tales, *Quarterly Journal of Economics* 90(4), pp. 599–617.

Akerlof, G. (2017). The importance of legitimacy, *The World Bank Economic Review* 30(Supplement 1), pp. S157–65.

Aldashev, G., Chaara, I., Platteau, J.-P., and Wahhaj, Z. (2012). Formal law as a magnet to reform custom, *Economic Development and Cultural Change* 60(1), pp. 795–828.

Amsden, A. H. (1989). *Asia's Next Giant: South Korea and Late Industrialization*, Oxford University Press, New York.

Amsden, A. H. (1992). *Asia's Next Giant: South Korea and Late Industrialization*, Oxford University Press on Demand, Oxford.

Anderson, S., François, P., and Kotwal, A. (2015). Clientelism in Indian villages, *American Economic Review* 105(6), pp. 1780–816.

André, C., and Platteau, J.-P. (1998). Land relations under unbearable stress: Rwanda caught in the Malthusian trap, *Journal of Economic Behavior and Organization* 34(1), pp. 1–47.

Aoki, M. (2001). *Towards a Comparative Institutional Analysis*, MIT Press, Cambridge, MA.

Arab News. (2022, 27 March). Japan condemns Houthi attacks on Saudi Arabia's oil facilities. *Arab News*. [online], available at: www.arabnews.com/node/2051236/world.

Auriol, E., and Platteau, J.-P. (2017a). The explosive combination of religious decentralisation and autocracy: The case of Islam, *Economics of Transition* 25(2), pp. 313–50.

Auriol, E., and Platteau, J.-P. (2017b). Religious co-option under autocracy: A theory inspired by history, *Journal of Development Economics* 127(July), pp. 395–412.

Auriol, E., Platteau, J.-P., and Verdier, T. (2021). *The Quran and the Sword*, EDI Working Paper Series, Oxford Policy Management, Oxford.

Axelrod, R. (1984). *The Evolution of Cooperation*, Basic Books, New York.

Axelrod, R. (1997). *The Complexity of Cooperation: Agent-Based Models of Competition and Collaboration*, Princeton University Press, Princeton, NJ.

Baland, J.-M., and Platteau, J.-P. (1996). *Halting Degradation of Natural Resources: Is There a Role for Rural Communities?* Clarendon Press, Oxford.

Baland, J.-M., and Platteau, J.-P. (1997). Wealth inequality and efficiency on the commons, Part I: The unregulated case, *Oxford Economic Papers* 49(3), pp. 451–82.

Baland, J.-M., and Platteau, J.-P. (1998). Wealth inequality and efficiency on the commons, Part II: The regulated case, *Oxford Economic Papers* 50(1), pp. 1–22.

Baland, J.-M., Bourguignon, F., Platteau, J.-P., and Verdier, T. (2020). Economic development and institutions: An introduction, in Baland, J.-M., Bourguignon, F., Platteau, J.-P., and Verdier, T. (eds), *The Handbook of Economic Development and Institutions*, Princeton University Press, Princeton, NJ and Oxford, pp. 1–20.

Balassa, B. (1988). The lessons of East Asian development: An overview. *Economic Development and Cultural Change*, 36(S3), S273–S290.

Banerjee, A., and Pande, R. (2007). *Parochial Politics: Ethnic Preferences and Politician Corruption*, Working Paper, Harvard University, Cambridge, MA.

Bardhan, P., and Mookherjee, D. (2020). Clientelistic politics and economic development: An overview, in Baland, J.-M., Bourguignon, F., Platteau, J.-P., and Verdier, T. (eds), *The Handbook of Economic Development and Institutions*, Princeton University Press, Princeton, NJ and Oxford, pp. 84–102.

Bardhan, P., Mitra, S., Mookherjee, D., and Nath, A. (2020). *How Do Voters Respond to Welfare vis-a-vis Infrastructure Programs? Evidence for Clientelism in West Bengal*, Mimeo.

Barrera, O., S. Guriev, E. Henry, and E. Zuravskaya, (2020). Facts, alternative facts, and fact checking in times of post-truth politics, *Journal of Public Economics*, 182, pp. 1–19.

Barro, R., and Lee, J. H. (2018). BarroLeeDataSet. [online], available at: www.barrolee.com/.

Basu, K. (2000). *Prelude to Political Economy: A Study of the Social and Political Foundations of Economics*, Oxford University Press, Oxford.

Basu, K., Jones, E., and Schlicht, E. (1987). The growth and decay of custom: The role of the New Institutional Economics in economic history, *Explorations in Economic History* 24(1), pp. 1–21.

Bates, R. H. (1989). *Beyond the Miracle of the Market: The Political Economy of Agrarian Development in Kenya*, Cambridge University Press, Cambridge.

Bauer, P. T., and Yamey, B. S. (1957). *The Economics of Under-Developed Countries*, Cambridge University Press, Cambridge.

Bayart, J.-F. (1993). *The State in Africa: The Politics of the Belly*, Pearson Education.

Berry, A., and William, C. (1979). *Agrarian Structure and Productivity in Developing Countries*, Johns Hopkins University Press, Baltimore, MD and London.

Bertho, F. (2013). Présentation de la Base de Données "Institutional Profiles Database 2012 (IPD 2012)", *Document de Travail de la DG Trésor Cahier 2013/07*.

Besley, T., and Coate, S. (1998). Sources of inefficiency in a representative democracy: A dynamic analysis, *American Economic Review* 88(1), pp. 139–56.

Besley, T., and Persson, T. (2009). The origin of state capacity: Property rights, taxation, and politics, *American Economic Review* 99(4), pp. 1218–44.

Besley, T., and Persson, T. (2010). State capacity, conflict, and development, *Econometrica* 78(1), pp. 1–34.

Binmore, K. (1992). *Funs and Games: A Text on Game Theory*, D.C. Heath and Co., Lexington, MA.

Binswanger, H. P., and Rosenzweig, M. R. (1986). Behavioural and material determinants of production relations in agriculture, *Journal of Development Studies* 22(3), pp. 503–39.

Binswanger, H. P., and McIntire, J. (1987). Behavioural and material determinants of production relations in land-abundant tropical agriculture, *Economic Development and Cultural Change* 36(1), pp. 73–99.

Binswanger, H. P., McIntire, J., and Udry, C. (1989). Production relations in semi-arid African agriculture, in Bardhan, P. (ed), *The Economic Theory of Agrarian Institutions*, Clarendon Press, Oxford, pp. 122–44.

Bisin, A., and Verdier, T. (2011). The economics of cultural transmission and socialization, in Benhabib, J., Bisin, A., and Jackson, M. O. (eds), *The Handbook of Social Economics*, Elsevier, vol. 1, pp. 339–416.

Bisin, A., and Verdier, T. (2001). The economics of cultural transmission and the dynamics of preferences, *Journal of Economic Theory* 97, pp. 298–319.

Bolton, P., and Dewatripont, M. (2005). *Contract Theory*, MIT Press, Cambridge, MA.

Boserup, E. (1965). *The Conditions of Agricultural Growth: The Economics of Agrarian Change under Population Pressure*, Allen and Unwin, London.

Boserup, E. (1981). *Population and Technology*, Basil Blackwell, Oxford.

Bossavie, L., Görlach, J.-S., Özden, C., and Wang, H. (2021). Temporary Migration for Long-term Investment, *Policy Research Working Paper No.9740*, World Bank.

Bourguignon, F. (1990). Growth and inequality in the dual model of development: The role of demand factors, *The Review of Economic Studies* 57(2), pp. 215–28.

Bourguignon, F., Houssa, R., Platteau, J-P, and Reding, P. (Eds.) (2023). *State Capture and Rent Seeking in Benin*, Cambridge University Press, Cambridge.

Bourguignon, F., and Platteau, J.-P. (2021a). Should a poverty-averse donor always reward better governance? *Economic Journal* 131(637), pp. 1919–46.

Bourguignon, F., and Platteau, J.-P. (2021b). *Aid Effectiveness: Revisiting the Trade-Off Between Needs and Governance*, Mimeo.

Bourguignon, F., and Verdier, T. (2000). Oligarchy, democracy, inequality and growth, *Journal of Development Economics* 62, pp. 285–313.

Bourguignon, F., and Verdier, T. (2012). The simple analytics of elite behaviour under limited state capacity, in Amsden, A. H., DiCaprio, A., and Robinson, J. A. (eds), *The Role of Elites in Economic Development*, UNU-WIDER Studies in Development Economics, Oxford University Press, pp. 251–80.

Bourguignon, F., and Wangwe, S. (Eds.) (2023). *State and Business in Tanzania's Development*, Cambridge University Press, Cambridge.

Bowen, J. R. (2003). *Islam, Law and Equality in Indonesia – An Anthropology of Public Reasoning*, Cambridge University Press, Cambridge.

Bowie, A. (1991). *Crossing the Industrial Divide: State, Society, and the Politics of Economic Transformation in Malaysia*, Columbia University Press, New York.

Bowles, S. (2004). *Microeconomics: Behavior, Institutions, and Evolution*, Russell Sage Foundation, New York, and Princeton University Press, Princeton.

Brandt, V. S. (1980). The agricultural sector in contemporary South Korea. *Asian Affairs: An American Review*, 7(3), pp. 182–94.

Broka, C., Guirkinger, C., and Platteau, J.-P. (2021). *Rapport des Données Baseline 2020 sur les Contraintes à la Production d'Ananas au Bénin*, Mimeo, University of Namur, Belgium.

Busia, K.-A. (2020). *The Position of the Chief in the Modern Political System of Ashanti: A Study of the Influence of Contemporary Social Changes on Ashanti Political Institutions*, Routledge, London (originally published by Oxford University Press, 1951).

Chabal, P., and Daloz, J.-P. (1999). *Africa Works: Disorder as Political Instrument*, James Currey, Oxford, and Indiana University Press, Bloomington, IN.

Chan, S. (2002). Economic performance and democratic transition: Stylized paradoxes and the Taiwan experience, in Chow, P. C. Y. (ed), *Taiwan's Modernization in Global Perspective*, Praeger, Westport, CT and London, pp. 173–93.

Chang, D. (1965). US aid and economic progress in Taiwan, *Asian Survey* 5(3), pp. 162–60.

Chaudhury, N., Hammer, J., Kremer, M., Muralidharan, K., and Halsey Rogers, F. (2006). Missing in action: Teacher and health worker absence in developing countries, *Journal of Economic Perspectives* 20(1), pp. 91–116.

Chayanov, A. V. (1966). *The Theory of Peasant Economy*, Irwin, Homewood, IL.

Cheema., A., Khwaja, A. I., and Qadir, A. (2005). Decentralization in Pakistan: Context, content and causes, *Faculty Research Working Papers Series, RWP05-034*, Harvard University, John F. Kennedy School of Government.

Cheng, T.-J. (2001). Transforming Taiwan's economic structure in the 20th century, *The China Quarterly* 165, pp. 19–36.

Cheng, T.-J., and Chu, Y.-H. (2002). State–business relationship in Taiwan: A political economy perspective, in Chow, P. C. Y. (ed), *Taiwan's Modernization in Global Perspective*, Praeger, Westport, CT and London, pp. 195–214.

Cho, Y. J. (1996). Government intervention, rent distribution and economic development in Korea, in Aoki, M., Kim, H.-K., and Okuno-Fujiwara, M. (eds), *The Role of Government in East Asian Economic Development*, Oxford University Press and World Bank.

Choo, H., Bark, S. I., and Yoon, S. B. (1996). Korea: Poverty in a tiger country, in Øyen, E., Miller, S. M., and Samad, S. A. (eds), *Poverty: A Global Review* (Handbook on International Poverty Research), Scandinavian University Press, pp. 86–99.

Chow, P. C. Y. (2002). Taiwan's modernization: Its achievements and challenges, in Chow, P. C. Y. (ed), *Taiwan's Modernization in Global Perspective*, Praeger, Westport, CT and London, pp. 3–28.

Chu, W. W. (1999). *Industrial Growth and Small and Medium-Sized Enterprises: The Case of Taiwan*, Mimeo, Academia Sinica.

Chun, S.-H. (2018). *The Economic Development of South Korea: From Poverty to a Modern Industrial State*, Routledge, New York.

Cohen, I., Dal Bo, E., Finan, F., Omala, K., and Schönholzer, D. (2021). Teacher Rotation and Student Outcomes: Experimental Evidence from Uganda, *EDI Project, Randomised Control Trials, Working Paper*, Oxford Policy Management, Oxford.

Collins, S. and Park, W.-A. (1989). An overview of Korea's external debt, in Sachs, J., and Collins, S. (eds), *Developing Country Debt and Economic Performance, Volume 3: Country Studies – Indonesia, Korea, Philippines, Turkey*, University of Chicago Press, Chicago, IL.

Colson, E. (1947). *Tradition and Contract: The Problem of Order*, Aldine, Chicago, IL.

Corey-Boulet, R. (2019, May 14). As Benin gears up for legislative elections, the opposition is left out. *World Politics Review*.

Cruz, A., Ferreira, I., Flentø, J., and Tarp, F. (Eds.) (2023). *Mozambique at a Fork in the Road*, Cambridge University Press, Cambridge.

Dal Bo, E., and Finan, F. (2020). At the intersection: A review of institutions in economic development, in Baland, J.-M., Bourguignon, F., Platteau, J.-P., and Verdier, T. (eds), *The Handbook of Economic Development and Institutions*, Princeton University Press, Princeton, NJ and Oxford, pp. 23–83.

Dal Bo, E., Dal Bo, P., and Eyster, E. (2017). The demand for bad policy when voters under appreciate equilibrium effects, *The Review of Economic Studies* 85(2), pp. 964–98.

Dasgupta, I., and Kanbur, R. (2005). Bridging communal divides: Separation, patronage, integration, in Barrett, C. B. (ed), *The Social Economics of Poverty: On Identities, Communities, Groups, and Networks*, Routledge, London and New York, pp. 146–70.

Dasgupta, I., and Kanbur, R. (2007). Community and class antagonism, *Journal of Public Economics* 91, pp. 1816–42.

Davidson, B. (1992). *The Black Man's Burden: Africa and the Curse of the Nation-State*, James Currey, Oxford.

Davidson, E., de Santos, A., Lee, Y., Martinez, N., Smith, C., and Tassew, T. (2014). *Bangladesh: Inclusive Growth Diagnostic*, USAID.

Dawson, J. (1998). Institutions, investment and growth: Nex cross-country and panel data evidence, *Economic Inquiry* 36, pp. 603–19.

Dawson, J. W. (2003). Causality in the freedom–growth relationship. *European Journal of Political Economy*, 19(3), pp. 479–95.

Delgado, C. L. (1992). Why domestic food prices matter to growth strategy in semi-open West African agriculture, *Journal of African Economies* 1(3), pp. 446–71.

Dercon, S. (ed), (2005). *Insurance Against Poverty*, Oxford University Press, Oxford.

Dercon, S., and Krishnan, P. (1996). Income portfolios in rural Ethiopia and Tanzania: Choices and constraints, *Journal of Development Studies* 32(6), pp. 850–75.

Devarajan, S., and Khemani, S. (2016). If Politics Is the Problem, How Can External Actors Be Part of the Solution?, *Policy Research Working Paper No. WPS7761*, World Bank, Washington, DC.

Dewatripont, M., and Roland, G. (1992a). The virtues of gradualism and legitimacy in the transition to a market economy, *The Economic Journal* 102, pp. 291–300.

Dewatripont, M., and Roland, G. (1992b). Economic reform and dynamic political constraints, *Review of Economic Studies* 59, pp. 703–30.

Dewatripont, M., and Roland, G. (1995). The design of reform packages under uncertainty, *American Economic Review* 85(5), pp. 1207–23.

Dincecco, M. (2017). *State Capacity and Economic Development*, Cambridge University Press, Cambridge.

Dincecco, M., and Katz, G. (2016). State capacity and long-run economic performance, *Economic Journal* 126(590), pp. 189–218.

Dixit, A. (1996). *The Making of Economic Policy*, MIT Press, Cambridge, MA.

Dixit, A. (2002). Incentives and organization in the public sector: An interpretative review, *Journal of Human Resources* 37(4), pp. 696–727.

Dixit, A. (2003). Some lessons from transaction–cost politics for less-developed countries, *Economics and Politics* 15(2), pp. 107–33.

Dixit, A. (2004). *Lawlessness and Economics: Alternative Modes of Governance*, Princeton University Press, Princeton, NJ and Oxford.

Dixit, A. (2007). Evaluating recipes for development success, *The World Bank Research Observer* 22(2), Fall.

Dixit, A. (2018). Anti-corruption institutions: Some history and theory, in Basu, K., and Cordella, T. (eds), *Institutions, Governance and the Control of Corruption*, Palgrave Macmillan, London, pp. 15–49.

Drèze, J., (2020). Policy Beyond Evidence, *World Development*, Vol. 127.

Durlauf, S. (2020). Institutions, development and growth; Where does evidence stand?' in Baland, J.-M., Bourguignon, F., Platteau, J.-P., and Verdier, T. (eds), *The Handbook of Economic Development and Institutions*, Princeton University Press, Princeton, NJ and Oxford.

Easterly, W. (2001). *The Elusive Quest for Growth*, MIT Press, Cambridge, MA.

Economist (2021). Education after COVID-19: Studying Ceara, 18–31 December, pp. 33–34.

Economist (2022a, January 29). Put Down Your Truncheons, p. 47.

Economist (2022b, April 2). Kenyan Voters Face an Invidious Choice in August, p. 36.

Ellis, S. (1999). *The Mask of Anarchy: The Destruction of Liberia and the Religious Dimension of an African Civil War*, New York University Press, New York.

Ensminger, J. (1992). *Making a Market: The Institutional Transformation of an African Society*, Cambridge University Press, Cambridge.

Ensminger, J. (1997). Changing property rights: Reconciling formal and informal rights to land in Africa, in Drobak, J. N., and Nye, J. V. C. (eds), *The Frontiers of the New Institutional Economics,* Academic Press, San Diego, CA, pp. 165–96.

Fafchamps, M. (1992). Solidarity networks in preindustrial societies: Rational peasants with a moral economy, *Economic Development and Cultural Change* 41(1), pp. 147–74.

Fafchamps, M. (1996). The enforcement of commercial contracts in Ghana, *World Development* 24(3), pp. 427–48.

Fafchamps, M. (2004). *Market Institutions in Sub-Saharan Africa: Theory and Evidence*, MIT Press, Cambridge, MA.

Fafchamps, M. (2020). Formal and informal market institutions: Embeddedness revisited, in Baland, J.-M., Bourguignon, F., Platteau, J.-P., and Verdier, T. (eds), *The*

Handbook of Economic Development and Institutions, Princeton University Press, Princeton, NJ and Oxford, pp. 375–413.

Feder, G. (1985). The relation between farm size and farm productivity, *Journal of Development Economics* 18(2/3), pp. 297–313.

Fei, J. and G. Ranis (1975). A model of growth and employment in the open dualistic economy: The cases of Korea and Taiwan, *The Journal of Development Studies* 11(2), pp. 32–63.

Fei, J. C. H., Ranis, G., and Kuo, S. W. Y. (1979). *Growth with Equity: The Taiwan Case*, Oxford University Press, Oxford.

Felipe, J., and Usu, N. (2008). Rethinking the Growth Diagnostics Approach: Questions from the Practitioners, *ADB Economics, Working Paper Series, No. 132*, Asian Development Bank.

Fernandez, R., and Rodrick, D. (1991). Resistance to reform: Status quo bias in the presence of individual-specific uncertainty, *American Economic Review* 81(5), pp. 1146–55.

Frank, C. R. Jr., Kim, K. S., and Westphal, L. E. (1975). *Foreign Trade Regimes and Economic Development*: South Korea, NBER Books.

Fukuyama, F. (2012). *The Origins of Political Order – From Prehuman Times to the French Revolution*. London: Profile Books.

Gazdar, H. (2000). State, Community, and Universal Education: A Political Economy of Public Schooling in Rural Pakistan, Asia Research Centre and London School of Economics, draft paper.

Geertz, C. (1973). *The Interpretation of Cultures*, Basic Books, New York.

Genicot, G., and Ray, D. (2020). Aspirations and economic behavior,' *Annual Review of Economics* 12, pp. 715–46.

Gerschenkron, A., (1962). *Economic Backwardness in Historical Perspective*. Cambridge, MA: Belknap Press of Harvard University Press.

Giblin, J. L. (2005). Some complexities of family and state in Colonial Njombe, in Maddox, G. H., and Giblin, J. L. (eds), *In Search of a Nation – Histories of Authority and Dissidence in Tanzania*, James Currey, Oxford, Kapsel Educational Publications, Dar es Salaam, and Ohio University Press, Athens, OH, pp. 128–48.

Gollin, D. (2014). The Lewis Model: A 60-year retrospective, *Journal of Economic Perspectives* 28(3), pp. 71–88.

Golub, S. S., and Mbaye, A. A., (2023). Benin's informal trading with Nigeria, in Bourguignon et al. (eds), *State Capture and Rent Seeking in Benin*, Cambridge University Press, Cambridge, Chapter 8.

Granovetter, M. (1985). Economic action and social structure: The problem of embeddedness, *American Journal of Sociology* 91(3), pp. 481–510.

Greif, A., and Tabellini, G. (2010). Cultural and institutional bifurcation: China and Europe compared, *American Economic Review Papers and Proceedings* 100(2), pp. 1–10.

Greif, A., and Tabellini, G. (2017). The clan and the corporation: Sustaining cooperation in China and Europe, *Journal of Comparative Economics* 45(1), pp. 1–35.

Greif, A. (1989). Reputation and coalitions in medieval trade: Evidence on the Maghribi traders, *Journal of Economic History* 49(4), pp. 857–82.

Greif, A. (1992). Institutions and international trade: Lessons from the commercial revolution, *American Economic Review Papers and Proceedings* 82(2), pp. 128–33.

Greif, A. (1993). Contract enforceability and economic institutions in early trade: The Maghribi Traders' Coalition, *American Economic Review* 83(3), pp. 525–48.

Greif, A. (1994). Cultural beliefs and the organization of society: A historical and theoretical reflection on collectivist and individualist societies, *Journal of Political Economy* 102(5), pp. 912–50.

Greif, A. (1998). Historical and comparative institutional analysis, *American Economic Review* 88(2), pp. 80–89.

Greif, A. (2002). Institutions and impersonal exchange: From communal to individual responsibility, *Journal of Institutional and Theoretical Economics* 158(1), pp. 168–204.

Greif, A. (2006). *Genoa and the Maghribi Traders: Historical and Comparative Institutional Analysis*, Cambridge University Press, Cambridge.

Greif, A., and Laitin, D. (2004). A theory of endogenous institutional change, *American Political Science Review* 98(4), pp. 633–52.

Guirkinger, C., and Platteau, J.-P. (2015). Transformation of the family farm under rising land pressure: A theoretical essay, *Journal of Comparative Economics* 43(1), February, pp. 112–37.

Guirkinger, C., and Platteau, J.-P. (2017). Transformation of African farm households: A short survey of economic contributions, *Journal of Demographic Economics* 83, pp. 41–50.

Guirkinger, C., and Platteau, J.-P. (2020). The dynamics of family systems: Lessons from past and present times, in Baland, J.-M., Bourguignon, F., Platteau, J.-P., and Verdier, T. (eds), *The Handbook of Economic Development and Institutions*, Princeton University Press, Princeton, NJ and Oxford, pp. 449–519.

Guirkinger, C., Goetghebuer, T., and Platteau, J.-P. (2015). Productive inefficiency in extended agricultural households: Evidence from Mali, *Journal of Development Economics* 116, pp. 17–27.

Gulesci, S., Jindani, S., La Ferrara, E., Smerdon, D., Sulaiman, M., and Young, P. (2021). A Stepping Stone Approach to Understanding Harmful Norms, *CEPR Discussion Paper No. DP15776*.

Gurnah, A. (2002). *By the Sea*, Bloomsbury Publishing PLC (French translation: *Près de la Mer*, Denoël).

Haggard, S., and Moon, C.-I. (1990). Institutions and economic policy: Theory and a Korean case study, *World Politics* 42(2), pp. 210–37.

Haggard, S., Kim, B.-K., and Moon, C.-I. (1991). The transition to export-led growth in South Korea: 1954–1966, *The Journal of Asian Studies* 50(4), pp. 850–73.

Hamilton, G. (1997). Organization and market processes in Taiwan's capitalist economy, in Orru, M., Woolsey Biggart, N., and Hamilton, G. (eds), *The Economic Organization of East Asian Capitalism*, Sage, Thousand Oaks, CA, pp. 237–93.

Hamilton, G. (1998). Culture and organization in Taiwan's market economy, in Hefner, R. W. (ed), *Market Cultures – Society and Morality in the New Asian Capitalisms*, Westview Press, Boulder, CO, pp. 41–77.

Haqqani, H. (2005). *Pakistan – Between Mosque and Military*, Carnegie Endowment for International Peace, Washington, DC.

Harrison, L. E., and Huntington, S. P. (2000). *Culture Matters: How Values Shape Human Progress*, Basic Books, New York.

Hasnain, Z. (2008). The politics of service delivery in Pakistan: Political parties and the incentive for patronage, 1988–1999, *The Pakistan Development Review* 47(2), pp. 129–51.

Hassan, M., and Raihan, S. (2017). Navigating the Deals World. Deals and Development: The Political Dynamics of Growth Episodes, 96.

Hassan, M., and Raihan, S. (2018). Navigating the deals world: The politics of economic growth in Bangladesh, in Pritchett, L., Sen, K., and Werker, E. (eds), *Deals and Development: The Political Dynamics of Growth Episodes*, Oxford University Press, Oxford.

Hattori, T., and Sato, Y. (1997). A comparative study of development mechanisms in Korea and Taiwan: Introductory analysis, *The Developing Economies* 35(4), pp. 341–57.

Hausmann, R., Rodrik, D., and Velasco, A. (2005). Growth Diagnostics, *The John F. Kennedy School of Government*, Harvard University, Cambridge, MA.

Hausmann, R., Klinger, B., and Wagner, R. (2008). Doing Growth Diagnostics in Practice: A "Mindbook", *CID Working Paper No. 177*, Harvard University, Cambridge, MA.

Hayami, Y. (1997). *Development Economics: From the Poverty to the Wealth of Nations*, Clarendon Press, Oxford.

Hayami, Y., and Kikuchi, M. (1981). *Asian Village Economy at the Crossroads: An Economic Approach to Institutional Change*, University of Tokyo Press, Tokyo (Japan).

Hayami, Y., and Kikuchi, M. (1982). *Asian Village Economy at the Crossroads*, University of Tokyo Press, Tokyo, and Johns Hopkins University Press, Baltimore, MD.

Hayami, Y., and Ruttan, V. (1985). *Agricultural Development: An International Perspective*, Johns Hopkins University Press, Baltimore, MD and London.

Helme, G., and Levitsky, S. (2004). Informal institutions and comparative politics: A research agenda, *Perspectives on Politics* 2(4), pp. 725–40.

Heybey, B., and Murrell, P. (1999). The relationship between economic growth and the speed of liberalization, *Journal of Policy Reform* 3(2), pp. 121–37.

Hicks, J. R. (1932). *The Theory of Wages*, Macmillan, London.

Hidalgo, C., and Hausmann, R. (2009). The building blocks of economic complexity, *Proceedings of the National Academy of Sciences of the United States of America* 106(26), pp. 10570–75.

Hirschman, A. O. (1958). The strategy of economic development (No. HD82 H49).

Hirshman, A. O. (1958). *The Strategy of Economic Development*, Yale University Press, New Haven, CT and London.

Ho, S. P. S. (1978). *Economic Development of Taiwan, 1860–1970*, Yale University Press, New Haven, CT.

Ho, S. P. S. (1979). Decentralized industrialization and rural development from Taiwan, *Economic Development and Cultural Change* 28(1), pp. 77–96.

Ho, S. P. S. (1980). Small-Scale Enterprises in Korea and Taiwan, *World Bank Staff Working Paper, No. 384*, Washington, DC.

Hoff, K., and Sen, A. (2005). The extended family system and market interactions, in Barrett, C. B. (ed), *The Social Economics of Poverty: On Identities, Communities, Groups, and Networks*, Routledge, London and New York, pp. 171–87.

Hoff, K., and Sen, A. (2006). The Kin System as a poverty trap, in Bowles, S., Durlauf, S. N., and Hoff, K. (eds), *Poverty Traps*, Princeton University Press, Princeton, NJ, Chap. 4.

Huang, S. W. (1993). Structural change in Taiwan's agricultural economy, *Economic Development and Cultural Change* 42(1), pp. 43–65.

Il, S.-K., and Koh, Y. (2010). *The Korean Economy, Six Decades of Growth and Development*, Korea Development Institute, Seoul.

Iliffe, J. (2005). Breaking the chain at its weakest link – TANU and the Colonial Office, Maddox, G. H., and Giblin, J. L. (eds), *In Search of a Nation – Histories of Authority and Dissidence in Tanzania*, James Currey, Oxford, Kapsel Educational Publications, Dar es Salaam, and Ohio University Press, Athens, OH, pp. 168–97.

Iliffe, J. (1995 [2007]). *Africans – The History of a Continent*, Cambridge University Press, Cambridge.

Johnson, C. (1987). Political institutions and economic performance: The government–business relationship in Japan, South Korea, and Taiwan, in Deyo, F. C. (ed), *The Political Economy of the New Asian Industrialism*, Cornell University Press, Ithaca, NY.

Johnston, B., and Kilby, P. (1975). Backward linkages: Fertilizer and farm equipment, in Johnston, B., and Kilby, P. (eds), *Agriculture and Structural Transformation: Economic Strategies in Late-Developing Countries*, Oxford University Press, New York, pp. 299–327.

Jomo, K. S., and Gomez, E. T. (1997). Rents and development in multiethnic Malaysia, in Aoki, M., Kim, H.-K., and Okuno-Fujiwara, M. (eds), *The Role of Government in East Asian Economic Development*, Oxford University Press and World Bank, pp. 342–72.

Jones, B. (2009). *Beyond the State in Rural Uganda*, Edinburgh University Press, Edinburgh.

Jones, E. L. (1981). *The European Miracle: Environments, Economies and Geopolitics in the History of Europe and Asia*, Cambridge University Press, Cambridge.

Kakar, S. (1978). *The Inner World: A Psychoanalysis Study of Childhood and Society in India*, Oxford University Press, Oxford.

Kanbur, R. (2017). W. Arthur Lewis and the roots of Ghanaian economic policy, in Aryeetey, E., and Kanbur, R. (eds), *The Economy of Ghana Sixty Years after Independence*, Oxford University Press, Oxford, pp. 16–27.

Kao, C.-S. (1991). Personal trust in the large businesses in Taiwan: A traditional foundation for contemporary economic activities, in Hamilton, G. (ed), *Business Networks and Economic Development in East and Southeast Asia*, Centre of Asian Studies, University of Hong Kong, Hong Kong, pp. 234–73.

Kaufmann, D., Kraay, A., and Mastruzzi, M. (2010). The Worldwide Governance Indicators: Methodology and Analytical Issues, *Policy Research Working Papers, No. 5430*, The World Bank.

Kennedy, P. (1988). *African Capitalism – The Struggle for Ascendency*, Cambridge University Press, Cambridge.

Khemani, S. (2015). Buying votes versus supply in public services: Political incentives to under-invest in pro-poor policies, *Journal of Development Economics* 177, pp. 84–93.

Khemani, S. (2019). What is State Capacity?, *Policy Research Working Paper, No. 8734*, World Bank, Washington, DC.

Khemani, S. (2020). Political economy of reform, in Dixit, A., and Hamilton, J. (eds), *Oxford Research Encyclopedia of Economics and Finance*, Oxford University Press, Oxford, pp. 1–28.

Kikuchi, M., and Hayami, Y. (1978). Agricultural growth against a land resource constraint: A comparative history of Japan, Taiwan, Korea, and the Philippines, *The Journal of Economic History* 38(4), pp. 839–64.

Kim, E. M., and Park, G.-S. (2011). The Chaebol, in Kim, B.-K., and Vogel, E. (eds), *The Park Chung Hee Era*, Harvard University Press, Boston MA.

Kim, K. S. (1991). The Korean Miracle (1962–1980) revisited: Myths and realities in strategy and development, *Working Paper No. 166*, Kelloggs Institute.

Kim, K.-H. (2004). Reflections on the problem of colonial modernity and "collaboration" in modern Korean history, *Journal of International and Area Studies* 11(3), pp. 95–111.

Kim, S. (2021). Land reform and postcolonial poverty in South Korea, 1950–1970, *Agricultural History* 95(2), pp. 276–310.

Kim, H.-A. (2011). State building; The military junta's path to modernity through administrative reforms, in Kim, B.-K., and Vogel, E. (eds), *The Park Chung Hee Era*, Harvard University Press, Boston MA.

Kirkpatrick, C., and Barrientos, A. (2004). The Lewis Model after 50 years, *The Manchester School* 72(6), pp. 679–90.

Koh, B. C. (1993). The war's impact on the Korean peninsula, *The Journal of American-East Asian Relations* 2(1), pp. 57–76.

Kong, T. Y. (2000). *The Politics of Economic Reform in South Korea: A Fragile Miracle*, Routledge.

Koo, A. Y. C. (1971). *Agrarian reform, production and employment in Taiwan, in International Labor Office (ILO)*, Agrarian Reform and Employment, Geneva.

Koo, Y. (2013). Evolution of industrial policies and economic growth in Korea: Challenges, crises and responses, *European Review of Industrial Economics and Policy (ERIEP)* 7. [online], available at: http://revel.unice.fr/eriep/index .html?id=3598.

Kuo, W. (1975). Effects of land reform, agricultural pricing policy and economic growth on multiple crop diversification, *Philippines Economic Journal* 14(1/2).

Kuran, T. (1995). *Private Truths, Public Lies: The Social Consequences of Preference Falsification*, Harvard University Press, Cambridge, MA and London.

Kuran, T. (2004a). The economic ascent of the Middle East's religious minorities: The role of Islamic legal pluralism, *Journal of Legal Studies* 33, pp. 475–515.

Kuran, T. (2004b). *Islam and Mammon: The Economic Predicaments of Islamism*, Princeton University Press, Princeton, NJ.

Kuru, A. (2009). *Secularism and State Policies Toward Religion: The United States, France, and Turkey*, Cambridge University Press, Cambridge.

Kuznets, S. (1955). Economic growth and income inequality, *The American Economic Review*, 45(1), 1–28.

Kuznets, S. (1966). *Modern Economic Growth: Rate, Structure and Spread*, Yale University Press, London.

Landes, D. (1998). *The Wealth and Poverty of Nations: Why Some Are So Rich and Some So Poor?*, *Little*, Brown and Co., London.

Lau, L. J. (1997). The role of government in economic development: Some observations from the experience of China, Hong Kong and Taiwan, in Aoki, M., Kim, H.-K., and Okuno-Fujiwara, M. (eds), *The Role of Government in East Asian Economic Development*, Oxford University Press and World Bank, pp. 41–73.

Ledeneva, A. (1998). *Russia's Economy of Favours: Blat, Networking and Informal Exchange*, Cambridge University Press, Cambridge.

Ledeneva, A. (2008). Blat and Guanxi: Informal practices in Russia and China, *Comparative Studies in Society and History* 50(1), pp. 118–44.

Lee, N.-Y. (2011). The automobile industry, in Kim, B.-K., and Vogel, E. (eds), *The Park Chung Hee Era*, Harvard University Press, Boston MA.

Lee, T.-H., and Chen, T.-E. (1979). Agricultural growth in Taiwan, 1911–1972, in Hayami, Y., Ruttan Vernon, W., and Southworth, H. M. (eds), *Agricultural Growth in Japan, Taiwan, Korea, and Philippines*, University Press of Hawaii, Honolulu, HI.

Levy, B. (2007). State capacity, accountability, and economic development in Africa, *Commonwealth and Comparative Politics* 45(4).

Lewis, D. (2011). *Bangladesh: Politics, Economy and Civil Society*, Cambridge University Press, Cambridge.

Lewis, W. A. (1965). *Politics in West Africa*, Oxford University Press, Oxford.

Lewis, W. A. (1954). Economic development with unlimited supplies of labour, *The Manchester School*, reprinted in Agarwala, A. N., and Singh, S. P. (eds), *The Economics of Underdevelopment*, Oxford University Press, Oxford, 1958, pp. 400–49.

Lewis, W. A. (1954). Economic development with unlimited supplies of labour, *Manchester School of Economic and Social Studies*, 22, 139–91.

Lewis, W. A. (1955), *The Theory of Economic Growth*, Richard D. Irwin, Homewood, IL.

Lewis, W. A. (1968). Reflections on unlimited labour, *Discussion Paper No. 5*, Development Research Project, Woodrow Wilson School, Princeton University, Princeton, NJ.

Li, J. S. (2003). The benefits and costs of relation-based governance: An explanation of the East Asian Miracle and Crisis, *Review of International Economics* 11(3), pp. 651–73.

Li, K.-T. (1995). *The Evolution of Policy Behind Taiwan's Development Success*, World Scientific Publishing, Singapore, New Jersey, London, and Hong Kong.

Lizzeri, A., and Persico, N. (2004). Why did the elites extend the suffrage? Democracy and the scope of government, with an application to Britain's age of reform, *Quarterly Journal of Economics* 119(2), pp. 707–65.

Luo, J.-D. (1997). The Significance of networks in the initiation of small businesses in Taiwan, *Sociological Forum* 12, pp. 297–317.

Lyon, S. M. (2019). *Political Kinship in Pakistan*, Lexington Books, London and New York.

Mahmud, W., Ahmed, S., and Mahajan, S. (2010). Economic reforms, growth and governance: The political economy aspects of Bangladesh's development surprise, in Brady, D., and Spence, M. (eds), *Leadership and Growth*, Commission on Growth and Development, The World Bank, Washington, pp. 227–54.

Majumdar, S., and Mukand, S. (2004). Policy gambles, *American Economic Review* 94(4), pp. 1207–22.

Malik, A., Mirza, R., and Platteau, J.-P. (2021). "Devolution Under Autocracies: Evidence from Pakistan", in Faguet, J.-P., and Sarmistha, P. (eds), *Decentralized Governance: Crafting Effective Democracies Around the World*, Palgrave, Chap. 7.

Malik, A., Mirza, R., and Platteau, J.-P. (2022). *Political Dynasties and Development under Competitive Clientelism: Evidence from Pakistan*, Mimeo.

Manusher Jonno Foundation (MJF). (2015). Rural Land Market in Bangladesh: A Situation Analysis, MJF, Uttaran, and Care Bangladesh. [online], available at: www .thedailystar.net/rural-land-market-in-bangladesh-a-situation-analysis-61897.

Markevich, A., and Zuravskaya, E. (2018). The economic impact of the abolition of Russian serfdom: Evidence from the Russian Empire, *American Economic Review* 108(4–5), pp. 1074–117.

Martimort, D. (1996). Exclusive dealing, common agency, and Multiprincipals Incentive Theory, *RAND Journal of Economics* 27, pp. 1–31.

Martin, N. (2016). *Politics, Landlords and Islam in Pakistan*, Routledge, London and New York.

Marx, B., Bazzi, S., and Hilmy, M. (2020). Islam and the State: Religious Education in the Age of Mass Schooling, NBER Working Paper No. 27073 (also CEPR Discussion Paper No. 14689).

Mauro, P. (1995). Corruption and growth, *Quarterly Journal of Economics* 110, pp. 681–712.

Mehmood, S., and Seror, A. (2019). Judicial Independence, Religion, and Politics: Theory and Evidence, *EDI Project, Case Studies, Working Paper*, Oxford Policy Management, Oxford.

Meier, G. M., and Baldwin, R. E. (1957). *Economic Development*, John Wiley & Sons, New York.

Migot-Adholla, S. E., Hazell, P., Blarel, B., and Place, F. (1991). Indigenous land rights systems in sub-Saharan Africa: A constraint on policy?' *World Bank Economic Review* 5(1), pp. 155–75.

Milgrom, P., and Roberts, J. (1992). *Economics, Organization and Management*, Prentice-Hall, Englewood Cliffs, NJ.

Mill, J. S. (1848 [1965]). *Principles of Political Economy*, Augustus M. Kelley, New York (Reprints of Economic Classics, based on the 7th edition, 1871).

Mohmand, S. K. (2019). *Crafty Oligarchs, Savvy Voters: Democracy Under Inequality in Rural Pakistan*, Cambridge University Press, Cambridge.

Monson, J. (2005). The tribal past and the politics of nationalism in Mahenge District, 1940–60,' in Maddox, G. H., and Giblin, J. L. (eds), *In Search of a Nation – Histories of Authority and Dissidence in Tanzania*, James Currey, Oxford, Kapsel Educational Publications, Dar es Salaam, and Ohio University Press, Athens, OH, pp. 103–13.

Mukandala, R. (2023). The civil service and economic development in Tanzania, in F. Bourguignon and S. Wangwe (eds), *State and Business in Tanzania's Development*, Cambridge University Press, Cambridge, Chapter 4.

Myint, H. (1958). The "classical theory" of international trade and the underdeveloped countries, *The Economic Journal* 68(270), pp. 317–37. Reprinted in Myint, H. (1971) *Economic Theory and the Underdeveloped Countries*, Oxford University Press, London and Toronto, pp. 118–46.

North, D. (1990). *Institutions, Institutional Change, and Economic Performance*, Cambridge University Press, Cambridge.

Nunn, N. (2008). The long-term effects of Africa's slave trades, *The Quarterly Journal of Economics* 123(1), 139–76.

Nurkse, R. (1953). *Problems of Capital Formation in Underdeveloped Countries*, Oxford University Press, New York.

OECD (2013). *OECD Investment Reviews: Tanzania*, OECD, Paris.

Okuno-Fujiwara, M. (1997). Toward a comparative institutional analysis of the government–business relationship, in Aoki, M., Kim, H.-K., and Okuno-Fujiwara, M. (eds), *The Role of Government in East Asian Economic Development*, Oxford University Press and World Bank, pp. 373–406.

Olken, B. A., and Pande, R. (2012). Corruption in developing countries, *Annual Review of Economics* 4(1), pp. 479–509.

Onoma, A. K. (2010). The contradictory potential of institutions: The rise and decline of land documentation in Kenya, in Mahoney, J., and Thelen, K. (eds), *Explaining Institutional Change: Ambiguity, Agency, and Power*, Cambridge University Press, Cambridge, pp. 63–93.

Orru, M. (1991). The institutional logic of small-firm economies in Italy and Taiwan, *Studies in Comparative International Development* 26, pp. 3–28.

Ostrom, E. (1990). *Governing the Commons: The Evolution of Institutions for Collective Action*, Cambridge University Press, Cambridge.

Park, A., and Johnston, B. (1995). Rural development and dynamic externalities in Taiwan's structural transformation, *Economic Development and Cultural Change* 44(1), pp. 181–209.

Park, Y. J. (1990). Korean patterns of women's labor force participation during the period 1960–1980, *Korea Journal of Population and Development* 19(1), pp. 71–90.

Partnership for Growth. (2011). Tanzania Growth Diagnostics: A Joint Analysis for the Governments of the United Republic of Tanzania and the United States of America'.

Platteau, J.-P. (1983). Classical economics and agrarian reforms in underdeveloped areas: The radical views of the two Mills, *Journal of Development Studies* 19(4), pp. 435–60.

Platteau, J.-P. (1991). Traditional systems of social security and hunger insurance: Past achievements and modern challenges, in Ahmad, E., Drèze, J., Hills, J., and Sen, A. K. (eds), *Social Security in Developing Countries*, Clarendon Press, Oxford, pp. 112–70.

Platteau, J.-P. (1994a). Behind the market stage where real societies exist, Part I: The role of public and private order institutions, *Journal of Development Studies* 30(3), pp. 533–77.

Platteau, J.-P. (1994b). Behind the market stage where real societies exist, Part II: The role of moral norms, *Journal of Development Studies* 30(4), pp. 753–817.

Platteau, J.-P. (1997). Mutual insurance as an elusive concept in traditional rural societies, *Journal of Development Studies* 33(6), pp. 764–96.

Platteau, J.-P. (2000). *Institutions, Social Norms, and Economic Development*, Harwood, Amsterdam.

Platteau, J.-P. (2004). The gradual erosion of the social security function of customary land tenure arrangements: The case of tribal societies in sub-Saharan Africa, in Dercon, S. (ed), *Insurance Against Poverty*, Clarendon Press, Oxford, pp. 247–78.

Platteau, J.-P. (2006). Solidarity norms and institutions in agrarian societies: Static and dynamic considerations, in Kolm, S., Mercier-Ythier, J., and Varet, G. (eds), *Handbook on Gift-Giving, Reciprocity and Altruism*, North Holland and Elsevier, Amsterdam, Vol. 1, pp. 819–86.

Platteau, J.-P. (2008). The causes of institutional inefficiency: A development perspective, in Brousseau, E., and Glachant, J.-M. (eds), *New Institutional Economics. A Guidebook*, Cambridge University Press, Cambridge, pp. 437–56.

Platteau, J.-P. (2011). Culture and development: An overview, in Platteau, J.-P., and Peccoud, R. (eds), *Culture, Institutions, and Development: New Insights Into an Old Debate*, Routledge, London, pp. 3–19.

Platteau, J.-P. (2014). Redistributive pressures in sub-Saharan Africa: Causes, consequences, and coping strategies, in Akyeampong, E., Bates, R. H., Nunn, N., and

Robinson, J. A. (eds), *African Development in Historical Perspective*, Cambridge University Press, Cambridge, pp. 153–207.

Platteau, J.-P. (2017). *Islam Instrumentalised: Religion and Politics in Historical Perspective*, Cambridge University Press, Cambridge (reviewed in Journal of Economic Literature 56(4), December 2018, pp. 1601–1603).

Platteau, J.-P. (2022). Enlightened autocrats: Lessons from bold experiments in the lands of Islam, in Basu, K., and Cordella, T. (eds), *Institutions, Governance and the Control of Corruption*, Palgrave Macmillan, London, pp. 235–86.

Platteau, J.P. (2022). Enlightened autocrats: Lessons from bold experiments in the lands of Islam, in Basu, K., Ghatak, M., Kletzer, K., Mundle, S., and Verhoogen, E. (eds), *Development, Distribution, and Markets*, Oxford University Press, Oxford, pp. 235–86.

Platteau, J.-P., and Oliveros, D. U. (2021). Cognitive bias in insurance: Evidence from India, *World Development* 44(August).

Platteau, J.-P., and Wahhaj, Z. (2013). Interactions between modern law and custom, in Ginsburgh, V., and Throsby, D. (eds), *Handbook of the Economics of Art and Culture*, vol. 2, Elsevier and North-Holland, pp. 633–78.

Polanyi, Karl (1957) *The Great Transformation*, Rineholt, New York.

Prakash, N., Rockmore, M., and Uppal, Y. (2019). Do criminally accused politicians affect economic outcomes? Evidence from India, *Journal of Development Economics* 141, Article 102370.

Price, R. M. (1975). *Society and Bureaucracy in Contemporary Ghana*, University of California Press, Berkeley, CA.

Querubin, P. (2012). Political reform and elite persistence: Term limits and political dynasties in the Philippines. In *APSA 2012 Annual Meeting Paper*.

Querubin, P. (2016). Family and politics: Dynastic persistence in the Philippines, *Quarterly Journal of Political Science*, 11(2), pp. 151–81.

Raihan, S. and Bourguignon, F. (2023). An Institutional Diagnostic of Bangladesh: Introduction, in Raihan et al. (eds), *Is the Bangladesh Paradox Sustainable?* Cambridge University Press, Cambridge. Chapter 1.

Raihan, S., Bourguignon, F., and Salam, U. (2020). *Is Bangladesh Paradox Sustainable? An Institutional Diagnostic*, EDI. [online], available at: https://edi.opml.co.uk/research/bangladesh-institutional-diagnostic/.

Raihan, S., Bourguignon, F., and Salam, U. (Eds.) (2023). *Is the Bangladesh Paradox Sustainable?* Cambridge University Press, Cambridge.

Ranis, G. (2004). Labor Surplus Economies, *Center Discussion Paper No. 900*, Economic Growth Center, Yale University, New Haven, CT.

Ranis, G. and Fei, J. (1961). A theory of economic development, *American Economic Review* 51(4), pp. 533–65.

Rasmusen, E. (1989). *Games and Information: An Introduction to Game Theory*, Basil Blackwell, Oxford.

Ray, D. (1998). *Development Economics*, Princeton University Press, Princeton, NJ.

Reno, W. (1995). *Corruption and State Politics in Sierra Leone*, Cambridge University Press, Cambridge.

Rhyu, S.-Y., and Lew, S.-J. (2011). Pohang Iron and Steel Company, in Kim, B.-K., and Vogel, E. (eds), *The Park Chung Hee Era*, Harvard University Press, Boston MA.

Riaz, A. (2016). *Bangladesh: A Political History Since Independence*, I.B. Tauris, London.

Rodrik, D. (2004). Institutions and Economic Performance: Getting Institutions Right, *CESifo DICE Report*, Institut für Wirtschaftsforschung, München Universität, 2(2), pp. 10–15.

Rosenzweig, M. R., Binswanger, H. P., and McIntire, H. (1988). From land abundance to land scarcity – The effects of population growth on production relations in agrarian economies, in Lee, R. D., Arthur, W. B., Kelley, A. C., Rodgers, G., and Srinivasan, T. N. (eds), *Population, Food and Rural Development*, Clarendon Press, Oxford, pp. 77–100.

Sahlins, M. (1965). On the sociology of primitive exchange, in Banton, M. (ed), *The Relevance of Models for Social Anthropology*, Tavistock Publications, London, pp. 139–236.

Sayigh, Y. (2019). *Owners of the Republic: An Anatomy of Egypt's Military Economy*, Carnegie Middle East Center, Beirut, and Carnegie Endowment for International Peace, Washington, DC.

Schneidewind, D. K. (2016). *Economic Miracle Market South Korea: A Blueprint for Economic Growth in Developing Nations*, Springer.

Schotter, A. (1981). *The Economic Theory of Social Institutions*, Cambridge University Press, Cambridge.

Schultz, T. W. (1964). *Transforming Traditional Agriculture*, Yale University Press, New Haven, CT.

Scott, J. C. (1976) *The Moral Economy of the Peasant: Rebellion and Subsistence in Southeast Asia*, Yale University Press, New Haven, CT and London.

Scott, J. (1972) *Comparative Political Corruption*, Prentice-Hall, Englewood Cliffs, NJ.

Sedjo, R. A. (1976). Korean historical experience and the labor-surplus model, *The Journal of Developing Areas* 10(2), pp. 213–22.

Sen, A. K. (1960). *Choice of Techniques*, Basil Blackwell, Oxford.

Sen, A. K. (1966). Peasants and dualism with and without surplus labor, *Journal of Political Economy* 74(5), pp. 425–50.

Sen, A. (1975). The concept of efficiency, *Contemporary Issues in Economics*, pp. 196–210.

Sen, B. (2018). The Rise of Landless Tenancy in Rural Bangladesh: Analysis of the Recent Evidence. Dhaka: Presentation Made at the 2018 Bangladesh Institute of Development Studies Research Almanac, pp. 11–12.

Sen, B., Dorosh, P., and Mansur, A. (2021). Moving out of agriculture in Bangladesh: The role of farms, non-farm and mixed households, *World Development* 144(August).

Seth, M. J. (2002). *Education fever: Society, politics, and the pursuit of schooling in South Korea*, University of Hawaii Press, Hawaii.

Seth, M. J. (2013). An Unpromising Recovery: South Korea's Post-Korean War Economic Development: 1953–1961, *Education About Asia*, 18(3), p. 42.

Seth, M. J. (2020). *A Concise History of Modern Korea: From the Late Nineteenth Century to the Present*, vol. 2, Rowman and Littlefield, Lanham, MD.

Shah, A. (2014). *The Army and Democracy: Military Politics in Pakistan*, Harvard University Press, Cambridge, MA and London.

Shapley, L. S., and Shubik, M. (1969). On the core of an economic system with externalities, *American Economic Review* 59(4), pp. 678–84.

Sheikh, M. Z. H., and Ahamed, Z. S. (2019). Military, Authoritarianism and Islam: A Comparative Analysis of Bangladesh and Pakistan, *Politics and Religion*, pp. 1–28.

Shipton, P. (1988). The Kenyan land tenure reform: Misunderstandings in the public creation of private property, in Downs, R. E., and Reyna, S. P. (eds), *Land and Society in Contemporary Africa*, University Press of New England, Hanover, NH and London, pp. 91–135.

Siddiqa, A. (2017). *Military Inc.: Inside Pakistan's Military Economy*, Penguin Random House, India.

Siddiqui, B. M., Di Maro, V., Mulaj, F., Maqueda, M. R., and Chen, D. (2021). Using machine learning to promote fairness and efficiency in Indian courts, *EDI Working Paper*, Oxford.

Smith, T. C. (1959). *The Agrarian Origins of Modern Japan*, Stanford University Press, Stanford, CA.

Sokoloff, K. L., and Engerman, S. L. (2000). History lessons: Institutions, factor endowments, and paths of development in the New World, *Journal of Economic Perspectives* 14(3), pp. 217–32.

Stewart, F. (1977). *Relevant Aspects of the Technology Problem in the Case of Developing Economies*, Université de Montréal, Centre de recherche en développement économique.

Stiglitz, J. (1989). Rational peasants, efficient institutions, and a theory of rural organization: Methodological remarks for development economics, in Bardhan, P. (ed), *The Economic Theory of Agrarian Institutions*, Clarendon Press, Oxford, pp. 18–29.

Sugden, R. (1986). *The Economics of Rights, Cooperation and Welfare*, Blackwell, Oxford.

Sugden, R. (1989). Spontaneous order, *Journal of Economic Perspectives* 3(4), pp. 85–97.

Teorell, J., Sundström, A., Holmberg, S., Rothstein, B., Alvarado Pachon, N., and Dall, C. M. (2021). The Quality of Government Standard Dataset, 21 January version, The Quality of Government Institute (www.qog.pol.gu.se), University of Gothenburg. doi: 10.18157/qogstdjan21.

Thorbecke, E. (1979). Agricultural development, in Galenson, W. (ed), *Economic Growth and Structural Change in Taiwan: The Postwar Experience of the Republic of China*, Cornell University Press, Ithaca, NY and London, pp. 132–205.

Tignor, R. L. (2006). *W. Arthur Lewis and the Birth of Development Economics*, Princeton University Press, Princeton, NJ.

Tilly, C. (1985). War making and state making as organized crime. In Evans, P. P., Evans, P. B., Rueschemeyer, D., and Skocpol, T. (eds), (1985). *Bringing the State Back In*. Cambridge University Press.

Udry, C. (1994). Risk and insurance in a rural credit market: An empirical investigation in Northern Nigeria, *Review of Economic Studies*, 61, 495–526.

Voigtländer, N., and Voth, H.-J. (2013). How the West "invented" fertility restriction, *American Economic Review* 103(6), pp. 2227–64.

Vromen, J. J. (1995). *Economic Evolution: An Enquiry into the Foundations of New Institutional Economics*, Routledge, London and New York.

Wade, R. (1982). The system of administrative and political corruption: Canal irrigation in South India, *Journal of Development Studies* 18(3), pp. 287–328.

Wade, R. (1985). The market for public office: Why the Indian state is not better at development, *World Development* 13(4), pp. 467–97.

Wade, R. (1988). The management of irrigation systems: How to evoke trust and avoid prisoners' dilemma, *World Development* 16(4), pp. 489–500.

Wade, R. (1990a). *Governing the Market: Economic Theory and the Role of Government in East Asian Industrialization*, Princeton University Press, Princeton, NJ.

Wade, R. (1990b). Employment, water control and water supply institutions: India and South Korea, in Gooneratne, W., and Hirashima, S. (eds), *Irrigation and Water Management in Asia*, Sterling Publishers, New Delhi.

Wang, W.-Y. (2002). Economic implications of the rule of law: The case of Taiwan, in Chow, P. C. Y. (ed), *Taiwan's Modernization in Global Perspective*, Praeger, Westport, CT and London, pp. 103–14.

Wilder, A. (2009). The Politics of Civil Service Reform in Pakistan, *Journal of International Affairs*, 63(1), pp. 19–37.

Wilson, J. Q. (2019). *Bureaucracy: What Government Agencies Do and Why They Do It*, Basic Books, New York.

Woo-Cumings, M. (1997). The political economy of growth in East Asia: A perspective on the state, market, and ideology, in Aoki, M., Kim, H.-K., and Okuno-Fujiwara, M. (eds), *The Role of Government in East Asian Economic Development*, Oxford University Press and World Bank, pp. 323–41.

World Bank (2007). *Bangladesh Paradox: Does Governance Matter to Growth*, Country Report, The World Bank, Washington.

World Bank (2017). *World Development Report: Governance and the Law*, The World Bank, Washington, DC.

World Justice Project (2019). *Rule of Law Index 2019 report*.

Wu, J. (2005). *Understanding and Interpreting Chinese Economic Reform*, Thomson South-Western, Mason, OH.

Yang, M. M. C. (1970). *Socio-economic Results of Land Reform in Taiwan*. East–West Center Press, Honolulu, HI.

Yoo, J. (2017). Korea's rapid export expansion in the 1960s: How it began, *KDI Journal of Economic Policy* 39(2): 1–23.

Yoon, Y., and Mudida, R. (2020). Social and economic transformation in Tanzania and South Korea: Ujamaa and Saemaul Undong in the 1970s compared, *Seoul Journal of Economics* 20(33), pp. 195–231.

Young, A. (1994). Lessons from the East Asian NICS: A contrarian view, *European Economic Review* 8(3–4), pp. 964–73.

Young, A. (1995). The tyranny of numbers: Confronting the statistical realities of the East Asian growth experience, *The Quarterly Journal of Economics* 110(3), pp. 641–80.

Young, P. (1998). *Individual Strategy and Social Structure*, Princeton University Press, Princeton, NJ.

Zahab, M. A. (2020). *Pakistan: A Kaleidoscope of Islam*, Hurst Publishers, London.

Zürcher, E. (2012). *The Young Turk Legacy and Nation Building: From the Ottoman Empire to Atatürk's Turkey*, I.B. Tauris, London.

Index

Footnotes are indicated by n. after the page number.

Printed in the United States
by Baker & Taylor Publisher Services